KOSOVO

KOSOVO

K O S O V O

How Myths and Truths Started a War

Julie A. Mertus

UNIVERSITY OF CALIFORNIA PRESS

Berkeley / Los Angeles / London

University of California Press
Berkeley and Los Angeles, California

University of California Press, Ltd.
London, England

© 1999 by Julie A. Mertus

Library of Congress Cataloging-in-Publication Data

Mertus, Julie, 1963–
    Kosovo : how myths and truths started a war / Julie A. Mertus.
        p.   cm.
    Includes bibliographical references and index.
    ISBN 0-520-20962-1 (alk. paper).—ISBN 0-520-21865-5 (pbk. :
alk. paper)
        1. Kosovo (Serbia)—History—Civil War, 1998– —Causes.
    I. Title.   II. Title: How myths and truths started a war.
    DR2087.M47   1999
    949.71—dc21   99-19044
                                                                  CIP

Manufactured in the United States of America

9 8 7 6 5 4 3 2

The paper used in this publication meets the minimum requirements
of ANSI/NISO Z39.48-1992 (R 1997) (*Permanence of Paper*).

*In memory of Jane Carey, who liked to tell stories,
and Irene Smith, who listened*

*Also in memory of Bajram Kelmendi, who along with his
two sons was murdered in March 1999, and for all the people of Kosovo and Serbia proper alike who support peace and
justice.*

In comparison with myth, history is fatiguing.

Ivo Zanić

*If, like truth, the lie had but one face, we would
be on better terms. For we would accept as certain
the opposite of what the liar would say. But the in-
verse of truth has a hundred thousand faces and
an infinite field.*

Montaigne

*What is truth? Truth is everything that we ought
not to say, because it is inadvisable, inopportune,
because such an utterance could not correspond
with our petty, selfish and monetary interest. . . . Is
truth of any use? No, because over the centuries
wanted posters have been regularly posted in search
of truth.*

Miroslav Krleža

*It is not dangerous to lose a battle. It is not even
that dangerous to lose a state. . . . Such losses can
be made up. It is dangerous, however, when one
begins to distort the truth, warp principles, corrupt
ideals, and poison traditions. Then the spirit suffers, craziness overcomes it, and self-destructiveness
crushes it. . . .*

Serbian nationalist in 1942
(quoted in Thomas A. Emmert,
Serbian Golgotha, 140)

Contents

Illustrations follow page 173.

Tables

Preface

The initial version of this book was completed in August 1998 and revised in the fall and winter of 1998–1999—before the NATO bombing of Kosovo in March 1999. The "hot spring" of 1999 is evidence that the international community have not heard and understood the voices in the stories documented in this book. If they had, they would have included Kosovo Albanian leaders in regional peace talks at a much earlier date.

Media accounts depicting Albanians as "terrorists" have played a role in creating the crisis of the Balkans today. Within Serbia, stories of Albanian "terrorists" were responsible for creating within the Serbian community a feeling of victimization and, once Serbs saw themselves as victims, they were one step away from being perpetrators. Outside of Serbia, stories of Albanian "terrorists" were partly responsible for the international community's failure to deal directly with Albanian political leaders.

As of this writing, the international community faces a terrible quandary. Milosevic has not moved one step closer toward signing a peace agreement. The very people NATO wants to help, Kosovo Albanians and anti-Milosevic Serbs, have been placed in great danger. Many have been murdered, tortured, or disappeared, including leading human rights and humanitarian activists and independent journalists. Many more have fled the country or are in hiding.

The absence of international monitors in Kosovo has given a green light to Serb "cleansing" of Albanians. A sea of humanity is headed

xi

toward Kosovo's borders. They are nearly all Albanians. When Kosovo Albanians cross the border, Serbs force them to leave their passports and identity papers behind. They will probably be unable to return without proof of citizenship. If bombing ends, the ethnic cleansing will only intensify. But if bombing continues and no other action is taken, the door-to-door slaughter of Albanians in Kosovo will also continue.

This book explains how the international community created this untenable situation by failing to support the Albanians in their initial passive resistance to brutal Serbian repression. Only after the world community failed to respond to their nonviolent quest for freedom did Albanians take up arms. Although the social movement that supports this quest comprises diverse ideologies, it is united by a single drive— the quest for freedom from oppression. Even defeated, Kosovo Albanians will never give up this dream. Albanian efforts to achieve autonomy or independence for Kosovo could destabilize the region for years to come.

Understanding the stories in this book is only a beginning. The international community has a responsibility to take action to address today's systemic and long-standing human rights and humanitarian violations in Kosovo and to do what it can to prevent such crises from happening again.

Acknowledgments

Many, many individuals in Kosovo, Serbia proper, Croatia, Slovenia, Macedonia, Montenegro, Albania and other parts of Europe and North America helped with various stages of this book. From providing hospitality during my two years in residence in the region, to locating sources of information and arranging interviews, to helping with visas and other technicalities, people of all nations of the former Yugoslavia had a part in assisting this project. The project could not have been possible without the assistance of a woman from Belgrade who fears to be named. She generously translated articles, gathered documents and provided a critical ear for discussion of each and every chapter. Individuals I can name who were particularly helpful include Genc Bucinca, Xheraldina Bucinca, Sevdie Ahmeti, Vjosa Dobruna, Shkelzen Maliqi, Dragan Čičić, Sanda Kosanović, Sonja Licht, Nataša Kandić Vesna Pesic, Aida Bagić and Jelena Savić.

This book was supported mainly by a research and writing grant from the John D. and Catherine T. MacArthur Foundation. It also benefited from the support of the Harvard Law School Human Rights Program, the Harvard Center for International Affairs, and the Fulbright Foundation. The archivists at *Vjesnik* and *NIN* were extremely useful in locating media clippings; human rights information was provided by the staff of Amnesty International, Human Rights Watch, the Human Rights Council of Prićtina, the Belgrade and Pričtina Helsinki Committees, the Humanitarian Law Fund of Belgrade and the New York offices of *Illyria*, the Albanian-American newspaper. The libraries of Harvard University were phenomenal in providing nearly everything else.

Lisa Kahane and Alice Mead provided one-time use of their photographs. More information on Lisa Kahane's portfolio on the Balkans can be obtained by e-mailing her at lkahane@interport.net.

Sections of this work have benefited from the editorial comments of Evan Camfield of the University of California Press and the suggestions of Sabrina Petra Ramet, Tom Cushman, Janet Lord, Joyce Neu, Keitha Fine and my editors and anonymous reviewers. I am also appreciative of the work of the many scholars who have written about the former Yugoslavia, and I am especially grateful for the advice of Shkelzen Maliqi, who encouraged me to focus on stories about the "Truth." The mistakes are all my own.

Comments on this book may be addressed to author at suitcase @igc.apc.org.

1. Yugoslavia, 1945–1989

2. Kosovo, 1998

Notes on Terms
and Concepts

Kosovo, Serbia Proper
and (Former) Yugoslavia

The geographic focus of this book is *Kosovo*. Until 1990, Kosovo was known as an "autonomous province" of Serbia, one of six Yugoslav republics. (The other autonomous province was Vojvodina.) From 1968 to the mid-1980s, Kosovo became increasingly more autonomous from Serbia. The history of the relationship between Serbia and Kosovo, as traced in the various Yugoslav constitutions, can be found in the chronology at the back of this book.

In 1989–1990, Kosovo was stripped of its autonomous status and became just a province of Serbia. All but two of the republics of what had been Yugoslavia became their own states—the countries of Slovenia, Croatia, Bosnia-Herzegovina and Macedonia. The remaining two republics, Serbia and Montenegro, called themselves *Yugoslavia*, and after the war ended in Bosnia-Herzegovina in 1995, most (but not all) members of the international community recognized this Yugoslavia. Kosovo has never been recognized as an independent country by any state other than Albania.

After years of simmering tensions in Kosovo, marked by human rights abuses perpetrated by Serbs against Kosovo Albanians, armed conflict erupted in Kosovo in 1998. The main arguments about the status of Kosovo are mirror opposites of one another. According to the dominant Serbian position, Kosovo is an inalienable component of Serbia in Yugoslavia. In making their argument, Serbs rely heavily on historical claims to land. Kosovo, they say, is so important to Serbian national identity that it is like a Serbian Jerusalem. They supplement these contentions with contemporary stories about human rights violations perpetrated by Kosovo Albanians against Kosovo Serbs, with the stories discussed in this book holding a central position in such discourse. When referring to Kosovo, Serbian officials use the name *Kosovo and Metohija* (or *Kosovo-Metohija,* or *Kosmet* for short).

According to the majority of Albanians living in Kosovo, the status of Kosovo came into question when Serbian politicians stripped it of its autonomy using impermissible and even illegal means. The break-up of Yugoslavia, they contend, threw open all questions of sovereignty within Yugoslavia, and Albanians living in Kosovo have voted for autonomy and established their own government. Kosovo Albanians make their own historical arguments regarding the longevity of their people in the region and for the centrality of Kosovo for Albanian national identity. They further underscore that years of gross Serbian human rights abuses against Albanians have made a continued union untenable. When referring to Kosovo, Albanians would use the Albanian-language name *Kosova* or *Kosovë*.

When using the term *Kosovo*, this book refers to the geographic area that has long been known as Kosovo. Use of this term, however, does not indicate a position on the larger issue of the political status of Kosovo today or in the future. When referring to Serbia without Kosovo and Vojvodina—"the rest of Serbia," if one considers those two formerly autonomous provinces to be part of Serbia—the book uses the term *Serbia proper*.

The term *Yugoslavia* when used in reference to the period before the most recent wars, refers to the internationally recognized state of the time, with its six constituent republics and, up until 1989, two autonomous provinces. When referring to the period after most of the republics became new states, *Yugoslavia* refers to Serbia proper, Kosovo and Montenegro.

Serbs, Albanians, Kosovo Albanians and Kosovars

This book is primarily about the building of national identity among Serbs living anywhere in Yugoslavia and Albanians living in Kosovo. The complication here is that Albanians of course also live in Albania (and in large numbers in Macedonia). In fact, Albanians are one of the most numerous diasporas in the world.

In this book the term *Kosovo Albanians* (or *Kosovar Albanians*) refers to Albanians in or from Kosovo, thus distinguishing them from Albanians from Albania, Macedonia and elsewhere. *Kosovo Serb* is used to specify Serbs living in Kosovo. The general terms *Kosovor* or *Kosovar* refer to anyone from Kosovo, including not only Albanians and Serbs but also Montenegrins, Croats, Muslims and Turks.

Language

One major dilemma in writing about Kosovo concerns whether to use Albanian or Serbian (until the break-up of Yugoslavia, "Serbo-Croatian") names of places. Sometimes the differences can seem minor, such as *Kosovo* (Serbian) versus *Kosova* (Albanian), and sometimes they can be enormous, such as *Uroścevac* (Serbian) versus *Ferizej* (Albanian). Throughout the 1970s and early 1980s, the Albanian language was used widely in Kosovo in official business. From the late 1980s onward, official business was conducted in Serbian. Serbs and Albanians together spoke Serbian, but among themselves Albanians spoke Albanian. Today, Serbs would rather speak their first language, Serbian, and Kosovo Albanians would rather speak the language they learn at home, Albanian. The majority of world atlases have always used spellings similar to those of the Serbian language. This book takes the easy way out by reverting to the atlases. Serbian is used for place names throughout, although this choice in no way signals a position on the language policy in Kosovo.

Nation, Ethnic Group, Ethno-National Minority

In this book, *nation* does not refer to a state. Rather, nations are groups united by real and imagined markers such as history, language and traditions.[1] Shared myths and memories hold key importance in the definition of nations. In Will Kymlicka's terms, " 'nation' means a historical community, more or less institutionally complete, occupying a given territory or homeland, sharing a distinct language and culture."[2] Leaders of nations attempt to advance purported common interests through organized political action; although they do not always desire their own state, nations often seek some kind of cultural and/or political autonomy.

Both Serbs and Albanians consider themselves to have these markers and to be nations, so this book uses the term to apply to both groups. This is contrary, however, to official usage in the former Yugoslavia. Under the 1974 Constitution of Yugoslavia, the nations (*narodi*) were Serbs, Croats, Slovenes, Macedonians, Montenegrins and Muslims. (Muslims were the last group to be added to this list.) Those with a "national homeland" in another state, such as Albanians and Hungarians, were considered to be "national minorities" (*manjina* or *narodnosti*); those without a homeland anywhere, such as the Rom, were labeled "ethnic groups." The chronology at the back of this book traces the development of these concepts in Yugoslavia.

The term *ethnic group* is also applied to both Serbs and Albanians, because they consider themselves to be ethnically distinct from each other. That is, they believe that they constitute a primary cultural unity and share common cultural interests. Ethnic groups exhibit, in varying degrees, the following factors: real or imagined common ancestry, shared historical memories, a link with a homeland, and one or more elements of a common culture, such as religion, customs and language.[3] Ethnic groups may be distinguished from nations in that ethnic groups need not seek to advance their interest through organized political action. When members of an ethnic group "interact regularly and have common interests and organizations at a collective level"[4] they are said to be *ethnic communities*. In this sense, ethnic communities may be equated with nations. References in this book to *ethnic Albanians* or *ethnic Serbs* are generally to people who are part of ethnic communities.

At times, the term *ethno-national* is used to collapse ethnicity and nation into a (slightly improper) nomenclature. *Ethno-national minorities* is something of a compromise between the more European use of "nation" and the American use of the term "ethnic groups." The wording "ethno-national" is useful as it underscores that members of the group in question locate solidarity at a collective level and that collective action may emerge from shared understandings of a unique past.

Sources and Methodology

The backbone of this work is a series of interviews conducted in Kosovo and Serbia proper in 1993–1995 and supplemented by subsequent interviews in Macedonia in 1996 and Kosovo in 1998. Apart from background interviews, which were conducted widely, the author focused on Albanians and Serbs who were students in 1981. When not specified, the author conducted all interviews. In some cases, the interviewee was hesitant to speak candidly with a foreigner, and interviews by local people solicited more open responses. Whenever the author did not conduct interviews, the interview was conducted by a Kosovo Serbian or Albanian independent researcher of the same age as the author. In all cases, factual statements were corroborated. References to secondary sources were included in order to provide a guide to further scholarship. Nearly all of these sources can be found in the Harvard University library. Hard-to-find Serbian language books were acquired largely through used book vendors in Belgrade.

The layered use of interview, text and interpretation provides a micro-examination of the development of national identity in Kosovo. While a macro-examination of the history of Kosovo is valuable as well,[5] a micro-analysis is needed if we are to understand how the telling of myths and truths started a war. Although tensions between Serbs and Albanians have long existed, the war in Kosovo was not preordained by ancient hatreds. Rather, the war was ignited by more recent storytelling. The goal of the methodology employed in this book is to shed light on the process of identity formation and to underscore the connection between a victimhood identity and the potential for conflict.

Notes

1. See, e.g., Benedict Anderson, *Imagined Communities: Reflections on the Origins and Spread of Nationalism* (London: Verso Books, 1991).

2. Will Kymlicka, *Multicultural Citizenship* (Oxford: Oxford University Press, 1995).

3. See generally Anthony D. Smith, *The Ethnic Origins of Nations* (Oxford: Blackwell, 1996); Donald Horowitz, *Ethnic Groups in Conflict* (Berkeley: University of California Press, 1985); Marcus Banks, *Ethnicity: Anthropological Con-

structions (London: Routledge, 1996); Nathan Glazer and Daniel P. Moynihan, *Ethnicity: Theory and Experience* (Cambridge, Mass.: Harvard University Press, 1975).

4. John Hutchinson and Anthony D. Smith in introduction to *Ethnicity*, ed. Hutchinson and Smith (New York: Oxford University Press, 1996), 6.

5. After this manuscript was completed, Noel Malcom and Miranda Vickers made significant contributions to our macro-understanding of the history of Kosovo. See Noel Malcolm, *Kosovo: A Short History* (New York: New York University Press, 1998), and Miranda Vickers, *Between Serb and Albanian: A History of Kosovo* (New York: Columbia University Press, 1998).

Introduction: Understanding Kosovo Through "Truths"

History as Myth and Experience

This book explains how myths and truths can start a war. It looks closely at Kosovo, but its most basic lesson applies to all of us. Our identities as individuals and as members of groups are defined through the telling and remembering of stories. Real or imagined, these stories shape our understanding of ourselves as heroes, martyrs, triumphant conquerors and humiliated victims.[1] The most dangerous identity is that of victim. Once we see ourselves as victims, we can clearly identify an enemy. Steeped in our own victimhood, we no longer feel bound by moral considerations in becoming perpetrators.[2]

The search for "truth" is integrally connected with the development of individual and group identity. How can we understand the "truth" about an event or idea? Our first impulse may be to "analyze it, find out what makes it distinct, grind it down to its simplest components."[3] Yet ideas and events cannot be so easily packaged and delivered. We live them. The ideas and events we experience interact and change in multilayered narratives, a storytelling forever changing and unconstrained by convention and reason. Such a state of disarray—our everyday lives—demands more than a little creativity. "To understand a subject is not to cut it down to size but to expand into it."[4] This book explores one way of expanding into the subject of national identity, a process of examining Truths.

Truths refer to one way of knowing the past. As Paul Cohen has explained, history comes in three keys: as fact, myth and experience.[5] Truths involve history as experience and myth rather than as fact. Truths underscore history as process rather than a fixed body of material.[6]

To understand this concept of history we must first accept a more complex analysis of the notion of "truth." Tzvetan Todorov has suggested two senses of the word: "truth adequation" (i.e., "factual truth") and "truth-disclosure" ("more or less truth").[7] The former is an all-or-nothing factual right or wrong. Either the policeman tortured the prisoner or he did not, whatever the attenuating circumstances. Either two ethno-national groups are shooting at each other or they are not. If, however, the question involves the causes of the ethno-national conflict and the policeman's motivations, we cannot point to a factual right or wrong answer. The answers for such questions "can only contain a more or less truth, since they endeavor to reveal the nature of the phenomenon, not to establish facts."[8] To understand how wars start, we need to do more than examine factual truth, we need to unravel the "more or less truths."

Although factual truth is important for courts of law, and for others who wish to assess blame and punish the guilty, it provides a poor guide for explaining why things happen or for predicting when they will happen. Individuals do not simply accepts facts as their truth. Knowledge of truth is not the product of reason operating independently of social and political relationships. Rather, truth can be understood as the product of complex power relations whereby Truth is produced through power and power is exercised in the production of Truth.[9]

Nowhere is this observation more true than with respect to areas encumbered by intergroup conflict. The day-to-day manifestations of the conflict, struggles over power, produce Truth. Individuals from each side of the conflict use the power they have to influence the meaning given to facts, experience and myth. Through their daily experiences and by listening to the experiences of others, they learn more about their own identity and that of their enemy. These are crucial lessons, for they frame how individuals and groups behave. As quiet sufferer, angry victim, proud martyr, misunderstood innocent, they turn their cheek, strike back, publicize their cause, or suffer silently. Their actions, informed by the power struggles around them and by what they accept as Truth, continue to contribute to the production of Truth.

Facts are rarely the driving force behavior human behavior. In terms of their bearing on ordinary human lives, experience and myth are far more persuasive and influential than factual truth.[10] With respect to Kosovo, Serbian officials are to blame for years of gross human rights abuses against Albanians; but in order to understand why these abuses continue and to predict future patterns of behavior, we must look beyond the facts of abuse and to other ways of knowing the past. We need to examine lived experience and evolving myth.

This is not to absolve anyone of agency in respect to their Truths. People are not unknowingly and blindly led to Truths. Rather, in a complex and self-perpetuating process, we seek out the Truths that best fit our own notions of right and wrong, our idea of who is good and who is evil. These notions all come from *somewhere:* from family, society, schooling, religion—the parts of our lives that wean us from ways of judging. "Socially and politically, we inhabit a world of unspoken premises, hidden dangers, subtle contradictions and quiet intractabilities, a world where nothing is quite as it seems to be, a world whose muscular realities warp and attenuate our values."[11] We may seem to move linearly, but we actually operate on several levels, dipping into our remembered and told Truths. Willingly, if not knowingly, and especially in times of danger, we fall back upon these notions and pad ourselves with the protective, comfortable coating of Truths.

An old Balkan tale tells of a man leafing madly through one newspaper after another. "Father, father, can I help you?" his son asks. "No," the man brushes the boy aside and continues skimming only the headlines of the papers. At last, he jabs his finger at one crumpled page and cries, "Here it is! I knew it all along." He throws the other papers on the floor and clings to his one headline. That the other papers contradict this story is irrelevant: He has found the Truth.

Truths can become so firmly a part of one's existence that to tell people to cast them away is to tell them to tear off a layer of their skin. Conflict resolution experts who insist on putting seven X's and seven Y's in a room and having them slug it out until they come to a compromise are asking people to alter their Truths. Yet Truths cannot be compromised. They are integral to our identity. We must hear Truths, see them, touch them, but not insist upon their immediate transformation. Only time can change the perception of experience and shape the telling of myths. Outsiders who demand an immediate retelling are perceived as illegitimate; any reshaping must come from within.

Each society has its regime of Truth, as Hannah Arendt has noted. Society determines the types of discourse that it values and makes function as true, and society determines as well the techniques and procedures accorded value in the acquisition of truth.[12] The holding of different Truths in and of itself does not cause conflict. Conflict arises only when one's Truths are constituted as degrading the "other." When Truths that are the foundation of national identity[13] are perceived to be in danger, members of that group may face the need to fight for their very survival. Under these circumstances, "convinced they know the Truth ... enthusiasts may regard lies for the sake of the truth as justifiable. They may perpetuate so-called pious frauds to convert the unbelieving or strengthen the conviction of the faithful."[14]

Allowing competing Truths to float through the air in the same space, unjudged and unquestioned, can be a revolutionary act. The Truths may always exist. But the very telling can provoke self-reflection and dismantle the link between Truths and the degrading of an oppositional "other." The telling may narrow the gap between Truths, creating a common bridge toward something else. Yet sometimes the divisions between peoples are too great, the fear too intense, the desire of some to maintain or gain power too overwhelming. The mere telling is not enough to stem conflict. Thus, we cannot stop after the telling. We must have the will to think of bold, even drastic interventions to change the status quo into a more peaceful *something else*.

Kosovo exemplifies a society in which the identities of two competing groups (there known as "nations") have long been tied to Truths about the other. Nonetheless, the war in Kosovo cannot be attributed to ancient hatreds. Rather, the conflict is the result of recent hatreds fueled by recent propaganda campaigns. The case of Kosovo illustrates what happens when political leaders exploit the most demeaning Truths about the other to create intense feelings of insecurity and victimization. This book provides a textured analysis of the context in which stories about the other have been told, received and remembered in Kosovo.

Such an analysis suggests the conditions which foster a politics rooted in antagonistic Truths: a culture of victimization and a history of real and imagined domination of one group over another,[15] long-term human political and social oppression of a disfavored ethno-national group, structural poverty, unmet human development needs, media manipulation of misunderstandings among the general populace, and the absence of civil and political institutions which allow for divergent opinions.[16] These are the conditions that we must address if we are to encourage the creation of peaceful and just societies wherein history as established fact is accepted as legitimate and experience and myth no longer drive a divisive wedge between oppositional groups. These are the stories we must hear if we are to foster institutions and processes that promote peace and justice for all.

The Importance of Kosovo Truths

Many outside observers do not know what to think about Kosovo. History appears to offer few interesting and intelligible clues. Outsiders tend to yawn when Kosovo Serbs (who now make up less than ten percent of the population) or Albanians (who comprise over 90 percent) reckon back fifty or five hundred years to support their claims to territory and tradition. But what about recent history? A void of analysis of recent history keeps us all ill-informed and unable to suggest the kinds of solutions that could lead to positive and long-lasting justice in the region. The kind of analysis that is most desperately missing is an analysis of history as told by the people of the Balkans themselves, history as experience and myth.

Popular accounts of Kosovo are marked by three lines of rhetoric that obfuscate what is really happening. First, the rhetoric of complexity: It is simply impossible to find out what is happening in the Balkans. . . . Albanians live in so many different places and their names are so hard to pronounce. . . . Second, the rhetoric of denial: Nothing ever changes in Kosovo; the situation never really worsens. Third, the rhetoric of Balkan primordialism: These people keep killing each other and there is nothing anyone can do. Serbs and Albanians just hate each other.

Each of the above assertions is wrong. Taking them in reverse order: Tension between Serbs and Albanians is longstanding, but they are not any more genetically prone to killing each other than any other groups with a history of unneighborliness. As in the rest of the former Yugoslavia, politicians have exploited for personal gain each and every sign of intergroup conflict. Serbs and Albanians can live peacefully as neighbors if their political, social and economic rights are respected. The international community could play a role in this process.

The situation in Kosovo has changed considerably since the signing of the Dayton Peace Accord in 1995. Most evidently, Serbian and Yugoslav forces are no longer waging war in other parts of the former Yugoslavia and thus are more available for war in Kosovo. Ruling Serbian politicians who promise to protect Serbs from their enemies may see war in Kosovo as essential to maintaining power. Conflict in Kosovo fosters conditions conducive to the perpetual re-election of politicians like Slobodan Milošević.

Another significant post-Dayton change is the emergence of Albanian actors challenging Ibrahim Rugova, the popularly elected Kosovo Albanian leader who led a campaign of passive resistance against Serbs. An influx of foreign dollars for independent Albanian media in Kosovo (mainly through the Soros Foundation) opened a space for criticism of Rugova and for discussion of more militant action. Rugova had led his people to believe that a favorable resolution on the Kosovo question would be included in any final peace treaty for Bosnia. When this did not occur, critics rose to the right and left of him. A few demanded that he take a more conciliatory stance with Serbs and enter into negotiations over specific economic matters, such as schools. A far greater number demanded more militant direct action for Kosova independence. Sporadic violence against Serbian police and civilians began in the summer of 1996. Although no one took responsibility for the earlier shootings (and most Kosovo Albanians called them staged incidents by Serbs), by the next year a militant Kosovo Albanian group, the Kosovo Liberation Army (KLA), admitted targeting police. In 1998, fighting between the KLA and Serbian police and army erupted into full-scale war, and by the middle of the year the KLA had captured one-third of the province. In June 1998, most Kosovo Albanians were keen to declare their support for the KLA and Rugova, despite their apparently oppositional stances.[17] An array of alternative Albanian politicians waited in the wings should either the KLA or Rugova fail to receive and maintain international and local favor. The collapse of KLA positions in Kosovo in September 1998 and the NATO threats of bombing Serbia in October 1998 created new political conditions within Kosovo that edged alternative Albanian politicians closer to the fore.

Finally, the situation in Kosovo is not hopelessly complex. The pattern of human rights violations in Kosovo, perpetrated by Serbians against Albanians, is undeniable. The U.S. State Department reported in 1997:

Police repression continued to be directed against ethnic minorities, and police committed the most widespread and worst abuses against Kosovo's 90-percent ethnic Albanian population. . . . Political violence, including killings by police, resulted mostly from efforts by Serbian authorities to suppress and intimidate ethnic minority groups. . . . Torture and other cruel forms of punishment, which are prohibited by law, continue to be a problem, particularly in Kosovo directed against ethnic Albanians. . . . Ethnic Albanians continue to suffer at the hands of security forces conducting searches for weapons and explosives. The police, without following proper legal procedures, frequently extract "confessions" during interrogations that routinely include the beating of suspects' feet, hands, genital areas, and sometimes heads. . . . Police use of arbitrary arrest and detention was concentrated primarily in Kosovo.[18]

Elisabeth Rehn, the UN Special Rapporteur on Human Rights in the former Yugoslavia, similarly reported on police brutality and torture against Kosovo Albanians.[19] In December 1996, the UN General Assembly adopted a resolution recognizing and condemning human rights abuses in Kosovo.[20] There is nothing unclear about the existence of human rights abuses in Kosovo.[21]

The Kosovo crisis is not difficult to understand as long as one keeps in mind that people are behind guns and politicians depend on people. Both sides now feel like victims; both sides now feel entitled to take some liberty in "taking back" what is rightfully theirs. Politicians manipulate public aspirations and fears in order to suit their own need to stay in power. These fears are grounded not only on factual events but also on events as remembered, refashioned and retold.

Much has been said about the recent rise of Balkan nationalisms, and particularly of virulent, antiliberal Serbian or Albanian nationalisms.[22] But few commentators have focused on the Truths that are the fodder of power-hungry nationalists, nor have they explored the process by which these Truths are perpetuated in preparation for war. And even fewer seem to remember that resurrection of Balkan power plays and the manipulation of a dark form of nationalism began at least twenty years ago in Kosovo, before the fall of the Berlin wall, before the first shot in Slovenia, the first raid into Vukovar, the first shelling of Sarajevo.

The events in Kosovo in 1981–1990 comprise a major chapter in the final years of Yugoslavia. Developments in Kosovo during these years "led to a fundamental realignment of politics in Serbia and the growth of dangerous, defensive, populist, and officially sanctioned nationalism."[23] An antidemocratic coalition within Serbia of nationalists and communists manipulated the myth of Kosovo to formulate nationalist ideology and produce propaganda. Serbs were said to be the victims of Albanians in Kosovo; they needed the protection of a strong leader like Slobodan Milošević. Populist gatherings — "meetings of truth" — on Kosovo became the main vehicle through which Milošević spread his message, as Mira Oklobdžija observes:

Mass gatherings in which the euphoria of newly found togetherness is engendered amidst glorifications of the national past are easier to perform when their antipode, "the other" who does not have all these good [heroic] qualities, is evoked. He [the Albanian, for example] is not "ours" and does not have the same heroic past. He has not only shown many times in history that he is against us but will surely act against us again if something or somebody doesn't put an end to his perfidious plans. . . . The new leaders . . . offered their services for the "organization of defense" and the "conquering of freedom."[24]

Incrementally, Milošević and his supporters applied this strategy to the rest of Yugoslavia, and the Serbian list of victimizers grew. In this way, "Kosovo provided the time-fuse, and Slobodan Milosevic provided the detonators for a chain reaction of explosions in which first Serbs and then Albanians, Slovenes, Croats, and others came to believe, often to the point of obsession, that part or all of their nation was already or could be faced with extinction."[25] In an atmosphere of economic and political insecurity, the victimization ideology begun in Kosovo caught on quickly. Serbs were called upon to protect themselves against their enemies throughout Yugoslavia.

Kosovo was not merely a place where things happened that could be subject to political manipulation. Kosovo was an abstraction, a set of national myths in the popular imagination. Over time, the nationalism became racialized, that is, difference was framed in terms of perceived physical differences in skin, noses, ears, IQ, sexuality. In this sense, nationalism became "written on the body."[26] Slurs against Kosovo Albanians shifted. No longer referred to as "white hats" (alluding to the hats worn by men in traditional Albanian dress), a sexualized imagery of Albanian men and women was adopted. In the mainstream Serbian and Yugoslav presses, Albanian men were declared to be rapists, although Kosovo had the lowest reported incidents of sexual violence in Yugoslavia. Albanian women were portrayed as mere baby factories, despite statistics indicating that the childbirth rates of urban Albanian women and those of other urban women in Yugoslavia were nearly identical.[27] Accused in the past of being culturally inferior, Albanians increasingly were depicted as genetically inferior as well. This is racism of the purest sort.

Kosovo gave a clear ethno-national "stamp and content to the interpretation of the collapse of the communist regime and its structures."[28] Kosovo was one of the central issues leading to the disintegration of the League of Communists into competing parties and to the dissolution of the Yugoslav federal arrangement.[29] Members of the party split over the use of force against Albanians in Kosovo, and the Serbian nationalism initially mobilized over Kosovo began to threaten other federal units.[30] What had begun as the "Kosovization" of Serbian politics spread to Yugoslav politics.

The seeds of war sown in Kosovo were rooted in the political aims of the powerful. From 1989 onwards Serbian leaders orchestrated a low-intensity state of siege in Kosovo, using police and paramilitary harassment and other human rights violations to cripple Albanian aspirations. With state-controlled media supporting his repressive tactics in Kosovo, Serbian President Slobodan Milošević did not need an all-out war in Kosovo to garner popular support and maintain power. Wars in Croatia and Bosnia-Herzegovina suited that task just fine. But as soon as the Dayton Peace Accord ended the fighting in Bosnia, Milošević turned his full attention to Kosovo. The emergence of militant Albanian groups in Kosovo further intensified Serbian feelings of victimization. These feelings served to erase any ethical responsibility to back peaceful resolution of the conflict.[31] Serbians were well prepared for the inevitability of more war.

From Facts of Abuse to Behavior-Guiding Truths

When I first began researching the role of Kosovo in the destruction of Yugoslavia, I wanted to document the factual truth and, in particular, to expose the facts about the Serbian oppression of Kosovo Albanians. But after spending two years traveling throughout Kosovo and Serbia proper, drinking coffees with Albanians and Serbs in their living rooms, cafés, human rights offices, clinics, weddings, funerals, political meetings, women's meetings, cultural celebrations, I came to realize that I had it all wrong. I was right about the abuse, but I was wrong in thinking that this was the central account that the international community had yet to hear.[32] For the most powerful diplomats, the facts could be crucial for determining and assessing blame and for taking action. The people of the region, however, pattern their behavior around what *they* believe to be true, based not on what some outside "expert" writes but on their own personal experiences and on the myths perpetuated by the local media and other popular storytellers. So for those who are interested in understanding and predicting behavior, what matters is not what is *factually* true but what people believe to be "Truth."

Serbs and Albanians structure their lives around Truths that are closely linked to their identity but that may have nothing (or everything) to do with factual truth or lies. In this context, the opposite of Truth is not necessarily a lie; rather, it is a competing Truth linked to an alternative self-image. The problem, I realized, is that local political leaders were manipulating particularly malignant strains of national Truths, aided by inaccurate and distorted media reports and deteriorating economic and social conditions. Understanding this process entails talking to local people about what they believe to be true and reading the local media, not the *New York Times, Le Monde* or *The Guardian*.

I came to understand another problem: most of the foreign conflict resolution groups and other nongovernmental organizations (NGOs) who travel to places like Kosovo have little awareness of local Truths. Yet Truths become the "hidden transcript"[33] of conflict, the storytelling that serves to define the competing identities of the parties in conflict, propelling and intensifying animosities. While no outsiders can ever hope to fully understand or resolve the Truths that have become part of the identities of competing groups, they cannot afford to ignore their existence. Unaware of competing Truths, NGOs cannot begin to understand the root cause of the conflicts, and thus cannot begin to address the problem in its complexity.

Not just for scholars of nationalism and the history of Yugoslavia, then, but also for NGOs and politicians interested in stemming ethnonational conflict, I decided to attempt to unravel the process of Truths. Most books on Kosovo, especially those from the region, tend to take a macro-examination of history, focusing on historical claims to the region and statistics on demographics and migration.[34] The questions of "who came first" and "who is the guest of whom" figure quite prominently in this discourse.[35] Serbs say that they arrived in the sixth or seventh century as part of the Slavic migration in the Balkans and that Albanians came much later;[36] some Serbs claim that many people who think they are Albanian today are simply "Albanized Serbs."[37] However, Albanians trace their roots in Kosovo to the Illyrians who, during the Roman Empire, populated the region;[38] some Albanians claim that Albanians have often been mischaracterized as Serbs because they were often forced to Serbianize their names.[39] Kosovo is integral to both group's competing national identities: the national awakening of Albanians occurred at the League of Prizren in 1878,[40] but Kosovo also contains places of significance to modern Serbian national identity, including the site of the Patriarchate of the Serbian Orthodox Church, established in 1346 in Peć.[41] Thus, as Sabrina Ramet has pointed out, the Kosovo debate is much like the Palestinian issue: "Two ethnic communities with distinct languages and religious traditions lay claim to the same territory with competing historical arguments as evidence."[42]

The crisis of Kosovo has been embittered by the continued emigration of Serbs and the high birth rate among Kosovo Albanians, two topics of choice among Balkan historians. Polemicists graph and chart birth rates among Serb and Albanian women, warning of a demographic time bomb.[43] Commentators argue about the number of Serbs or Albanians who were allegedly forced to leave Kosovo during various time frames.[44] And on top of everything, hate propaganda proliferates. For more than eighty years, "Serbian propaganda [has] simultaneously dehumanized Albanians, presenting them as utterly incapable of governing themselves and as the sort of element that ought to be exterminated, and elevated them to the level that warranted their assimilation."[45]

The fact remains that Kosovo has become increasingly populated by ethnic Albanians who refuse to give up their language and culture and that, despite Serbian hegemonic control over the region, Serbs keep leaving. Nevertheless, Serbian nationalists continue to claim Kosovo as their Jerusalem, as the essential part of Serbianity. Milan Komnenić, for example, writes: "Kosovo is Serbia, and that is the way it has to be. If some 20 have fallen, tomorrow 20 times as many and 400 times as many may fall. We have to defend every foot of our territory, every foot of our spirituality. . . . This is the cherished center of our spirituality and out entire identity."[46] Despite such heroic utterances, the willingness of most Serbs to sacrifice themselves for Kosovo is "less widespread than their (self-proclaimed) leaders admit."[47] This explains why Milošević and other Serbian leaders have to supplement national animus with an organized campaign of hysterical propaganda, employing journalists and intellectuals to shape Truths for popular consumption.

Instead of duplicating earlier macro-examinations of Kosovo history and debates over medieval history, migration or demographics in Kosovo, I engage in a micro-examination of recent history, selecting both a time frame and a geographic focus that has generally been overlooked in academic literature. In addition, I employ a methodological approach that combines a close media analysis with historical, political, sociological and ethnographic analysis. Just as life is interrupted and perpetuated by storytelling, I move these Truths along with excerpts of oral histories and other storytelling devices. (For the reader who is unfamiliar with Yugoslav history, a review can be found in the chronology at the conclusion of this book. This chronology shows how the "national question" in Yugoslavia began long before the most recent crisis).

The core of the present study analyzes nine years following Tito's death, 1981–1990, tracing the line of Truths from Kosovo to Belgrade (and from there to Ljubljana, to Sarajevo, to Srebrenica). Four Truths serve as markers to divide this time period: the 1981 Student Demonstrations, the Martinović Case, the Paraćin Massacre and the Poisoning of Albanian Schoolchildren. While other Truths existed during this time period, these incidents were particularly instrumental in the reshaping of political and social life in Kosovo, Serbia proper and, ultimately, all of Yugoslavia. The 1981 student demonstrations drew world attention to Kosovo; although the demonstration was portrayed as a "counter-revolutionary" attack against Yugoslavia, it sparked the first criticisms of Tito's legacy and helped (re)shape the debate over centralization/decentralization of Yugoslavia. Next, the Martinović case made Kosovo a Serbian problem; the Serbian and Yugoslav press saw the case as an attack by Albanian nationalist separatists against Serbs. The incident opened the floodgates for more open nationalistic propaganda and sparked Serb feelings of victimization. In contrast, the Paraćin massacre turned Kosovo into a Yugoslav problem, leading to the military buildup of Kosovo and providing ample material for Milošević's populist-nationalist campaign. Finally, the "poisoning of Albanian schoolchildren" made Kosovo once again a Serbian-Albanian problem, cementing the division between the two groups; the incident created the pretext for the Serbian takeover of Kosovo police stations and other government functions and added new fuel to Milošević's drive for major constitutional changes, as well as ushering in the creation of a parallel Kosovo Albanian society. Chapter Five, "Lessons from Truths," explains how nongovernmental organizations can improve their work in Kosovo by deepening their understanding of the root cause of conflict.

My intent is to provide a case study that will add to existing literature on nationalism and storytelling, and to accounts of Balkan history during the period just prior to the wars in Croatia and Bosnia-Herzegovina. As many readers will have in mind the most recent events in Kosovo, the book does include two dated postscripts, one analyzing the situation in Kosovo as of July 1997 and the other critiquing humanitarian, political and military developments as of July 1998.

Ultimately, as Vesna Pešić has noted, "Yugoslavia's demise was in

Kosovo. The federation was politically unequipped to protect its citizens—Serbs and ethnic Albanians in this case—because it had no nonviolent instrument (above all, the rule of law) at its disposal to neutralize and pacify these types of [ethno-national] conflicts."[48] Outsiders may be useful in helping to create institutions and mechanisms for the nonviolent resolution of future conflicts in the Balkans and elsewhere, but in order to be effective they must begin to understand the Truths that can start wars. Kosovo illustrates well the important role played by history as experience and myth in shaping human behavior. The main propellant behind war in Kosovo was not ancient history and ancient hatreds but, as this book shows, recent hatreds manipulated by a carefully orchestrated, fear-mongering media campaign. These stories became the Truths for Kosovo Serbs and Albanians, serving to guide their behavior as perpetrators and victims. We must hear these stories of Truth—for our very survival.

Notes

1. Tzvetan Todorov illustrates this point in *Conquest of America* (New York: HarperCollins, 1994).

2. Paul Arthur, Professor of Politics at the University of Ulster, has made this point in the context of the conflict in Northern Ireland. Conversation with author, Washington, D.C., October 1998.

3. Robert Grudin, *On Dialogue: An Essay in Free Thought* (New York: Houghton Mifflin Company, 1996), 34.

4. Ibid.

5. Paul A. Cohen, *History in Three Keys: The Boxers as Event, Experience and Myth* (New York: Columbia University Press, 1997).

6. For history as process, see Hannah Arendt, *Between Past and Future: Eight Exercises in Political Thought* (New York: Penguin Books, 1954), 85.

7. Tzvetan Todorov, *The Morals of History,* trans. Alyson Waters (Minneapolis: University of Minnesota Press, 1995), 90.

8. Ibid.

9. Michel Foucault, *Power/Knowledge: Selected Interviews and Other Writings 1972–1997,* trans. Colin Gordon (New York: Pantheon, 1980), 131–32.

10. See Cohen, *History in Three Keys,* 3.

11. Grudin, *On Dialogue,* 20.

12. Hannah Arendt, *The Origins of Totalitarianism* (New York: Harcourt Brace, 1951), 72.

13. I adopt the concept of national identity as theorized by Bhikhu Parekh: national identity is not a substance but a cluster of tendencies, neither fixed

nor alterable at will, and periodically redefined. See Bhikhu Parekh, "The Concept of National Identity," *New Community* 21, no. 2 (1995) 255–68.

14. Sissela Bok, *Lying: Moral Choice in Public and Private Life* (New York: Vintage Books, 1979).

15. For the development and application of the model of domination as the rooted cultural-historical pattern in Kosovo, see Srdja Popović, Dejan Janča and Tanja Petrovar, eds., *Kosovski čvor: Drešiti ili seći?* (Belgrade: Chronos, 1990), 8. Dušan Janjić has also identified a "heritage of authoritarianism." See Janjić, "Resurgence of Ethnic Conflict in Yugoslavia: The Demise of Communism and the Rise of the 'New Elites' of Nationalism," in *Yugoslavia: The Former and the Future: Reflections by Scholars from the Region*, eds. Payam Akhavan and Robert Howse (Washington, D.C.: The Brookings Institute, 1995), 33.

16. Other factors include a culture of not accepting blame for social problems. See chapter five, on conflict resolution, for this factor.

17. Author's interviews in Kosovo, June 1998.

18. U.S. State Department, *Country Reports for Human Rights Practices for 1997* (Washington, D.C.: U.S. Government Printing Office).

19. Elisabeth Rehn's report on Kosovo is in her submission to the Commission on Human Rights, UN Doc. E/CN.4/1998/15.

20. UN General Assembly, UN Doc. A/RES/51/111 of 5 March 1997.

21. Human Rights Watch, the International Helsinki Committee, the Humanitarian Law Fund and the International Crisis Group are among the international nongovernmental organizations that have documented human rights abuses in Kosovo and analyzed their implications. See bibliography.

22. Živko Surčulija, drawing from Isaiah Berlin, has described antiliberal nationalism as being "turned completely to the past instead [of] to the future . . ." and which "appears out of the fear of anything new, of freedom, modernization and of development." Živko Surčulija, "Nationalism and Post-Communism: The Role of Nationalism in Destroying Former Socialist Federations with Particular Emphasis on the Case of Yugoslavia," *Balkan Forum* 3, no. 2 (June 1995), 160.

23. Bogdan Denitch, *Ethnic Nationalism: The Tragic Death of Yugoslavia* (Minneapolis: University of Minnesota Press, 1994), 116.

24. Mira Oklobdžija, "The Creation of Active Xenophobia in What Was Yugoslavia," *Journal of Area Studies*, no. 3 (1993), 95.

25. Dennison Rusinow, "The Avoidable Catastrophe," in *Beyond Yugoslavia: Politics, Economics and Culture in a Shattered Community*, eds. Sabrina Petra Ramet and Ljubiša S. Adamovich (Boulder, Colo.: Westview Press, 1995), 19–20. I may disagree with Rusinow regarding only the precise ordering of nationalisms.

26. I take this phraseology from Jeanette Winterson, who used it in a different context in *Written on the Body* (New York, Vintage Books, 1994).

27. See Julie Mertus, "Gender in the Service of Nation: Female Citizenship in Kosovar Society," *Social Politics: International Studies in Gender, State and Society* 3, no. 2/3 (Summer/Fall 1996).

28. Mirjana Kasapović, "The Structure and Dynamics in the Yugoslav Po-

litical Environment and Elections in Croatia," in *The Tragedy of Yugoslavia: The Failure of Democratic Transformation*, eds. Jim Seroka and Vukašin Pavlović (Armonk, N.Y.: M. E. Sharpe, 1992), 30.

29. Denitch, *Ethnic Nationalisms*, 122.

30. Ibid.

31. See Pierre Taminiaux, "Sacred Text, Sacred Nation," in *Textured Nation: Cross-Disciplinary Essays on Cultural and National Identity*, ed. Laura Garcia-Moreno and Peter C. Pfeiffer (Columbia, S.C.: Camden House, 1996), 91–104.

32. On Serbian oppression of Kosovo Albanians, see Helsinki Watch and International Helsinki Foundation, *Yugoslavia: Crisis in Kosovo*, eds. Julie Mertus and Vlatka Mihelić (New York: Human Rights Watch/Helsinki Watch, 1990). I have also written about human rights abuses in Kosovo in op-eds in *The New York Times* and *The International Herald Tribune*.

33. This term is developed by James C. Scott in *Domination and the Arts of Resistance: Hidden Transcripts* (New Haven: Yale University Press, 1990), 198.

34. Two exceptional broad historical accounts on Kosovo were published after this manuscript was completed. See Noel Malcolm, *Kosovo: A Short History* (New York: New York University Press, 1998), and Miranda Vickers, *Between Serb and Albanian: A History of Kosovo* (New York: Columbia University Press, 1998). One of the best accounts on the recent wars in Yugoslavia by journalists is Laura Silber and Allan Little, *The Death of Yugoslavia* (London: Penguin Books, BBC Books, 1995). Another journalist, Tim Judah, has written a history of Serbia in which he includes Kosovo; see Judah, *The Serbs: History, Myth and the Destruction of Yugoslavia* (New Haven, Conn.: Yale University Press, 1997).

35. In connection with these claims, Michel Roux asks, "Does anyone have a right, based on this or that period of the past, to make themselves the exclusive 'owners' of a territory?" Michel Roux, *Les Albanais en Yougoslavie: Minorit (nationale, territorie et développement)*. Paris: Maison des Sciences de l'Homme, 1992, 21.

36. For two recent accounts, see Dimitrije Bogdanović, *Knjiga o Kosovu*, 3d ed. (Belgrade: Srpska akademija nauka i umetnosti, 1996); and Djordje Jevtić, *Bitka za Kosovo, šest vekova posle I* (Priština: Novi Svet, 1995).

37. See Djoko Slijepčević, "Concerning the Albanization of the Serbs," *The South Slav Journal* 5, no. 4(18) (winter 1982/83), 8–14.

38. See Rexhep Ismajli, *Kosovo and the Albanians in Former Yugoslavia* (Kosovo: Kosova Information Center, n.d.), 7.

39. Arshi Pipa, "The Other Albania: A Balkan Perspective," *The South Slav Journal* 8, nos. 1–2 (spring-summer, 1985). Ivo Banac has written that although Albanians "have a point in claiming that Christian names do not necessarily convey Slavs, . . . it is hard to believe that a 'Radihna, son of Dabiživ' or a 'Prijezda, son of Relja' has any Albanian ancestry. . . ." Ivo Banac, *The National Question in Yugoslavia: Origins, History, Politics* (Ithaca, N.Y.: Cornell University Press, 1984), 294–95n. 9.

40. The League of Prizren was formed primarily to organize political and military opposition to the dismemberment of Albanian-inhabited territory by the Ottoman Empire. The League united Albanian nationalists in their demands for administrative and cultural autonomy. Over time, the League turned

to demanding total autonomy. See Vickers, *Between Serb and Albanian,* 44–45. See also Derek Hall, "Albanian Identity and Balkan Roles," in *Reconstructing the Balkans: A Geography of the New Southeast Europe,* eds. Derek Hall and Darrick Danta (New York: John Wiley & Sons, 1996), 122–23.

41. George W. White, "Place and its Role in Serbian Identity," in *Reconstructing the Balkans,* eds. Hall and Danta, 44–45.

42. Sabrina Ramet, *Social Currents in Eastern Europe: The Sources and Meaning of the Great Transformation* (Durham, N.C.: Duke University Press, 1991), 174. Marko Milivojević has similarly referred to the potential "Lebanonization" of Kosovo. Marko Milivojević, "Descent into Chaos: Yugoslavia's Worsening Crisis," *The South Slav Journal* 12, nos. 1–2 (spring-summer 1989), 7.

43. For more measured accounts of demographics, see Hivzi Islami, "Demographic Problems of Kosova and other Ethnic Albanian Territories," in *The Kosova Issue: A Historic and Current Problem,* ed. Jusuf Bajraktari et al., 139–45 (Tirana: Institute of History); and Srdjan Bogosavljević, "A Statistical Picture of Serbo-Albanian Relations," *Republika* 6, special issue 9 (February 1994), 19 (published also in Serbian as "Statisticka slika srpsko-albanskih odnosa").

44. See chapter 2, note 78, for a comparison of some of these figures.

45. Banac, *The National Question in Yugoslavia,* 293. See appendix of this book for a survey of recent stereotypes of Albanians held by Serbs and Hungarians.

46. Milan Komnenić, quoted in Gale Stokes, *The Walls Came Tumbling Down: The Collapse of Communism in Eastern Europe* (New York: Oxford University Press, 1993), 302n.33.

47. Mark L. Almond, *Europe's Backyard War: The War in the Balkans* (London: Heinemann, 1994), 201.

48. Vesna Pešić, "Serbian Nationalism and the Origins of the Yugoslav Crisis." Paper prepared for the U.S. Institute for Peace, 1996 (available on the internet at http://www.usip.org/oc/sr/pesic/pesic.html#exp).

ONE

The 1981 Student Demonstrations

Laying the Foundation: 1971–1981

When reforms against repression begin, repression becomes less tolerable: so goes the Machiavellian proposition.[1] Nowhere does this maxim hold more true than in Kosovo. From 1971 to 1981, Albanians in Kosovo progressively gained rights and, in the process, experienced unparalleled progress in the fields of education, science and culture. With the opening of the University of Priština in 1969, Kosovars had access to Albanian-language instruction in primary, secondary and university classes;[2] institutes for Albanian literature and culture were opened; and cultural ties between Albania and Kosovo were permitted, leading to an influx of books from Albania to Kosovo, the exchange of visiting professors and even the planning of joint film productions.[3] Although not perfect, the national "key" system—akin to proportional affirmative action—assured Albanian representation on managerial boards of state enterprises, in civil service and in provincial and federal government. During 1978–79, the vice-president of the federal Presidency (which after the death of Tito became a collective body) was a Kosovo Albanian, Fadil Hoxha, making him the highest-ranking Kosovo Albanian ever in Yugoslavia. Within the framework of Yugoslavia, then, Kosovo Albanians had never achieved so much in such a short time.

At what appeared to be the zenith of Kosovo Albanian achievements, those who seemed to be benefiting the most from the reforms, the young intellectuals, decided to take action to push for even greater change. The improved conditions for Albanians in Kosovo had created a better educated, healthier and more ambitious population. But also, by opening the door for hope, the improvements had tapped discontent.[4] As a result, the decade of 1971–1981 was characterized by "a growing confidence among local Albanian leaders, who felt uneasy under Serbian 'paternalism,' as well as an increasing number of mass protests, demonstrations, and riots that rejected it unconditionally."[5]

The staging of Albanian demonstrations at this time period confounded Serbs. After all, things seemed to be going so well. "Minority rights of Albanians in Kosovo until 1989 were guaranteed beyond and in excess of international standards," legal scholar Vladan Vasilijević notes.[6] The sentiment among Serbs was along the lines of: "We had given them everything, even their own university, their own government."[7] But Albanians did not want to be in the position of being *given* anything. Despite the reforms, notes Sami Repishti, a U.S.-based academic originally from Kosovo, "the feeling of dependency on Serbia . . . remained a major source of friction and deep dissatisfaction."[8] Moreover, Kosovo Albanians felt a personal affront at not being considered a "nation" but only a "nationality," a lower status under the nomenclature of Yugoslavia. The insult of Yugoslavia not considering Albanians a "nation" could not be compensated with a university, nor with a provincial government.

In 1981, Yugoslavia was composed of six nations—Slovenes, Montenegrins, Croats, Serbs, Macedonians and Muslims—and all the rest of the groups of people were considered "nationalities" or "ethnic minorities." "Muslims"—ethnic Slavs who had converted to Islam during Ottoman rule—were the last group to be given the status of a nation (in 1968), having been allowed the appellation on the federal census in 1961. The term "Muslim" did not refer only to religion; the practicing of Islam was neither necessary nor sufficient for inclusion in this group. (For example, Muslim Albanians were not considered to be part of this national grouping of Muslim.) Rather, "Muslim" referred to a group defined by a bundle of markers of distinctiveness: language, culture, economic life, real and imagined history and a sense of territoriality.[9] Albanians living in Yugoslavia pointed out that they had all those markers. There were more Albanians in Yugoslavia than there were Montenegrins; why should the latter be a nation while the former were not? The only reason, it seemed, was that they were considered to have a nation elsewhere—Albania—and thus they could not "have two." Some feared that the promotion of an Albanian nation within Yugoslavia would challenge the country's territorial integrity. Promotion of a Muslim identity in Bosnia-Herzegovina was thought to help serve as a buffer against territorial claims from Croatia and Serbia and, thus, promote the continued existence of Yugoslavia, but promotion of an Albanian Kosovar identity was viewed as a threat to Yugoslav unity. Some Albanian commentators suggest that Yugoslavia, being at its core a Slavic country, would never give a non-Slavic population, such as the Albanians, the status of a "nation."[10]

As a mere "nationality," Kosovo Albanians did not have the right to their own republic. The heart of the political tensions in Kosovo rested in this denial of republic status.[11] Nevertheless, constitutional changes introduced in 1969, 1971 and 1974 gave Kosovo greater autonomy and the ability to forge direct links with federal authorities.[12] Under the 1974 Constitution for the Federal Republic of Yugoslavia, Kosovo was considered an "autonomous province" of Serbia.[13] This made Kosovo a "quasi-republic," with a government, constitution, police, courts, school system, industry and economic institutions—almost everything except the right to secede from the federation, a right that the full-status republics possessed. As Albanian political leader Azem Vllasi has observed, "Kosovo functioned as a republic in the federal state of Yugoslavia and we were not [a republic] only by name."[14] But for Kosovo Albanians, almost was not good enough. The rights of the territorial unit known as "the Autonomous Province of Kosovo" were still at least formally tied to the Constitution of the Republic of Serbia.[15] Shedding every trace of dependence on Serbia became Kosovo Albanians' primary goal.

Albanian national consciousness, like other forms of national consciousness in the Balkans and elsewhere, was formed in large part in relationship to a real and imagined historical past, as written, told and shared. In Yugoslavia, the line was thin between permissible exploration of culture and condemned "counterrevolutionary" behavior, "hostile propaganda," or acts deemed to be "incitement of national hatreds." Still, by and large, the rules of the game were well known.[16] Kosovo Albanians pushed the envelope when in 1978 they held a series of festivities commemorating the League of Prizren centennial. The League, the primary symbol of the Albanian "national awakening," had called in 1878 for a unified Albanian state and full autonomy for all Albanian-inhabited territories in the Ottoman empire.[17] To mark this seminal event, nearly every predominately Albanian town in Kosovo held celebrations of Al-

banian literature, song and history. Local and federal authorities tolerated the gatherings, hoping that they would provide some kind of ca-
tharsis. However, leaflets printed and distributed in connection with
these events were condemned as illegal, and in some places verbal confrontations erupted between Albanians and police.[18]

The League of Prizren events, the blossoming of Albanian literature
and folk festivals, and the flying of the Albanian flag alongside the Yugoslav (at a time when the flying of a Serbian or Croatian flag would
have been met with a jail sentence) — all of these steps were seen by many
Yugoslavs as unwise indulgence of Albanian nationalism. Indeed, some
commentators have described Yugoslavia's attitude toward expressions
of national sentiment by Kosovo Albanians during 1971–1981 as "laissez-
faire."[19] However, a review of arrest records at the time show that the
authorities were far from indifferent. The treatment of nationalist demands in Kosovo, Sabrina Ramet notes, "exemplifie[d] conflict resolution in communist Yugoslavia: jail the troublemakers but grant their
non-disintegrative demands."[20]

From 1971 to 1981, public expression of political dissent was suppressed in all parts of Yugoslavia,[21] but the greatest percentage of political prisoners were Kosovo Albanians.[22] The decade began with a stiff
warning to those with national or "reformist" sentiments: the silencing
of dissent in Croatia in 1971, when Tito removed the reformist leadership
of the League of Communists.[23] Taboo subjects included nationalism
(and any criticism of the unity of different ethnic groups), criticism of
the structure of government of Yugoslavia, including the operations of
the League of Communists and its leadership, and any challenges to
basic domestic or foreign policies.[24] Although some national cultural
events were tolerated, such as the League of Prizren events, the authorities maintained discretion to control and prosecute anything deemed
to be organized national activity and, in particular, any acts considered
separatist.

During the 1970s, several trials were held in which Albanians were
convicted for plotting the secession of Kosovo from Yugoslavia.[25] Yugoslav security forces announced at this time that they had discovered
at least seven underground Albanian separatist organizations operating
in Kosovo and two in Macedonia; the purported leaders, usually students at the University of Priština, were arrested and given lengthy
prison sentences. Student demonstrations in Priština in 1974 led to at
least 100 arrests.[26] According to official Yugoslav reports, between 1974
and 1981, at least 618 Albanians were accused of nationalist and irreden-

tist activities in Kosovo; of these, 89 received prison sentences ranging from one to fifteen years, and another 503 were charged for the lesser offense of making nationalist statements.[27]

Many of the Albanians who were arrested, like other political prisoners at the time, were harshly treated: "Albanians were beaten into insanity, had their arms and legs broken under torture, were forced to conduct prolonged hunger strikes and were shot inside solitary cells. The worst case was registered in the Idrizovo prison [Skopje, Macedonia] . . . , when 'six Albanians were beaten by prison guards with twisted whipcords for refusing to go to solitary cells.' Two prisoners died; the other four, badly maimed, saw their jail sentences increased."[28] In the Idrizovo case, a federal investigation resulted in the imprisonment of the prison director and five guards.[29] Albanian prisoners staged massive riots in 1978 to protest alleged mistreatment of Albanian prisoners and discriminatory behavior by Serbian prison guards.[30]

The rising expectations of Kosovo Albanians concerning the strengthening of their national rights were both helped and hindered by publicity surrounding state retaliation against Albanian political expression. Any Kosovo Albanian who voiced any political opinion whatsoever risked being branded as an "irredentist," a person who sought to unite all the members of his or her ethno-national group in an autonomous state. Arrests of Kosovo Albanians served to create martyrs for the Albanian community. Many of those fined or arrested were not in fact irredentists but rather small-time graffiti writers or fourth-hand readers of underground publications who happened to get caught.[31] Nevertheless, these unlucky ones took their place among real and imagined Kosovo Albanian leaders as the emerging heroes.

On the other hand, repression drove the Albanian national movement, like other national movements at the time, underground. Organized in highly secretive cell-like structures, with "webs" of individuals reporting to each other in a fashion that minimized their knowledge of even each other's identity,[32] the movement could hardly be populist. Cells were intentionally kept small to minimize the possibility of infiltration, so "recruitment" was not a key goal; communication among movement members was limited; movement propaganda of any type, from crude fliers to the hand-to-hand circulation of mimeographs, was considered risky and thus restricted. Under such conditions, planning a strike or demonstration was extremely difficult and entailed great risk.[33]

In addition to political crimes, Kosovo Albanians were increasingly accused of other crimes against Serbs and Montenegrins, such as breaking up Serbian and Montenegrin gravestones, defacing the property of the Orthodox church and physically assaulting Serbian priests, nuns and farmers. With accusations far outnumbering investigations or convictions for crimes, Serbs accused the local Albanian police and other Kosovar authorities of failing to prosecute crimes against Serbs and Montenegrins.[34] While not agreeing with all of the accusations, even today's leader of Albanians in Kosovo, Ibrahim Rugova, has admitted that Albanians did not "behave as they should have" and that "some people were out of control" during this period.[35]

Belgrade officials would later plead ignorance of the mounting national tensions in Kosovo, accusing Kosovar politicians of withholding information from them. Some commentators have alleged that Kosovo Albanian party leaders were operating in concert with the accused separatists, or that at the very least they had sympathy for their actions. Others suggest that provincial leaders quieted any news of Albanian-Serb conflict for fear that publicity would lead to a crackdown and a lessening of their power. And still others suggest that no cover-up existed at all: If Belgrade did not know, it was because Belgrade did not want to know. Indeed, information did exist about the purported separatist groups and their leaders. Provincial leaders and the Albanian-language daily *Rilindja* (an organ of the provincial party) had explicitly warned about the growing problem posed by Albanian separatist groups.[36] The Belgrade dailies continually quoted Kosovo's provincial party chief Mahmut Bakali as saying that Kosovo was under control—that "the efforts of the enemies have not found wide support among the masses . . . [and] the devotion of the Albanians to Tito's Yugoslavia is durable and indestructible."[37] Yet the same dailies also ran articles warning about separatist activities and impending doom in Kosovo.[38]

The international press also began speculating about the fate of Kosovo. In April 1980, Agence France Press quoted Tito as saying that "Kosovo is now the biggest problem confronting Yugoslavia," and *Le Monde* in May 1980 speculated, "Whatever the future may be, the mere existence of a Yugoslav Albania in Kosovo, bordering on Tirana's Republic of Albania, will, as a matter of course, present serious problems in the not too distant future."[39]

Dissatisfaction among Kosovars was compounded by the dire economic situation in Kosovo. Although development aid was pumped into Kosovo through a federal fund for development of underdeveloped areas at a rate far higher than in any part of the country (see table 1),[40] the economic ventures in the province had little impact on the quality

Table 1 *Percentage Distribution of the Federal Credit Fund for the Development of Economically Underdeveloped Republics and Provinces, 1985–1990*

	1985	1986	1987	1988	1989	1990
Bosnia- Herzegovina	25.18	31.05	28.52	21.30	28.32	24.11
Montenegro	9.99	8.32	9.47	7.19	7.66	5.98
Macedonia	25.27	14.91	17.85	16.35	18.84	16.65
Kosovo	39.56	45.73	44.15	55.17	45.18	53.26

SOURCE: *Statistical Yearbook of Yugoslavia*, 501, as cited in Dragomir Vojnić, "Disparity and Disintegration: The Economic Dimension of Yugoslavia's Demise," in *Yugoslavia: The Former and the Future: Reflections by Scholars from the Region*, eds. Payam Akhavan and Robert Howse (Washington D.C.: The Brookings Institute, 1995), 102.

of people's lives. Instead of boosting the province's industrial output and creating jobs for workers, the funds had been directed disproportionately into the administrative sector of the bureaucracy and to heavy industry dinosaurs. As a result, while the pockets of the well-connected had been lined with federal cash, the general population of Kosovo saw little improvement in everyday life. One quarter of all employed Kosovars were government employees,[41] but few jobs existed outside the government sector. The unemployment rate in Kosovo was the highest in the country—27.5 percent—compared to a mere 2 percent unemployment in Slovenia, the most prosperous republic, the same year.[42]

Meanwhile, conditions in other federal units improved, widening the development gap between Kosovo and all other republics. The per capita income in Kosovo declined from 48 percent of the Yugoslav average in 1954, to 33 percent in 1975, to 27 percent by 1980.[43] According to calculations by Serbian economists, Albanians continued to earn less than members of other ethnic or national groups; moreover, Albanians earned far less in Kosovo and in Serbia proper than in any other part of Yugoslavia (see table 2).

The regional disparities were related to "a complex interplay of economic, political, social, cultural and historic factors, which made the officially declared goal of reduction of the enormous inherited economic disparities and social inequities among Yugoslav nations very difficult to achieve."[44] The gaps between the more developed federal units (Slovenia, Croatia and Serbia) and the less developed units continued to widen, and within the group of "less developed" units Kosovo progressively slipped farther and farther to the bottom. In 1947, the level of

Table 2 Per Capita National Income (in Dinars) by Republic and Ethnic Group in 1981

	All Nations	Monte-negrins	Croats	Mace-donians	Muslims	Slovenes	Serbs	Albanians	Hun-garians	Poles	Roma	Yugo-slavs*	Others
Average for Yugoslavia as a whole	89,466	80,745	105,316	63,448	60,236	158,353	85,051	34,099	117,913	106,507	67,654	110,861	96,690
Percentage of average for Yugoslavia as a whole	100.0	90.3	117.7	70.9	67.3	177.0	95.1	38.1	131.8	119.0	75.6	123.9	108.1
Bosnia-Herzegovina	61,511	88,522	57,885	84,725	60,346	91,101	59,665	75,535	87,937	58,456	64,970	79,762	70,506
Croatia	114,660	144,958	114,461	148,937	151,415	164,457	98,906	144,505	110,252	124,274	150,700	127,531	124,669
Macedonia	57,643	73,503	72,768	60,950	57,260	81,709	63,948	45,133	68,904	60,538	54,476	68,329	58,373
Montenegro	69,709	71,385	96,813	81,371	45,184	86,348	87,989	63,628	100,000	86,667	74,439	96,396	78,380
Serbia proper	85,892	105,993	122,400	108,432	52,652	135,579	85,286	36,797	123,867	118,933	73,399	115,550	87,703
Vojvodina	114,863	124,688	112,235	116,336	116,978	119,416	113,654	111,123	118,870	117,114	106,408	121,348	107,246
Kosovo	29,684	36,495	20,096	43,750	26,200	41,691	35,250	28,443	38,095	40,741	39,876	36,435	34,456
Serbia as a whole	82,660	98,745	108,997	110,087	46,927	128,241	88,672	29,149	118,903	116,279	68,947	117,265	95,788
Slovenia	160,905	199,658	176,973	185,401	195,151	158,637	195,491	196,423	102,675	180,882	147,944	189,106	188,829

*Citizens of Yugoslavia were permitted (indeed, encouraged) to identify themselves not as any nationality but as Yugoslavs. Few did so.

SOURCE: Kosta Mihailović, *Regionalna stvarnost Jugoslavije* (Belgrade: Ekonomika, 1990), 153.

development of the more developed parts of Yugoslavia was twice as high as that of Kosovo, Macedonia, Montenegro and Bosnia-Herzegovina. In 1980, the level of development for Macedonia, Montenegro and Bosnia-Herzegovina had grown to two-and-a-half times that of Kosovo, while the level for Yugoslavia as a whole was four times Kosovo's.[45]

The discrepancies between more and less developed regions in Yugoslavia can be seen in a comparison of basic indicators for regional development, as measured by GMP (Gross Material Product), GMP per capita and average growth of GMP. Kosovo lagged behind the country average in all of these measures. (See table 3.) In addition, although Kosovo and the other less developed areas significantly increased their fixed assets per worker, the return on the investment was low. In her analysis of data from this period, Vesna Bojičić has found that although the investment ratio was higher in Kosovo than the Yugoslav average, "in order for less developed parts of the country to achieve the same economic performance as more developed republics, the investment input *had* to be significantly higher." Once the data on population growth is added to the equation, "a vicious circle of poverty emerges, with per capita income in poorer areas growing only slowly, from a low base."[46] Some analysts point to the uneven regional development in Yugoslavia as a critical factor in the country's disintegration.[47] With respect to Kosovo, these disparities constituted one of several factors fanning national tensions.

Another aspect of the economic situation that exacerbated national tensions was the inferior position of Kosovo Albanians in comparison with the Kosovo Serbian minority, whose proportion of the total population in Kosovo had fallen from 23.6 percent in 1961 to 13.2 percent in 1981. Fred Singleton has observed a colonialist phenomenon at play in Kosovo. Within Kosovo, Serbs still held a disproportionate share of the senior positions in the professions, especially in technology, medicine and law. "The situation bore a resemblance to the position of many newly independent Third World countries," Singleton notes, "where posts requiring high technical qualifications were still held by expatriate Europeans whilst the new universities became centers for the propagation of the national culture."[48]

The discrepancies Singleton mentions are not readily discernible from employment statistics. In 1980, the number of Albanians among the employed population of Kosovo (64.9 percent of total employed) was 12.6 percentage points lower than their share of the population (77.5

Table 3 Basic Indicators of Regional Development in Yugoslavia

	Percentage of Yugoslav population		Percentage of Yugoslav GMP		GMP per capita, as a percentage of Yugoslav average		Average annual percentage growth of GMP, per capita		Fixed assets per worker	
	1953	1988	1953	1988	1953	1988	1956	1988	1952	1987
Bosnia-Herzegovina	16.7	18.8	14.4	12.8	83	68	4.6	3.3	82	95
Montenegro	2.5	2.7	1.8	2.0	77	74	5.0	3.9	46	137
Croatia	23.2	19.9	26.7	25.4	122	128	4.6	4.8	101	110
Macedonia	7.7	8.9	5.2	5.6	68	63	5.1	4.1	69	74
Slovenia	8.8	8.2	14.3	16.7	175	203	5.2	4.5	122	134
Serbia proper	26.3	24.8	25.4	25.0	91	101	5.1	4.3	106	82
Vojvodina	10.0	8.7	10.0	10.3	94	119	5.3	4.8	95	102
Kosovo	4.8	8.0	2.2	2.2	43	27	5.1	2.6	89	92
Serbia as a whole	41.1	41.5	37.6	37.5	86	90	5.1	4.2	113	91
Yugoslavia as a whole	100.0	100.0	100.0	100.0	100	100	4.9	4.0	100	100

SOURCE: Dijana Pleština, Regional Development in Communist Yugoslavia: Success, Failure and Consequences (Boulder, Colo.: Westview Press, 1992), 180.

percent), while the number of Serbs in Kosovo with jobs (25.6 percent of the total employed) was 12.4 percentage points higher than their share of the population.[49] On the other hand, because more Serbs were *seeking* jobs, the Serbs' share of the *un*employed in Kosovo was consistently higher relative to their share of the population. In sum, the economic situation in Kosovo was bad for everyone. (See also table 4.)

Who is to blame for Kosovo's economic woes of unemployment, inflation, food shortages, housing crises, weak infrastructure and poverty? The highest ranking Kosovar economist, Riza Sapunxhiu, who in 1981 was vice-president of the economy, contends that any criticism about the state of economy in Kosovo in 1981 was unwarranted. "We were doing everything we could," he says. "People were impatient."[50] Similarly, although he believes that economic reforms could have been improved, Dragomir Vojnić attributes much of the developmental difference between the regions to a "historical inheritance" that could not easily disappear.[51] The people who lived in Kosovo, however, looked for a target for their frustrations. Kosovo Albanians were most likely to blame federal or republic officials for historically neglecting the region and for pursing poor economic plans. In particular, as some economists have pointed out, "the developed regions had more manufacturing industry, with less developed regions predominately basic-industry oriented."[52] For three decades, Kosovo had produced raw materials that were then processed in Serbia proper and elsewhere, making Kosovo dependent on other parts of Yugoslavia for finished goods.[53]

In addition to the economic planning, many Serbs pointed to the waste, inefficiency and incompetence of the Albanian bureaucrats who took over in the 1970s, as well as the large Albanian family structure that greatly taxed social resources.[54] Commentators on both sides say the situation was made worse by the "exodus of experts" from Kosovo, mainly Serbs and Montenegrins who moved to other parts of Yugoslavia in the late 1960s and early 1970s after Ranković's reign ended.[55] Serbs most often contend that the experts had been forced out due to the discriminatory policies of Kosovo Albanians.[56] Albanians contend that the emigration resulted from "the loss of privileges they had enjoyed and their reluctance to accept the equality of the Albanians."[57]

Instead of combating the economic disparities, the University of Priština offered only a palliative and ultimately destructive alternative. Instead of immediately joining the ranks of the unemployed, the best and brightest of Kosovo could attend the university, where their expectations would increase and sense of self would develop; but upon grad-

Table 4 *Unemployment in Kosovo by Nationality*

	1970	% of Total	1980	% of Total	1981 (as of June)	% of Total
Albanians	48,590	76.0	52,926	76.1	52,170	77.6
Serbs	11,216	17.6	11,812	17.0	10,202	15.1
Montenegrins	1,490	2.4	1,405	2.0	1,267	1.8
Turks	412	0.7	464	0.7	447	0.7
Muslims	691	1.2	1,228	1.8	872	1.4
Roma	982	1.6	1,361	1.9	1,301	2.0
Other	610	0.5	390	0.5	890	1.3
Total	63,991	100.0	69,586	100.0	67,149	100.0

SOURCE: *Rilindja,* Priština, March 6, 1982 (as cited in Peter Prifti, "Kosova's Economy: Problems and Prospects," in *Studies on Kosova,* eds. Arshi Pipa and Sami Repishti [Boulder, Colo.: East European Monographs, 1984], 143). Similar figures appear in other sources.

uation they would still not find a job in their field. University graduates could find little work in Kosovo apart from "the inflated administrative machine and in the cultural institutions which had also been the recipients of [federal] funds which ought to have been spent on projects of greater economic relevance."[58] Opportunities in the rest of Yugoslavia were even worse, especially for those who were educated only in the Albanian language. Meanwhile, the resentment of the Serb and Montenegrin population toward the numerous Albanian students grew; the students were accused of monopolizing the few opportunities that did exist and of overburdening republic and federal coffers that had to foot the bill for their education.[59]

The problem was compounded by the chosen courses of study at the university. Instead of training students for technical careers in a modern age, the university specialized in liberal arts, in particular in Albanian literature and culture.[60] Competition for the few jobs that existed in this field was fierce. Also, lacking a sufficient supply and breadth of Albanian-language textbooks in these subjects, the high schools and universities imported texts from Albania. Given Albania's different ideological bent, these texts necessarily included ideological and philosophical undercurrents contrary to those produced in Yugoslavia. Tito had originally envisioned the cultural exchange between Kosovo and Albania as a bridge along which Yugoslavia would be able to exert influence over Albania.

For the most part, however, there was only one-way traffic from Albania to Kosovo, and the young Kosovar students were "like a very parched sponge, immediately avid to absorb anything that helped to illuminate their past history and made sense of their contemporary situation."[61] Those who were university students in 1981 contend that they looked beyond the ideological leanings of the books to the cultural content.[62] Nonetheless, the books, the students and the educational system would later be blamed for the growing discontent at the University of Priština.

By 1981, the student population in Priština had ballooned to over twenty thousand—nearly one in ten adults in the city.[63] Kosovo had the dubious honor of having the highest ratio of both students and illiterates in Yugoslavia. The Albanian nationalist movement in Kosovo found its most vocal supporters and leaders among the young, educated unemployed. Tito was aware of this growing danger during his last visit to Kosovo (and one of his last pubic experiences) on October 16, 1979. He warned members of the party that "Kosovo must truly be the concern of all our peoples of the entire Yugoslav union," and that "more development is in the interest not only of Kosovo, but all of Yugoslavia."[64] Kosovo did not need just more development funds, it desperately needed more efficient social and economic strategies that were more attentive to the region's national tensions. These improvements never came. Instead, within a year of Tito's death, the University of Priština would erupt in the worst violence in Yugoslavia since the end of the Second World War.[65]

The Truths of the 1981 Demonstrations

Those who were university students in Kosovo in 1981 remember the initial demonstrations as small-scale protests for better food in the school cafeteria and improved living conditions in the dormitories.[66] These protests, on March 11, 1981, involved an estimated two thousand students. Some say they lasted a couple of hours, others that the demonstrations lingered for nearly two days. According to interviews with participants, there was little advance knowledge of the action—nor could there have been, as police would have disrupted the protest before it began. Most students who joined in the demonstrations say that they just happened to be at the university when they heard and saw fellow students beginning to gather.[67] Before long, the protesters had expanded their concerns to demand better conditions for Albanians in Kosovo.[68] Police dispersed the demonstrators. The next day, Tanjug, the official Yugoslav press agency, described the demonstrations as having been provoked by "hostile elements . . . attempting to exploit the discontent of certain students over the quality of food at the school cafeteria."[69]

After two weeks of calm, the protests resumed in Prizren (southern Kosovo) on March 25, and again in Priština on March 26, when Albanian students occupied a dormitory. This time, the demonstrations grew violent. The Priština daily *Rilindja* reported that thirty-five people were wounded and twenty-one students arrested in this second wave of protests.

No longer a student protest but a mass revolt, the unrest moved across Kosovo. Six cities erupted on April 1 and 2, bringing tens of thousands of miners, workers, teachers, students, civil servants, Albanians from all walks of life onto the streets. Rioters allegedly marched with young children in front, as shields, as they moved against police, throwing rocks and smashing store windows. The federal government declared a state of emergency, bringing in federal troops and helicopters to patrol cities, major roadways and borders. Paratroopers occupied an airfield strip in Priština; the entire province was sealed off; a curfew was imposed;[70] schools and factories were closed and all signs of normal life came to a standstill. At one point up to thirty thousand federal troops patrolled the province; Kosovars experienced their presence as a "military occupation."[71]

A news blackout and a near-total ban on foreign journalists kept the world ill-informed about what was happening. According to the Albanian protesters, police used excessive force to control the crowds, turning on civilians with batons, tear gas and firearms. Reportedly, some Albanian members of the police and army turned coat and joined the demonstrations. The crowd shouted slogans and carried placards demanding "Kosovo Republic," "Stop the Exploitation of Trepča [a mine in Kosovo]," "Protect the Rights of Albanians Outside Kosovo," "Improve Living Conditions for Students and Workers," "Stop Repression, Free Political Prisoners," "Down with the Greater-Serbia Chauvinism."[72] Some demonstrators also were reported to have boasted pro-Albania messages, such as: "We Are Enver Hoxha's Soldiers," "Down with Revisionism, Long Live Marxism-Leninism,"[73] "We Are Albanians, Not Yugoslavs," and "We Want United Albania!"[74] Kosovar protesters argue that the pro-Albania themes were not supported by the majority of people who took to the streets.[75] Regardless, once the media blackout was lifted, local journalists would zero in on these more controversial signs, presenting them as the demonstrators' key political demands.[76]

In an effort to squelch the demonstrations, the police moved quickly to arrest those they suspected of being ringleaders. Witnesses contend that people were arrested at random merely for participating in the demonstrations.[77] The arrests backfired, as they provided another reason for further protest: demanding the release of those arrested.[78] On April 3, demonstrations spread to Kosovska Mitrovica, Vučitrn and Uroševac from there to nearly every municipality within Kosovo. Yugoslav authorities accused the protesters of being armed. The Yugoslav press reported that by the end of April eleven people had died; Amnesty International reported that the number may have been as high as three hundred;[79] some Kosovars claimed that almost one thousand were killed.[80]

Despite intense police pressure and numerous arrests, the protesters would not leave the streets. The second week in May, thousands of students and supporters once again occupied the dormitories at the University of Priština, and police once again used tear gas and clubs to disperse the crowd.[81] Elementary and public schools, which had been closed during the first wave of unrest and reopened two weeks later, were declared closed for the summer.

The events in Kosovo had a tremendous impact on Albanians living in other parts of Yugoslavia. Demonstrations broke out in Tetovo, in northwestern Macedonia. Protestors there called for the establishment of an Albanian-language university and, alternatively, for the inclusion of "Albanian parts" of Macedonia into Kosovo.[82] A number of "incidents" were also reported in Montenegro, from graffiti writing to the formation of unauthorized, purportedly separatist organizations. Similar unrest was reported in towns in southern Serbia and Zagreb.

The Yugoslav press approached the 1981 demonstrations with unusual caution. The local press had run independent, on-the-spot reports of the 1968 Kosovo demonstrations, but in 1981 they ran only the official statements provided by provincial, republic and federal leaders.[83] The first statement to come out of the Kosovo League of Communists Provincial Committee, which was later approved by the Serbian and Yugoslav League of Communists, labeled the demonstrations "a component of the organized actions by domestic and foreign enemies working for Al-

banian nationalism and irredentism, a component of the counterrevolutionary struggle against the socialist self-managing system."[84] According to the Yugoslav press, the demonstrations were against everything
Yugoslavia stood for: "The demonstrations and the disturbances, organized by hostile, anti-self-managing and irredentist elements, are
aimed at causing instability in Kosovo, provoking confrontations between Albanians and members of other nations and nationalities in Kosovo and Yugoslavia, and breaking the brotherhood and unity achieved
in their common struggle during the National Liberation War and the
period of socialist development. They are also aimed at overthrowing
the political system of socialist self-management."[85] Calling the demonstrations counterrevolutionary served to hide the larger national, social and economic issues behind the unrest. Instead of addressing the
root causes of conflict, the public was invited to speculate about the
"organized work of internal and external enemies."[86]

Who were the domestic and foreign enemies? Conspiracy theories
abounded, and in the new post-Tito era the press and the public were
more free to explore them. Conspiracy theories fall on particularly fertile
ground in the Balkans. Mihailo Crnobrnja has noted the intransigence
of such theories in post-Tito Yugoslavia: "Though such a theory can be
challenged, it is extremely difficult to refute partial and individual statements by its adherents. When faced with an individual statement by a
conspiracy-theory zealot, a rational person runs the risk of appearing
naive or uninformed, especially if the conspiracy theory comes from such
authoritative sources as academies of science, the leadership of political
parties, or individual political leaders who have a considerable following."[87] For these reasons, history as myth in the Balkans—as opposed
to history as fact—is often colored by theories of conspiracies. The theories about the 1981 demonstrations all sounded at least a little possible,
especially when presented in a piecemeal fashion and when delivered to
audiences looking for anything that could help them make sense of their
lives.

The spread of the conspiracy theories about the 1981 demonstrations
helped to unleash nationalist sentiment, convincing many that there was
indeed an identifiable "enemy" who was being helped by someone else
(either from "inside" or "outside"), as well as diverting attention from
political quarrels and shifting responsibility for the failures of economic
and social policies onto someone else. Two kinds of Truths were to
emerge from the 1981 demonstrations: Truths about Kosovo Albanian
participants and Truths about the "outsiders."

TRUTHS ABOUT THE KOSOVO
ALBANIAN PARTICIPANTS

Many commentators believe that the 1981 demonstrations, with perhaps the exception of the first protests on March 11, were in no way spontaneous student rallies but rather organized political events. While some believe that "outsiders" (such as the secret police of Serbia, Albania and/or the Soviet Union—see discussion below) instigated or even orchestrated the unrest, other commentators believe that Kosovo Albanian groups played a role as well. Zachary Irwin has summarized the three Albanians groups most often said to have been involved: "(1) those desiring Kosovo be granted greater control and formal republic status; (2) those who desired a regime inspired by Albania's 'Marxism-Leninism' [and who wanted to unite with Albania]; (3) and those whose anti-Communist or militant Islamic stance was equally hostile toward Belgrade and Tirana [the capital of Albania]."[88] This characterization is only partially supportable. Placards carried by the demonstrators and interviews with participants suggest that at least the first two groups were included, although those supporting a Kosovo republic far outnumbered those with Marxist-Leninist goals. To some extent "anti-Communists" were involved as well. Within the group seeking republic status, ideological differences existed, pitting those self-identified as communists with those who questioned communist ideology—so-called anti-Communists.[89]

As for the third grouping in Irwin's list, however, there is little evidence that groups with a "militant Islamic" stance were participating in any way. Although the vast majority of Kosovo Albanians are Muslim and only an estimated fifty thousand are Catholic and a handful other denominations, Islam has never been a basis of organization for political action in Kosovo. Albanians identify themselves primarily as Albanians, not as Muslims or Catholics. Common history, myths, traditions and language (with different dialects) hold them together, not a common religion.[90] Moreover, most Kosovo Albanians, like other residents of then-Yugoslavia, are not dogmatic adherents to any faith. It is not uncommon in Kosovo for communities that are mixed Muslim, Catholic and atheist to respect both Islamic and Christian holidays. Furthermore, with respect to the 1981 demonstrations, some *khojas* (Islamic leaders) in Kosovo had explicitly refused to support the protests.[91]

Despite all of the evidence to the contrary, the Truth for some Serbs—and for westerners similarly fearful of the "Oriental Other"—is that Islamic fundamentalism must be at the heart of Albanian actions in Kosovo. Pushing the "Muslim terrorist" button in the 1990s is easy. In a book on Kosovo published in Belgrade in 1992, Dušan Bataković says that Kosovar Albanians set fire to the Peć Patriarchate in March 1981, and that the event brought to the "surface again the religious intolerance that remained the deepest layer of [Albanians'] obsession against Serbs."[92] Samuel Huntington's "clash of civilizations" thesis attracts adherents like Bataković, who warns: "A deep driving force of all tectonic disturbances in Kosovo and Metohija emerged from layers beneath the deceptive communist reality and the inheritance of centuries long conflict of different nations: a class of two civilizations, the Christian and the Islamic. . . ."[93] This characterization of the conflict ignores the fact that Kosovo Albanians are both Muslim and Christian and that Kosovo Albanians have never identified themselves in terms of religious identity. Resistance against the Serbs was just as much a part of Kosovo Albanian Catholic culture as of Kosovo Albanian Muslim culture.

In contrast, the Truth for most Kosovo Albanians is that the participants in the first set of demonstration were in fact students, who above all wanted better economic conditions—and then also republic status for Kosovo. Although the March 11 organizations were planned by *someone,* most Albanians believe that someone to be a group of students. Kosovars remember people taking to the streets in the second wave of demonstrations, in the last week of March, to protest economic, social *and* political conditions in Kosovo; most protestors say they wanted republic status for Kosovo, not Kosovo's unification with Albania. The massive April demonstrations, Kosovars suspect, were more carefully planned, perhaps by Kosovar groups working with outsiders.

Analysts have identified at least five major Kosovo Albanian underground groups active in the early 1980s.[94] Groups that purportedly called for the unification of Kosovo with Albania included the Movement for a National Liberation of Kosovo (MNLK), the Group of Marxist-Leninists of Kosovo (GMLK) and the Red Front. Groups seeking republic status for Kosovo within Yugoslavia included the Communist Party Marxist-Leninist of Yugoslavia (PKNLSHJ) and the Movement for an Albanian Republic in Yugoslavia (LRSHJ). The last organization appears to have been formed after the demonstrations, by a unification of the first three organizations.[95]

Whether any of these organizations had a part to play in the 1981 demonstrations (and if so the extent of that role) is unclear. Association with these organizations was never taken lightly. The mere mention of the name of any of these organizations in Kosovo was and is dangerous. The leaders in exile of the MNLK, Jusuf and Bardhosh Gervalla, and the leader of the GMLK, Kadri Zeka, were shot in Germany in an incident that has been attributed to Yugoslav hit men. The founder of LRSHJ, Nuhi Berisha, was shot by police in Priština in January 1984, reportedly during a shoot-out.[96]

Today, most Albanians who took part in the demonstrations strongly deny an association with any of these groups. Some Albanians who stayed away from the 1981 demonstrations did so precisely because they had heard Marxist-Leninist groups were involved.[97] "I am not and have never been Marxist-Leninist," said one woman who was arrested and sentenced to prison following the demonstration, "They said that I am, but I am not!"[98] "I wanted a Kosovo Republic," said a man who had been sent to jail at the same time. "I was not for the goals of any of those organizations."[99]

Even those who admit to being leaders of separatist groups deny primary responsibility for the organization of the 1981 demonstrations. Hydajet Hyseni, for example, reportedly a founder of the GMLK, was sentenced to fifteen years in prison on November 17, 1982, for involvement in nationalist activity, including purported leadership of the 1981 demonstrations. Hyseni had been in hiding, however, and was not in the country during the time of the first demonstration (March 1981). He says he returned to the country and spoke at the second demonstration, but that the demonstration had been organized by others.[100]

The conflicting statements of participants and bystanders to the 1981 demonstrations, as well as those made by federal, regional and provincial authorities, have produced multiple Truths. The identities of the Kosovo Albanians who played the largest role in the demonstrations may never be known.

TRUTHS ABOUT THE ROLE OF OUTSIDERS

Serbs, Albanians and other commentators inside and outside the region also have speculated about the involvement of outsiders—that is, people outside Kosovo Albanian communities—in the 1981 demonstrations. Many Kosovo Albanians now attribute the second wave of demonstrations to the Serbian secret police and/or other Serbian "elements" who wanted to create the pretext for a crackdown against Kosovo Albanians. Two additional theories also gained broad appeal: either Tirana or pro-Soviet elements had a role in the demonstrations, acting alone or, more likely, working with either local Albanians or Serbian police.[101] Interestingly, versions of these theories (though vastly different) are accepted among both Serbs and Albanians.

The Tirana Conspiracy. The mildest version of this theory speculates that propaganda from Tirana fostered the conditions that led to the unrest. But some charge that the government of Albania had a direct hand in the 1981 demonstrations. Serbs and Albanians have been attracted to two very different strains of this theory: Some Serbs believe that Tirana was working directly with Kosovo Albanians in order to promote Albanian goals, while some Kosovo Albanians believe that Tirana was working with Serbs in order to crush Albanians in Kosovo.

There is no direct proof of Albanian involvement. Instead, those who accept this theory point to the behavior of the demonstrators (that is, waving pro-Albania placards), the Marxist-Leninist orientation of some Kosovo Albanian underground organizations,[102] and Tirana's unusually loud and prolonged response to the 1981 events, which was in marked contrast to its silence following the 1968 demonstrations in Kosovo. In 1981, leaders in Albania lashed out against the "response of the Yugoslav leadership to the lawful demands of the people of Kosova," terming it "repression with fire and steel" and attributing it to the "savage terror of the Great-Serb chauvinists."[103] According to *Zeri i Popullit*, the main Albanian press and an organ of the government, in Kosovo "streets were running with blood," "hundreds of people were wounded and killed" and "several thousand were arrested."[104] In order to make sure that its positions was heard, the Albanian government even assembled a collection of articles from *Zeri i Popullit*, translating the collection into English and distributing it to the foreign press.

According to the Albanian officials, the demonstrations had nothing to do with Kosovo Albanians wanting to join Albania. Rather, the editors of *Zeri i Popullit* asserted: "Any objective person, any unbiased observer, can see and immediately understand that the basic causes of the recent events in Kosovo are the great backwardness of the region, the poverty and the suffering of its people, and the lack of democratic freedoms and political rights. The demonstrations had erupted as the result of a[n] intolerable situation which has been going on for tens of years and the increasingly gloomy prospects of ever emerging from this situation."[105] Apart from the economic demands, *Zeri i Popullit* said, "the demonstrators made political demands for greater freedom, for democratic rights as well as for the granting of the status of a republic within the Yugoslav Federation to Kosova."[106]

In other articles, *Zeri i Popullit* explicitly endorsed Kosovo Albanians' demand for the status of a "nation" and a "republic" under the Yugoslav system of government, asking:

Why does the leadership of the Federation [of Yugoslavia] not study the demands for a republic . . . in a fair way, why does it not interpret them as demands which stem from the Constitution of the Socialist Federal Republic of Yugoslavia itself, but rush in to describe them as "hostile, counter-revolutionary demands which ruin the stability and destroy Yugoslavia"? Do not the Albanians of Kosova have all the features and characteristics that constitute a nation, do they not live in a compact territory, do they not have their common language, culture, spiritual make-up, are they not capable of governing themselves, but need the tutelage of someone else, are they so few in number that they are not worthy of being raised to the rank of a republic . . . ?

. . . Those who are really to blame for the situation must be found, but they are not in Kosova, nor in . . . Albania, as is being hinted and implied in some quarters. To find them one must probe deeper into the policy pursued by the Yugoslav leadership.[107]

The Albanian paper suggested that those to blame can be found by reading the memorandum of Vasa Čubrilović on the expulsion of Serbs from Kosovo, addressed to the royal Serbian government in 1937—in other words, Serbian Chauvinists.[108] The editors emphasized that they spoke out about events in Kosovo out of concern for injustice toward fellow Albanians, much as others support or criticize the Solidarity movement in Poland, but not because of any greater meddling in the internal affairs of Yugoslavia.[109]

Despite these strong disclaimers, Yugoslav and Serbian authorities saw Albania as interfering with an "internal matter." In particular, Belgrade perceived Tirana to be questioning the territorial integrity of Yugoslavia when *Zeri i Popullit* boldly wrote: "The Treaty of London, the Treaty of Versailles, or any other imperialist treaty cannot be imposed to the detriment of the Albanian people."[110] In response to criticism from Yugoslavia, the editors of *Zeri i Popullit* saved its harshest accusations for Serbian leaders: "Leading Serbian personalities in particular, and certain organs of the press which are run by them, set up a furious propaganda campaign against [Albania] full of the most monstrous slanders and lies, distort the character of the relations between our two countries and even go so far as open provocations."[111]

If Albania was, as some Serbs suggest, helping Kosovo Albanians in 1981, that move would have been against Albanian policy. Albania had worked hard at isolationism, creating its own form of ideological purity. Kosovo Albanians, with their free practice of religion, ownership of property and bourgeois notions of life, would certainly have disrupted this purity. Albania had indeed beamed its television and radio programs and sent books over the border to Kosovo, but it did little more to encourage Kosovo Albanians to "unite with the motherland." Indeed, never wanting to create tensions with Yugoslavia, Albania had even returned members of illegal Kosovar groups who had sought shelter within its borders.[112]

At the time of the demonstrations, Kosovo Albanians also publicly denied that the demonstrations had any political connections with Albania. In 1981 very few Kosovars supported unification with Albania.[113] Although Kosovo had adopted the literary language used in Albania rather than one based on its own dialect, Kosovars were content to read the books published in their own "Kosovo Republic" in Yugoslavia, not Albania. Before the doors had opened to Albania, Kosovars could fancy romantic visions of their "motherland," but by 1981 these dreams had been deflated by the stories brought back by tourists who had witnessed the poverty of Albania firsthand. Kosovars also were not thrilled with the condescending attitude of Enver Hoxha, the ruler of Albania. A widely heard saying in Kosovo, Miranda Vickers has observed, was: "Enver Hoxha should remember that he is head of state and head of a party, but not head of a nation."[114] Given the prevailing skepticism toward Albania, the number of Kosovars who carried placards in the 1981 demonstrations reading "We Are Enver Hoxha's soldiers" was likely to have been extremely small.

Recently, however, Kosovo Albanians have started to talk openly about Tirana's probable involvement, but not according to any scenario put forth by the Yugoslav or Serbian leadership. According to one thesis popular among some Albanians (living both in Kosovo and Albania), at least the second wave of demonstrations was part of a conspiracy between supporters of Enver Hoxha and Serbs. Under this theory, Hoxha was displeased with the opening of relations between Kosovo and Albania because Albanians visiting Kosovo were bringing back word that the economic situation in Kosovo was not as bad as portrayed in Albanian propaganda. Hoxha wanted nothing more than to see Kosovo isolated. Thus, he conspired with the Serbian secret police in order to ensure that an unsuccessful demonstration would be held, one that could be easily crushed.

In an interview with Serbian journalists that was printed in Belgrade in 1995, this theory was supported by none other than Azem Vllasi, one of the leading Albanian politicians, who had held high federal posts until his ouster in 1990. Vllasi says:

One thing is for sure: what happened in 1981 was not growing or was not prepared or organized all in Kosovo. . . . It is undeniable that there was a certain role of the Albanian secret service Sigurimi, who were in connection with that smaller part of our émigrés abroad who supported the position of the regime of Enver Hoxha. Actually, before the demonstrations, more and more information had reached Albania about Albanians in Kosovo and their significant advancement, their education in the mother tongue, the existence of the university, the academy of sciences, Albanian-language TV programs, that they had achieved a high cultural level and also that their living standard was significantly higher than the one in Albania. . . . Knowledge such as that was shaking the positions of the Albanian regime of that time until 1981, when the propaganda in Albania started to feed on information on Yugo-repression in Kosovo and on Serbian pressures against the autonomy of Kosovo and the national freedoms of Albanians, which was unfortunately was actually happening.

There are some indications about . . . cooperation of certain circles of the state security from Belgrade and Sigurimi around discovering and arresting people from Kosovo who were involved in the happenings [in 1981].[115]

The cooperation with Sigurimi backfired. Vllasi says that some of those who had been imprisoned for organizing the 1981 demonstrations told him that one of the members of their group went to Albania after the demonstrations to "get instructions" from Sigurimi. Following this person's return, the entire group was arrested, apparently having been double crossed. Vllasi and others who support this thesis underscore that those cooperating with the Sigurimi were a minority, but that their influence doomed the protest. If the demonstrators had not protested in favor of Albania, Vllasi contends, the local political leadership of Kosovo would have supported them.[116] Vllasi's allegations in this regard appear to be a transparent piece of misinformation, as the political leadership of Kosovo in 1981 still strongly supported the official Yugoslav line.

After Enver Hoxha's death in 1982, Albanian television reportedly ran a special report on the 1981 demonstrations supporting a variant of the thesis that Hoxha's men had held the reins. Given the timing of the broadcast—just after the purges in Kosovo following revocation of Kosovo's autonomy—an especially large number of Kosovo Albanians were in Albania to watch the report. Their reactions were various: "We already knew," "We suspected," "That's just propaganda to discredit Hoxha," or, most commonly, "Even if that happened, I was there at the demonstration for another reason."[117]

The Soviet Conspiracy. One popular version of this theory, believed by many both inside and outside the region, attributed the demonstration to Cominformists—pro-Soviet, anti-Tito communists.[118] Following the 1981 demonstrations, public policy circles in Washington and elsewhere warned, "There is concern that 'Cominformist' (pro-Soviet) elements in Kosovo and Albania have attempted to exploit Albanian dissent in order to forestall a rapprochement between Belgrade and Tirana, and provoke a restoration of Serbian dominance."[119] This theory draws on the belief, popular in some circles, that within Serbia an underground political movement was hard at work that included ex-Cominform supporters, ex-Chetniks and Ranković supporters (Serbian hard-liners on Kosovo), sharing a common platform of "Serbian Chauvinism."[120]

The idea is that pro-Soviet elements, working either independently or with various Serbian "opposition actors," encouraged or even staged one or both sets of demonstrations. There is no agreement on who these opposition actors were. At that time, "opposition" could mean anything against the policy of the Yugoslav League of Communists at the time, such as unitarists in a time of decentralization, or those opposed to economic reform in a time of liberalization.

Among the most vocal supporters of the Cominform theory was Albania, which speculated that Moscow's silence on events in Kosovo exposed the existence of a "secret Soviet–Great-Serb collaboration."[121] The escalation of an Albanian-Yugoslav quarrel would serve Soviet interests by shaking the existing stability of the Balkan Peninsula and further weakening Yugoslavia, which, *Zeri i Popullit* said, was already falling apart. In what would prove to be a chillingly accurate political estimation, the Albanian press wrote:

They are saying nothing about what is occurring in Kosova because they want the Great-Serb clan to operate there without any hindrance, to go to the limit in its adventure, to play all its cards and reach the point from which there can be no turning back, when they are left with only one option—to fall back into the lap of the Soviets. Moscow has calculated that the Serbian "iron fist" which is striking at Kosova at present, will be raised against Bosnia, Croatia and Slovenia tomorrow. When this time comes, and it is already obvious that it will not be long delayed, the Serbian clan will be in dire need of the aid of the Soviets.[122]

Whether a Soviet-Serb (or Russian-Serb) conspiracy over Kosovo ever actually existed, the accuracy of the Albanian prophecy has won adherents to this theory today.

Following the Truths

The attempts of the Communist Party to suppress information about the unrest in Kosovo proved futile. Eventually, "the dam burst and a torrent of articles soon flooded the Yugoslav press, criticizing party behavior in Kosovo, exposing the depths of inter-ethnic friction between Serbs and Albanians in Kosovo, and upbraiding those [provincial] party figures who had endeavored to withhold information from the party."[123] The Yugoslav press eventually reported that "a wave of 'hostile activities' " swept Kosovo, Serbia proper, Macedonia and Albanian-populated parts of Montenegro, as young Albanians went on a rampage. According to Sami Repishti, these activities included defacing government buildings, desecrating communist monuments and Serbian cemeteries, writing slogans on walls, throwing stones at passing trains and government cars, and especially distributing antigovernment material.[124] The Kosovo state president, Ali Shukria, appealed for Kosovars to act honorably and with restraint. He asked, "How would Albanian families feel if their graves were desecrated and their religious objects damaged?"[125] Relations between Serb and Albanian neighbors and workers became increasingly strained. According to both Kosovo Serbs and Albanians, 1981 was the year in which many previously harmonious relationships between members of different groups grew sour or broke off completely.[126]

The backlash against Albanians began immediately. In Macedonia, Montenegro, Serbia proper and Kosovo, Slavs began to boycott Albanian owned stores and bakeries, cutting their sales by as much as 85 percent.[127] Cooperation between Albania and Kosovo came to a standstill,[128] as the movie deals, exchange of visiting professors and booming tourism between Albania and Yugoslavia came screeching to a halt. The University of Priština was prohibited from using textbooks from Albania; from then on, the university texts were to be books translated from Serbo-Croatian.

Emigration from Kosovo, by all groups, increased after the 1981 demonstrations. Estimates of migrations vary widely. Many believe that thirty thousand Serbs and Montenegrins left Kosovo during 1981 through 1987, although even these figures are contested.[129] During the 1980s a large number of Albanians left as well, usually young men looking for work in other parts of Yugoslavia and abroad.[130] Albanians who left during this period attributed their migration to poor economic conditions;[131] in contrast, Serbs who left frequently blamed the party for failing to protect them from discrimination and harassment by Albanians.[132]

Mandatory party meetings were held throughout Kosovo in which Albanians were to pledge their support for the party. Tanjug, the press agency, accused local Albanian party leaders of conspiring with the protesters, claiming that "the inescapable conclusion is that much of the Kosovo party is either implicated in the unrest in some way or is sympathetic to the growing secessionist movement. The Kosovar Party organization and the security apparatus are permeated with Albanian counterrevolutionaries and irredentists."[133]

Kosovar leader Mahmut Bakali, the head of the League of Communists of Kosovo, was accused of misleading Belgrade about the extent of the unrest in Kosovo and forced to resign. He was replaced by his predecessor, Veli Deva, a man thought to be harder on Tirana. Federal authorities also purged many Albanians from other government posts, removing the secretaries for education and culture, international affairs, economics, and information; the president of the university and two rectors; the Priština party secretary; and several minor officials, all of whom were ethnic Albanians. One Serb was forced to resign as well, the Province Council chairman, for inflammatory statements. All of those purged were replaced with members of the old guard, some of whom had held high positions during the Ranković era.[134]

The demonstrations led to severe "preventative measures," that is, the arrest and containment of those suspected of being likely to protest again. On June 9, 1981, Interior Secretary-General Herljević reported to the federal Assembly that the situation was coming under control:

During these past days, preventative and repressive measures were taken against 1,700 people . . . 506 persons were sentenced for petty offenses.[135] For participating in the demonstrations, 287 persons; 38 for assisting; 31 for attempting to organize demonstrations; 46 for spreading hostile slogans; 104 for openly hostile attitudes. Criminal procedures were initiated against 154 persons. Among them, there are 39 members of illegal organizations; 29 are main organizers of demonstrations; others have demonstrated tendencies for vandalism. The majority of those against whom criminal procedures were initiated are intellectuals. . . ."[136]

Many young Albanians were arrested for taking part in the demonstrations and for various "verbal offenses" or minor vandalism following the disturbances. The trials, which rarely lasted more than a few hours, were expedited during the summer months, with no independent observers present to ensure that the charges of irredentism were proven at a fair trial.[137] From July 1 to September 9, 1981, 226 students and workers, most of whom were under the age of twenty-five, were tried, convicted and sentenced to up to fifteen years in prison.[138] One could receive up to six years in prison for the mere writing of the slogan "Kosovo Republic" or for penning pro-Albanian poetry. The severity of the sentences was harshly attacked. Eventually, 60 percent of the sentences for "verbal crimes" were reduced on appeal by the Supreme Court of Kosovo, but the lengthy sentences for "organized activity" were not disturbed.[139]

In 1982, Amnesty International's newly adopted prisoners of conscience list included eight youths sentenced in Priština for advocating republic status for Kosovo; three university students and a high school pupil charged with irredentism in Vranje (southern Serbia proper); and two Albanian men charged with selling tape-recorded Radio Tirana broadcasts and writing poems in praise of Albania.[140] The extreme youth of those arrested after the demonstrations had a tremendous impact on Kosovo Albanians, shaping the future of not only the arrested but also their relatives and friends, who would forever mark time in relation to the 1981 demonstrations.[141] The age of the arrested would also become an issue for Serbian nationalists, who would argue that the state had intentionally failed to arrest the real leaders and that "Even the deliberately draconian sentences handed down against young offenders have been designed to incite and spread ethnic hatred."[142]

Accompanying the arrests and trials of student demonstrators were a series of arrests of those suspected of taking part in underground Albanian organizations. On February 3, 1982, the provincial Secretary for Internal Affairs, Mehmet Maliqi, claimed to have uncovered thirty-three illegal groups, describing the support of Albanians for even the most radical groups as "massive."[143] Although these groups may have claimed left-wing, Marxist-Leninist ideology, their ideology was based more on Albanian nationalism, and their goal was republic status for Kosovo and/or unification with Albania. Their methods were usually the peaceful distribution of propaganda. As noted above, Hydajet Hyseni, the purported founder of one of the illegal organizations, GMLK, was sentenced to fifteen years in prison in 1982. The authorities had hunted

Hyseni down alone. More typically, the accused were arrested en masse. Usually the accused were young intellectuals who lived in the same town, attended the same university or had other connections; relatives were often accused together. Often a similar collection of people would be arrested in another town and accused of being a "branch" of the same organization. In July 1982, for example, a court heard the case of a school teacher, Nazmi Hoxha, and fifteen of his fellow teachers, students and friends. They were convicted of belonging to the GMLK and of producing and distributing leaflets calling on Albanians to take part in boycotts and strikes, of writing "subversive slogans" (such as "Kosovo Republic") and of distributing "subversive literature" (originating in Albania or Albanian émigré circles).[144] Nazmi Hoxha received a fifteen-year prison sentence, and his codefendants received various sentences of up to thirteen years.

Whether Kosovar Albanians were writing nationalist graffiti and passing around propaganda from Albania is not in dispute. Whether those convicted were members of Albanian separatist and/or Marxist-Leninist organizations is less clear. Some of the young people accused of belonging to Marxist-Leninist organizations credibly testify that they were never Marxist-Leninists and they simply wanted to use their right to assembly and speech (guaranteed not only in international conventions but in the Yugoslav Constitution) to "do something for [their] people."[145] Even if some of the accused were Marxist-Leninist separatists, the mass roundups, mistreatment during detention and speedy trials virtually assured that some people would be convicted for being in the wrong place at the wrong time, or for knowing the wrong people. For most Kosovar Albanians, these trials simply demonstrated injustice against Albanians. For many Serbs (and to a lesser extent Yugoslavs), the trials exposed deep and dangerous Albanian conspiracies that, if not extinguished, might explode.[146]

The Yugoslav governments' response to the phenomena known as the "1981 student demonstrations" changed political discourse in Yugoslavia in four ways that would prove critical to the ability of the country to sustain itself in the future.

First, by defining the demonstrations as counterrevolutionary,[147] Yugoslavia could dodge having to see the underlying social, economic and ethno-national concerns, and in doing so upped the stakes over Kosovo — and Yugoslavia itself. As Mahmut Bakali explains, "It became a Yugoslav problem because of the wrong decision of Yugoslavia to label it 'counterrevolutionary.' In Communist logic, the counterrevolution is doomsday. I thought at that time not to call the demonstration counterrevolutionary, but to give it a more logical explanation. My suggestion was to make a peaceful bypass, to address the students' concerns and continue."[148] Federal officials were perhaps writing the future of Yugoslavia when they equated the demands for a Kosovo republic within Yugoslavia with the call for a Kosovo republic outside Yugoslavia. Less drastic solutions to ethno-national conflict were effectively cut off.

Second, as Miranda Vickers has observed, "The fact that the problem could only be contained by force played into the hands of government hard-liners."[149] Within Serbia a new measure for political acceptability was set: those who were "hard" on Kosovo (which meant hard on Albanian nationalism) had a possibility of being in; those who were perceived as "soft" were out. Anyone who called for improvement of the economic situation in Kosovo as the solution had a limited political life span, unless he or she also somehow "spit on Kosovo."[150]

Third, the demonstrations sparked criticism about the previous policies of Tito and the party. After the 1981 demonstrations, Serbs talked of the "past mistakes" of the party and, implicitly, of Tito (usually without mentioning him by name).[151] Tito's liberal attitude toward Tirana was seen as one "mistake" that had to go. Miloš Minić, a party leader in Serbia, went so far as to blame Tito for permitting Kosovo Albanian students to be misled: "Tito was always his own foreign minister and Enver Hoxha used this soft line of Tito's so that an open flirtation was possible in Kosovo. We should have explained this Albanian variant of Socialism, we should not have left our people so completely uninformed about it. If we had done so, there would be fewer misled people in Kosovo. We have to correct this without turning everything into a campaign against Albania and the Albanian people."[152] Some Serbian leaders were less forgiving than Minić. In any event, this statement was among the very first to be critical of Tito's legacy.

Finally, all of these changes encouraged Serbian politicians to begin exploiting the Kosovo issue to their gain. Nationalists were encouraged to speak more openly. Sensing the popularity of the nationalist appeal, would-be nationalists were encouraged to follow along. Although much of the Yugoslav press was still trying to assuage national unrest, blatantly nationalistic articles began to appear in books and in less mainstream publications. In 1981, for example, Stevan Moljević wrote of a "homogeneous Serbia that had to embrace the whole ethnic territory on which

Serbs live."[153] These words would never have appeared in Tito's day.

"The 1981 demonstrations had a tremendous impact," Kosovo Albanian leader Ibrahim Rugova has noted, "but the course of history was already changing."[154] Long before the 1981 student demonstrations, political life in Yugoslavia was characterized by national tensions, regional economic disparities, and ideological and political differences between republics. Controlling these problems had led the government to adopt what were seen at the time to be creative reforms: decentralization of political and economic institutions and encouragement of certain forms of cultural pluralism.[155] The 1981 demonstrations were not the beginning of the problem, but rather the start of serious examination of the shortcomings of these reforms. Each failure would be explained differently and exploited by politicians from every nation and nationality, in each republic. While the other republics pushed for greater decentralization of political and economic institutions and enhanced cultural pluralism, Serbian politicians demanded centralization, the unity of Serb lands, a decrease in cultural pluralism for Albanians and an increase in the protection and promotion of Serbian culture.

In time, Albanians would lose more than they ever imagined. Looking back, Kosovar Albanians would wonder whether the 1981 demonstrations should have occurred at all. "The demonstrations were our handicap," Mahmut Bakali would say in 1995. "They were not needed at the time."[156] Azem Vllasi, an Albanian politician who would appear close to Milošević until their falling out in 1989, would agree, "We weren't ready. The 1981 demonstrations did more harm than good."[157] On the other hand, the demonstrations would be endorsed in retrospect by Albanian leaders who had held high posts in 1981 but failed to offer support to the protesters. The man who would be the last Kosovo Albanian member of the Yugoslav Presidency (until his ouster in 1991), Riza Sapunxhiu,[158] would reflect, "The 1981 demonstration caught me by surprise. I thought things were going well . . . I was surprised then, but now I see the need for the demonstrations."[159] Sevdie Ahmeti, an academic turned activist, would point to the one undisputed "achievement" of the demonstrations: "Only after 1981 did the world find out that Albanians existed in Kosovo."[160]

Still, over the next eight years, 584,373 Kosovo Albanians—half the adult population—would be arrested, interrogated, interned or remanded.[161] Albanians would not only lose their demand for a Kosovo republic—they would lose their status under the 1974 Constitution. And Yugoslavia would be lost altogether.

Notes

1. Sabrina Ramet has applied this proposition to Kosovo. See Sabrina P. Ramet, *Nationalism and Federalism in Yugoslavia, 1962–1991,* 2d ed. (Bloomington, Ind.: Indiana University Press, 1992), 190.

2. Serbs have tended to attribute many problems in Kosovo to Albanian-language instruction, from Albanians' preservation of a strong national identity to Kosovo's low development rate. *Kosovo Knot,* the independent study conducted in 1990 by Belgrade liberals, found that "the weak cultural integration of Albanians in Yugoslavia" can be explained by "the influence of traditionalism, . . . customary law, attachment to property, the mother language and religion, which are leading to the isolation and are limiting integration [of Albanians] within the Yugoslav boundaries." Srdja Popović, Dejan Janča and Tanja Petrovar, *Kosovski čvor: Drešiti ili seći?* (Belgrade: Kronos, 1990), 14.

3. Miranda Vickers, *The Albanians: A Modern History* (London and New York: I. B. Tauris, 1995), 204.

4. For discussions of the origins of this dissatisfaction, see Elez Biberaj, "Kosovo, The Struggle for Recognition," *Conflict Studies,* no. 137 (London: Institute for the Study of Conflict, 1982); and Steven K. Pavlowitch, "Kosovo: An Analysis of Yugoslavia's Albanian Problem," *Conflict Studies*, no. 138 (London: Institute for the Study of Conflict, 1982). For Biberaj's update on the problem, see Elez Biberaj, "Kosova: The Balkan Powder Keg," *Conflict Studies,* no. 258 (London: Institute for the Study of Conflict, 1993).

5. Sami Repishti, "Human Rights and the Albanian Nationality in Yugoslavia," in *Human Rights in Yugoslavia,* eds. Oskar Gruenwald and Karen Rosenblum-Cale (New York: Irvington Publishers, 1986), 255.

6. Vladan A. Vasilijević, "Kosovo: Exercise and Protection of Human Rights," in *Conflict or Dialogue: Serbian-Albanian Relations and the Integration of the Balkans,* eds. Dušan Janjić and Shkelzen Maliqi (Subotica: Open University, 1994), 82. The rights that were granted to Albanians, Vasiljević suggests, were a mistake, because Albanians, "[b]y availing themselves of the rights they were granted," became "collaborators in a mass movement of non-Albanian populations out of Kosovo . . ."

While "minority rights" may have been in line with international standards, many laws and practices throughout Yugoslavia violated international law, such as prosecution of "verbal offenses," the holding of prisoners for prolonged periods without charges and without counsel, torture and mistreatment in custody. These laws and practices were applied not only to Kosovo Albanians but to all dissenters.

7. Quote drawn from interviews by author with Serbian university students in Belgrade in 1994 and Priština in 1995. Statements such as "What more did they [Albanians] want from us?" were the most common responses given by Serbs when asked about the 1981 demonstrations.

8. Repishti, "Human Rights and the Albanian Nationality," 255.

9. For the failure of the "Yugoslav" identity to catch on in Bosnia and the

need to recognize the Muslim nation, see Fritz Hondius, *The Yugoslav Community of Nations* (The Hague: Mouton, 1968), 341, and for a discussion on the origins of Muslim identity, see Sabrina Ramet, "Primordial Ethnicity or Modern Nationalism: The Case of Yugoslavia's Muslims Reconsidered," *The South Slav Journal* 13, nos. 47–48 (spring-summer, 1990), 1–20. See generally Noel Malcolm, *Bosnia: A Short History* (New York: New York University Press, 1994); H. T. Norris, *Islam in the Balkans: Religion and Society between Europe and the Arab World* (London: Hurst, 1993).

10. On the question of the national status for Albanians, Muhamedin Kullashi asks: "Why should Macedonians, Montenegrins or Muslims be recognized as nations while Albanians should remain the status of a national minority? Does it imply the usual difference in Yugoslav legal-political ideology between Slavic peoples (Serbs, Croats, Montenegrins, etc.) who are 'state-building' and those who are not, e.g. Albanians, as they are not of Slavic origin?" Muhamedin Kullashi, "Kosovo and the Disintegration of Yugoslavia," in *Conflict or Dialogue: Serbian-Albanian Relations and the Integration of the Balkans*, eds. Dučan Janjić and Shkelzen Maliqi (Subotica: Open University, 1994).

11. See Miloš Mišović, *Ko je tra'io Republiku: Kosovo 1945–1985* (Belgrade: Narodna Knjiga, 1987).

12. Anton Logoreci, "A Clash between Two Nationalisms in Kosova," in *Studies on Kosova*, eds. Arshi Pipa and Sami Repishti (Boulder, Colo.: Eastern European Monographs, 1984), 189.

13. For the history of this development, see Kurtesh Salihu, *The Origin, Position, and Development of the Socialist Autonomous Province of Kosova* (Priština: Center for Marxist Studies, 1982). For one of the most concise analyses of the 1974 Constitution and its contribution to the collapse of Yugoslavia, see Vojin Dimitrijević, "The 1974 Constitution and Constitutional Process as a Factor in the Collapse of Yugoslavia," in *Yugoslavia: The Former and the Future: Reflections by Scholars from the Region*, eds. Payam Akhavan and Robert Howse (Washington, D.C.: The Brookings Institute, 1995), 45–74, and for a thorough examination of the constitution's framework for negotiating conflict, see Steven Burg, *Conflict and Cohesion in Socialist Yugoslavia* (Princeton: Princeton University Press, 1983), 242–300. The constitution itself is published as *Ustav Socijalističke Federativne Republike Jugoslavije* [The Constitution of the Socialist Federal Republic of Yugoslavia] (Belgrade: Dopisna Delavska Univerza, 1974).

14. Interview with Azem Vllasi, Priština, April 1995, in *Kosmet ili Kosova*, eds. Bahri Cani and Cvijetin Milivojević (Belgrade: NEA, 1996), 93.

15. For an elaboration on the differences between the status of a republic and that of a province, see Sami Repishti, "The Evolution of Kosova's Autonomy within the Yugoslav Constitutional Framework," in *Studies on Kosova*, eds. Pipa and Repishti, 216–25.

16. Thanks to Sabrina Ramet for this insight.

17. See Derek Hall, "Albanian Identity and Balkan Roles," in *Reconstructing the Balkans: A Geography of the New Southwest Europe*, eds. Derek Hall and Darrick Danta (New York: John Wiley & Sons, 1996), 122.

18. Repishti, "Human Rights and the Albanian Nationality," 256.

19. Zachary T. Irwin, "Law, Legitimacy and Yugoslav National Dissent:

The Dimension of Human Rights," in *Human Rights in Yugoslavia*, eds. Gruenwald and Rosenblum-Cale, 182.

20. Ramet, *Nationalism and Federalism*, 192.

21. See Nikola R. Pašić, "Political Persecutions in Yugoslavia: A Historical Survey," in *Human Rights in Yugoslavia*, eds. Gruenwald and Rosenblum-Cale, 49–106; Amnesty International, *Yugoslavia: Prisoners of Conscience* (London: Amnesty International, 1982).

22. See Amnesty International, *Yugoslavia: Ethnic Albanians—Victims of Torture and Ill-Treatment by Police* (New York: Amnesty International, 1992).

23. Ivo Banac, "Serbia's Deadly Fears," *The New Combat* (autumn 1994), 40.

24. U.S. State Department, *Country Reports for Human Rights Practices 1981* (Washington, D.C.: Government Printing Office, 1982), 925.

25. See Repishti, "Human Rights and the Albanian Nationality," 255.

26. Ramet, *Nationalism and Federalism*, 193.

27. "Report to the Federal Assembly," Tanjug (Yugoslav press service), June 8, 1981; *Rilindja*, June 9, 1981.

28. Repishti, "Human Rights and the Albanian Nationality," 253–54 (citing "Albanian Prisoners in Idrizovo Appeal for Help," *Der Spiegel*, April 22, 1978, p. 18).

29. Ibid.

30. Ramet, *Nationalism and Federalism*, 194.

31. The author interviewed some of those arrested who described themselves in these terms.

32. Descriptions of operations of Albanian national movements in 1971–1981 are drawn from author's interviews. See immediately following this chapter for an interview in which a man describes the formation of such movements.

33. See immediately following this chapter for an interview with man arrested as a leader of the demonstrations.

34. This position is represented in Alex N. Draganich and Slavko Todorovich, *The Saga of Kosovo: Focus on Serbian-Albanian Relations* (Boulder, Colo.: Eastern European Monographs, 1984), 170–73.

35. Interview by author in Priština, spring 1995.

36. Ramet, *Nationalism and Federalism*, 195. Some Serbian leaders complain that this information was deliberately issued in the Albanian language in order to keep them as Serbian speakers ill-informed.

37. Ibid. (citing *Politika*, March 30, 1980, p. 8).

38. Ibid. (citing Tanjug, November 1, 1980).

39. Quoted in Repishti, "Human Rights and the Albanian Nationality," 257.

40. See Božidar Jovanović, "Poratni društveno-ekonomski koreni nacionalizma," in *O albanskom i drugim nacionalizmima*, Sveske (Sarajevo), January 12, 1985.

41. Vickers, *The Albanians*, 204.

42. On Kosovo, see Dragan Avramov et al., *Demografski razvoj i populaciona politika SAP Kosova* (Belgrade: Institut drustvenih nauka, Centar za

demografska istrazivanja, 1988), 82. On Slovenia, see Dennison Rusinow, *Yugoslavia: A Fractured Federalism* (Washington, D.C.: Wilson Center Press, 1988), 71.

43. Rusinow, *Yugoslavia,* 70.

44. Vesna Bojičić, "The Disintegration of Yugoslavia: Causes and Consequences of Dynamic Inefficiency in Semi-Command Economies," in *Yugoslavia and After: A Study in Fragmentation, Despair and Rebirth*, eds. David A. Dyker and Ivan Vejvoda (New York: Longman, 1996), 40.

45. Peter Prifti, "Kosova's Economy: Problems and Prospects," in *Studies on Kosova*, eds. Pipa and Repishti, 1984, 147.

46. Bojičić, "The Disintegration of Yugoslavia," 41. The economic plan announced at the start of 1981 set investment activity in Kosovo at 35.7 percent lower than in the year before, giving little hope for improvement. Prifti, "Kosova's Economy," 135.

47. See, e.g., Dijana Pleština, *Regional Development in Communist Yugoslavia: Success, Failure and Consequences* (Boulder, Colo.: Westview Press, 1992); Dragomir Vojnić, "Disparity and Disintegration: The Economic Dimension of Yugoslavia's Demise," in *Yugoslavia: The Former and the Future*, eds. Akhavan and Howse, 75–111. According to Vojnić one of the greatest sources of friction leading to the disintegration of Yugoslavia was the tension between less developed parts of Yugoslavia, which favored a more centralized economy, and the developed parts (in particular Slovenia and Croatia), which favored decentralization. Pp. 102–3.

48. Fred Singleton, *A Short History of the Yugoslav People* (New York: Cambridge University Press, 1985), 273.

49. Prifti, "Kosova's Economy," 142.

50. Interview by author.

51. Vojnić, "Disparity and Disintegration," 111.

52. Bojičić, "The Disintegration of Yugoslavia," 42–43.

53. Hivzi Islami, "Demographic Reality in Kosova," in *Conflict or Dialogue*, eds. Janjić and Maliqi, 33.

54. Darko Hudelist quotes an interview with Shkelzen Maliqi in which he suggests that Albanian graduates of universities in Yugoslavia were being passed too easily and with little skills to prepare themselves for their jobs. Darko Hudelist, *Kosovo, bitka bez iluzija* (Zagreb: Center for Information and Publicity, 1989), 140. In addition to demographic reasons, Alex Draganich and Slavko Todorovich write that "other explanations given are Albanian backwardness, lack of management skills, corruption, investing in unproductive prestige enterprises, unrealistic and over-ambitious planning, and growing unemployment." Draganich and Todorovich, *The Saga of Kosovo,* 162.

55. Prifti, "Kosova's Economy," 148.

56. See, e.g., Milan Vučković and Goran Nikolić, *Stanovništvo Kosova u razdoblju od 1918. do 1991. godine* (Munich: Slavica Verlag, 1996), 126–32.

57. Islami, "Demographic Reality in Kosova," 49.

58. Singleton, *A Short History of the Yugoslav People*, 272.

59. According to the federal government, twice as much was spent on education per pupil in Kosovo as elsewhere in Yugoslavia. Miranda Vickers,

"The Status of Kosovo in Socialist Yugoslavia," *Bradford Studies on South Eastern Europe*, no. 1 (1994), 28.

60. Prifti, "Kosova's Economy," 148.

61. Logoreci, "A Clash Between Two Nationalisms," 190.

62. Interviews by author.

63. The original figures for the academic year 1981–82 set the number of students at some 45,000, but that figure was changed to 20,434 currently enrolled students at the University of Priština and 8,174 enrolled in other institutions of higher learning in Kosovo. Hugh Poulton, *The Balkans: Minorities and States in Conflict* (London: Minority Rights Group, 1991), 61. Poulton observes, "Whatever the actual figure, it was a far higher percentage than for other areas in the country."

64. Josip Broz Tito, *Borba za novi svet* (The Struggle for a New World) (Belgrade: Pres kliping, 1982), 234.

65. Crampton, R. J. *Eastern Europe in the Twentieth Century* (New York and London: Routledge, 1994), 387.

66. Interviews by author with numerous participants in the demonstrations.

67. See remembrances of former students in chapter one.

68. A minority of people interviewed recall that at these early demonstrations some students even called for Kosovo to become a republic within Yugoslavia. Most of the interviewees thought that the cry for a "Kosovo Republic!" was not heard until the next wave of demonstrations.

69. Tanjug, March 12, 1981.

70. Young Serbs and Albanians alike say that the long-lasting curfew had a profound influence on their development by disrupting their childhood and adolescence. See interviews following this chapter for remembrances of Kosovo Serbs and Albanians.

71. Vickers, *The Status of Kosovo*, 30.

72. Repishti, "Human Rights and the Albanian Nationality," 259.

73. Ibid.

74. *NIN*, April 12, 1981.

75. Interviews by author.

76. See, e.g. Tanjug, October 29, 1981.

77. Indeed, the author has interviewed many people who were arrested even though they were not the organizers of any demonstrations.

78. For one account, see Christopher Bennett, *Yugoslavia's Bloody Collapse: Causes, Course and Consequences* (New York: New York University Press, 1995), 89.

79. Amnesty International, *Yugoslav Prisoners of Conscience* (London: Amnesty International, 1985), 12.

80. Vickers, *The Albanians*, 205.

81. Interviews by author.

82. Such a change, some commentators have warned, would not only have disrupted the operations of Macedonia but also destabilized Yugoslavia's relations with Greece and Bulgaria, countries that have long disputed the boundaries of Macedonia. See Peter Prifti, *The Kosovo* (Cambridge, Mass.: MIT Center for International Studies, 1972), 267.

83. Repishti, "Human Rights and the Albanian Nationality," 258.

84. *Rilindja*, April 7, 1981. Emphasis added.

85. Ibid. Note that self-management was one of the unique components of the Yugoslav system. See the 1974 constitution. Vojin Dimitrijević has described the system of self-management as "atomized and incomprehensible and, as such, unable to influence political decisionmaking." Dimitrijević, "The 1974 Constitution and Constitutional Process," 71.

86. *Vjesnik*, April 16, 1981.

87. Mihailo Crnobrnja, *The Yugoslav Drama*, 2d ed. (Montreal & Kingston: McGill-Queen's University Press, 1996), 125.

88. Irwin, "Law, Legitimacy and Yugoslav National Dissent," 181.

89. This conclusion is drawn from author's interviews with members of these groups.

90. As one Kosovo Albanian leader explained, "The issue isn't religion. Serbs think of religion as a 'second level ethnic difference'—in other words, an important signifier of ethnicity. Albanians have always been defined by language, history and a common way of life—not by religion." Risa Sapunxhiu, a former World Bank official and Kosovo's representative on Yugoslavia's federal collective Presidency until his forced resignation in March 1991. Interview by author in Priština in 1995.

91. Gzime Starova, "The Religion of the Albanians in the Balkan European Context," *Balkan Forum* (Skopje) 1, no. 4 (September 1993), 201–4.

92. Dušan T. Bataković, *The Kosovo Chronicles* (Belgrade: Plato, 1992), 212.

93. Ibid., 213. See also Samuel P. Huntington, *The Clash of Civilizations and the Remaking of World Order* (New York : Simon & Schuster, 1996). A critique of this thesis is beyond the scope of the present project.

94. Dušan Janjić offers a longer and slightly different list in "Socialism, Federalism and Nationalism in (the Former) Yugoslavia: Lessons to Be Learned," *Journal of Area Studies*, no. 3 (1993), 116 n.14. See also Radovan Petrović, "Kontrarevolucionarne akcije nacionalista i iredentista na Kosovu—Napad na bratstvo-jedinstvo i integritet SFRJ," *Bezbednost* (Belgrade) 1–2 (1982), 191.

95. Poulton, *The Balkans*, 62. The author's own interviews indicated the existence of all of these organizations except for the Red Front, and also the existence of other pro-Republic cliques (not large enough to be called groups) that either did not have names or that had names that the members do not wish to reveal. As the goals of Kosovo have shifted, these groups have been transformed as well.

96. Poulton, *The Balkans*, 62.

97. Interview by author. See interviews following this chapter for stories of the demonstration.

98. Interview by author.

99. Interview by author.

100. Interview by author.

101. Mahmut Bakali is one of the those who has said that the Serbian secret police was involved. Interview by author.

102. Ivo Banac, *With Stalin Against Tito: Cominformist Splits in Yugoslav Communism* (Ithaca, N.Y.: Cornell University Press, 1988), 267.

103. *About the Events in Kosova: Articles from "Zeri i popullit" and Other Press Organs* (Tirana: The 8 Nentori Publishing House, 1981), 3. An earlier collection of articles from Tirana can be found in *The Truth about the Plight of the Albanians in Jugoslavia* (Tirana: Zeri i Popullit, 1961).

104. Ibid.

105. Ibid., 5–19 (translation of "Why Were Police Violence and Tanks Used Against the Albanians in Kosovo?" *Zeri i Popullit*, April 8, 1981).

106. Ibid., 3.

107. Ibid., 13 (*Zeri i Popullit*, April 8, 1981).

108. Ibid.

109. Ibid., 20–41, 26 (citing "Who Incites Hostility Amongst the Peoples of Yugoslavia?" *Zeri i Popullit*, April 23, 1981).

110. Ibid., 13 (*Zeri i Popullit*, April 8, 1981).

111. Ibid., 4.

112. Vickers, *The Albanians*, 213.

113. Out of the fifty-some people the author interviewed about their participation in the demonstrations, none said they wanted unification with Albania. Gale Stokes has similarly observed that "from the initial riots in 1968, through the second wave of the demonstrations in 1981, right up to the civil war of 1991, the leaders of every major Albanian movement stoutly denied any interest in joining Albania and demanded only that Kosova become a republic in Yugoslavia." Gale Stokes, *The Walls Came Tumbling Down: The Collapse of Communism in Eastern Europe* (New York: Oxford University Press, 1993), 232.

114. Vickers, *The Albanians*, 204.

115. Bahri Cani and Cvijetin Milivojević, *Kosmet ili Kosova* (Belgrade: NEA, 1996), 96. In 1981, Vllasi was president of the Socialist Youth of Yugoslavia. Later he would be president of the Provincial Conference of the Socialist League of Working People of Kosovo.

116. Ibid.

117. Interviews by author. These Kosovar Albanians either had emigrated "permanently" or, more likely, were temporarily staying in Albania while studying or simply waiting for the wave of repression to pass.

118. Cominform was the International Communist Movement orchestrated from Moscow. Following Tito's break with Stalin in 1948, Cominformists in Yugoslavia were arrested en masse, tortured and imprisoned under extremely harsh conditions. See Ivo Banac, *With Stalin Against Tito*; Mirko Vidović, "Tito's Gulag and Human Rights," in *Human Rights in Yugoslavia*, eds. Gruenwald and Rosenblum-Cale, 118. See also Hamilton Fish Armstrong, *Tito and Goliath* (New York: Macmillan, 1951), and Milovan Djilas, *Tito: The Story from the Inside* (New York: Harcourt Brace Jovanovich, 1980). The Cominformists became active again in the 1970s, holding a secret meeting in Bar in 1974 where they announced the creation of a new "Yugoslav Communist Party." Pašić, "Political Persecutions in Yugoslavia," 82.

119. Prifti, *The Kosovo*, 267 (citing Louis Zanga, "The Meaning of the Latest Demonstrations in Kosovo," *RFE Research Report* 115 (January 3, 1975), 3–7).

120. Dennison Rusinow, *The Yugoslav Experiment: 1948–1974* (Berkeley: University of California Press, 1977), 224.

121. "The Events in Kosova and the Secret Soviet–Great-Serb Collaboration," *Zeri i Popullit*, June 5, 1981 (as translated and reprinted in *About the Events in Kosova*, 104–12).

122. Ibid., 107.

123. Pedro Ramet, "Yugoslavia 1982: Political Ritual, Political Drift, and the Fetishization of the Past," *South Slav Journal* 5, no. 3 (17) (autumn 1982), 15.

124. Repishti, "Human Rights and the Albanian Nationality," 260.

125. *ATA* (Tirana), 6 January 1991, trans. in FBIS *Daily Report* (Eastern Europe), 9 January 1981, 16.

126. In interviews with over one hundred Kosovo Serbs and Albanians, most people point to 1981 as the time in which their personal relations with members of the other group soured.

127. Ibid.

128. Vickers, "The Status of Kosovo," 206.

129. Vickers, *The Albanians*, 206, citing Steven K. Pavlowitch, *The Improbable Survivor: Yugoslavia and Its Problems: 1918–1988* (London: Hurst, 1988), 87. See also chapter 2, note 78. For historical analysis, see also Vučković and Nikolić, *Stanovništvo Kosova*, 47; B. Perunčić, *Pisma srpskih konzula iz Prištine, 1890–1910* (Belgrade: Narodna Knjiga, 1985).

130. Prifti, "Kosova's Economy," 144; Vučković and Nikolić, *Stanovništvo Kosova*, 147.

131. See Hivzi Islami, *Demographic Reality in Kosova* (Priština: Kosova Information Center, n.d.). Hivzi Islami has written that after 1981 Albanians left due to police pressure and thus were political refugees. In 1996, he estimated that 400,000 Albanians from Kosovo and from other parts of the former Yugoslavia were working in Europe, with about 120,000 in Germany, 95,000 in Switzerland and 35,000 in Sweden. Hivzi Islami, "Demographic Problems of Kosova and Other Ethnic Albanian Territories," in *The Kosova Issue: A Historic and Current Problem* (Tirana: Institute of History, 1996), 143.

132. The thesis that Serbs and Montenegrins suffered from a "system of discrimination" that forced them to leave was developed in a sociological study completed for the Serbian Academy of Sciences and Arts. See Ruža Petrović and Marina Blagojević, *Migracije Srba i Crnogoraca sa Kosova i Metohije* (Belgrade: SANU, 1989). An English summary can be found in Marina Blagojević, "Serbian Migrations from Kosovo from the End of the '60s: Social Factors," reprinted from *Serbs and Albanians in the 20th Century* (academic conferences of the Serbian Academy of Sciences and Arts, vol. LXI, Department of Historical Sciences, no. 20) (Belgrade, 1991).

133. Tanjug, June 23, 1981.

134. Repishti, "Human Rights and the Albanian Nationality," 263.

135. The Code for Petty Offenses allowed for fines or imprisonment for up to sixty days. Poulton, *The Balkans*, 61.

136. Repishti, "Human Rights and the Albanian Nationality," 262–63 (citing *Rilindja*, June 9, 1981).

137. Logoreci, "A Clash Between Two Nationalisms," 191.

138. "More Than 300 Persons Were Sentenced," *New York Times*, October 19, 1981, A4.

139. Poulton, *The Balkans,* 61.

140. Oskar Gruenwald, "Yugoslavia's Gulag Archipelago and Human Rights," in *Human Rights in Yugoslavia,* eds. Oskar Gruenwald and Karen Rosenblum-Cale (New York: Irvington Publishers, 1986), 19.

141. See interviews following this chapter.

142. See Kosta Mihailović and Vasilije Krestić, *Memorandum of the Serbian Academy of Sciences and Arts: Answers to Criticisms* (Belgrade: Serbian Academy of Sciences and Arts, 1995), 127.

143. Branka Magaš, *The Destruction of Yugoslavia: Tracking the Break-Up, 1980–1992* (London: Verso, 1993), 12–13.

144. Poulton, *The Balkans,* 63.

145. Interview by author.

146. Interview by author.

147. See Popović, Janča and Petrovar, eds., *Kosovski čvor,* 16.

148. Interview by author.

149. Vickers, "The Status of Kosovo," 32.

150. Interview with Serbian opposition politician in 1994: "To be in politics today, you must spit on Kosovo."

151. Vickers, *The Albanians,* 206.

152. Vickers, "The Status of Kosovo," 35 (citing *Vjesnik*, May 8, 1981).

153. Stevan Moljević, "Homogena Srbija," *Zbornik dokumenata i podataka o narodnooslobodilačkom ratu naroda Jugoslavije* (Belgrade), 14(2) (1981), 1–10.

154. Interview by author.

155. U.S. State Department, *Country Reports for Human Rights Practices 1981,* 920.

156. Interview by author.

157. Interview by author.

158. Riza Sapunxhiu is also one of Kosovo's most accomplished economists. In 1981, he was vice-president of the economy. In 1982, he became an official at the World Bank.

159. Interview by author.

160. Interview by author.

161. Mark Thompson, *A Paper House: The Ending of Yugoslavia* (London: Vintage, 1992), 128.

Young People Remember
the 1981 Demonstrations

In 1994 and 1995, more than fifty young Kosovars were interviewed about their memories of the student demonstrations of 1981. In order to enhance the willingness of people to speak freely about the incident, the young Serbs were questioned by a young Serbian journalist from Priština, and the young Albanians were questioned by a young Albanian journalist from Priština. To complement these interviews, the author conducted her own interviews.

Among the questions asked were: What were you doing at the time of the 1981 demonstrations? What do you think happened? What did the demonstrators want? Did the demonstrations have an influence on your life?

Kosovo Albanians

The sections following this one contain the stories of two Kosovo Albanians, one man and one woman, who were imprisoned following the demonstrations. Because these stories are included in depth, the interviews with Albanians in this section include only one story of an alleged organizer (the first story), along with the observations of Albanian bystanders and minor participants.

MAN, AGE 22 IN 1981, BORN IN A VILLAGE NEAR UROŠEVAC, LIVING IN UROŠEVAC

The real demonstrations [in Priština] began on March 26. They started in the student center. The professors, Azem Vllasi and [other Albanian] political leaders tried to stop it. I was not the organizer of the demonstrations, but I had a part in it. There were three aspects to our demands: one, an economic aspect . . . ; two, a political aspect, [emphasizing] what Macedonian and Serbian authorities were doing [to Albanians]; three, and a national aspect—we wanted to say that we *know* that we are Albanians. There were some theories then that Albanians are not a nation. . . . The politicians were trying to convince us that we were wrong.

[After three or four hours of talking with the politicians], we were aware that the politicians who had come [to the demonstrations] had come [only] to convince us that if we didn't stop they would use police force. The anger of people was growing and growing. No one was saying "Kosovo Republic" before then. . . . We wanted to speak to [politicians] high [in the] political structure. They didn't come—they were busy with the passing of the baton for Tito's birthday.

[Suddenly] the order was given to shoot [tear gas]. There were about one thousand students then. Part of the students ran to the north side of the student center; part of us went to one of the student buildings, building number four. . . . I was in [building number four]. . . . [The police] surrounded us. They shot tear gas inside the rooms and when we ran out, they beat us some more. It was impossible not to be beaten. . . . The police lined the halls and beat us when we walked down the corridor. . . . They gathered us and took us to jail according to some kind of list. Fortunately, I was not on that list. [He was later arrested and charged with "irredentism."]

The international community thought everything was OK in Yugoslavia. We had to find a way to show them that something was wrong. . . . We told the world that Albanian people are divided and convinced them that the communist regime was offensive. One of our biggest demands was for democracy. It was the first anti-Communist demonstration in Europe. . . .

WOMAN, AGE 15 IN 1981, BORN
IN PRIŠTINA, LIVING IN PRIŠTINA

I was in the second grade of high school during the demonstration. I was there because everyone else was. I was insecure and frightened because it was my first time participating in something like that. I think that the first demonstrations [on March 11] started because people were dissatisfied and I think that Serbs organized [the large demonstrations on April 1 and 2] in order to draw attention away from other crises in Serbia.

I don't know if the demonstrations were a good thing. We didn't get what we asked for and it brought a lot of bad consequences. After that, we had the police in our lives every day and we lost our schools completely. One of my cousins was arrested after the demonstrations and my entire family was very upset. My mother asked me to stay away from any politics.

WOMAN, AGE 19 IN 1981, BORN
IN PRIŠTINA, LIVING IN PRIŠTINA

I did not participate in the demonstration but I saw the masses. I was very emotional. There was so much police brutality. The demonstrations were organized by the people who had a wrong political view. Young people were used by them. But the goal of the last demonstrations [in 1989] was independence and freedom from Serbs. In 1989, we were not used.

She could not specify what political view was held by the demonstrators, only that it was "wrong" and that young Albanians had been duped into accepting it.

WOMAN, AGE 14 IN 1981, BORN
IN PRIŠTINA, LIVING IN PRIŠTINA

I did not attend the 1981 demonstrations, but I saw them. Everyone saw them. I think that the demonstrations happened because a group of [Albanian] intellectuals could not watch the people suffering any more. . . . I am disappointed in the way demonstrations are organized in Yugoslavia. All of them are done with no success. It seems like everything that they [Albanian political leaders] do is without any success. There is no hope for young people here [in Kosovo].

WOMAN, AGE 15 IN 1981, BORN
IN PODUJEVO, LIVING IN PRIŠTINA

I was in the second grade of high school during the demonstrations. After we heard the voices of the crowd, we jumped through the window and joined the demonstrations. It was very emotional and I was kind of confused. We thought that those demonstrations were organized by students who wanted better conditions at the university.

Those students really suffered bad consequences later [when they were harassed] by police. When I think about the demonstrations, I know that maybe things would have been different for me if I were older [because I would have been arrested too]. That makes me feel strange. . . . I [now] believe that the 1981 demonstrations were planned and organized by Serbia.

Responses to the question "Who started the demonstrations and why?" varied widely. Many of the young Albanians interviewed thought that the demonstrations had been organized by Serbia. Only a tiny number suspected Tirana.

MAN, AGE 13 IN 1981, BORN IN VILLAGE
NEAR PRIZREN, LIVING IN PRIŠTINA

I was still in school and I was involved in the demonstrations, although I was not sure of their purpose. We all just went. I saw the crowd being beaten by the police. I felt great for being there. The reason [for the demonstration] was that students were not satisfied and [also] the goal was juridical independence of Kosovo from Serbia. [The 1981 demonstrations] affected my life because for the first time I experienced police horror. That made my conviction in independence even more strong.

MAN, AGE 12 IN 1981, BORN
IN PRIŠTINA, LIVING IN PRIŠTINA

I was in school and I saw demonstrations. I saw that people had strong will, but they were so naive. I was too young to attend. I was confused because I never saw any demonstrations before. The demonstrations were organized by the [Yugoslav or Serbian] state security and they wanted just to destabilize the position of Albanians in Kosovo. Yes, [the demonstrations] really affected me. I lost my ideals.

MAN, AGE 15 IN 1981, BORN IN PRIŠTINA, LIVING IN PRIŠTINA

I was in high school when I saw the crowd shouting and the police throwing tear gas, but I did not join the demonstration. I was afraid. I think the goal was to separate Kosovo from Serbia. Those demonstrations affected me by strengthening my political beliefs. Also, everything changed for the young people. We had to become serious very fast. No sports, no clubs, no carefree walking. I feel sorry for those who are younger than me because [at least] I had some childhood.

MAN, AGE 23 IN 1981, BORN IN PRIŠTINA, LIVING IN PRIŠTINA

I was not here during the 1981 demonstrations but I can say that it was more tragic for the people who were outside [of Kosovo]. We couldn't do anything to help. . . .The demonstration was a game by the Serbs to show that they were strong, to show us what they can do to us. But they didn't succeed in that—they will never succeed. Those demonstrations affected the relationship between nations a lot [i.e., between Serbs and Albanians]. Even my own [Serbian] friends changed. I changed too. I could no longer trust. . . . Everything got worse.

MAN, AGE 20 IN 1981, BORN IN PRIŠTINA, LIVING IN PRIŠTINA

I was a student at that time and I participated in the demonstrations. No one knew who was leading the demonstrations. I heard that there was a protest about the food [at the university]. . . . [In the later demonstrations] we were for a "Kosova Republic." I think for some people the goal of the demonstration was independence for Kosovo and merging with Albania. These events encouraged the awakening of the [Albanian] national consciousness. I am a nationalist and I feel very proud of that.

WOMAN, AGE 19 IN 1981, BORN
IN PRIŠTINA, LIVING IN PRIŠTINA

In 1981 I was a student, but I was not involved in the demonstrations because I thought [at that time] that they were Marxist-Leninist. But I saw the crowd. I think that the demonstration shouldn't have happened. The goals of the protestors were independence and democratization but they were never achieved. Every day since then our lives have gotten worse.

MAN, AGE 22 IN 1981, BORN
IN PRIŠTINA, LIVING IN PRIŠTINA

At the time of demonstrations, I was working. I stopped work and joined, shouting together with other people. We wanted independence for Kosovo in 1981 and we never succeeded. The demonstration changed my life because ever since then I have been involved in politics.

MAN, AGE 17 IN 1981, BORN
IN PRIŠTINA, LIVING IN PRIŠTINA

I was in high school and I saw the crowd and the police violence. I participated and I hated police at that time. I felt good when police were running after us. After Tito's death nobody felt secure anymore about living in ex-Yugoslavia, and people went back to their ethnic roots. The goal of the demonstrations was to show who was who, to show who belongs to which nationality. I always thought of myself first as Albanian, but the demonstrations made me think more about what that means and what I can do for my people.

WOMAN, AGE 16 IN 1981, BORN
IN PRIŠTINA, LIVING IN PRIŠTINA

The demonstrations were not organized by the people who attended those demonstrations but by somebody else. We were accused of chauvinism and separatism [and that wasn't what we wanted]. But the [attacks on us] made us more strong and more united. There were some people who wanted a Kosova republic before the demonstrations, but now we all wanted the same thing—and not joining Albania like they said. We wanted to be a part of Yugoslavia, but not to be with Serbia. Now that Yugoslavia is gone, our plans have to change. . . . But Kosovo [as a part of] Serbia would never be for us [a solution].

MAN, AGE 21 IN 1981, BORN IN PRIŠTINA, LIVING IN PRIŠTINA

I was working at that time and I was involved in the demonstrations with all of my friends. We were shouting and police were beating us. At first it was not so violent but then suddenly it was very, very violent. We were all together and I felt secure, not afraid. It was as if the tanks and guns were only there to watch us. It was like a celebration for me and my friends. Then, when the fighting started, we all tried to run away. One of my friends died from a police beating. We had been together in the crowd and then we lost each other. The next time I saw him, he was dead.

We were not satisfied and we were out to ask for a Kosovo republic. We did not succeed. I think a lot about that demonstration, who started it and why. The demonstration taught me about the power of the military and the police, that they can kill but they can't change our minds about freedom.

MAN, AGE 17 IN 1981, BORN IN PRIŠTINA, LIVING IN PRIŠTINA

I was in high school and I was not involved in the demonstrations because I was not clear what was happening. I saw people running away from the police. Students were not satisfied about the university and they started it. I was not a part of the university so I didn't go. I was afraid of having problems. Now I am even more afraid.

MAN, AGE 14 IN 1981, BORN IN PEĆ, LIVING IN PRIŠTINA

I was in high school and I didn't participate because I was young. I saw the crowd beaten by the police and heard the shouting. [At that time] I thought that the students caused the demonstrations, but now I know that the goal was the independence of Kosovo.

From that time the gap between Serbs and Albanians widened. I lost my friends who are now on the other side.

MAN, AGE 21 IN 1981, BORN
IN PRIŠTINA, LIVING IN PRIŠTINA

I was a student and participated in the demonstrations. We all participated if we were around. I didn't know about it before [it happened], and I'm not sure how it was planned. I saw the arrogance [of the police] and I felt weak. [Now I think that] the demonstrations were organized by people who wanted to see us [Albanians] move towards destruction.

The goal was to destroy us. That was the beginning of the creation of the Greater Serbia.

Serbs

WOMAN, AGE 11 IN 1981, BORN
IN PRIŠTINA, LIVING IN PRIŠTINA

I was at home during the 1981 demonstrations. I was scared. I could see the tanks from my window and how the demonstrators would run and hide from the tear gas. I felt lost. I didn't know what was going on. The demonstrations were at first students' and then political. First, they asked for better student standards and then for the republic. Now they are not demonstrating anymore but nothing has changed.

I have some memories from that period which influenced my life. After the demonstrations, I was very much hurt that the neighborhood [Albanian] children were forbidden to socialize with us. Their mother forbade it.

WOMAN, AGE 26 IN 1981, BORN IN
KOSOVSKA MITROVICA, LIVING IN NOVI SAD

I was in Mitrovica at the time and I survived the demonstrations. I saw so much hatred on their [Albanian] faces and I could not understand where was that coming from. Were they brought up in a wrong way or seduced? Weren't we all taught that we are supposed to live together? I was very hurt and disappointed and that, unfortunately, resulted in my hatred against them for they betrayed me.

I couldn't understand the real reason why they didn't want to live with us any more. It was probably because Albanians had all the rights at that time, all the power. They say, "Give somebody power to see what is he like," and that was it. Simply they felt too powerful and they wanted everything at once. You can see for yourself what they achieved by that . . . Actually this regime enabled many people to earn money through illegal means. Corruption was the only thing the regime achieved. I feel hurt that that the present authorities in Kosovo [Serbian] are aggressive in the same way and maybe even more towards Albanians than the Albanian authorities were towards Serbs. You don't achieve anything by that.

Those protests influenced me a lot to leave Mitrovica. I spent thirty years of my life there. I have tried to forget that. It is hard to hate; I hated those people because they hated me. That's why I moved to Čačak [and then to Novi Sad]. I wanted to escape that.

WOMAN, AGE 15 IN 1981, BORN IN PRIŠTINA, LIVING IN BELGRADE

I was at home during the demonstrations and since I was living in the center of the city I was watching what was going on. I saw them [Albanians] gathering and being beaten by the police after the police hour, how they were chased away and, of course, I saw all of those many potholes left behind by the tanks on the streets.

I was very curious to find out what was going on. The whole thing was weird because it happened so suddenly. The demonstrations were caused by the leaders of the irredentist party, which envisioned the annexation of Kosovo by Albania. They officially demanded a Kosovo republic, but who knows what else they wanted to achieve. Those demands were never realized. Their present demands are still without foundation and impossible. . . . The demonstrations helped me to understand what's happening today [the war in Yugoslavia]. It is all part of the same, isn't it?

MAN, AGE 28 IN 1981, BORN IN KOSOVSKA MITROVICA, LIVING IN NOVI SAD

During the demonstrations I was driving a truck [so I wasn't in Kosovo], but I was afraid for my family. . . . [After the 1981

demonstrations] I certainly saw many attempts at protesting. Especially miners from Trepča. Huge lines of people who were allegedly
on a hunger strike for ten days—but they walked ten and more kilometers without any problems. . . . After all of those protests I had
conflicts with my colleagues. I felt anger. Yes, I decided to leave the
unhealthy environment. . . .

The reasons for demonstrations? Greater Albania. The reason is the
same today. Actually I have the impression that Šiptars [a derogatory
Serbian term for Albanians] from Kosovo don't like those from Albania and that they [Kosovars] would most like to be independent, I
mean a separate state. . . .

WOMAN, AGE 16 IN 1981, BORN
IN PRIŠTINA, LIVING IN BELGRADE

I was at school during the demonstrations. I saw the
way it looked. First I saw the police and after them the demonstrators.
I was scared and nothing was clear to me. Actually I did not understand the demonstrations as [something done by] irredentists. I
thought that the students were protesting because of the bad nutrition
at the university. Actually, their goals were separation from Yugoslavia. That never changed; the motive is still the same. Those demands
are unofficially realized but officially it doesn't look that they are.

Those events totally changed both my life and the way I experienced the world. I became more and more frustrated. I knew that I
had learned a big lie [about "brotherhood and unity"]. When I could
go to Belgrade, I did.

WOMAN, AGE 14 IN 1981, BORN
IN PRIŠTINA, LIVING IN PRIŠTINA

During the demonstrations, I was at a neighbor's house.
[She was a] female neighbor, a teacher. [She] used to collect all of us
younger ones to socialize in some kind of constructive way because
we were not going to school. That way parents worried less because
they had to work. . . . I saw many of them [Albanians] running away
from the tear gas, but I heard them better, because they were very
loud. I felt weird, I couldn't leave the house and I was a little mad
because of that. After that they proclaimed the police hour [curfew]
and I couldn't socialize in a normal way with my peers, and that was
my first time to fall in love. That was not the best [time]. . . .

I was not completely sure about the cause of the demonstrations but I was connecting that to the fact that there were many more Albanians here than us Serbs. I remember that they were asking to change the Constitution, and also I know that now they want back the [Constitution] from 1974. The main slogan was "Kosovo Republic." I think that nothing changed and that they still want independence. . . . The demonstrations had a big influence on my life in the way that many of my friends moved away, including my boyfriend at the time.

MAN, AGE 16 IN 1981, BORN IN PRIŠTINA, LIVING IN PRIŠTINA

I went [to the demonstration] to see how it looks. At the beginning there were really only students and mainly those who came from villages. I knew most of the Prištinians and there were only few of them there. It was a crowd dressed in red-black [Albanian national colors]. To me it looked like a football game. Like a crowd of bewildered club supporters.

I actually felt great. Something was going on. Instead of doing it during the night we were partying during the day. All day long. Only now I can see that the whole thing was not that amusing. I was not interested in the causes at the time. I didn't know exactly what were they looking for and how they envisioned that republic. I am not sure even today what they actually want. What do they achieve by boycotting the state in which they live?

Nothing can be achieved through demonstrations. For me, they are simply disloyal citizens. The Constitution is what it is and they have the same rights as any other citizens. The fact that they don't like them is something else.

Several Kosovo Serbs who witnessed the demonstrations described the crowd as "bewildered" and not knowing what they were doing. The press at the time described the crowd in identical terms.

MAN, AGE 17 IN 1981, BORN IN PRIŠTINA, LIVING IN PRIŠTINA

I was at the high school at that time. I saw the demonstrators, police, tanks, airplanes. . . . Some demonstrators were carrying metal bars. At the beginning I was a little afraid, but later I got used to that and then curious about what was happening. As much as I could, I found a way to see [what was happening].

The demonstrations were caused by the Albanian wish to separate from Yugoslavia and join Albania. Nothing changed until today and everything comes around to their desire for their own state.

The demonstrations had a huge and deep impact on my life. I spent half of my youth under the regime of the police hour [curfew]. I don't know how to define some of the feelings and avoid being too extreme. In comparison to other young people in other parts of the country, we didn't have a freedom of movement. There was no freedom at all—for anyone. . . .

MAN, AGE 14 IN 1981, BORN
IN PRIŠTINA, LIVING IN PRIŠTINA

I was at school. They were in the school yard, breaking the windows. My mother came to pick me up and she brought me home. I saw them. In one word—a mob. At the time I was a little confused and scared, but after my mother took me I felt miserable and I tried to run away from her, to go back to school and stay with my friends.

Their demands were same as they are today—separation from this state. It did not come true. . . . I became more cautious with people of Albanian nationality.

MAN, AGE 15 IN 1981, BORN
IN PRIZREN, LIVING IN PRIŠTINA

I was a kid and I was going to school. After the demonstrations I didn't even go to school. . . .

I saw people walking down the streets and shouting, but I didn't know what. I was not very scared but happy as any other kid [would be] because I was not going to school. At that time I was not interested in the reasons. It was like an unexpected holiday and very strange because we [kids] were happy and the parents were not.

I was not thinking about it then but now I think that their demands were not justified, that they actually had more than they needed. The demands were following that direction, but since 1991, when they [Serbian authorities] discontinued the Kosovar Assembly, they [Albanians] have much less power then they had before. . . . In 1990, I felt what freedom means.

MAN, AGE 16 IN 1981, BORN IN PRIŠTINA, LIVING IN PRIŠTINA

I was in high school and in the classroom on April 1 when they demonstrated for the first time. I saw the crowd heading towards the student dorms.

It was all the same to me, but everybody around me was upset and therefore I was upset as well. I was sixteen at that time and I had a very unclear picture about what the Albanians wanted when what all of the Serbs were talking [about was] that they [could not] find a job because they were Serbs or because they didn't speak Albanian.

I think that their demands were ridiculous and that they made a strategic mistake for doing it [the demonstrations]. It is a fact that Serbs are still moving out [of Kosovo] but now in a lower number because there are fewer of them left.

[The demonstrations] influenced me because I started seriously to realize that I live in multinational surroundings and that it is not all the same for all of us. No matter what your last name is and what language you are using, you should have some rights. I think about these things, although I was not raised that way.

Demonstrations had occurred twice earlier in March, but many people, Serbs and Albanians alike, refer to the April 1 demonstrations as "the first."

MAN, AGE 17 IN 1981, BORN IN PRIŠTINA, LIVING IN PRIŠTINA

I was seventeen and I was still at the high school. I saw the way it looked—a bewildered mob. I was circling the whole day to reach my home, but I couldn't because I live in the center and the demonstrations were there. I slept over at my friend's house and managed to get in touch with my parents only later in the night. I was terrified and surprised. I thought maybe there would be a war.

The demonstrations were caused by the national minority having too many rights. That's why they wanted to have a state within a state. Their demands were the republic within the federation. Today they want the independent, ethnically clean Kosovo joined with Albania and Albanians in Macedonia. . . .

The demonstrations had a huge negative influence on my life. I think that several generations got stranded in their development because of reasonable parental concern and expectation of the worst [i.e., real war]. We were not allowed to go out [downtown], we had to be careful about the places we went to, about the people we socialized with; prohibitions and fear were all over. I still feel the consequences of that [paranoia and fear].

WOMAN, AGE 9 IN 1981, BORN IN PRIŠTINA, LIVING IN PRIŠTINA

I was with my family. I didn't see a lot, just the tanks passing through the town, small groups of demonstrators with flags and so on. I felt weird, hurt in some way. I did not know how to accept that.

They shouted a lot of things, but mostly they were asking for the republic. As long as I remember they had proclaimed it [the republic] on several occasions, but never officially. Some people say that that's the way to forge the history later. The demonstrations had a tremendous influence on my life. My parents are of different nationalities [Serb and Albanian] and some people started to avoid me and there was a lot of arguing at home. I was very confused. I don't like to talk about politics.

Born in 1972, this woman would have been too young to remember Albanians proclaiming a republic in 1968, and perhaps on any other occasion prior to 1981. Many young people, Serbs and Albanians alike, "remember" things they are too young to have known first hand. Whether they actually experienced what they know, however, is irrelevant. However it is gained, their knowledge forms part of their present day Truth.

The intermarriage rate among Serbs and Albanians is extremely low. However, some intermarriages do occur, touching all parts of Kosovo. In the region known as Has, for example, a part of Kosovo that is nearly 100 percent ethnic Albanian, the son of one well-established Albanian family married a Serbian woman he met at the University in Belgrade. Together, they attend weddings and other celebrations in Has, though they live in Belgrade, where mixed marriages are more common. After 1981, many of the Serb-Albanian couples in Kosovo moved to Serbia proper or to other parts of Yugoslavia.

WOMAN, AGE 13 IN 1981, BORN
IN PRIŠTINA, LIVING IN BELGRADE

During the demonstrations everyone was sitting at
home worrying and so did I. [My parents] sent me to Belgrade for
three months to visit relatives. When I came back, I saw a lot of police
and army. Everyone else had had some time to get used to that, but
seeing it all at once was a shock. I thought that the national hatred
was responsible for all of that. They [Albanians] were asking for the
republic in order to separate, and that cannot happen. . . . The demonstrations speeded up my departure from Kosovo.

MAN, AGE 24 IN 1981, BORN
IN PRIŠTINA, LIVING IN PRIŠTINA

I was at home. I saw all sorts of things, various violent
behaviors, people throwing stones, people who were ordered to
gather and go in circles [and make some kind of blockade]. I was terrified by the level of the demonstrations. It was totally unexpected. I
don't think that they really knew what they wanted. Their demands
are known [today] — Kosovo republic.

Those happenings influenced the gap between Serbs and Albanians
in all respects. A widening, you can say. Every part of our lives [be-
came] further and further apart. And today, we live in the same place
but we are like strangers.

WOMAN, AGE 15 IN 1981, BORN
IN PRIŠTINA, LIVING IN PRIŠTINA

I saw larger groups of demonstrators being chased by
the police. I was not very scared. That was the first time. At that age
the whole thing looks interesting. I was especially surprised by the appearance of the tanks, which made me feel a bit more safe and scared
at the same time.

That was the time when the line was drawn between the Serbs and
Albanians. I was not thinking about the reasons at that time. I didn't
see them then. I think that there is no real reason [for Albanian past
and present demands]. They want "Kosovo Republic," but I think
that the majority did not know what they wanted. I was not afraid of
those demands at the time, but now I am afraid of them because I am

afraid that they are not the ones who are making decisions about it and that they will get Kosovo through some political way.

I had more Albanian friends before [the demonstrations] and I did not make a distinction between the nationalities. [After the demonstrations] what nationality [one was] became the most important thing. I didn't like that at all.

MAN, AGE 15 IN 1981, BORN IN PRIZREN, LIVING IN PRIZREN

I was watching the demonstrations. A crowd following a small group of people [the leaders]. To me the whole thing looked crazy. It was as if they didn't have any goals and they didn't know what they were doing. Something like — where one goes everyone goes. The whole thing was caused by a small group of people. Individuals. It didn't come from the [ordinary] people. This was the politics of a clique. . . . They wanted "Kosovo Republic," the same thing they want now.

MAN, AGE 18 IN 1981, BORN IN PRIŠTINA, LIVING IN PRIŠTINA

I was coming home from school. I was caught in the crowd, but I thought that it was a welcome for some politician. When I saw the police and heard the shooting I knew that it was something else.

At the time, I didn't have the answer for what it was and what could it be. I was not afraid at the beginning. Now I think that they did a great thing for their nation. Their demands were not realized in the way they had demanded in the demonstration, but [through the influence of] the wrong politics of the time and also now because of the population explosion [i.e., the high birth rate among Albanians]. This is an Albanian Kosovo, just look around you. The police did not stop anything except for our lives.

[The demonstrations] affected me because I learned about the prewar state [i.e., what a prewar state looks like and how it feels]. And [the demonstrations] created cohesion and [the sharing of a] similar opinion among the people of my generation. We [young Kosovo Serbs] became closer to each other.

MAN, AGE 20 IN 1981, BORN
IN PRIŠTINA, LIVING IN PRIŠTINA

I was watching what was going on. I saw a bewildered crowd that was unreasonably trying to destroy everything around [them]. Conflicts, fights, police, violence. . . . I felt very insecure.

They tried to conquer a part of Serbia. Their demands were totally unjust and [they were part of] the politics that has nothing to do with sanity.

Of course it had an influence on me. Now I look at those people in a different way than before. The relationship between us changed, and since I live among them, my whole life changed. We always have to be careful now.

MAN, AGE 16 IN 1981, BORN
IN PRIŠTINA, LIVING IN LONDON

First, those were not student but nationalistic demonstrations. I saw them many times and it was more or less the same — shouting, breaking, conflicts with the police. The causes are nationalistic tendencies, same as now. That cannot be realized in this state. Maybe in another one.

I was not afraid, I was appalled. That influenced me a lot. I decided to leave this city [Priština]. I knew I had no future there.

WOMAN, AGE 18 IN 1981, BORN
IN PRIŠTINA, LIVING IN PRIŠTINA

It was horrifying. The city turned black all of a sudden. Full of police, full of mad people. I was afraid and I didn't understand why was it happening. Now I think that it had to be like that. Tensions were building up! They exploded! They exploded at the wrong moment! . . .

I think that they [Albanians] lost a lot and that they are far away from the achievement [of their goals]. Me, I don't have any interest in politics. I just want to forget about everything [and just live life]. It is a little hard here, you know? [Laughing nervously.] I am still afraid of what could happen. I saw about the war [in Croatia and Bosnia-Herzegovina] on TV, and I am very afraid.

WOMAN, AGE 14 IN 1981, BORN
IN PRIŠTINA, LIVING IN PRIŠTINA

I was going to school at that time. I saw very little of the whole thing. I was sitting at home and I was not allowed to go out on the street. I didn't go to school for a while. I was shocked.

They demanded a republic, an ethnically clean Kosovo. That didn't happen. Kosovo has been multinational for centuries. Since the Turkish times.

No one asks us [young people] what to do [about the situation in Kosovo]. I don't think anyone cares about any of us [living in Kosovo].

WOMAN, AGE 11 IN 1981, BORN
IN PRIŠTINA, LIVING IN BELGRADE

I was a student. During the demonstrations I was in Niš. My father is in the military and during that time he was mobilized.

At that time I thought that those demonstrations were caused by the antistate, separatist element. That is what everyone was saying. I was young and I didn't understand that. I only knew that it was something dangerous that had to be prevented.

[The demonstrations were] an attempt to drag the public's attention to the state of Serbian-Albanian relations. . . . Because of the demonstrations, my father was relocated to Priština in order for the Army to show its presence. I stopped seeing him so often. Of course I was afraid for him. My whole family knew that Kosovo was dangerous.

MAN, AGE 20 IN 1981, BORN
IN PRIŠTINA, LIVING IN PRIŠTINA

Every day I was on the roof of the building watching what was going on. I even saw how the police killed the demonstrators. I was shocked. I think about it sometimes.

The demonstrations were caused by political interests. Then they [Albanians] were demanding a republic and now they want autonomy.

The demonstrations made me think about war. I never want to

fight in a war. I don't have hate for anyone. I saw the war [in Bosnia-Herzegovina] on TV and I know people who fought there. I saw the refugees here, so miserable and angry. They have nothing! And so many dead neighbors. I wouldn't want anyone to attack my family because I would [be forced to defend them]. But I want to avoid it. Only a crazy person would enjoy that.

WOMAN, AGE 16 IN 1981, BORN IN LIPLJAN, LIVING IN LIPLJAN

I was going to school at the time. I didn't see very much of that. I only remember that we didn't go to school and that everything changed after that.

The reason [for the demonstrations] was the unsatisfactory living conditions [at the university]. As I remember, they [Albanians] were asking for improvement in nutrition and then they were asking for "Kosovo Republic." Now they are demanding separation from Yugoslavia and joining with Albania. Fortunately it didn't happen.

It influenced my life because I was not allowed to go out. There was a police hour [curfew]. And I started to be afraid. Before that, I didn't have these fears.

WOMAN, AGE 17 IN 1981, BORN IN VUČITRN, LIVING IN KRAGUJEVAC

I was still in school at the time. There was a terrible chaos in Vučitrn. They were passing through the streets and shouting. They were wearing black and red scarves. The police blocked the streets. I was terrified. I was afraid of war.

The demonstrations were caused by the hatred that had existed forever. They wanted to chase us away from Kosovo because they wanted an independent Albanian state. . . .

My whole youth was slowed down.

One Man Accused of Being the Ringleader

"Afrim"[1] had been waiting for me for over an hour. I enter a small back room filled with men smoking cigarettes. They stand and we all shake hands. My translator politely asks for privacy. All but one of the men shuffle out into the antechamber. An unassuming man in a gray suit remains behind. At one time he was "public enemy number one" for Serbia. He had been arrested and tried as one of the founders of an illegal Kosovo Albanian Marxist-Leninist organization and accused of plotting the 1981 demonstrations. I tell him that I've heard that he was a leader in the 1981 student demonstrations. "A leader?" Afrim says quietly. "No, but I did have something to do with it."

He wrings his hands nervously and looks down at his shoes. We sit less than three feet apart on hard wooden chairs. "You can talk about whatever you want to remember and I'll just take notes," I assure him. He begins slowly, with his general views on Kosovo. It's something of a prepared speech. The historical claims to Kosovo. The oppression at the hands of Serbian authorities. The desire for freedom. I try to let him say whatever he needs to say, but Afrim can sense my impatience. He stops abruptly. I know you know a lot about this place, his manner tells me, but I have my own story to tell. Afrim examines me in silence. He has not yet decided whether he will actually tell me anything. He starts his prepared speech again, edging around the 1981 demonstrations in broad strokes, as if he too had only read about them in the paper or heard the tale from a neighbor.

Then, after more than half an hour has passed, Afrim starts speaking about himself, cautiously and deliberately:

I became involved when I was twenty years old. The movement consisted entirely of creating certain "circles." We would distribute forbidden literature, write articles, pamphlets, that sort of thing. The goal of this propaganda was to increase the consciousness of Albanians, to uncover Serbian policies, to establish the preconditions for a wider democratic movement.

There were various organizations, all clandestine. The ones that were the most clandestine lasted longer. The Yugoslav secret service was very widespread; there was a lot of shadowing of people. The whole situation was really Orwellian. You know, like big brother watching you. We would try to combat this by setting things up so each person knew at most two other people in the circle. This way even if someone was tortured into talking, they couldn't be sure about more than two names. But the police could even uncover organizations consisting of only two people. They were so strong. They could break you.

In the 1970s and 1980s, Albanians made up 80 percent of the political prisoners in Yugoslavia. Now it is different. It is worse. We are bugged all the time, even in prison. When I was in prison, I could not write letters. And today my correspondence is monitored, my phone tapped, my movements shadowed on the street. I have the same feeling that I had when I was in jail. There never was more oppression. . . .

The 1981 demonstration was spontaneous. Opposition groups operating clandestinely had an impact, of course, but they [the demonstrators] were not linked with any organized movement. Albania provided indirect support through propaganda. But I don't think Albania had that much to do with it. It was the students, and it wasn't really organized.

We were cautious. We didn't want an uncontrolled explosion. We were aware that the political leadership of Kosovo was not ready to turn to that phase. Among the former leadership of Kosovo there was disagreement about what to do.

What was happening in Poland at the time had an indirect impact as well. It gave us hope. It showed us that a movement was possible. In general, democracy in Eastern Europe had a pro-western perspective. The opposition had an anti-Communist and social aspect in Poland. In contrast, in Kosovo the opposition had a national character. Instead of being anti-Communist, the Kosovo movement was anti-colonialist and nationalist.

At first, the movement in Kosovo was called reactionary or coun-terrevolutionary. In court trials and in the newspapers, Albanians were called "ballists,"[2] labeled as counterrevolutionaries, considered enemies of the socialist revolution. By the end of the 1980s, counterrevolution-aries had gained the sympathy of western countries, so the regime tried to label Albanians as Stalinists.

[The organizations were most often described as "Marxist-Leninist," not Stalinist.]

But of course we were not Stalinists — the greatest outside influence came not from Stalinists but from the west and Albanian immigrants in the United States. The identification with brother Albania was actu-ally weak. It was on the level of fantasy. Most activists knew nothing about Albania. Since they had never been there, they could afford grand illusions. It is similar to the orphan child who has never known her mother; she can easily glorify her. I was one of those who once had these fantasies about Albania.

In 1978, I was a journalist but I was also still studying. The secret police came and kidnapped me in the middle of the market. I had been warned that I was shadowed by the police. I was twenty-four years old. There were about half a dozen of them. They came in two cars and forced me into one of them. I was sent to a forest twenty-four kilometers from here [Priština] in Lipan [Lipljan], where there was a hunters' lodge used by the officers of the secret police. Some high-ranking police officers interrogated me. They alleged that I was the author of some poetry in clandestine publications. They told me to admit it. I refused. I was offered a chance to become a collaborator. If I refused, I would be sentenced to at least eight years in prison and the police would hurt my family. They tried to blackmail me with every threat possible. I still refused.

Sometime after midnight, I was brought to my apartment, which was being guarded by police. I was told to report to the police station the next morning. During the night, I managed to escape. I can't say exactly how, but I know Priština very well and I went through some small streets. I knew where the uninhabited homes were. I had had it all planned in case I had to use them.

For four years I lived clandestinely. I was the father of three young kids and I couldn't see my family. During this period, I saw my chil-dren only two times, and only when they were sleeping. I missed their entire childhood, these four years and the ten that followed. Being only a few kilometers away from them in hiding and not being able to see them was very difficult. I spent the whole time writing poetry. I felt like a rabbit—there were hunters all around me.

On March 11 [1981], I was in Switzerland. I had trouble with my health, so I came back [secretly, right before the student demonstrations]. To me, the student demonstration appeared to be very peaceful, not political. Still, the press and political leaders branded it as the deeds of hooligans, and the regime embarked on arresting students. I didn't have anything to do with these [first] demonstrations.

There was a festival with the passing of the baton for Tito's birthday. [Young people would carry a baton from town to town in a grand relay throughout Yugoslavia, culminating on May 25, Tito's birthday and a national holiday.] The baton passing was already widely discredited throughout Yugoslavia, but most discredited among Kosovo youth. [During the time of the baton race,] many students were arrested and tensions increased. I thought what was happening on that March 11 was nothing special.

The March 11 demonstrations were a spontaneous reaction of students to the unfavorable conditions at the university in Priština and the interference of authorities in the general operation of the university. The students wanted an autonomous university. There were protests elsewhere in the university system—in Novi Sad and Sarajevo. The demonstrations didn't really appear to be anything special. . . .

I came back from Switzerland before the March 26 demonstrations, but I didn't participate. The second demonstrations combined both social and political demands. Some things we [the opposition groups] had written were in the students' demands. After the students were back in their dormitories, the Belgrade police broke into their rooms and beat the students brutally, including those who were not demonstrators.

The mass demonstrations began on April 1. All [Albanian residents of Kosovo] participated, not just the students. The entire square was filled. The primary demand was for a republic of Kosovo within Yugoslavia. They also called for decreased police pressure and improved economic conditions. . . .

I went to the April 1 demonstration dressed as a worker. It was the first time I had appeared publicly [since 1978]. I considered my presence a public necessity. It was better to have us old activists known by the police appear, than to risk the new activists. The glass was full then. Everyone was out. I do not regret that I appeared. The smallest thing that a person can do is to stand with youth, with the people. I insisted that the demonstration not turn into an anti-Serbian demonstration, though the regime was Serbian. Some Serbs supported us, both before and after the demonstration, but very few did so.

[Adem] Demaqi [negotiator for the Albanians] demanded talks, but officials ignored him. I joined the demonstration by noon, after people had been protesting for hours. During the entire demonstration, people did not eat or drink anything. We did not want to provoke anyone, so we did not enter any building. There was a kind of euphoria among the crowd. We thought that our demand for a separate republic would be met with the support of all the other Yugoslav republics.

The demonstration was surprisingly restrained. About forty thousand people were in the square for hours. People gave different speeches. Some were celebratory. Some talked on behalf of workers, teachers, students. . . . I addressed the audience from a tree in front of the leadership of the Communist committee. We thought there would be talks. If there wasn't a promise of talks, the people would have dispersed earlier. The police could have given a warning. We thought there were going to be talks. . . .

Then suddenly it erupted into the first wave of tear gas and shootings. . . . Many of those who tried to go to the main square were killed. Everyone was running and hiding wherever they could. The police were running after people, beating, shooting, rounding people up for arrest. Chaos. . . .

I managed to run away. I stayed with a Turkish family. The father in the family was in the police [but] the entire family supported the demonstrations. Many Serbs took people in as well. Some Serbs and Turks took part in the demonstrations. They also supported the demands for decentralized power in Kosovo. . . .

I went back into hiding. In December 1981, I was arrested. It's not clear how they found me.

[His speech slows. He becomes obviously pained.]

Thousands of people were arrested during that time. They followed all activists. I really don't know how they found me.

Early in the morning on the fifteenth of December, special [police] units surrounded the house where I was sheltered. They broke into the apartment and arrested me together with a roommate. Initially I was kept in Priština, and then sent to Skopje [Macedonia], to a building in a forest. They kept me in the forest for two months without even bringing me before an investigative judge. I wasn't permitted to see a lawyer for four months and my family was forbidden to see me for even longer.

I was moved to a lot of prisons. I learned later that I was kept one month in Sarajevo. I had no idea; I had understood myself to be in Belgrade. They blindfolded me whenever they moved me.

[Pause. Someone brings in a cup of coffee and a glass of water for each of us, and then leaves. Afrim takes a sip of coffee. He shifts in his chair and leans forward. He begins speaking faster. The words march out.]

The prison in the forest was built so the detainee could not hurt himself. I was safeguarded by police who stood in the cell twenty-four hours a day. I wasn't allowed to sleep for the first seven days.

They made me stand; I could only sit when they talked to me. As soon as I would close my eyes, they would click their guns or put them down hard on the table to make noise. Two people would talk about how they were going to liquidate me.

I was subjected to various forms of torture: hunger, thirst, the use of chemicals. A Swiss doctor who treated me later said that I had been given narcotics.

They beat me on every part of my body. When I asked for a glass of water, they gave me something that made my head light. The inspectors kept telling Albanian jokes. They told me to laugh. If I didn't laugh, they would beat me some more. They invited other people to come and watch. After they gave me the water, I couldn't stop myself from laughing.

They forced me to take medicines. They broke one of my teeth by forcing a spoon into my mouth. When I refused to open my jaws, they would beat me and pry my mouth open.

They gave me dinner. I felt pains and they gave me pills. I felt dizzy from the pills and began having visions. I saw colors and snakes and horrible things. The inspector was lifting me up, saying, "Where are you, my hero?" I was outside my body watching him.

I remember having to drink some mineral water. I poured half of my water into the glass of the inspector. My glass had a different color than the others. It looked like it was covered in oil. I drank it. I realized that I could not concentrate on anything they wanted from me.[3] They became more and more aggressive. In the back of my head, I heard them saying, "Who was . . . who was . . . ?" When I came to my senses, I realized that I was sleeping with my head on the table. They asked me, "What happened to you? You slept on the table."

Of course they made me confess to something.

To what?

To everything. To tell you the truth, they had ample evidence. I wrote poetry in clandestine publications and participated in the preparation and distribution of written propaganda. They wanted to construct links between Kosovo Albanians, the official leadership, western circles. . . . They talked about the poetry I wrote . . . the speeches [I gave, but] they wanted a conspiracy.

I can't remember the day I signed. Too many days. I signed a statement saying that I did this and that.

What?

I don't remember. They forced me to speak and then they made me take back my opinion. I don't remember even what I said I did.

I knew how police acted. I had experience. The worst was when they would stage my execution. A couple of guards kept talking about killing me. They said they would be the ones to do it to me. They told me that only one person knew I was in prison—my roommate—and he doesn't exist anymore and that I would be found dead in Germany and that I would be accused of assassinating my friend. They would say, OK, come with us. . . .

One day they blindfolded me, put me in a car and took me into the woods. I think it was the woods. They pushed me against the tree and asked me if I had anything to say. They put a gun near my head and I heard a click.

I really thought they would kill me. I tried to keep standing. I wanted to die standing. For some reason that was so important. To be standing. I didn't want to faint or fall to my knees. I knew about some young Albanians whom police had driven to the border and then shot, later saying that they were trying to escape. I had no idea where I was. I thought I was at the border.

You know what the worst thing was? When they did this a second time, I didn't even care. And then when they did it again, I wanted to be dead. I actually wanted them to shoot me.

The security inspectors were my main torturers. I knew some of them personally. They were both Serbs and Albanians. The Albanians in particular tried to prove themselves loyal in front of the Serbs.

How do you feel about the Albanian guards?

I felt sorry for these men. All of them, not just the Albanians. I don't blame them, any of them. They were just the apparatus of torture. They were the main victims. The experience of being a torturer crushed many men who survived two or three wars.

How did you survive?

I would imagine my children growing up. I grew my first mustache in jail. I wrote poetry. . . . I was together with men who had been imprisoned for poetry and pamphlets. The torturers did not succeed in crushing us, because we were convinced that we never did anything evil in our entire lives. We were against the regime, but not against Serb citizens.

In one of my poems, a person gets arrested and tortured. He laughs and says, there are worse things. He's scolded and humiliated, and he says there are worse things. He's tied up and left hanging by his feet, and he says there are worse things. He's asked, what could be worse? He says, it would be worse if I were in your shoes. This conviction, that we did nothing wrong, was very hard on the body, but good on the mind.

We prisoners were together. We could feel the prospect of democracy on the horizon. Spring was coming, we would say. No, they could not break us. . . .

When I entered a prison in Niš, complete hatred existed between the Albanian and Serbian prisoners, and this hatred was stimulated by the guards. One Albanian was placed in a cell with four or five Serbs. In my cell, there was a maniac killer. Albanians would do everything they could to be put in solitary confinement to escape. After some time passed, a very young guard said, "I'm on duty here and I can't do it any more." [The guard stopped encouraging the prisoners to hate each other.] This guard liked some of the inmates—he had hate too, but he realized to what he had been assigned.

The attitudes in the prison eventually changed. The conditions in the prison were very bad. We would have joint protests and hunger strikes. In a way, we were protected by the Serbian prisoners; some of them would take the blame for us if they could [because the guards would punish them less.] The Albanian prisoners helped the Serbian prisoners too. We were the ones who were visited by the Red Cross. When the Red Cross came, we would pass messages for the Serbian prisoners. The conditions in the prison eventually changed. I spent the last five years of my prison term in Niš; in the beginning we had no coffee, tea or juice and no exercise. We changed all that.

Yesterday I was stopped in the street by a former prisoner, a Serb. He hugged me right there on the street. He said, I realize you are right, the policies against you are wrong.

I am convinced that my friends saved me. During the trial of my friends, I was being held at a psychiatric clinic in Belgrade. My friends refused to talk about me in the trial unless they were informed about where I was and what was happening to me. Amnesty International immediately reacted and I am convinced that that is why I am here today.

I think I was in that clinic for about three months. It was after the place in the forest, that's all I know. I had no watch, no newspapers, no window. It was hard . . . to mark the passing of time.

They told me that I was being held for psychological observation. They kept giving me injections that would make me dizzy. I kept having hallucinations. Every time I would try to stand, I would fall down. Each days the guards would beat me up without pretext. That was the routine.

They were no longer trying to get me to talk. They stopped asking me questions. They were just trying to make me crazy. They would bring me really sick things as food. They brought me the unshaven skin of a pig and tried to force me to eat it. When I refused to eat it, they said, you went on a hunger strike. Then they tied me onto a bed and forced a tube into my nose. They said they were giving me artificial nourishment. I heard that they would stick the tubes into a guy's anus too, as a form of humiliation. They didn't do this to me.

This was the place [in the hospital clinic] where a lot of prisoners committed suicide. I didn't have the chance. I don't know what I would have done if I had the chance. I had to be treated in a special care ward. I saw people who were brought in as ordinary healthy men and who died in my presence.

They told me that there was a civil war going on in Kosovo and that my entire family was arrested. I kept asking to see my family. They gave me one last wish before execution. I said it was to see my children again and that, dead or alive, I wanted to be brought back to Kosovo. They said, you will see your family.

I had been held for over five months before I could see my family. The guards brought me into a small room and there they all were. My family could hardly recognize me and I could hardly talk. They told me afterward that my wish had only caused panic in my family.

[Afrim begins to cry. He stands up abruptly and leaves the room. Moments later he returns. He apologizes and says he wants to continue.]

The international groups got me out of there [the psychiatric hospital]. [He believes that Amnesty International had demanded that he have a trial.] They brought me to Priština for a trial. It was a complete farce. My punishment had been decided when my friends were convicted earlier. I was sentenced to fifteen years in jail. The prosecution had no evidence of any involvement in violence. [His appeal was unsuccessful.]

I was sent back to Belgrade to the Central Prison, where I was held in solitary confinement. I could meet my family once a month, and could occasionally read a Serbian paper. The beatings stopped.

To pass the time, whenever I had paper I would write poems and make drawings. Even in solitary, there was solidarity with other prisoners and prison guards. I had some pills to take for my pain, but I didn't trust them. I would slip the pills to the other prisoners who would dispose of them. The other prisoners went together each day on a walk in the yard. I went alone. . . .

One prison guard would talk to me each day for fifteen or twenty minutes; he used to say that he just wanted to break the monotony. He told the ones who distributed food to give me more. He told me that while he was in the military an Albanian saved his life, and that he visits the Albanian in his home in Kosovo. He said that from his visits in Kosovo, he knew that the things in the newspapers weren't true. He was a Montenegrin. Albanians never know what a good thing he did. One can't speak in general terms that all Serbs are bad. Ironically, it was my prison time that gave me the most contact with the kindness of Serbs.

I eventually got out of solitary and then was sent to a few other prisons before ending up in Niš. . . .

The day I was released was the most difficult day of my life. When nonpolitical prisoners were released they were smiling; those who remained were sad. With us, those who walked out cried and those who remained were happy. To go out looked like an injustice. There was no question that to go out and see your family would be wonderful. But it is a very hard feeling to see a prison from the outside. There are still many young Albanians in prison who are absolutely innocent. I

felt like I should change places with some of them. I know I can survive prison, but I don't know about them. I met the boys they had
arrested in the Paraćin case [see chapter three] and I am absolutely
convinced that those boys had nothing to do with what happened. I
worry about those boys.

I remember that day when I walked out. . . .

[He cries and turns away.]

I have seen police shoot at school kids. A Serb police officer
shouted at me and told me to back off. I have seen an officer on a
bridge pushing kids down. What he was doing was pushing them out
of the gunfire. The bullets flew by and none of the kids were hurt.
The pupils were crying. The officer led them down the road and into
a house.

We hear only about cases: cases of arrests and murders. One has to
think about what the children have experienced. If they are not dead
or wounded, they are not a case. No one thinks about them. A man
gets beaten in the middle of town—what happens to the children who
are watching? What happens when it is their father?

I have a three-year-old child. The other day, I told him that we
were going to the village, and he said, "Daddy, will there be police
there?" Now, how did he learn that? I have not told him anything
about police. When we go by police barricades, I see him watching. I
try to see what he is thinking.

I never want to tell him about these things. I have never told my
other children what happened to me . . . not even my wife, my
mother, myself. Today . . . this is the first time.

I won't sleep tonight. I have revealed more. . . .

No, don't worry, I am O.K.

There is one more thing I want to tell you. There was this Serbian
police officer who was sent to the prison in Niš. He had killed someone when he was driving drunk. When I saw him the first time—he
was a very big man—he could hardly wait for a chance to provoke
me. My friends warned me not to talk to him. They said he was a spy.
After a while, we became friends. He said he would kill anyone who
would hurt me. . . . He told me that police would practice ways to kill
irredentists. He said that he had been told that Albanians in Kosovo
were tying down Serb parents and raping their children. He had been
anxious to take action [in retaliation]. He had supported the paramilitary groups in Kosovo. That was the good thing to do, he had been

absolutely convinced. When he was in Niš, this guy defended two Albanians who were beaten by prison guards. That was the most significant victory.

I think more communication with Serbs would help liberate all of us. Many Albanians do not understand me.

Notes

1. Names of the interview subjects in this section have been changed.

2. The Balli Kombeter was an anti-Soviet, antiroyalist (against the return of King Zog) Albanian resistance movement during WWII which wanted Albania to retain Kosovo after the war. After Italy surrendered in 1943 and Germany took major cities in Albania, members of the Balli Kombeter cooperated with the pro-Nazi government in Tirana. See Barbara Jelavich, *History of the Balkans: Twentieth Century* (Cambridge, England: Cambridge University Press, 1983), 274–75; Ivo Banac, *With Stalin Against Tito: Cominformist Splits in Yugoslav Communism* (Ithaca, N.Y.: Cornell University Press, 1988), 209. It was very common for Serbian nationalistic propaganda to charge, without evidence, that pro-Nazi organizations were still operating within certain ethno-national groups, usually Croatian or Albanian, but also Slovene and Bosnian Muslim. See Michael A. Sells, *The Bridge Betrayed: Religion and Genocide in Bosnia* (Berkeley: University of California Press, 1997), 57.

3. Several prisoners in Yugoslavia, of all ethno-national backgrounds, have described a similar scenario, in which they drank something offered by the guards and then were unable to concentrate and even hallucinated. Interestingly, the stories of Albanian political prisoners in the 1980s are nearly identical to those of prisoners in the 1990s held captive by military and paramilitary troops during the war in Croatia and Bosnia-Herzegovina. Observations are drawn from the authors' own interviews with released prisoners, 1993–1996.

One Woman Tried As an Irredentist

I knew the legend of "Mirita" long before I met her. Mirita is one of the martyrs of the 1981 demonstrations. The authorities had not only arrested and imprisoned Mirita, they had killed her boyfriend while she was in jail. Each year, the boyfriend's hometown remembers the day on which he was killed as if it were a national holiday. And whenever Mirita visits Albanian activists in any part of Kosovo, she is received with the respect due an elder — although, at times, she still is the youngest.

Mirita labors long hours working on human rights cases, doing the kind of work no one wants to do, phoning, faxing, typing. She works long hours for Albanian-language newspapers, sacrifices, doesn't sleep. She attends the appropriate political events, visits the families with people in prison, works, works, works. She rarely talks about herself; she rarely talks at all.

I wonder what kind of life Mirita would have if not for the 1981 demonstrations. A trained lawyer, maybe she would be receiving clients, making money, getting married, having children. Maybe she would be the one traveling to countries facing human rights crises, maybe she would be the one hypothesizing about other people's conflicts. Or maybe she would just be a poet, a writer, a women's rights activist. Maybe should would enjoy being anonymous.

I learn over time that Mirita's real love is poetry; she won a prize for a poem that she wrote about women's rights. I learn that she spends long hours working on stories to please the newspaper so she can slip in the stories she wants to write — stories on women's rights. I learn that she dreams every day about traveling outside the country, that she has been invited to numerous inter-

national symposia, that she always has at least some hope of attending but in the end can never make it. Her passport was taken in 1981, before she had ever traveled anywhere at all. With Yugoslavia broken into separate states, she can no longer even visit relatives in Croatia.

"I'm stuck," Mirita shrugs. I note the edge of desperation. Another lead on a passport has turned sour. "Sometimes I don't think I'll ever get out of here." Mirita is tired, very tired. We are sitting around a neighbor's dining room table sipping coffees. I try to be encouraging: surely someone will help her get her passport. We both know that it will take a miracle. The problem isn't that Mirita is a big threat to Serbia; the problem is that she is only a little fish. Most of the big fish have their passports. But the little fish are not important enough—to anyone.

"Do you still have that tape recorder?" Mirita asks suddenly. "Now," she decides, "is a good time to tell you my story."

When I remember my childhood and school days, I cannot recall one bad moment. All of my girlfriends were just ordinary girlfriends. I never asked about their nationality. I think that I did not even know for sure what nationality meant. None of us thought about those things. It was probably different among adults, but I am sure that there was tolerance between nations and mutual understanding in Kosovo at that time. My grandmother used to talk about the difficulties our family had because of its origin. I started to think about those stories much later on. But when I was young, I thought that those [national conflicts] are things that belong to the past and that I should not pay any attention to them.

In the fourth grade of high school I was forced for the first time to think of myself as an Albanian. I was listening to Radio Tirana's program and there I heard a song that I really liked. The next day, my art professor heard me singing it in the school hallway and he yelled at me: "I don't want to hear you *ever* singing that again!" I was completely shocked; he was Albanian too. I asked him for the reason and he replied—"You must not mention Albania, you know where you live." I really could not understand him.

The same year at the graduation celebration a similar situation occurred. We were singing various songs, and among others some Albanian [songs] too. Professors terminated the celebration because of "nationalistic songs." One professor, a Montenegrin, who liked me reacted then worse than the others. He said: "I know you Albanians. I should learn Albanian to find out when and how you are insulting me." He is now one of Kosovo's functionaries and he calls us "Šip-tari."

I started to think about things which were strange to me until then. I started to remember my grandmother's stories about how a lot of people in Kosovo perished because of the crime of "verbal misdemeanors." [This is a reference to the prohibition in Yugoslavia and Serbia against speech deemed to be inciting national hatreds.] My mother warned me every time I listened to Radio Tirana. She insisted that I should turn the volume down; she was afraid that some of the neighbors might report us. We were not allowed to listen to this station. I did not want to obey that [prohibition], because I thought that it is my right to listen to anything I want to. I even managed to find some so-called forbidden books, and all of that had a great influence on the formation of my own attitude about the need for Albanians to be equal with all others.

When I got to the university I met my boyfriend. He was active in a student organization. I did not know exactly what they were doing, and in the beginning I was not very interested in finding out. Later, when I asked him to tell me more, he avoided giving me any answers. On the eleventh of March, 1981, the first student demonstrations were held in Kosovo because of the bad conditions in students' dormitories. At one of the previous classes our professor warned us not to be foolish, and to not ask for our rights out in the streets but [instead] in school. He said that education is our most powerful weapon. I am not sure that I really understood his warning at the time. I knew little about the things that were going on then.

On March 26 I saw a lot of people in the street. I asked a friend what was going on, and my friend told me that the demonstrations are beginning and she asked me if I wanted to join the crowd. We both did.

[Although demonstrations had already occurred two weeks earlier, most people refer to March 26 or April 1 as "the demonstrations."]

The demonstrators sought republic status for Kosovo. Soon police forces appeared, insisting on dismissing the demonstrations. They told us to go home. We did not obey, so they used tear gas several times, but the crowd would always come back again and again. Everything lasted for a few hours.

On April 1 and 2, demonstrations were held again, but I did not participate because of my mother. She threatened to kill herself if I went out. I had to stay at home because I knew how concerned she was. Those demonstrations were bloody. A lot of people were killed. These events changed the attitude I had until then. I didn't feel like an equal citizen anymore. I wanted to do something. . . .

I insisted that my boyfriend tell me what he was doing and what kind of organization it was. He said that he would explain everything only if I got involved in the work too. I didn't want to become a member of any kind of political organization, but I thought that something with broader goals would be OK. I demanded that I not be registered as a member. He told me that he is involved in the work of a group that is promoting the idea of establishing the republic of Kosovo within Yugoslavia. It didn't look like a bad idea. . . .

[The group was later accused of being Marxist-Leninist and "counterrevolutionary," charges Mirita denies.]

I continued with my studies and started to read more and more of the prohibited Albanian books. I offered those books to my colleagues after I would finish reading them. On April 16 I went to the center of the town together with my sister to buy shoes for myself. I noticed that we were being followed by a man. Soon, four other men joined him. At first I thought that I was imagining things, but my sister was convinced that they were following us. We ran into a shoe store and asked the clerk to let us hide behind the counter. He let us stay in the back room. We were very frightened.

I knew that those men from the police and that they were following me. By that time my boyfriend had been in hiding from the police for six months. He warned me that I could have problems with the police and advised me to take care and be cautious.

A little later, the clerk came to us and said that the policemen had gone, so we left the store. We started to walk toward our house. On the way there we saw them again. They were standing on the sidewalk looking at me and shaking their heads in a half-threatening way.

We started running toward the house. It was then when I remembered that two days before a man had come to our house to ask for a room we were renting. We never rented rooms before and we told him that. He apologized, said that it must have been some kind of mistake and went away. My boyfriend was very suspicious about that visit. He said that it was a policeman, and it turned out that he was right.

As soon as I got into the house I told my brother to take all of my [forbidden Albanian] books immediately out of the house. We agreed that he should hide them at somebody's place and so he did. I didn't tell my mother what happened, but I went to my uncle's house in the evening and told him everything that was going on. On the same night police broke into my family's house and searched it, but they never found anything. Then they came to my uncle's house too. I managed to escape and hide myself at a neighbor's house. When they left my uncle advised me to go and report myself to the police, but I didn't want to listen to him. For the next couple of weeks I hid in my friend's house.

As soon as I went back home the police arrested me. They took me to the police headquarters and one of the inspectors started to investigate me. He offered me a coffee, which I refused, saying that I never drink it. A little later a woman inspector joined him. She addressed me by the name "Viktoria" and asked me why I had been hiding. I said that it was not true but she continued questioning me, calling me "Viktoria" all the time. I remained silent. She became very rude and violent. She pulled my hair and shouted at me, demanding to know why I was not answering. I told her that my name is Mirita and not Viktoria. She replied that she knew very well what my conspirator name was. I kept telling her that I had only one name.

Eventually, they gave me some kind of document to sign. I refused. Then they told me that I had to go to see a doctor because I didn't look very healthy. I said that I felt very well and that I didn't need a doctor, but they took me there by force and gave me some kind of injection. I became completely numb.

Then they took me to the prison in Mitrovice [Kosovska Mitrovica]. The police who took me there told the guards that they mustn't do anything with me before asking. They locked me in the cell. I was half conscious. In the evening I started having terrible convulsions. I suppose that it happened both because of the psychological shock and the injection that I had received. One of the guards wanted to call a doctor, but the others reminded him of the instructions they got from the Priština policemen. But eventually a doctor came and he said that he didn't care what anyone said, that I was ill and that I needed help. He injected me with a sedative.

For the next three months they filled me with injections. I felt numb most of the time. In my dreams I had horrible hallucinations. Every second day they would interrogate me, and every session was psychological torture. Sometimes police would slap me and make me stand in the corner on one leg. They insulted me and tried to provoke me in various ways. Despite my very bad psychological and physical condition, I was trying to concentrate as much as I could during the investigations. I believe that it helped me a lot. The most important thing was to not let them provoke aggression or any emotions. . . . Only after going back to the cell would I allow myself to cry.

There were some other women in my cell, and that was a thing which made my imprisonment more bearable. I was never in solitary confinement. They fed us normally, but our cells were full of roaches, bedbugs and lice. But that was hardly the most unbearable thing. I suffered terrible convulsions and nightmares. I had been on drugs for eight months, and that was ruining both my physical and mental health. I asked a doctor for help and he gave me some kind of pills which caused a horrid pain in my stomach. Soon I threw all of them out.

We often listened to the cries from the male part of the prison. Once we held a protest by hitting the doors of our cells. A guard, who was wearing a completely bloody shirt, ran in and threatened to beat us up the same way if we didn't shut up. One of the prisoners said: "So what!" He took her out of the cell and brought her back totally bruised. They were more than clear that they could do whatever they wanted to us.

My interrogations seemed to have a few phases. At the beginning they didn't ask me much about my boyfriend, but later they started to question me about him. I didn't want to tell them anything except that we had a relationship and that I didn't know anything about his work. They kept wanting me to talk about organizations and things like that but I didn't know anything.

I was sentenced to two years of imprisonment. [Apparently, she was convicted because one of the recipients of forbidden Albanian literature had said that he received it from Mirita.] After thirteen months of being in a maximum security penitentiary, they transferred me to the medium security prison in Lipljan. It was much better there. If nothing else they stopped giving me drugs, but my nightmares didn't abate.

After I got out of the jail my life completely changed. I found out that the police had killed my boyfriend on January 11, 1984. After a long period of hiding, somebody had reported him and his friend. Police surrounded the house they were in and asked them to surrender. They didn't want to, and so police shot them in an attempt to capture them.

My hallucinations started again very intensively. I was recovering for seven years. I also wanted to finish my studies, because I thought that it would help me to go back to a normal way of living. But there was a big disappointment waiting for me at the university. There were blacklists with the names of some students [who were forbidden to attend]. My name was also on it. Professors were left to choose whether they wanted to obey those lists or not. Most of my teachers told me that those lists didn't mean anything to them and that I was as much their student as anyone else. But two gave me a hard time. I would appear at the exam and they would simply drive me away. I was persistent. I tried to appeal to their conscience, which they apparently didn't have at all. They would say that it was forbidden for them to allow me to attend the exam and that I should leave the class. After a long time of stubbornness and with a lawyer's help, I finally managed to graduate [with a degree in law].

Unfortunately, I never got a job in my specialized area.

TWO

"Impaled with a Bottle": The Martinović Case, 1985

Laying the Foundation: 1981–1985

As politicians in other parts of Yugoslavia experimented with the void of control created by the absence of Tito, so did those in Kosovo and Serbia proper. The early 1980s were a time of building and consolidating political strategies for both Kosovo Albanians and Serbs. Both were influenced by the larger Yugoslav context, which was embroiled in an economic crisis and political disarray. The 1981 demonstrations and their aftermath also had a profound influence on the development of their plans, dictating both the feasibility and desirability of any subsequent actions.

Instead of crushing a movement, the widespread arrests of Kosovo Albanians following the 1981 demonstrations rekindled Kosovo Albanian nationalism and helped form a mass movement for change. Much of the Kosovo Albanian opposition, which had previously operated underground, was pushed into the public eye. While some leaders went into hiding, others, including many who were not in fact leaders but simply unlucky enough to be arrested, were transformed by their arrests into heroes for present and future generations. Albanian opposition members spoke publicly not only at the 1981 demonstrations but also at subsequent protests at the trials of those accused of leading the demonstrations. These events gave young Kosovo Albanians a sense of pride and national identity, and energized many to become politically active for the first time.[1]

According to Shkelzen Maliqi, the Albanian movement had two main streams: one largely illegal (the Enverists), composed of "Marxist Leninist groups, though without any common leadership or even a basic, agreed upon platform." The other stream was "semi-legal (Titoists), composed of intellectual and cultural organizations and institutions, management bodies within industry, and later on (late 1988–early 1989) even within parts of the state administration, the Assembly, and the League of Communists."[2] As the 1980s progressed, the more radical elements of the Albanian underground seemed to fade away, as the new popular movement cast aside Marxist-Leninist terminology and shied away from affiliation with Tirana.[3] Although some individuals and groups still set their sights on uniting Kosovo with Albania, a consolidated front was portrayed to the world media: Kosovo Albanians wanted a republic within Yugoslavia. The crackdown following 1981 gave greater credibility and urgency to Kosovo Albanians' second demand: human rights according to international standards.

The Albanian diaspora grew increasingly active in publicizing the plight of Kosovo Albanians and in pushing the Kosovo Albanian national agenda.[4] Photographs from the 1981 demonstration of the Yugoslav army training its guns on Albanian children and a body count confirmed by international journalists steered world attention to human rights abuses in Kosovo. Countries that had previously found it politically and economically expedient to ignore human rights abuses in Yugoslavia now were forced to pay some attention to the issue.[5] In 1983, an Albanian émigré group published a complaint by a group of Kosovo Albanian political prisoners in which they describe the ill-treatment they had received at the Gospić prison, including severe beatings on their limbs and genitals along with verbal abuse.[6] At the same time, another émigré group wrote an open letter to the UN Secretary General listing the names of fifty-seven academic staff at the University of Priština who had been arrested, expelled or publicly reprimanded in an attempt to deter future demonstrations.[7]

Most Kosovo Albanians advocated nonviolent means for achieving republic status for Kosovo. After the 1981 demonstrations died down, the activities of most Kosovar activists consisted solely of creating and passing around pamphlets with such slogans as: "Kosovo Republic!" and "Long Live the 1981 Revolution!"[8] However, in the early 1980s a minority advocated a more radical approach. In mid-1982 the press publicized two murders that many claimed were nationally motivated—one of a young Serb, the other of a Montenegrin, both allegedly killed by

Kosovo Albanians.[9] In the first six months of 1984, a group of Kosovo Albanians were arrested and charged with having caused nine explosions in Priština; another group was accused of having smuggled arms, ammunitions and explosives into Yugoslavia for irredentist activity in Kosovo; others were accused of firing at members of security forces, hijacking a police vehicle or issuing threats of armed uprisings if Kosovo was not given the status of a republic.[10]

According to the official statistics of the federal Secretary of Internal Affairs, by July 1982 more than 700 persons had been arrested in Kosovo for what was considered anti-Yugoslav, Albanian nationalist-irredentist activity, and 320 had been put on trial.[11] The president of the Provincial Committee of the League of Communists of Kosovo, Ilijaz Kurteshi, reported that by October 1983 a total of 595 individuals had been sentenced to prison in connection with the 1981 demonstrations.[12] Furthermore, the federal Secretary for Internal Affairs claimed to have broken up seven illegal Albanian groups in Kosovo and Macedonia in 1983, involving 130 individuals.[13] Each year following the 1981 demonstrations, roughly sixty percent of those charged with political crimes in Yugoslavia were Kosovo Albanians.[14]

Kosovo Albanians contend that many of the charges against them were fabricated in order to support the mass firing or arrest of Kosovo Albanian intellectuals and Party members. After the 1981 demonstrations, the government implemented a policy euphemistically known as "differentiation," that is, mass purges designed to separate out the "good Albanians" from the bad ones by firing all those from their jobs who would not disavow the calls for Kosovo to become a republic.[15] While governments throughout Eastern Europe used this method of economic marginalization, the "special feature of differentiation in the Kosovo conflict is that it is specially applied to ethnic Albanians, in the form of overt, racial discrimination by the government with regard to jobs and party positions."[16] By July 1982, some one thousand members of the League of Communists of Kosovo (LCK) were expelled, and some basic units of the LCK were dissolved altogether.[17] The authorities also dismissed thousands of university professors and elementary and secondary teachers from their posts.[18]

Anti-Albanian sentiment had grown in Serbia since the 1981 demonstrations and nationalist rumblings among Kosovo Serbs were gathering steam. Encouraged by Dobrica Ćosić[19] and other Belgrade intellectuals, Kosovo Serbs began telling to the press their own stories of human rights violations against Serbs and Montenegrins in Kosovo. Led by Miroslav Šolević, Kosta Bulatović and Boško Budimirović, Kosovo Serbs circulated their first protest petition, declaring "This is our land. If Kosovo and Metohija are not Serbian then we don't have any land of our own."[20] Although this petition was signed by less than seventy-five people, it signaled the beginning of a series of Serbian protest petitions.

Another event that presaged things to come was the funeral of Aleksandar Ranković, the former Yugoslav Minister of the Interior and Vice President (1945–1966), who had ruled over Kosovo with draconian anti-Albanian policies.[21] For Kosovo Serbs, Ranković's name is synonymous with peace and order; for Albanians, the name invokes suffering and misery.[22] Ranković's funeral in 1983 turned into a Serbian "nationalistic event," with a reported one hundred thousand people in attendance shouting his name. Kosovo needed a Ranković, they urged, to keep Albanians in control.[23] Significantly, the funeral was the first public demonstration in Serbia against Titoism.[24]

Still under the influence of Titoist policies that strictly limited expressions of national disunity, local authorities and the state-sponsored Yugoslav press did their best to ignore the demands of the protest petition and to minimize the nationalist attributes of Ranković's funeral. As in Tito's days, unrest in Kosovo attributed to Albanians was branded as "counterrevolutionary" and as "subversions of brotherhood and unity," while unrest that may have been attributed to Serbs was overlooked entirely.[25]

The official line in 1984 was that the political situation in Kosovo was under control, although Serbs and Montenegrins continued to leave Kosovo in large numbers. A report of the meeting of the Yugoslav Presidency on January 24, 1984 (facilitated by Nikola Ljubičić, general of the JNA), published in the Belgrade daily *Politika*, stated that "the political-security situation in Kosovo is improving all the time, but despite all of the measures taken one of the important tasks coming out of the Platform on Kosovo has not been fulfilled: emigration is continuing; during the last year alone [1983] almost four thousand Serbs and Montenegrins left."[26] The report went on to say that Serbs and Montenegrins were being forced to sell their homes at below market price, and that Albanian harassment of Serbian and Montenegrin landowners were being investigated by the (mainly Albanian) police as lower offenses (misdemeanors) and not as criminal acts. "All of this," the report found, "is encouraging irredenta which is openly or clandestinely creating an atmosphere of tension and insecurity," causing Kosovo to be abandoned "not only by those who are unemployed, but also by experts and economically strong households."[27]

Nevertheless, the 1984 report on Kosovo and the press accounts of its contents attempted to paint as rosy a picture as possible. After all, the easiest way to run afoul of the authorities was to write or say anything that could be considered to be "inciting national hatreds" or derogatory toward any national or ethnic group.[28] Tito had long ago declared the "national question" to be resolved "in principle" in Yugoslavia. In the aftermath of the 1981 demonstrations, however, both Kosovo Serbs and Albanians knew better. Nationalism was not the only factor organizing their lives, but it was an increasingly important one. Especially with the decentralization of power that had occurred following Tito's death, Serbs were beginning to think that there was no real "Yugoslav" interest defending their rights.[29] And with the amount of development aid to Kosovo reduced during the economic crisis of 1983, Kosovo Albanians were also beginning to wonder if they had a friend in the other republics.[30]

Tensions between ethno-national groups were kindled by the worsening economic crisis. By 1983, Yugoslavia's accumulated foreign debt, mainly to the International Monetary Fund and to western banks, had reached $20 billion; interest repayments of $5 billion consumed 23 percent of export earnings.[31] Foreign creditors came knocking, demanding debt repayment and restructuring. An austerity program was launched in order to reduce inflation, which had then risen to 30 percent. The IMF stabilization program for Yugoslavia had little chance of success.[32] As Vesna Bojičić explains:

Supply-side bottlenecks originating in the economic system itself represented a major cause of the crisis. What systematic changes were implemented had little impact on these bottlenecks, as they did not change the basic incentive structure of the system. Thus, at the very least, the IMF-style austerity programme stood little chance of success. Its immediate effect was a sharp drop in demand and imports, which further lowered the levels of output and aggravated the economic and political crisis. The impact was particularly severe in less-developed parts of the country.[33]

The people of Yugoslavia were hit hard by a slate of foreign currency controls, import restrictions, gasoline rationing, power cuts, shortages of consumer goods and a 20 percent devaluation of the dinar. Within a year over one million workers, 18 percent of the work force, would be unemployed. Real wages fell by 8.5 percent in 1983 and 9 percent in 1984.[34] It is no wonder that the U.S. State Department noted at the time, "By and large, the [Yugoslav] Government and the party were preoccupied with the country's economic problems and reform of the economic system."[35] Still, the cracks in the "brotherhood and unity" facade were too large to ignore, though too controversial to address.

The Martinović "Truth"

On May 1, 1985, according to Yugoslav newspaper reports, a Serbian peasant, fifty-six-year-old Djordje Martinović, had been attacked in his field by two unknown Albanian men who tied him down, mistreated him and forced a bottle into his rectum, bottom first. They left him unconscious and bleeding. After he came to his senses, the papers reported, he crawled to the nearby hospital.[36]

The press originally reported this account as factually correct, not adding, for example, that the story was "according to Martinović." This style of journalism was not unusual in Yugoslavia where "facts were scarce"[37] and journalism was often a means to an end. Stories of Albanian persecution of Serbs were becoming the medium for populist mobilization of Serbs against their enemies; Martinović's story soon led this trend. Before anyone had been accused of a crime, journalists hinted obliquely that Kosovo Albanians must have been responsible for the crime. The Belgrade daily *Politika*, for example, ended one account: "In his family, sorrow and bitterness. They told us that buyers [Kosovo Albanians] for that field [in which Martinović had been abused] had come several times, but the Martinovićs' [property] was not for sale."[38] Given the large number of Serbs migrating from Kosovo in the early 1980s, the "Property for Sale" sign was one of the most powerful symbols of the Serbian-Albanian conflict. Albanians were being accused of pressuring Kosovo Serbs to sell them their property so that they could make Kosovo exclusively Albanian. The ending of the *Politika* account implied that the Martinović case indicated the lengths to which Albanians were prepared to go in order to lay their hands on Serbian possessions.

According to press reports, Martinović's version of the story was initially accepted as truth by local authorities (who were mainly Albanian), but the locals quickly changed their minds. The Zagreb publication *Danas* wrote that immediately after the incident, Kosovo Albanian leaders in Gnjilane "gathered and gave a statement for the public in which they condemned the 'despicable crime' and demanded from the municipal persecution bodies an urgent investigation to find the perpetrators."[39] Almost immediately, however, they grew suspicious of Martinović's allegations. "Only three days later," *Danas* reported, "the same municipal leadership gathered and issued a different statement, in which, among other things, they said that 'the internal injuries of Djordje Martinović are accidental consequences of a self-induced practice. . . .'"[40]

Public investigators in Priština also reported that Martinović's wounds had been self-inflicted. While still in the Priština hospital, they said, Martinović had confessed to Colonel Novak Ivanović, the commanding officer of the JNA garrison in Gnjilane, where Martinović worked as a clerk. The "prosecutor made a written conclusion from which it appears that the wounded performed an act of 'self-satisfaction' in his field, [that he] put a beer bottle on a wooden stick and stuck it in the ground. After that he sat 'on the bottle and enjoyed.' "[41] The examining physician at the Priština medical facility, an Albanian, later confirmed that Martinović had indeed "confessed" and that a medical examination indicated that the wound was self-inflicted.[42]

Individual citizens and associations sent letters and petitions to federal and local authorities demanding more information about the case. On May 11, the deputy to the Minister of Internal Affairs of Serbia issued a statement announcing that the special commission in Serbia would review the case and "in time" give the factual truth to the public.[43] In the meantime, Martinović was transferred from the hospital in Priština, where he had had an operation, to the Medical Military Academy (VMA) in Belgrade.

The investigation of the Martinović matter grew more contentious as groups of medical experts offered conflicting opinions. The Zagreb weekly magazine *Danas* chronicled the many conflicting reports surrounding the case:

May 1, 1985: The medical center in Gnjilane informed Gnjilane police at 5:30 P.M. that they were treating a heavily injured man named Djordje Martinović who claimed that he had been hurt by two individuals of Albanian nationality.

May 2, 1985: The Investigative Judge authorized the work of the Secretariat of Internal Affairs [SUP] of Gnjilane and a team of the provincial SUP to investigate the case; the investigators neglected to make wax models of the footprints at the crime scene or take fingerprints from the pieces of glass found there [but other work of the expert investigators, the paper said, compensated for these failures].

May 5, 1985: The Presidency of the Municipal Conference of the SSRN [Socialist League of the Working People] of Gnjilane issued a statement about the attack on Martinović, characterizing it as "a pre-conceived barbarian act of the enemy."

May 6, 1985: The SUP of Gnjilane filed [a criminal complaint] against the unknown perpetrator, and the municipal prosecutor sent a demand to the SUP for [an investigation into the incident].

May 7, 1985: The provincial SUP of Kosovo and the municipal court in Gnjilane issued a statement that Martinović had confessed that the injury was self-inflicted.

May 8, 1985: The Presidency of the Municipal Conference of the SSRN of Gnjilane issued a statement according to which it was "discovered that this despicable act was done by Djordje Martinović himself."

May 18, 1985: [In an abrupt change,] the federal public prosecutor gave instructions to the municipal public prosecutor in Gnjilane to suggest to the Investigative Judge of the municipal court that the unknown perpetrator committed a criminal act of violence with the motivation of an enemy (on May 25, 1985, the municipal public prosecutor agreed with this assessment of the federal public prosecutor in its statement to the Investigative Judge of the municipal court).

May 18, 1985: Authorized SUP workers sent a report to the municipal prosecutor finding that "criminal acts of false accusation" and the "criminal act of spreading false news" had occurred in the case of Djordje Martinović [because the allegations that Martinović's wounds were self-inflicted were false].

May 22, 1985: The Investigative Judge interrogated Martinović in VMA [the Military Medical Academy in Belgrade] and Martinović responded that he had been attacked by two persons of Albanian ethnicity.

May 23, 1985: One inspector of the republic and one of the municipal SUP talked to Martinović with the permission of the Investigative Judge, and then Martinović was again interrogated by the Investigative Judge. Martinović stated for the record that he was not attacked but had injured himself.

June 22, 1985: The liaison committee to the executive chamber of the Kosovo Assembly received an official statement of the municipal prosecutor in Gnjilane about the measures undertaken and the progress of the investigation; but after two days the municipal prosecutor was informed that the leadership bodies of the SAP [Socialist Autonomous Province] of Kosovo were opposed to announcing the results as stated. [Thus the federal public prosecutor did not issue the official report but instead gave information at the request of individual delegates.]

June 25, 1985: At the suggestion of the municipal public prosecutor, the Investigative Judge asked the VMA for the opinion of its medical team of experts [which differed significantly from the opinion of the experts from the Institute for Forensic Medicine in Priština].

June 26, 1985: The Investigative Judge received the report and opinion of the experts from the Institute for Forensic Medicine at the Medical Faculty in Priština, in which it says that until the traumatic event Martinović "did not express any signs of homosexual or bisexual deviations."

July 20, 1985: The VMA sent only the conclusion of its team of medical experts to the Investigative Judge, which, among other things, found that the investigation should rule out anal onanism.

August 25, 1985: Again at the suggestion of the municipal public prosecutor, the Investigative Judge ordered another complete evaluation by the VMA medical experts [who were joined by an expert from the Skopje Institute for Forensic Medicine].

September 31, 1985: The Investigative Judge questioned all of the evaluators in an attempt to eliminate differences, but all of the experts adhered to their original written findings and opinions.

November 1, 1985: The Investigative Judge ordered a new evaluation of the medical evidence, to be undertaken by a new team of experts.

November 15, 1985: The new team of experts handed in their opinion, concluding that the strong mechanical force could have been produced by other persons but also by the powerful pressure of the body weight.[44]

In sum, there were at least four sets of opinions: the Priština authorities' finding that the wound had probably been self-inflicted; the initial finding of the VMA, the military hospital in Belgrade, finding that the wound could not have been self-inflicted; the second finding of the VMA (after an expert from Macedonia was added to the research team) agreeing with the VMA's earlier finding; and the finding of the new team of experts (requested by the Investigative Judge) which concluded that the wound could have either been self-inflicted *or* committed by others. By failing to give one authoritative version of the case, the provincial and federal authorities increased suspicions on both sides that something was being hidden from the public.[45]

During the first few months following the incident, many Belgrade newspapers and magazines (such as *Večernje novosti, Politika ekspres, Komunist* and *Duga*) actively promoted the version in which Martinović's injuries had been self-inflicted. In time, however, the event was described more and more often as a misdeed of Albanian separatists, or simply of Albanians.

The press wondered, "Was that a dirty assault in which a fifty-eight-year-old clerk was impaled on a bottle . . . by Albanian nationalists? Or was it Martinović's sexual act that went wrong? . . . What had really happened on May 1 in the field outside of Gnjilane became a favorite subject of morbid speculations among Yugoslavs, from Rom boys in the streets to the Belgrade landladies and up."[46] The press's exploration of the most intimate and "morbid of Martinović's injuries" prepared "almost every Serb . . . to explain why he couldn't have done it to himself."[47]

Many papers questioned the validity of the local police investigation (conducted mainly by Kosovo Albanian police), charging that the investigation had been conducted unprofessionally and "negligently," as "not all of the details and prints were recorded [at the site of the alleged act of violence]."[48] Most Yugoslav papers carried stories in which Martinović claimed that he had been forced into making a false confession by Colonel Ivanović.[49] (In connection with these claims, the colonel (then retired) eventually sued Martinović for libel.)[50]

Given the speculation surrounding the case, Martinović's family felt compelled to come forward and testify that Martinović had no "deviant sexual tendencies." Sympathetic accounts of the case did not fail to mention that Martinović was a grandfather and that he was married. Martinović's wife came forward, telling the press that the confession had been coerced, that Colonel Ivanović had "interrogated" Martinović for almost three hours while he still lay in the hospital, and that the Colonel had promised that Martinović's children would receive employment in exchange for the confession.[51] Martinović's son, Sreten, told the press that his father would not have done such an act to himself and that he had been attacked simply because he was a Serb.[52] "Friends are telling us," Sreten is quoted as saying, "[Albanian] irredentists did it in revenge. . . . They don't care who the victim might be. As long as it is a Serb."[53]

Over a year and a half after the Martinović case had begun, the Presidency of the Federal League of the Socialist Alliance of the Working People of Yugoslavia (SSRNJ), the influential Yugoslavia-wide mass organization, issued its own statement on the case. It found that the first statement made by the municipal leadership of Gnjilane (saying that Martinović had been attacked) was a "prejudicial interference with the work and the affairs of the state organs" and that the second statement had "brought suspicion and confusion in the public." The Presidency also said that the regional Secretariat of Internal Affairs of Kosovo and the regional court in Gnjilane had made a "hasty decision" when making a statement on May 8, 1985, that Martinović had injured himself. "It is most probable that their intention was to put an end to the whole case by issuing this statement. But the further development of the events and political climate created in the public have shown that it was a mistake." The SSRNJ statement pointed to the role of the press in creating a volatile social atmosphere. While some of the papers had helped to stabilize the situation, others supported sensationalism, fueling emotions and "provoking" the public. The Presidency stated that all "three nationalisms" (Serbian, Montenegrin and Albanian) were fueled by the case, and it called on political representatives to act responsibly in resolving the matter.[54]

No one was ever arrested in connection with the case; yet the press and public continued to hypothesize as to the involvement of Albanians and the misconduct of local (Albanian) authorities. Although the nationality and number of the perpetrators were never established, journalists wrote as if they were known. For example, *Illustrovana Politika* stated that "two unknown criminals disfigured the unfortunate man . . . display[ing] all the brutality of the methods of the Albanian nationalists. . . ."[55] Another widely reported rumor was that the culprits had been relatives of Zijah Shemsiu, an Albanian who had been accused of antistate activities. Mr. Shemsiu had died in prison on May 1, 1985; his father and two brothers were said to have wanted to avenge his death by picking on the first Serb they saw—Martinović just happened to get in their way. This rumor could not have been true, because all three men had been in prison at the time Martinović had been attacked.[56] Additional rumors claimed that other attacks had been attempted but the assailants were chased away, or that the police and local authorities had kept quiet the existence of similar attacks.[57]

Martinović's lawyer, Velimir Cvetić, spread yet another rumor. The press reported that Cvetić discovered that a day before Martinović was "abused," a meeting was held in the Kosovo Albanian village of Prilepnica. The Albanian "Council of Elders" purportedly decided on that occasion that three Serbs and Montenegrins were "to be massacred as savagely as possible" in retaliation for the death of a young Albanian weapons smuggler in prison. According to this account, Martinović was chosen as the first victim to be attacked by three masked Albanians.[58]

Four years after the Martinović assault, Živorad Mihajlović offered a new version of the case. He contended that Martinović had reported some of his Albanian neighbors to the police for receiving into their house "various people, bringing some [written] materials." The police, however, were Albanian, so they double-crossed Martinović. Mihajlović ventured that there was no difference between the official institutions and that part of the population disposed to irredentism. All Albanians, he claimed, secretly promote the agenda of separatism. The assailants, having learned of Martinović's actions from the police, assaulted him in retaliation. The police and local authorities knew that twelve more Serbs had been attacked by Albanians and three had been disfigured, Mihajlović said, but local authorities failed to take action.[59] Mihajlović's account and other stories fed speculation that the attack on Martinović was part of a coordinated campaign against Serbs, and that provincial and republic authorities were not doing enough to keep order in Kosovo.

In the end then, each side had something to believe as Truth. Kosovo Albanians focused on Martinović's early confession, which they contend was not coerced, and the report of the Priština police and medical examiners. To this day, former Kosovo Albanian medical staff will say that the evidence indicated that the wound was self-inflicted.[60] The persistence of Belgrade authorities in contradicting their colleagues in Priština, they argue, was part of a deliberate attempt to stir up anti-Albanian sentiment. By failing to come out with clear information, some contended, the "political leadership [was] allowing national emotions to overwhelm Serbian citizens more and more each day and for radical Serbian political circles to [intensify their] loud demand for an 'extraordinary situation' in Kosovo."[61] Thus, for most Kosovo Albanians the Truth was that Martinović committed the act himself and then tried to blame it on Albanians when things went wrong. The whole affair was then used by Serbian nationalists to provoke anti-Albanian feelings.

Some Kosovo Albanians would quietly agree that Martinović could have been attacked by Albanians and that the local police could have bungled their investigation. Yet the need to avoid collective blame pushed Albanians into denying any possibility of Albanian responsibility. "I am ashamed to think that Albanians could have done this," one Kosovo Albanian woman said, "The expert testimony conflicted, so we don't know what happened for sure. Where I take offense is that Serbs automatically accused all of us of being there with the perpetrators. It was as if we all had done the attack."[62] No matter what happened in the case, Kosovo Albanians today contend, the crime was in no way condoned by Albanian political and community leaders.

On the other hand, most Serbs focused on Martinović's claims that his confession had been coerced and the accounts of the Belgrade and Skopje medical authorities that found the wound must have been caused by others. For many Serbs then, the Truth was that Martinović was "another victim at the hands of savage Albanians" and that the incident was a particularly egregious example of the Albanian conspiracy to drive Serbs from Kosovo.[63] Supporters of this theory pointed out that "the irredentists got what they wanted"—Martinović's family reportedly sold the field where the incident took place.[64]

Each side's public reaction to the case further entrenched the other's position. Kosovo Albanians' flat denial of the incident was played up in the Serbian community to support the allegation that all Kosovo Albanians were blindly supporting each other's evil deeds. In the same vein, the contradictory statements surrounding the investigation only served to strengthen Serbian rumors that the police were allied to the irredenta and that Albanians enjoyed state protection to act as they chose. Many Serbs attributed the failure to identify and arrest a culprit to a deliberate refusal of authorities to assist Martinović. For Kosovo Serbs, the Martinović case was viewed as representative of the kind of incidents they had been reporting since the late 1960s: Albanian violence against Serbs and misconduct of Albanian police investigators and other Albanian authorities.

Most of the finger-pointing regarding the Martinović case occurred at the republic and province levels. Under the 1974 Yugoslav Constitution the justice system of Kosovo enjoyed relative autonomy, and criminal investigations were usually carried out on the level of the republic or province. Nevertheless, the failure of the federal authorities to issue a single statement about the case fostered Serbian distrust of the federal government. "After Martinović," as one Kosovo Serb remembered, "we knew that the government wasn't really prepared to protect the Serbian people."[65]

An assault of Serbs on Serbs would not have received such public scrutiny, nor would have an attack on Serbs by Albanians in earlier times. Apart from its cruelty, the Martinović case was singled out because the incident propelled the nationalist agendas brewing in the mid-1980s. The popular slogan after Tito's death had been "After Tito, Tito": the Titoist vision of "Brotherhood and Unity" among all nations would continue after Tito's death. But the mere utterance of the name "Djordje Martinović" was enough to disprove the official notions of national harmony. Although the Martinović case was not the single turning point of the 1980s, it did mark a distinct change in direction. While most of the Yugoslav press had previously downplayed nationalism, the press after Martinović trumpeted national conflict. By the end of 1985, Tito's luxurious yacht would be sold for hard cash and his island retreat would be turned into a national park.[66] Times were changing.

Following the Truths

After the Martinović incident, the actions of Kosovo Albanians were no longer branded "counterrevolutionary" acts against all of socialist Yugoslavia.[67] Rather, they became Albanian nationalist threats to the Serbian nation. From 1981 to 1987, the crime rate in Kosovo was the lowest in Yugoslavia.[68] There were five interethnic murders in all of Kosovo during this period, two cases in which Albanians murdered Serbs and three in which Serbs murdered Albanians.[69] Pushing that reality aside, Serbian intellectuals began to construct the case of the Albanian "genocide" against Serbs in Kosovo.[70]

The Serbian press carried story after story on the victimization of Kosovo Serbs. The Belgrade weekly *NIN*, for example, screamed in its headline: "Why are we still surprised by drastic cases from Kosovo?" The article reprinted a report of a meeting of the Yugoslav Presidency on conditions in Kosovo. According to the report, in the first three months of 1985 there were six hundred subversive slogans, pamphlets and fliers distributed among ethnic Albanians in Kosovo; fifteen suspicious fires and explosions which had destroyed or damaged the social property or private property of Serbs and Montenegrins; four "sabotages and diversions"; ten cases of "storming" the cars of public transportation; eight cases of "insulting Tito's personality"; and twelve attacks on police officers. The number of Serbs living in Kosovo, the report said, decreased 7 percent during the four years after the 1981 demonstrations, and during 1984 more than 3,400 Serbs had migrated from Kosovo.[71]

Taking advantage of the public uproar caused by the Martinović case, Kosovo Serbs created a petition to the assemblies of Serbia and Yugoslavia in October 1985. Boasting over two thousand signatures this time, the petition demanded radical measures to safeguard all constitutional rights and to halt the exodus of Serbs from their homes. These words, again crafted with the help of Serbian nationalists in Belgrade, set forth the core arguments for stripping Kosovo of its autonomous status. Although the petition would be denounced by party leaders, it succeeded in drawing considerable public attention to the demands of Kosovo Serbs.

Each step in the subsequent buildup of Serb nationalism would be helped along by the Martinović undercurrent. The next major Serb petition on the Kosovo issue, submitted by Belgrade intellectuals to the assemblies of Yugoslavia and Serbia in January 1986, also evoked the power of Martinović. As discussed more fully in the next chapter, this petition was instrumental in elevating the issue of Kosovo and Serbian nationalism to the top of the Yugoslav political agenda. After accusing the authorities of "calming down the public by means of untrue statements, ideological interpretations and the hushing-up of violence, the equation of victims' cries and criminals' cunning," the petition exhorted: "The case of Djordje Martinović has come to symbolize the predicament of all Serbs in Kosovo. It is difficult to find a crime so horrendous, but it is totally impossible to find another country where the entire legal system is so mobilized in order to cover up the crime."[72] Warning that "a long, fatal genocide here in Europe" was being committed in Kosovo, the January 1986 petition used Martinović to invoke the folklore of Serbian victimization:

History and memories still alive tell us that the exodus of Serbs from Kosovo and Metohija has been going on for three centuries. Only the mentors of those who are pushing out Serbs have changed; instead of the Ottoman Empire, Austria-Hungary, Fascist Italy and Nazi Germany, this role is now filled by the state of Albania and by the ruling institutions of Kosovo itself. Instead of forced Islamization and Fascism—Stalinized chauvinism. The only new feature is the blend of hatred and genocide hidden beneath the Marxist veil.

The methods have not changed either. The new Deacon Avakum [a victim of Ottoman times] is called Djordje Martinović. . . . [73]

Newspaper headlines similarly compared the Martinović incident to horrors committed "in the time of Turks."[74] And the Memorandum of the Serbian Academy of Sciences and Arts, also discussed more fully in the next chapter, bluntly stated that the Martinović case was "reminiscent of the darkest days of the Turkish practice of impalement."[75] Živorad Mihajlović, the Serbian author who wrote a book on the Martinović case, explained these references: "Here we are dealing with the remains of the Ottoman Empire. [Albanians] stuck him to a stake, this time just wrapped in a bottle. In the time of the Turks, Serbs were being impaled too, though even the Turks were not the ones who did it, but rather their servants—Arnauts [an old Serbian term for Muslim Albanians]. This, what is going on in Kosovo today, is a unique method of cruelty."[76]

"Impalement by a beer bottle" became "a metaphor for five centuries of real, but also mythical Turkish acts of impalement, all of which were a key demonic element in the national traditions any mythology regarding the horrors of Turkish oppression."[77] Every Serbian school child knows about the horror of impalement from national folk ballads, national novels, national plays and other national traditions. As Serbian Nobel Laureate Ivo Andrić graphically detailed in *The Bridge on the Drina*,[78] Turks would fix Serbian rebels on a stake, running it from rectum to neck, working carefully so as to avoid any vital organs. Still alive, the victim then would be hoisted upright for the entire town to witness a slow and painful death.

Equating the Martinović case with an impaling and Kosovo Albanians with the Ottoman Turks had an enormous impact on Serbian consciousness. Worsening economic conditions in Serbia and the political and social uncertainty created by Tito's death had already made many Serbs feel victimized. The impalement metaphor worked well to further feelings of endangerment and to propel the desire for historical revenge.

The Martinović case was compared as well to another of the main symbols of Serbian victimization, the Jasenovac death camp. "Martinović was a Jasenovac for one man," academic Brana Crnčević said in a comment that was widely printed in the Belgrade press.[79] The Ustaše, the Croatian fascist forces, murdered hundreds of thousands of Serbs, Jews, Gypsies and Croatian Communists at Jasenovac. Serbian nationalists set the number of Serbs killed as high as seven hundred thousand; Croatian nationalists, with Franjo Tudjman at their head, have placed it below sixty thousand.[80] The exact number of victims aside, the intent of the camp was to eliminate entire groups of people based on their ethno-national background and/or political beliefs. Thus, many commentators argue that the crime committed at Jasenovac was genocide.

In Yugoslavia any comparisons with Jasenovac were explosive, especially given the years of silence during the Tito regime on the crimes committed by the Ustaše.[81] Tying Martinović to Ustaše cruelty revitalized collective prejudices, not only toward Albanians but to Croats as well. As with the impalement analogy, the use of Jasenovac as a metaphor generated feelings of victimization among Serbs and fostered the desire for historical revenge. Although such historical analogies did not work with all members of the Serbian populations in Yugoslavia, Serbian political leaders found that they were extremely useful in promoting a Serbian national program. Martinović became the poster boy for the Serbian nationalist cause. Photos were published of Martinović together with avowed Serbian nationalist Bishop Amfilohije Radović and one of the leaders of the Serbian protests in Kosovo, Miroslav Šolević.[82] Martinović's name was commonly invoked whenever there was an attack on Kosovo Albanians; for example, the opening sentence of a story about the disqualification of an Albanian judge asked, "How many people emigrated from Kosovo because of the Martinović case?"[83]

Continued reports about Martinović kept the case alive. A 485-page book devoted to the Martinović case was published in 1986; the initial print run sold fifty thousand copies.[84] A year and a half after the incident, the press reported with horror that Martinović still suffered from his injuries. According to one account, five Belgrade doctors had suggested that he see a specialist in London, but until his ongoing condition was leaked to the press local authorities had refused to pay for his care.[85] In 1991, Belgrade newspapers reported that Martinović was to receive compensation from the state for the injuries he had suffered because the state had not investigated his case properly and because, although no one had ever been convicted, the municipal court in Belgrade had found that the crime was committed by "Šiptar terrorists."[86] (Šiptar is the derogatory Serbian term for Albanians.)[87]

Four years after the incident, one of the Albanian doctors who had purportedly treated Martinović in the Gnjilane hospital, Dr. Remzi Aliu, was accused of malpractice in his treatment of a patient in 1985. According to the Serbian account, Aliu had botched a routine gall bladder operation on Verica Palamarović, and his subsequent medical treatment had aggravated her condition. Eventually, Aliu sent the woman to a hospital in Skopje, where she died four days later. A Serbian journalist writing in 1989 concluded: "In simple terms, Dr. Remzi Aliu killed Verica Palamarović and in order to hide his crime he sent her to the hospital in Skopje."[88] Kosovo Albanian physicians, however, charge that Aliu was being scapegoated and that he did not act with malicious intent against any patients of any background.[89] Serbian journalist accounts of the charges against Aliu tied him closely to the Martinović case, suggesting that he had intentionally committed malpractice (in order to cover for the Albanian irredenta) in that case as well by transferring Martinović from Gnjilane to a hospital in Priština, instead of moving the wounded man immediately to the modern and better equipped hospital in Belgrade.[90]

Four years after Martinović, a Serbian woman in Kosovo invoked his name as a symbol of her own suffering. In complaining during 1989 demonstrations in Kosovo that Albanians received special treatment, she stated that Martinović haunts her. "I enter the store in Obilić and they [the Albanians] tell me, 'Madam, you forgot the bottle.' They are making allusions to the sufferer Martinović. I crawl into my apartment and I am silent, silent."[91]

A spate of new articles on the Martinović case appeared in 1989. Journalists reminded the public that Martinović was still "waiting for justice."[92] Again the crime was compared to an impaling, with Brana Crnčević declaring that Martinović was "the last Serb fixed to a stake packed into a bottle."[93] The same year, Velimir Cvetić, Martinović's lawyer, contended that when his client came to visit him at his house outside Belgrade, a stranger came and stood outside in the middle of the night, shouting threats in Serbian and Albanian. Cvetić said the stranger told him that he should prepare to shelter other Serbs who, like Martinović, would be expelled from Kosovo.[94]

More than ten years after the alleged assault, Martinović' s image as the martyr of all Serbian people is alive and well. An elderly Kosovo Serbian woman living in a predominately Albanian village whispers to her foreign guests that although her first neighbor is Albanian and their children went to school together, "Martinović shows you just never know about these people."[95] An educated young Serb in Priština says that "Martinović's suffering is all of ours." And a peace activist in Belgrade in 1995 admits, "Since Martinović, whenever I hear of an Albanian accused of a crime, I think first that he is guilty. I know this is not the right way, but I do."[96]

In sum, whenever the public needed to be reminded about the victimization of Serbs and the barbaric nature of Albanians, the image of Martinović could conveniently be invoked. What had actually happened in the case was no longer important. What mattered was what the Serbian public felt. The power of the Martinović case lay in its ability to invoke the primary imagery of Serbian oppression: the Turkish brutality of impaling, Jasenovac, the "for sale" sign on the property of Kosovo Serbs. The handlers of the Martinović case also successfully manipulated a brand of nationalism laced with racism. As a violent crime of the most "unspeakable nature," the act itself was written on the body. While slurs against Albanian-language speakers or Albanian "white hats" (referring to the traditional white skull caps worn by Albanian men) were cultural, blanket acceptance of allegations of Albanian sexual misdeeds were corporal, that is, racist.

Although the exodus of Serbs from Kosovo had long been discussed in academic circles and stories of Kosovo Albanian violence had appeared before in the press, the Martinović incident pushed the situation of Kosovo Serbs into the mainstream of Serbian public debate. It became a national issue, not a matter of "counterrevolution." Federal and republic authorities were criticized for respecting the principle of noninterference with the internal affairs of the province and for not ensuring that "a court of law determine and acknowledge the truth."[97]

Finishing his book on Kosovo shortly after the Martinović case, Dimitrije Bogdanović, a noted Serbian historian, warned that Albanians were taking revenge against Serbs and Montenegrins:

The striking slogan [chanted by Albanians] was "What are you waiting for, why aren't you leaving, do you want us to throw you out?" . . . Terror against the Serbian and Montenegrin population is rising, and those things done illegally in secret earlier are now continued with higher intensity and with complete freedom. Propaganda against the "Greater-Serbia hegemonism" is taking an openly anti-Serbian course. The education of Serbian children is suffering great setbacks, highly qualified experts of Serbian nationality are physically assaulted, and in that chaotic atmosphere, emigration of Serbs and Montenegrins is assuming the character of a great escape.[98]

The reference to "propaganda against 'Greater-Serbia hegemonism' " alludes not only to Albanian propaganda but to the widespread feeling throughout Yugoslavia since WWII that other nations needed to protect themselves against Serbian domination.[99] The "hegemonistic heritage" also stemmed from "the old Cominform political line according to which the prewar Serbian bourgeoisie was held to be the only hegemonistic power in Yugoslavia. . . ."[100] In the 1980s, Serbs would continually cry that the rhetoric of "Greater-Serbian hegemonism" was being used to oppress Serbia. Another Serbian academic, Vladan Vasiljević, has explained the power of the argument: "There is a lot of danger in the thesis of Greater-Serbian domination between the two wars, calling for the 'punishment' of the majority nation in the form of long-term economic, cultural-social marginalization, which logically generated the feeling of being sacrificed. It took only the skill to use, and even misuse, that feeling, to have it turn all at once into hatred toward everyone else."[101]

Serbs were tired of being "sacrificed." Moving from Bogdanović's analysis of Kosovo to an argument that Serbs everywhere are oppressed was easy. After all, Bogdanović had concluded from his study that Serbs' very existence was in danger: "It is now a question of the survival of the entire Serb nation. It is not the fate of the Albanian nation which is at stake but that of the Serbs. . . . The position of the Serbs in the Balkans is much too delicate to be examined in light of present events. It is being increasingly concealed under a thick veil of mystification. The historic memory of a whole people is being wiped out, the very foundations of its national consciousness being undermined."[102] Only Serbs, he implied, could save themselves.

Galvanized by the outpouring of public sympathy, Serbian nationalists began to organize around the issue of Kosovo, enlisting Belgrade intellectuals in service of their cause. Much to the dismay of the rest of Yugoslavia, Serbian nationalism was becoming increasingly fashionable. The rapidly rising Communist leader Slobodan Milošević looked on with interest. Having gained the number one spot in the party organization in Belgrade in 1984, Milošević started to talk about Serbian victimization by pressing Serbian economic grievances. By 1987, he would embrace the cause of Serbian grievances in Kosovo.

Notes

1. See interviews following chapter one with young Kosovo Albanians on the impact of the 1981 demonstrations.

2. Shkelzen Maliqi, "The Albanian Movement in Kosova," in *Yugoslavia and After: A Study in Fragmentation, Despair and Rebirth*, eds. David A. Dyker and Ivan Vejvoda (New York: Longman, 1996), 139. Maliqi writes that both of these movements failed to impose themselves "more powerfully as a continuous force" because of their "failure to free themselves from the ideology of communism." Ibid.

3. Information drawn from author's interviews with Albanians accused of being members of such groups. See also the interviews following chapter one with the man accused of being a ringleader.

4. For a brief discussion of the Albanian diaspora, see Derek Hall, "Albanian Identity and Balkan Roles," in *Reconstructing the Balkans: A Geography of the New Southwest Europe*, eds. Derek Hall and Darrick Danta (New York: John Wiley & Sons, 1996), 130–31.

5. Note that the U.S. State Department reports on human rights for Yugoslavia become longer and more detailed with respect to Kosovo following the 1981 demonstrations.

6. The report is mentioned in Amnesty International, *Yugoslavia: Prisoners of Conscience* (New York: Amnesty International, 1982).

7. "Memorandum—The Albanian Kosovar Youth in the Free World," New York, September 20, 1990.

8. According to Serbs, the slogans were much more venomous and treacherous. One journalist, Miloš Marković, made this list of slogans he claimed to see during 1982:

> Kosovo—republic or war!
> Kosovo Republic together with Preševo [Macedonia]!
> Kosovo Republic, old desire!
> Enver Hoxha will come and it will be a republic!
> Long live proud Kosovo with Enver Hoxha at its head!
> Long live the 1981 revolution!
> Unification of Albanians of all regions!
> We are Albanians, not Yugoslavs!
> Cherish Albanianism!
> The Albanian flag is older than brotherhood and unity!
> Enver Hoxha, you have seven hearts—you will have the
>   treasure of Kosovo too!

Rise Albanians, the time has come!
Long live the Albanian Communist Party!
We want an ethnically clean Kosovo!
Serbs—out!
Down with Serbs and all Serbia!
Serbian monks—to be moved as soon as possible from Kosovo!
We love Kosovo without Serbs!
Ramiz [an Albanian in the federal government] brother, don't be a
    friend with a Serb—stab him with knife!
Serbs don't leave, stay to be our servants!
Belgrade is the filthiest town in Yugoslavia!
We don't want police from Niš and Belgrade!
All Serbs drop dead, long live Enver!
Down with whores like Yugoslavia!
Down with Titoism!
Down with Serbian chauvinism and infamous Titoism!
Trepča [mine] is working for others!
Trepča is working, Belgrade is being built!
We want Trepča, we want Obilić [a town in Kosovo],
    we want Albanian Kosovo!
Go for it, brother Albanians!

Listed in Milorad Djoković, *Kosmetski dosije* (Požarevac: Prosveta, 1990),
97.

9. U.S. State Department, *Country Reports for Human Rights Practices 1982*
(Washington, D.C.: Government Printing Office, 1983), 1061.

10. See Hugh Poulton, *The Balkans: Minorities and States in Conflict* (London: Minority Rights Publications, 1991), p. 65.

11. U.S. State Department, *Country Reports for Human Rights Practices 1982*,
1062.

12. U.S. State Department, *Country Reports for Human Rights Practices 1983*,
1175.

13. Ibid.

14. See U.S. State Department, *Country Reports for Human Rights Practices*
for 1982, 1983 and 1984.

15. Poulton, *The Balkans*, 65.

16. Helsinki Watch and International Helsinki Federation, *Yugoslavia: Crisis
in Kosovo*, eds. Julie Mertus and Vlatka Mihelić (New York: Human Rights
Watch/Helsinki Watch, March 1990), 37.

17. Sabrina P. Ramet, *Nationalism and Federalism in Yugoslavia, 1962–1991*,
2d ed. (Bloomington, Ind.: Indiana University Press, 1992), 197.

18. The Serbian press in Kosovo, *Jedinstvo*, carried many stories about such
dismissals. See for example the coverage on March 1, 1984 (reported in Hugh
Poulton, *The Balkans*, 65). See also U.S. State Department, *Country Reports for
Human Rights Practices 1984*, 1152.

19. Dobrica Ćosić is a famous Serbian writer who had long romanticized

Kosovo as the heartland of Serbia. In 1968, he had been expelled from the Central Committee of the Communist Party for accusing Kosovo Albanians of anti-Serbian propaganda. He later was an active member of the Committee for Freedom of Speech, which defended those prosecuted for expressing their political views. In June 1992 he was elected President of the Federal Republic of Yugoslavia, and discharged from duty in June of 1993.

20. Laura Silber and Allan Little, *The Death of Yugoslavia* (London: Penguin Books, BBC Books, 1995), 33.

21. For accounts of the Rancović era, see Steven Burg, *Conflict and Cohesion in Socialist Yugoslavia* (Princeton: Princeton University Press, 1983), 66–69; Paul Shoup, *Communism and the Yugoslav National Question* (New York: Columbia University Press, 1968), 140.

22. Many Kosovo Serbs interviewed by the author wished for the return of the kind of "order" that Ranković had brought to Yugoslavia. See interviews following this chapter for stories of Serbs who left Kosovo. On the other hand, rare was the interview with Kosovo Albanian villagers when someone did not mention Ranković's name and associate it with some evil deed against Albanians.

23. See Slavoljub Djukić, *Izmedju slave i anateme—Politička biografija Slobodana Miloševića* (Belgrade: Filip Višnjić, 1994), p. 36.

24. Mark L. Almond, *Europe's Backyard War: The War in the Balkans* (London: Heinemann, 1994), 176.

25. As the U.S. State Department human rights report in 1983 noted: "Unorthodox, public expression of dissent is frequently suppressed, particularly when it involves the verbal expression of local nationalisms, which the Government considers incendiary. . . . 65 percent of all political crimes in 1982 fell into the 'verbal' category, and most of the political trials reported in the press involve[d] the verbal offenses of 'hostile propaganda,' 'inciting national hatreds,' and 'damaging the country's reputation.' " U.S. State Department, *Country Reports for Human Rights Practices 1983*, 1177. See also Slavko Curuvija and Ivan Torov, "The March to War (1980–1990)," in *Yugoslavia's Ethnic Nightmare: The Inside Story of Europe's Unfolding Ordeal*, eds. Jasmika Udovički and James Ridgeway (New York: Lawrence Hill Books, 1995), 79.

26. Darko Hudelist, *Kosovo, bitka bez iluzija* (Zagreb: Center for Information and Publicity, 1989), 20 (quoting 1984 report published in *Politika*). The Platform on Kosova was the federal political and economic plan for stabilization of the Kosovo situation. The Platform reflected the attitude that Serbs were being victimized by Albanians and, thus, a political solution would protect Serbs from Albanian aggression and at the same time guard against irredentism.

27. Ibid.

28. U.S. State Department, *Country Reports for Human Rights Practices 1984*, 1149, 1151. The probability that an indictment would be brought against someone charged with "subversive propaganda" in Kosovo was extremely high. In 1979–1988, 94 percent of those accused in Kosovo of "subversive propaganda" were indicted, compared with a 74 percent Yugoslav average, 68 percent in Croatia and 61 percent in Serbia. Srdja Popović, Dejan Janča and Tanja Petrovar, eds., *Kosovski čvor: Drešiti ili seći?* (Belgrade: Kronos, 1990), 66.

29. See Miranda Vickers, "The Status of Kosovo in Socialist Yugoslavia," *Bradford Studies on South Eastern Europe*, no. 1 (1994).

30. Peter Prifti, "Kosova's Economy: Problems and Prospects," in *Studies on Kosova*, eds. Arshi Pipa and Sami Repishti (Boulder, Colo.: Eastern European Monographs, 1984), 157.

31. Fred Singleton, *A Short History of the Yugoslav People* (New York: Cambridge University Press, 1985), 276. For an analysis of the importance of debt to the Yugoslav system, see David Dyker, *Yugoslavia: Socialism, Development and Debt* (London: Routledge, 1990).

32. For a critical analysis of these programs, see J. Prasnikar, J. Svejnar and M. Klinedinst, "Structural Adjustment Policies and Productive Efficiency of Socialist Enterprises," *European Economic Review* 36, no. 1 (1990), 179–201.

33. Vesna Bojičić, "The Disintegration of Yugoslavia: Causes and Consequences of Dynamic Inefficiency in Semi-Command Economies," in *Yugoslavia and After: A Study in Fragmentation, Despair and Rebirth*, eds. David A. Dyker and Ivan Vejvoda (New York: Longman, 1996), 35.

34. Marko Milivojević, "The Uneven Impact of Economic Adjustment in Yugoslavia," *South Slav Journal*, vol. 7, no.3/4 (autumn-winter 1984).

35. U.S. State Department, *Country Reports for Human Rights Practices 1983*, 1172.

36. Martinović eventually recounted the following scenario to reporters:

Two young men in disguise attacked me and tied my eyes, my hands and legs. They spoke Albanian and later it seemed to me that there were more of them. They took off my clothes, they beat me, massacred me with the broken bottle and tortured me until I fainted out of pain. When I came back to consciousness, with the last bits of my strength, with the unbearable pains in my abdomen, I stumbled somehow to the Gnjilane hospital. From there they urgently transferred me to the surgical department of the Priština hospital.

See Dragan Živanović, "Anatomija slučaja Martinović" (The Anatomy of the Martinović Case), *Arena*, no date.

37. Mark Thompson, *A Paper House: The Ending of Yugoslavia* (London: Vintage, 1992), 129. For analysis of the role of the media in Yugoslavia generally, see Françoise Hampson, "Responsibility of and for the Media in the Conflicts in the Former Yugoslavia," in *Yugoslavia: Collapse, War, Crimes*, ed. Sonja Biserko (Belgrade: Centre for Anti-War Action and Belgrade Circle, 1993), 79–113; *Forging War: The Media in Serbia, Croatia and Bosnia* (London: Article 19, 1994); Jasmina Kuzmanović, "The Media: The Extension of Politics by Other Means," in *Beyond Yugoslavia: Politics, Economics, and Culture in a Shattered Community*, eds. Sabrina Petra Ramet and Ljubiša S. Adamovich (Boulder, Colo.: Westview Press, 1995), 83–98.

38. *Politika*, May 4, 1985.

39. Djuro Zagorac, "Drama u iščekivanju rešenja" (Drama in the Expectation of the Solution), *Danas*, August 6, 1985, 23.

40. Ibid.

41. Ibid.

42. Interview by author.

43. Tanjug, "Nemir zbog slučaja Martinović" (Restlessness because of the

Martinović Case), July 18, 1985 (purportedly reprinting an article by Kristina von Kol in the Swiss daily newspaper *Neue Züricher Zeitung*, July 16, 1985).

44. Zorica Nikolić, "Točka sa tri točke" (A Full Stop with Three Dots [implying that although something is officially concluded it is not yet over]), *Danas*, November 11, 1986, 27–28.

45. Mark Thompson concludes that in the Martinović case, "In due course the courts and the medical examiners agreed that the man was unbalanced and his wounds were self-inflicted; but who cared?" (*A Paper House*, 129). A review of the media and interviews with Serbs and Albanians about the case, however, does not show agreement on any theory.

46. Tanjug, "Reuters on Martinović Case from Kosovo," July 31, 1985 (purportedly reprinted from Reuters).

47. Ibid.

48. Nikolić, "Točka sa tri točke," *Danas*, November 4, 1986.

49. *Borba*, December 18, 1985; *Intervju*, March 15, 1986; *Vjesnik*, October 24, 1986.

50. "Poziv na dvoboj" (Call for a Duel), *Illustrovana Politika*, May 9, 1989.

51. Zagorac, "Drama u iščekivanju raspleta," *Danas*, August 6, 1985.

52. Jevrem Damnjanović, "Martinovićeva kuća na prodaju" (Martinović's House on Sale), *Illustrovana Politika*, November 26, 1985, pp. 22–23.

53. Ibid.

54. Tanjug, "Saopćenja unijela nemir" (Statements Caused Restlessness), *Borba*, October 29, 1986.

55. "Poziv na dvoboj," *Illustrovana Politika*, May 9, 1989.

56. "Martinović kao tužilac" (Martinović as a Prosecutor), *Politikin svet*, July 23, 1986 (reporting both the rumor and that it could not be true).

57. "Poziv na dvoboj," *Illustrovana Politika*, May 9, 1989; "Čak i sekretar zna istinu" (Even the Secretary Knows the Truth), *NIN*, February 5, 1989.

58. "For Saving the Face of Kosovo Bigwigs," *Politika Ekspres*, July 7, 1989.

59. Živorad Mihajlović, *Podzemni rat na Kosovu i Metohiji, 1389–1989* (Belgrade: Jugoslovenska Estrada, 1986).

60. Interviews by author.

61. Tanjug, "Nemir zbog slučaja Martinović,'" July 18, 1985.

62. Interview by author.

63. Interviews by author.

64. Damnjanović, "Martinovićeva kuća na prodaju," *Illustrovana Politika*, November 26, 1985.

65. Interview by author.

66. R. J. Crampton, *Eastern Europe in the Twentieth Century* (New York: Routledge, 1994), 386.

67. Vesna Pešić has made this point. See Vesna Pešić, "Serbian Nationalism and the Origins of the Yugoslav Crisis," prepared for the U.S. Institute for Peace, 1996; available on the internet at http://www.usip.org/oc/sr/pesic/pesic.html#exp.

68. See Milan Vučković and Goran Nikolić, *Stanovništvo Kosova u razdoblju od 1918. do 1991* (Munich: Slavica Verlag, 1996), 130.

69. See Thompson, *A Paper House*, 129–30.

70. See, for example, Radosav Stojanović, *Živeti s' genocidom: Hronika kosovskog beščašća, 1981–1989* (Belgrade: Sfairos, 1990); Živorad Mihajlović, *Podzemni rat na Kosovu i Metohiji, 1389–1989* (Belgrade: Jugoslovenska Estrada, 1989); Milan Komnenić, "The Kosovo Cataclysm," in *Kosovo 1389–1989: Special Edition of the Serbian Literary Quarterly on the Occasion of 600 Years since the Battle of Kosovo*, ed. Alex Vukadinović, 141–50 (Belgrade: Serbian Literary Quarterly, 1989); Dimitrije Bogdanović, *Knjiga o Kosovu* (Belgrade: Srpska akademija nauka i umetnosti, 1986).

71. Hudelist, *Kosovo, bitka bez iluzija*, 23 (citing *NIN* article). Compare the estimates in: Živorad Igić, *Kosovo i Metohija (1981–1991): Uvod u jugoslovensku krizu* (Priština: Jedinstvo, Oktoih, 1992), 201 (35,000 Serbs and Montenegrins left between 1981 and 1988); Vuksan Cerović, *Kosovo: Kontrarevolucija koja teče* (Belgrade and Priština: Nova Knjiga, 1989), 17 (35,000 Serbs and Montenegrins left Kosovo between 1981 and 1989); Bogdanović, *Knjiga o Kosovu*, 253 ("at least 66,000 people came from Kosovo [to Serbia] in the period 1961 to 1981"); Djordje Jevtić, *Bitka za Kosovo, šest vekova posle I* (Priština: Novi Svet, 1995), 22 (concluding that 50,000 Serbs and Montenegrins left Kosovo in the 1980s); Hudelist, *Kosovo, bitka bez iluzija*, 23 ("In the 2.5 years after the [1981] demonstrations, 5,025 Serbs and Montenegrins left Priština, among whom many had a job and apartment"); Ruža Petrović, *Migracije u Jugoslaviji* (Belgrade: Istraživačko izdavački Centar SSO Srbije, 1987), 108 (from 1971 to 1981, 37,031 Serbs and 5,280 Montenegrins left Kosovo).

72. "Documents, Petition to the Assembly of the Socialist Federal Republic of Yugoslavia and to the Assembly of the Socialist Republic of Yugoslavia," dated January 21, 1986, reprinted in *South Slav Journal* 9, no. 1–2 (spring-summer 1986), 109.

73. Ibid.

74. See M. Janković, "Zločin kao u vreme Turaka" (Crime Like in the Time of Turks), *Politika Ekspres*, January 14, 1991.

75. See Kosta Mihailović and Vasilije Krestić, *Memorandum of the Serbian Academy of Sciences and Arts: Answers to Criticisms* (Belgrade: Serbian Academy of Sciences and Arts, 1995), 129. For a discussion of the Memorandum, see chapter three.

76. "Čak i sekretar zna istinu," *NIN*, February 5, 1989. See also radio interview with Živorad Mihajlović by Milica Ostojić-Pusara, reporter for Radio Belgrade (cited in Mihajlović, *Podzemni rat na Kosovu i Metohiji*).

77. Slaven Letica, "The Genesis of the Current Balkan War," in *Genocide after Emotion: The Postemotional Balkan War*, ed. Stjepan G. Meštrović (New York: Routledge, 1996), 95.

78. Ivo Andrić, *The Bridge on the Drina*, trans. Lovett F. Edwards (New York: Macmillan, 1959).

79. "Istina o Martinoviću" (The Truth About Martinović), *Politikin Svet*, May 1, 1991.

80. Michael A. Sells, *The Bridge Betrayed: Religion and Genocide in Bosnia* (Berkeley: University of California Press, 1997), 61. For estimates of how many Serbs and other persons were killed by the Ustaše, see Aleksa Djilas, *The Con-*

tested Country: Yugoslav Unity and Communist Revolution, 1919–1953 (Cambridge, Mass.: Harvard University Press, 1991), 102–27.

81. See Bette Denich, "Dismembering Yugoslavia: National Ideologies and the Symbolic Revival of Genocide," *American Ethnologist* 21, no. 2 (May 1994), 367–90; Paul Mojzes, *Yugoslavian Inferno* (New York: Continuum, 1994), 129–35.

82. *Politikin Svet*, October 5, 1988.

83. "Disqualification of Judge Asked For," *Illustrovana Politika*, February 25, 1986.

84. Noel Malcolm, *A Short History of Kosovo* (New York: New York University Press, 1998), 338, citing S. Spasojević, *Slučaj Martinović* (Belgrade, 1986).

85. Miroslav Zarić, "Na redu operacija London" (Operation London Next), *Večernje Novosti*, November, 21, 1986.

86. R. P., "Djordje Martinović dobio spor" (Djordje Martinović Won the Litigation), *Politika*, July 17, 1991. See also "Istina o Martinoviću," *Politikin Svet*, May 1, 1991.

87. Albanians call themselves "Shqiptar," which sounds similar to the non-Balkan ear. Both sides recognize today that the Serbian term "Šiptar" is offensive.

88. Mihajlović, *Podzemni rat na Kosovu i Metohiji,* 195.

89. From interviews by author.

90. At this time, Serbian health care workers started to come forward, accusing Aliu of misconduct in connection with the Martinović case. See Mihajlović, *Podzemni rat na Kosovu i Metohiji,* 196.

91. Dušanka Pjevac, "Poseban tretman za demonstrante," in *Kosmetski dosije,* ed. Milorad Djoković, 17 (Požarevac: Prosveta, 1990).

92. "Djordje Martinović i dalje čeka" (Djordje Martinović Is Still Waiting), *Illustrovana Politika*, January 9, 1993.

93. Ibid.

94. B. S. M., "Nova akcija zastrašivanja" (New Action of Terrorizing), *Večernje Novosti*, January 6, 1989.

95. Interview by author. "First neighbors" are close neighbors, generally next door.

96. Interview by author.

97. This criticism was part of the Memorandum of the Serbian Academy of Sciences and Arts. See Mihailović and Krestić, *Memorandum of the Serbian Academy of Sciences and Arts,* 129. For a discussion of the Memorandum, see chapter three.

98. Bogdanović, *Knjiga o Kosovu,* 247. Emphasis added.

99. Wayne S. Vucinich, "Nationalism and Communism," in *Contemporary Yugoslavia: Twenty Years of Socialist Experiment,* ed. Wayne S. Vucinich (Berkeley: University of California Press, 1969), 243.

100. Zdenko Antić, "Serbian Problems," *The South Slav Journal* 11, no. 4 (winter 1988). Aleksa Djilas has written that "[w]hile there was no Serbian hegemony in economic affairs, Serbs predominated in the state administration, diplomatic corps, and the military." Aleksa Djilas, "Fear Thy Neighbor: The Breakup of Yugoslavia," in *Nationalisms and Nationalities in the New Europe,*

ed. Charles A. Kupchan (Ithaca, N.Y.: Cornell University Press, 1995), 203 n.4.

101. Vladan A. Vasilijević, "Kosovo: Exercise and Protection of Human Rights," in *Conflict or Dialogue: Serbian-Albanian Relations and the Integration of the Balkans*, eds. Dušan Janjić and Shkelzen Maliqi (Subotica: Open University, 1994), p. 81.

102. Bogdanović, *Knjiga o Kosovu*, 247.

INTERVIEWS

Serbs Who Left Kosovo

In 1995 and 1996, over thirty interviews were conducted on this subject. Among the questions: Why did you leave? What is happening in Kosovo?

DJURIĆ BOŠKO, LIVING IN KRALJEVO, IN A PLACE CALLED "LITTLE ALBANIA"

Before World War II, Kosovo was almost 50 percent Serbs. After the war that number decreased to 45 percent because some people escaped from Kosovo during the war and then they were not allowed to come back. The government prohibited Serbs from going back to Kosovo, supposedly because they would disturb the agrarian structure. Under that disguise somebody was promoting his politics, and we all see where it brought us today. Our people were always under pressure and they [the Albanians] were always getting favors from the Central Committee and from the Serbian government and from the Yugoslav government. They were given everything and everything was taken away from us, all our rights. Therefore, finally they succeeded in expelling us.

In 1941 our home and all of our belongings were burned to the ground, and when we came back we got nothing from the community. They considered us to be dangerous for "brotherhood and unity." In 1941 Albanians devastated everything in Kosovo and Kolašin [Montenegro], so we went back to a desolate land.

I was a police officer for thirty-two years but I had to leave. . . . My neighbor was watering his yard and then he would "forget" to turn off the water and my basement would be full of water. Then they would go through my yard swearing and shouting: "Go, move out, what are you doing here." My kids had problems at work. Serbs were never given promotions, so my children moved away. One went to Pančevo and the second one is here. When they moved here, I had to withdraw too. My younger son had been a traffic cop [in Kosovo] and he worked together with an Albanian police officer. A bird ran into the windshield of [my son's police car]. They [the Albanian officers] didn't trust him that it was a bird and they kept badgering him to pay for that windshield. For me, this is just one form of oppression. People destroyed whole factories and nobody was questioned. It was not safe to walk during the night time. Kids were frequently assaulted [by Albanians] and also beaten.

One day I went to buy some coal and after I started to speak Serbian they told me that there was no coal for me and that someone had already paid for the coal in the store. There were two young men and approximately a ton of coal. When I returned the next day, that coal was still there and the boss told me that he could not help me.

It was an organized policy. They also had help from the republic governments, for example from Croatia, Slovenia and Bosnia. Serbia never had any influence in Kosovo even though it was Serbian territory. They are unified and they work in concert with each other— [you can tell that] somebody is ruling them because they are really obedient. I cannot talk to my son because we always fight—we [Serbs] are such people, while they are doing everything like moles, secretly and behind one's back.

Resolving the conflict in Kosovo depends mostly on foreign policy [of political leaders, not on what the people want]. Albanians have huge support from outside and therefore they don't agree to living jointly with Serbs. They want an ethnically clean Kosovo. As long as they have the support from outside there won't be peace there. If they get independence, they will expel the few remaining Serbs from there, and again that is not a solution.

Their natality is, I think, the greatest in Europe. Every woman of theirs gives birth to ten to fifteen children, and very few Serbs have more than two or three kids. Emigrants from Albania were coming too. Even the SUP [Secretariat of Internal Affairs] was buying properties in Kosovo for them. They were buying everything for them:

plows, cattle, furniture. They got some special documents as Albanian citizens [because] they couldn't have our citizenship, [but still] the state bought all those things for them. Officially, all that was given to those emigrants was temporary, just to use those things and not to own them, but those people are still there.

The exact number of Albanian emigrants from Albania is unknown. Officially, the number is quite low. In recent years, most emigrants from Albania have been Serbian.

The natality rate of Albanian women living in cities is actually very similar to that of urban Serbian women in Kosovo. Similarly, the number of children in families living in villages is approximately the same for Serbs and Albanians, although slightly higher for Albanians.[1]

VUKAŠINOVIĆ DRAGOLJUB, BORN IN PEĆ, NOW LIVING IN NOVO SELO (BY VRNJAČKA BANJA IN SERBIA)

My family and I were living in Peć. As a young boy I was friends equally with Serbs and Albanians. My best friend was Albanian. At that time I didn't feel that there were any problems about the difference in nationalities, but after I got married and started to look for a job problems came up. Wherever I asked for a job I was refused, because all of the executives were Albanians who were employing their compatriots. At that time 70 percent of the population in Peć was Albanian.

A few times my wife and both sons were exposed to unpleasantness and threats by Albanians, but I cannot say that there were any open physical and more serious confrontations. That was Tito's Communist times. We were all living well and therefore we thought less about politics. My father raised seven kids on only one salary.

Albanians are in fact an easily frightened people. They get courageous and dangerous only when they are in a big majority. That is why they were getting in our vineyards and stealing our grapes, because they knew that there were not enough of us to defend ourselves.

The reason Serbs started to leave Kosovo was mostly the intimidation we felt living among them as a minority. That is why my father left Peć in 1979, and I was already in Kraljevo with my family, where I came because of the problems with employment. We managed to sell the house in Peć for the market price. For that money we bought this house here in Novo Selo. Local Serbs from here accepted us pretty well, although there were some sporadic incidents between us "Kosovars" (that is how they call us here) and the indigenous people from here.

In the meantime, we were visiting our relatives and friends in Peć. Our former Albanian neighbors always greeted us in a nice way. I believe that Serbs and Albanians can live together, but under the condition that there are equal numbers of them so nobody is a minority. That is why Serbs should go to live in Kosovo and create total discipline, to stop the absolute chaos down there.

A SERBIAN WOMAN AND HER HUSBAND, FORMERLY LIVING IN OBILIĆ IN KOSOVO, NOW LIVING IN GLOGOVAC, SERBIA

WIFE: I was in my own house minding my own business when I heard a loud noise. When I went out to see what the noise was, I thought that somebody was having a good-bye party. But as they approached, I saw that they were turning buses upside down, throwing stones at the Serbian houses and stores. Then this stone hit me and blood started to spurt out on my cheek and somehow I dragged myself back to my house. I woke up my husband to go to the Priština emergency hospital. When we got there, there was not a Serbian living soul. It seemed like all the nurses and doctors were Albanians, but fortunately one nurse was Serbian and she told me: "Don't say what hurt you, it is going to be even worse." And I said the neighbor's kid threw a stone at me, by accident not deliberately. The Albanian doctor told me to lie down and they started to prepare some kind of injection for me. They would have poisoned me for sure; they would have done something to me, so I got up and said that I don't want it, and he said: "I don't care. If you want it it's OK, if you don't want it you don't have to." So I went back home to our doctor, he was Macedonian, and he received me and gave me injections against poisoning every half hour.

After twenty days my kids went to Priština. They got their salaries and went to buy themselves some shoes. They went in the afternoon, after the working hours, because Priština was near, fifteen to twenty minutes away. We waited for them and they didn't show up until late in the evening. After they came back, they immediately went to the bedroom, saying that they were tired. My daughter-in-law went to their room to see what they bought, and then she saw they were completely beaten up and that's why they didn't want me to see them. There were two of them and two more girls at the bus stop, waiting to come back home. They were talking in Serbian and then a bigger group of Albanians came by and started to mistreat them and beat them without any reason, just because they were talking in Serbian, which means because they were Serbs. It is their fortune that they are silent by nature or else they would have been stabbed with knives by those Albanians.

And so, they [Albanians] made us sell our house just after we started to live decently. Now we are trying to make our living decent again, but what we had we will never have again. It is true that it is quiet here and peaceful, but my soul suffers for what we left in Kosovo. There isn't a single night that I don't dream about our house in Obilić.

HUSBAND: My wife went to the store to buy some groceries and she knew nothing. I was working the night shift and because of that I was sleeping at home. As they [Albanians] were throwing stones at people, one of the bigger stones hit her on the ear. It hit her from the front and I was afraid that it would kill her for sure because it was big. I have a hunting gun, and I told her why didn't she wake me up? I was in that kind of state that I would have gone there and killed whoever I could have killed and wouldn't have cared what they would do to me.

They were teasing women and children the most. You couldn't fight them because there were always a lot of them. In our street in Obilić there were no Albanians. But the first Montenegrin who sold his house to an Albanian earned a lot of money. The Albanian who bought his house started to say that the whole street will soon belong to his family, Dedinjac. Now, after fifteen years there are only two Serbian houses left in that street. All of the other ones belong to Albanians. Serbs were 90 to 95 percent of Obilić's population and now there is only 30 percent left. Albanians from all over Kosovo, Peć and Metohija were buying houses there. The ones who bought my house came from Preševo.

After the first house was sold to an Albanian all of the other [houses of Serbs] were cheap to buy. I sold my house. It had four or five additional buildings; I had a garage; the house had a fence; I had sidewalks everywhere, a nice yard, pig pens, hen houses and everything else. After I sold it and went to Serbia . . . I couldn't afford to buy anything else but this shack. . . . They are saying that we got a lot of money from them, but maybe they paid better around Prizren, because the soil is more fertile there. There, they were competing [over] who was going to buy the house and the property first. Their goal is that [at least] one [Albanian] get into the place. For that first guy, everybody collects money, and they pay a good price for the Serbian house. But as soon as one moves in, others start coming as well. Albanians are not very likely to go to places that are all Serbian.

Those Serbs who didn't move out of Kosovo, they all built something here in Serbia in case there were demonstrations or [something] similar [in Kosovo]. Also, when they retire they want to be safe here in Serbia.

We have land down there and I cannot work on it. We have a lot of family left down there. While we were living in Obilić we worked on that piece of land, but Albanians were always making some damage [to it]. I went to the police to complain and they told me: "Negotiate with him." What was the use of negotiating when he did damage a hundred times before I caught him? It meant that you were forced to sell that land for as much as he offered you. And if any other Albanian wanted to buy it for a higher price he could not, if somebody had reserved it earlier. . . . That is why you cannot get a real price for your house and land. My household was completely equipped and I had to leave it all.

One of my sons adapted well here and he got married. But this older one would go back [to Kosovo] tomorrow if I told him so. And honestly speaking, I am nostalgic too. If I could I would go back there now. Everything is fine here, but there are no people that I went to school with, or that I worked with, or that I was friends with, that I went to dance with. I don't have those people here. I have three brothers left there. One of my brothers was killed by an Albanian taxi driver, but what can you do about it—nothing. That Albanian first escaped, and then after they caught him he said: "Let's make peace." Well fuck it, let me kill him first and then we can make peace, and not first he kills my brother and then "Let's make peace." He never spent one day in jail and he killed my brother on the spot. He was speeding and it was an inhabited area where you mustn't go faster than sixty kilometers per hour.

Until this [situation] in Kosovo gets regulated, [Serbian] people won't go back for sure, because it is not safe there at all. I don't know what kind of law this is. . . . Albanians poisoned their youth [with hateful thoughts]. The older ones don't think the same. I worked with them, you know, and I asked them several times: "What the hell is going on?" And they would say that they had to do [everything] the way they were ordered to, because if they disobeyed then fifteen or twenty people would come in the evening to their house and tell them that this was the last warning and if they didn't listen they would kill them. So one time all Albanians, both workers and directors, got the order to leave the workplace on a certain day at noon, and nobody stayed. But there are honest people with whom you can work. But students and youth are poisoned. . . .

MAN FROM CRKVENA VODICA (A VILLAGE NEAR OBILIĆ), NOW LIVING IN GLOGOVAC, SERBIA

Until 1968, when they removed Ranković [the Yugoslav internal affairs minister and vice president from 1945 to 1966, who ruled over Kosovo with an iron fist], living in Kosovo was decent. Everything was fine and there was order. Then, when student demonstrations started in 1965, '66, '68, Kosovo gained autonomy and everything else until Milošević came to power. Albanians were a majority and now they are an even bigger majority. When there were job offers it was a condition that nine out of ten people had to be Albanian, or the condition was to [be able to] speak Albanian. They finished school too fast, they were buying their diplomas. So a boss comes to you and he is illiterate and he is leading a [workplace]. There were a lot of problems. Experts were running away to other places in Serbia. All those Serbian engineers are [now] experts somewhere else in Serbia. Power plants in Kosovo were working properly while they were running them, but after the semiliterate Albanians became the executives, everybody who was worth something left in a hurry.

There were Albanians in our village. They were indigenous and so were we and with them we never had any problems. They were even brothers-in-oath, godfathers to our children, but Albanians who came later were mean.

I was the executive of a branch of the bank and the director was Albanian. We had around fifty employees of both nationalities and we cooperated well. In 1981, it turned out that most of them were for THEIR thing together with the director. . . . You had to write bilingually. Also, you would go to the store and you would speak Serbian and he would speak Albanian and you would have to understand each other.

It was the same thing in hospitals. You couldn't go and get cured in a human way. There was a story about this midwife doctor, Merkurka, who delivered female Serbian babies with their hips deformed. All the Serbian girls she had delivered had the same deformation of the hips. No Serbian women dared to go there and give a birth to a kid.

Here we have a second neighbor [that is, a neighbor two houses away] who killed an Albanian kid in a car accident. He was not guilty but what can you do, a kid was killed. After they told him [the neighbor] that they would kill either him or his kid, he had no other choice but to escape. Down there in Kosovo you cannot live under the threat of blood vengeance . . . not being able to send your child to school or to the store. Such life is worthless. With things like that nobody can help you, no law, no police, nobody.

MIODRAG CVETKOVIĆ, LIVING IN RIBNICA (NEAR KRALJEVO)

During the Yugoslav Kingdom, Albanians had all rights, they had a representative in the Senate, most of the municipality presidents were Albanians, even in places where Serbs were the majority. . . . They had [it] all. And it is not true that they were robbed by the agrarian reform and colonization. In 1929, they got the fertile land and Serbs got woods they had to clear for fields. In 1941, Albanians turned against both Serbs and the country which gave them all of that. . . . Our state couldn't solve one of the most important problems, and that is that Albanian emigrants were not political but economic emigrants and that they were inhabiting Kosovo from WWII until Tito's death. There are more than five hundred thousand emigrants from Albania inhabiting Kosovo for sure. . . . [2]

Albanians were very sneaky in putting pressure on Serbs. Those pressures date from 1945, when the government forbade Serbs to go back to Kosovo. Just look at the ratio of the ethnicities there. In 1941 it was fifty-fifty, and now it is 10 percent — 90 percent and you can easily see what it means. . . . I was lucky not to be in those [Army] formations that turned away those poor people [who wanted to return to Kosovo after WWII,] but I know [about] it. And that is when Serbian insecurity started.

The breaking point was when Ranković fell. While he was in
power, safety was the most important thing. Since then, the terrible psychological tortures began. Serbs were labeled as Greater
Serbian nationalists and Chetniks. This was helped also by Serbian
politicians in high places at that time. For example, after Ranković
fell, Serbs had to learn Albanian or they would lose their jobs. So
you had forty- or fifty-year-old people sitting behind desks in the
school. Then Albanian professors would be mean and cancel the
whole class if anybody was late for it. Then rapes started to occur
more and more often. Most frequently the victims were girls, then old
women. Also, Albanians were making terrible damage to Serbian
properties. If you look at the fields, you can easily tell which ones are
Albanian and which ones are Serbian. All the Serbian ones are destroyed.

Around twenty years ago, our area had 44 percent Serbs, and now
I don't believe that there are more than 10–12 percent. For example,
Vitina was a center of the area, and until 1961 there were no Albanian
houses there. It was inhabited only by Serbs, and now two-thirds of it
is Albanian. The first Albanian moved in there in 1962 and their tactic
was to get into the center of the place first and then they automatically
move all over. First they buy one house and then slowly, one by one,
[they buy them all]. . . . In Vitina only the center of the city is still
Serbian and everything around it is Albanian. Two days ago I came
back from there, and the Albanians are giving nine thousand deutschmarks for one hundred square meters in the zone that is attractive for
them. But if you have property in the area where everything else is
owned by Albanians, you can hardly get even a hundred deutschmarks
for one hundred square meters. . . .

Starting in 1968 until 1974, people [Serbs] were selling their properties for nothing. From 1976 until 1980 Albanians paid good prices,
and now they pay well if they think it is in their interest, and if it
is surrounded by Albanian properties they don't even bother [to
pay much] because they think of it as it already belonging to them.
One big, bad thing was that the government bought houses from
Serbian emigrants and gave them to Albanian immigrants. The
United Nations gave 40 percent and our government 60 percent,
so half of the villages were bought and all of that went through
the SUP of Kosovo. This affected Serbs a lot. There are those emigrants who still don't have Yugoslav citizenship and they have property. . . .

[He is referring to an alleged United Nations–sponsored resettlement of refugees from Albania in Kosovo. Many Kosovo Serbs blame the UN for the presence in Kosovo of Albanians from Albania.]

The way that Albanians bought the houses was that no matter what the commission would say about the price, they would agree on one price among themselves and then offer it to the owner of the house. No other Albanians were allowed to offer a better price. For example, the teacher from our village sold his house for half of the real price, because that was the only offer he had. His father had bought that land in 1925 and he had paid for it in cash.

Everything [in Kosovo] is malfunctioning and there is great feeling of insecurity. The worse thing is that there is no hope. During the existence of the group called Božur [an organization for the return of Serbs to Kosovo] in 1986–87 there was some kind of hope there, there was a hope that something would happen. Something could have been done and the problem would have been solved, but everything fell apart.

The big changes [with Milošević] are worthwhile only in that Albanians aren't able any more to rape, rob and kill openly. Nothing else is good. The [rule of] authority is totally dead and everything is in anarchy for both Serbs and Albanians. Corruption is everywhere and nothing works.

There are no reasons why we shouldn't live together but I am positive that it is impossible here because in Serbia we have complete anarchy, everybody does what they like. If it doesn't get arranged that Serbs have equal power in Kosovo, Albanians will be a total majority. Albanians made an ethnic cleansing in Kosovo and now Americans are rewarding them for that. This is what we have to solve before we start even talking about joint living. . . .

I have been fighting [for Kosovo for Serbs] since 1968 and I have been punished for that. In 1974, I sent fifty-five densely typed pages to Tito and described the whole situation to him. After that I was hunted and arrested. I believed that I shouldn't leave but stay and fight, and now I understand that it is without any purpose. There [in Kosovo] a man does not see a hope. Those hopes have vanished or have been destroyed. There is no sense to anything.

We started to build this house [in Serbia] in 1981 and finished it in 1985 and until this January [1995] it was empty. We were waiting for the situation to change, but nothing ever happened.

In interviews with Serbs from Kosovo, Americans are frequently mentioned as the culprits. The state of corruption this man describes was indeed widespread, but not unique to Kosovo. It was endemic to all of Serbia.

SUNDIĆ ZVEZDAN, BORN
IN KOSOVSKA MITROVICA, LIVING
IN DUBRAVA (NEAR VRNJAČKA BANJA)

I moved to Vrnjačka Banja in 1986 because I managed to get a job here. Until 1980, living in Kosovska Mitrovica was pretty decent. We were more or less friendly with Albanians, who were 50 percent of the city population. During the Albanian demonstrations and conflicts in Kosovo, I was serving in the army out of [Kosovo]. After I came back home I could feel a huge tension in the relationship between the two peoples. Somehow we all started to socialize only with our own compatriots.

At that time I was supposed to go to the University of Priština, but because of the situation I decided to study in Belgrade. After finishing my studies in 1986, I went back to Kosovska Mitrovica but interethnic relations were getting worse and worse. We [Serbs] started to feel insecure about our future in Kosovo and Metohija because the number of Serbs was rapidly decreasing. Those who hadn't moved out yet were thinking about it. My wife and I decided to start our life somewhere else, and so we left for Serbia.

Our relationships with locals here in Vrnjačka Banja were not the best at the beginning, mainly because of the difference in mentality. My parents still live in Kosovska Mitrovica. They are not as close with their Albanian neighbors as they were before, but their relations are decent.

I still think that without drastic changes in Kosovo, Serbs there don't have any future. I am afraid that Kosovo will become for Serbia the same as Northern Ireland for Great Britain. The only solution is that all Albanians get kicked out of Kosovo. If they didn't have foreign support they wouldn't dare asking for something that doesn't belong to them, like autonomy, or even more, a republic. If it wasn't for that politics we would be living peacefully with each other like we did before. Since I don't believe that the political situation in Kosovo will become better, I am not thinking about going back there.

Notes

1. See Srdjan Bogosavljević, "A Statistical Picture of Serbo-Albanian Relations," *Republika* 6, special issue 9 (February 1994), 19 (published also in Serbian as "Statistička slika srpsko-albanskih odnosa").

2. No credible published sources contain such a high estimate for the number of emigrants from Albania. See Tim Judah, *The Serbs: History, Myth and the Destruction of Yugoslavia* (New Haven, Conn.: Yale University Press, 1997), 150.

THREE

"A Shot Against Yugoslavia": The Paraćin Massacre, 1987

Laying the Foundation: 1985–1987

The "Paraćin Massacre" occurred in 1987, less than two years after the Martinović case. In that short span, Serbian politicians and would-be politicians had begun to use Kosovo as a central organizing tool in their campaign to gain power not only over Kosovo but over all of Yugoslavia. Serbian demands for constitutional changes to take control over Kosovo and to change the structures of power within Yugoslavia were picking up steam. The moves that would help seal the future for Kosovo were coming not from Priština but from Belgrade. Serbian intellectuals were at the vanguard.

In January 1986, a group of some two hundred prominent Belgrade intellectuals sent a petition to the Yugoslav and Serbian national assemblies decrying the treatment of Serbs in Kosovo. The charges against Kosovo Albanians were heinous: "Old women and nuns are being raped, youngsters beaten up, cattle blinded, stables built from gravestones, churches and old shrines desecrated. . . ."[1] Endorsing the October 1985 petition of Kosovo Serbs, this new petition blasted Serbian and Yugoslav leaders for failing to take action and for remaining "indifferent to [the] desperate cry for help and [the people's] awakened consciousness." In apocalyptic tones, the petition cautioned: "People denied rights are running out of time and they are already attempting to organize themselves and assume responsibility for their own fate. No nation will give up its right to exist, and the Serb people are not and do not want to be an exception." If Kosovo was to become "ethnically pure," the petition warned, "this would inevitably lead to fresh national and international conflicts." Yet, it contended, no one would listen to Serbs: "Under the guise of the struggle against 'Serbian hegemonism,'[2] the Serb nation and its history have been subjected for decades to a show trial. The first objective is an ethnically 'pure' Kosovo, to be followed by further conquests of Serbian, Macedonian and Montenegrin lands."[3]

The authors of the petition stressed that "we do not wish any evil or injustice to the Albanian people and we support its [sic] democratic rights," and that "we also condemn all injustices ever committed by the Serbs against the Albanian people." Despite this statement, the petition also implicitly endorsed the demand to strip Kosovo of its autonomous status, declaring that "genocide in Kosovo cannot be halted without deep social and political changes in the whole country," including "a change in relations between the Socialist Autonomous Provinces and the Socialist Republic of Serbia, or indeed the whole of Yugoslavia." The present constitutional arrangement, it alleged, constituted a "policy of a gradual handover of Kosovo to Albania, capitulation with no capitulation being signed, a policy of national betrayal."

Reading the names on the petition provides a good summary of those who would decide to jump on the bandwagon of nationalism. However, even some of the Belgrade intellectuals who did not sign the petition later attempted to justify their colleagues' behavior. "You have to understand," one Belgrade antiwar activist explained in 1994, "those were different times."[4] Or, as another Belgrade antiregime activist said, "Just because someone signed the petition on Kosovo, they did not automatically become nationalist—or a supporter of Milošević."[5] For many Belgrade liberals at that time, the petition seemed "just a freedom of speech issue."[6] So deeply ingrained was the sense of injustice that most Serbs felt regarding Kosovo that they failed to make a connection between Serbian claims to Kosovo and Greater-Serbian nationalism.

The petition of Belgrade intellectuals helped to fuel the campaign of Kosovo Serbs and Serbian nationalists everywhere. Under the direction of Belgrade Serb nationalists in 1986, the Committee of Serbs and Montenegrins (a Kosovo protest group) collected fifty thousand signatures, purportedly all from Kosovo Serbs and Montenegrins, demanding greater rights for Serbs in Kosovo.[7] Republic and federal authorities characterized this protest as a "provocation," arresting the person whose name appeared first on the list of signatures. Several hundred Kosovo Serbs protested the arrest by staging a sit-in at the man's house, and eventually he was freed. Kosovo Serbs then attempted to organize a massive march from Kosovo to Belgrade, but local authorities prevented them from carrying out their plans.

One of the most important events for Serbian nationalists occurred in September 1986, when the Memorandum of the Serbian Academy of Sciences and Arts (SANU) was leaked to the press and published in the Belgrade daily *Večernje novosti*.[8] In three years, the document would be called a "platform or pamphlet for political action" for Slobodan Milošević[9] and even "a blueprint for war."[10] Its authors maintain that the document is not nationalistic,[11] and that SANU was independent of the official policies of Serbia and Milošević.[12] Nonetheless, the document triggered shock waves in Yugoslavia in 1987 precisely because of its admonitions on "the status of Serbia and the Serb nation"[13] — content which is decidedly nationalistic under nearly any definition of "nationalism."

Today, the wording of most of the Memorandum, especially the arguments on the economic structure of Yugoslavia,[14] may appear somewhat benign in light of subsequent developments in the region. But in 1986 the content was stridently defiant, in particular the continued references to the victimization of and discrimination against the Serb nation, the suggestions for reworking the 1974 Constitution to allow for greater centralization (at a time when Yugoslavia was becoming increasingly decentralized), and the warning that Kosovo was the most potent of the political crises coming "close to the flash point of complete destabilization of Yugoslavia."[15] The most foreboding attribute of the Memorandum was that it left open whether Serbs could ever achieve justice within the Yugoslav arrangement, as Ivo Banac has observed: "The novelty of the memorandum was its questioning of Yugoslavia as the optimal solution for Serbs. Usually, the non-Serb national movement hurled accusations at Yugoslavia on account of various Serbian advantages in the common state. Now, the leading Serbian intellectual institution cast its own aspersions on Yugoslavia."[16] Whether the Memorandum served as a springboard for Milošević's policies or the developing platform of Milošević's advisors formed the content of the Memorandum, the similarity between the Memorandum and Milošević's platform in 1988–1990 is undeniable.[17]

Along with its attack on the economic system, bureaucratic inefficiencies and the monopoly of Communist party leadership, the Memorandum assailed the 1974 Constitution of Yugoslavia, which had decentralized power to the republic level and had given Kosovo and Vojvodina the status of autonomous provinces. These and other related measures were said to be a violation of the "self-determination of nations."[18] Serbs, the authors said, were particularly disadvantaged:

Over the past two decades, the principle of unity [of the state] has become weakened and overshadowed by the principle of national autonomy, which in practice has turned into the *sovereignty* of the federal units [the republics, which as a rule were not ethnically homogeneous, except for Slovenia]. The flaws which from the very beginning were present have become increasingly evident. Not all the national groups were equal: the Serbian nation, for instance, was not given the right to have its own state. The large sections of the Serbian people who live in other republics, unlike the national minorities, do not have the right to use their own language and script; they do not have the right to set up their own political and cultural organizations or to foster common cultural traditions of their nation together with conationals. The unremitting persecution and expulsion of Serbs from Kosovo is a drastic example showing that those principles which protect the autonomy of a minority (the ethnic Albanians) are not applied to a minority within a minority (the Serbs, Montenegrins, Turks and Romas in Kosovo).[19]

The Memorandum viewed the political and economic policies of Yugoslavia, and in particular the "special legal and political status" of Serbia (that is, the creation of the two autonomous provinces) as reflecting "the desire to keep the Serbian people constantly under control."[20] Serbia, alone of all the republics, is not allowed its own state. "A worse historical defeat in peacetime cannot be imagined."[21] The Memorandum blamed Slovenia and Croatia for this debacle. Using what would soon become a cliché of the Serbian nationalist platform, the Memorandum said that the watchword of the federal policy was, "A weak Serbia ensures a strong Yugoslavia."[22] The two most developed republics, Slovenia and Croatia, had been able to accomplish their national programs because they had control over the federal leadership while the Yugoslav economic and political system had deliberately left Serbia politically disadvantaged and economically underdeveloped. "Nothing would be more normal now than for them [Slovenes and Croats] to defend the system. . . ."[23]

According to the Memorandum, only the redrawing of the Yugoslav political system could correct the disadvantaged position of Serbs. The Memorandum called for "political democratization and the infusion of new blood, genuine self-determination and equality for all members of the Yugoslav nations, including the Serbs, [and] full exercise of human, civil, and economic and social rights. . . ."[24] Since Albanians were not considered to be a "Yugoslav nation," their status under this formulation is uncertain at best. While the document stressed that the human rights situation must improve if Yugoslavia is to call itself "a civilized and enlightened society," the focus is on civil liberties, the sort of violation that the authors of the Memorandum would be most likely to encounter personally:

In Yugoslavia "verbal crimes" are still prosecuted; books are still being banned and destroyed, and plays are taken off repertory if they are deemed "ideologically unacceptable." Public expression of opinions is trammeled; association, assembly, and public demonstrations are prohibited; exercise of the constitutional right to send petitions of protest to government agencies is branded as a hostile act; the organizers of protest strikes are hounded; elected officials have turned into a farce of self-nomination.[25]

The section on human rights, not surprisingly, fails to mention human rights abuses committed against Kosovo Albanians. It also does not include in its generic listing of potential abuses those experienced more frequently by Kosovo Albanians, such as police torture, arbitrary arrest and detention, the denial of fair public trials, arbitrary interference with privacy and the right to free movement within the country and to foreign travel.

The Memorandum did prominently feature Kosovo, however, using the familiar story of Serb victimization there as a springboard to portents of doom for Serbs who live anywhere outside of their "motherland." The authors opened their section on Kosovo by asserting: "In the spring of 1981, open and total war was declared on the Serbian people, which had been carefully prepared for in advance in the various stages of administrative, political and constitutional reforms."[26] In other words, responsibility for the situation rested with the republic and federal authorities who had created the 1974 Constitution and safeguarded it against changes. By failing to take decisive action against Kosovo, these authorities only encouraged separatist Albanians: "The five years of ethnic Albanians' war in Kosovo have convinced its organizers and protagonists that they are now stronger than they ever dared dream and that they enjoy support from various power centers in the country which is incomparably greater than that which the Kosovo Serbs receive from the Republic of Serbia, or this republic [Serbia] from other republics in

Yugoslavia."[27] The Memorandum further claimed that "the physical, political, legal and cultural genocide of the Serbian population in Kosovo and Metohija is a worse defeat than any experienced in the liberation wars waged by Serbia. . . ."[28] Those responsible for the defeat included not only federal authorities and the Communist Party of Yugoslavia but also "generations of Serbian politicians . . . who are always on the defensive and always worried more about what others think of them . . . than about the objective facts affecting the nation whom they lead."[29]

The destiny of Kosovo, the Memorandum cautioned, "can no longer be fobbed off with empty words, convoluted resolutions, vague political platforms; it has become a matter of Yugoslav concern."[30] For the Memorandum's authors, Kosovo was just the beginning, as "Serbs in Croatia have never been before as jeopardized as they are today," and thus "solution of their status is a question of overriding importance."[31] The Memorandum crescendoed with a call for a Serbian national awakening: "The Serbian people must be allowed to find themselves again and become an historical personality in their own right, to regain a sense of their historical and spiritual being, to make a clear assessment of their economic and cultural interests, to devise a modern social and national program which will inspire present generations and generations to come."[32]

Had the above stanza of the Memorandum spoken not of "Serbian people" but of Albanian, Croatian, Slovene, Muslim, Bosniac,[33] Macedonian, Montenegrin, Hungarian, or any other "people," it would have likely come under attack by its authors. No other group had so bluntly stated its national demands, at least not without suffering repercussions.[34] It came as no surprise then when the press throughout Yugoslavia, including the Serbian press, strongly assailed the Memorandum and SANU. For its part, SANU denied responsibility for the Memorandum, stating that it was simply a draft by a group of academicians, not an officially authorized document of the academy. (Later, however, two of the authors, Kosta Mihajlović and Vasilije Krestić, confirmed that the first thirty pages of the text "can be considered to have been approved by the Committee.")[35]

Politicians throughout Yugoslavia attacked the Memorandum, and even Belgrade leaders decried its contents. Serbia's President, Ivan Stambolić, spoke out against the Memorandum in a speech at Belgrade University on October 30, 1986: "The so-called Memorandum is not new. It is the old chauvinist concern for the fate of the Serbian cause with the well-known formula that Serbs will win wars but lose the peace. . . . In short, the so-called Memorandum, more precisely, with an easy conscience, could be entitled 'In Memoriam' for Yugoslavia, Serbia, Socialism, self-management, equality, brotherhood and unity. . . . Essentially, it is diametrically opposed to the interests of Serbs throughout Yugoslavia."[36] Nevertheless, in a sign that nationalist-oriented speech was becoming a bit more free, no one took legal action against either the authors or the press that had printed the Memorandum.

Official criticism aside, the Memorandum was silently and privately endorsed by many Serbs, who saw it as simply confirming what they already believed. While the Memorandum's critique of Yugoslavia's political and economic situation was widely endorsed, it was the text on Kosovo that had particular resonance among the growing Serbian populist movements, in Kosovo and elsewhere. The message here was simple: Albanians (or someone else) have always been the evil Other; Serbs have always been the victims. Even for those who did not believe in the ideology of nationalism, the rhetoric served as a means to other ends. As Lenard Cohen has observed, "Disillusioned with the failure and unpopularity of the Titoist system, and with socialism's inability to resolve multiethnic conflicts, many Serbian intellectuals tended to opportunistically view . . . Serbian nationalism as a new avenue to influence political affairs."[37]

Slobodan Milošević, then the newly (self-)designated leader of the League of Communists of Serbia, was one of the few Communists who did not publicly castigate the Memorandum. Apart from an unpublicized speech in front of a select group of secret policemen,[38] he did not speak out against the document at all. Instead, he began to use language strikingly similar in both tone and scope to that of the Memorandum. He chose a propitious location for announcement of his platform, Kragujevac, a workers' city on Kosovo's border and a main destination for Serbs leaving Kosovo. There, he told party activists, "Serbia does not seek to be more of a republic than other republics, but, it is certain, she cannot permit herself to be less of a republic than the others. The fact that Serbia has two socialist autonomous provinces in her composition cannot be a reason for her to be reduced to her inner territory." In ominous tones, Milošević warned that changing the status of Kosovo "would be difficult to achieve" because "areas [i.e., other republics] and individuals whose interests are imperiled will be against [change]."[39]

The Kragujevac speech proved to be a mere warm-up for 1987. At the beginning of the year, Milošević addressed a rally near Belgrade, calling for a reduction in the autonomy of Kosovo and Vojvodina and proclaiming, "Serbia will be united or there will be no Serbia."[40] Then, in what would be his most important career move to date, Milošević traveled to Kosovo on April 24, 1987, to hear first-hand the complaints of Kosovo Serbs. The purported purpose of the trip was a meeting with the Albanian representatives to the Presidency of the Central Committee,[41] Azem Vllasi and Kolë Shiroka, and selected representatives of Serbs and Montenegrins living in Kosovo, but in time the trip would be remembered as a Milošević one-man show.

A large public protest had been prepared in advance of the April 25 meeting at the Braća Krajnović house of culture in Kosovo Polje. Fifteen thousand Serbs were waiting for Milošević. As soon as he arrived, the crowd began shouting in unison: "We want freedom! We want freedom!" (This had a double meaning, as Milošević's first name means "free.") Police escorted Milošević through the swarming crowd and into the run-down building. When the small auditorium quickly filled to capacity, police formed a cordon around the building, but the crowd still pressed to get in. The crowd grew increasingly restless and began chanting slogans such as "We are Tito, Tito is ours." Swinging their batons, police pushed the protesters back. At some point, the demonstrators began throwing rocks at the police and shouting "thieves, thieves" and "murderers." According to some journalists, the organizers of the demonstration had conveniently parked a truck filled with stones next to the demonstration.[42]

Accounts in the Yugoslav press of police conduct at the demonstration vary considerably. According to the Zagreb magazine *Danas*, the police pushed back the crowd and defended themselves against the onslaught of rocks, but no one was seriously injured.[43] In contrast, the Belgrade weekly *NIN* reported that the (predominantly Albanian) police started to beat people "on command" and that after "some women fell on the ground, they passed them and cruelly hit those who were running away."[44] The report made later by the Priština SUP did concede that "several police officers used rubber sticks and hit a few people on their legs," and in fact disciplinary measures were taken against six police officers in connection with the incident.[45] The discrepancy between these different reports gave all possible sides something to believe.[46] According to many Yugoslavs and Kosovo Albanians, Serbs were getting out of control. On the other hand, according to many Serbs, the police were at fault.

In any event, the rock throwing had not quite died down by the time

Vllasi and Milošević went outside to address the crowd. The politicians could not be heard above the roar, and so they waited for speakers to be set up. According to some press reports, the crowd meanwhile continued shouting about the abuses committed by Albanians. One man close to Milošević screamed, "They are beating us. Why do they beat us?" Milošević was reported to have told the crowd in response, "No one shall beat these people!" This statement was later interpreted as Milošević's promise to protect Serbs from Albanians. Some commentators contend, however, that Milošević directed these words to the police after one of the protesters had complained that *the police* were beating them. Regardless, the first interpretation has become the Truth, and the uttering of the words "no one shall ever beat you again" is remembered as the seminal moment in Milošević's career, the point at which he turned into the protector of the Serbian nation.

With the Belgrade media on hand to capture the moment, the appreciative crowd began chanting in unison "Slobo, Slobodo," punning on Milošević's first name and the Serbian word for "freedom." Milošević told the crowd, "You should stay here. This is your land. These are your houses. Your meadows and gardens. Your memories. You shouldn't abandon your land just because it's difficult to live, because you are pressured by injustice and degradation. It was never part of Serbian and Montenegrin character to give up in the face of obstacles, to demobilize when it's time to fight. . . ."[47] In what would be called the Night of Hard Words, the protestors took their turn at the podium, outlining their grievances against Albanians, telling stories of rape, murder, harassment, employment discrimination and other wrongs. The event lasted until six in the morning. Before the sun rose, Milošević, a good Communist, had been transformed into a good nationalist.[48] It would only be a matter of time before an uneasy coalition of nationalists and Communists would elect him president of Serbia and follow him into war.

Breaking with the tradition of minimizing coverage of national conflict, the Yugoslav media broadly covered the events in Kosovo Polje. Even the traditionally Communist newspaper *Borba* featured a report with the headline "A New Phase." As the author of the article later explained: "We argued that at Kosovo Polje the Serbs and Montenegrins had held a convention, articulating their national goals. In the 'socialist' Serbia and Yugoslavia of the time, where the slightest expression of nationalism was taboo, this bordered on the impermissible."[49]

Capitalizing on the momentum of the Kosovo Polje speech, Milošević called a special meeting of the Yugoslav Communist Party on Kosovo on June 16, 1987. To mark the event, three thousand Kosovo Serbs were transported to Belgrade, where they were to protest in Pioneer Park, across from the federal Assembly in downtown Belgrade. They fulfilled their role well, disrupting the meeting by shouting curses at the political leaders in attendance, accusing them of being thieves. Above all, the crowd demanded that Kosovo's autonomy be revoked. Eventually the crowd disbanded, but it had achieved its goal: the problem of Kosovo had become the problem of Yugoslavia. After Milošević's arrival on the Kosovo scene, the headlines of leading Belgrade papers such as *Politika* began to issue nationalist warnings: "Serbia and SFRY [the Socialist Federal Republic of Yugoslavia] won't give Kosovo away," "There won't be any tyranny on this soil," "We don't want greater rights than others but we want equal rights with others," "The law has to be applied."[50] In Kosovo, the law was already being applied to weed out potential Albanian political leaders. In 1986, some one hundred Kosovo Albanians, allegedly irredentists, had been prosecuted on charges of hostile activity and conspiracy to overthrow the state.[51] The demands for more prosecutions in 1987 only intensified police action against Albanians.

Meanwhile, the economy of Yugoslavia continued to spiral downward. In the first months of 1987, inflation had reached 130 percent (annually), unemployment stood at an all-time high, and the foreign debt rested at $20 billion, placing Yugoslavia ninth among the world's largest debtors.[52] The worsening economic conditions in Kosovo did little to stem the tide of Serbs fleeing for Serbia proper and Albanians fleeing for other parts of Yugoslavia, Germany, Switzerland and any other place that would take them. To prevent Serbs from leaving Kosovo, the Serbian Assembly passed an unusual law in 1987 restricting land sales between individuals. Individual sales of property would be allowed by the republic's Secretariat for Finance only if "the sale did not influence a change in the national structure of the population or emigration of the members of the certain nation or national minority and when that transaction does not cause restlessness, or insecurity or inequality with the citizen members of another nation or national minority."[53] The law produced a situation in which neighbor turned in neighbor for violating the provisions, thus further heightening animosity between Serbs and Albanians.

At the federal level, the political crisis only deepened. Further fragmentation of political power, from the federal to the republic level, had led to political chaos and "the withering legitimacy of the Party and the system as a whole."[54] With the party on its sickbed, the Yugoslav army, diehard party members and soon-to-be-former party members stood watch. It was in this context that Aziz Kelmendi's shots were heard throughout Yugoslavia.

The Truths about the Paraćin Massacre

On September 3, 1987, Aziz Kelmendi, a young Albanian soldier of the Yugoslav army, opened fire in his army barracks in the Serbian town of Paraćin, killing four soldiers (one Serb, two Bosnian Muslims, one Slovene and Croat) and wounding five others. The military reported that after a search Kelmendi was found dead, having apparently committed suicide. Eventually, eight soldiers—six Albanians, one Muslim and one Rom—would be convicted of helping Kelmendi in the attack.

The attack was immediately reported as an attack against the entire country. The headlines in *Politika* and *Borba,* Belgrade's widely read dailies, blared "Kelmendi Shot at Yugoslavia" and "Shots at Yugoslavia." *Borba*, for example, carried this front-page story:

Belgrade, Sept. 3—This morning at dawn in Paraćin, the most absurd shots that were ever heard echoed in one of the barracks of JNA. Soldier Aziz Kelmendi, of Albanian nationality, shot treacherously with an automatic rifle at his friends while they were sleeping. After his fire, four soldiers were dead, while five more of them were wounded.

The victims of Aziz Kelmendi could have been prepared for any kind of surprise except for this one. This was the only way Kelmendi could have killed them.

His shots were insane, but his crime is much more than that. With his rounds, which everything indicates were not incidental, he aimed at one of the steadiest pillars of Yugoslav unity and Yugoslav stability—at the JNA [the Yugoslav army]—and moreover he aimed at the most sensitive pulse of its being—our young recruits, who have always proudly worn its uniform.

Kelmendi actually shot at Yugoslavia. He obviously didn't choose his victims. All of those at whom he shot wore the same uniform, the uniform of the Yugoslav People's Army—the same Tito's caps, same stars, and they were almost from all of the parts of Yugoslavia—Serbia, Bosnia and Herzegovina, Croatia, Slovenia, Montenegro.

And with that, with that Yugoslav dimension of the crime, this morning's massacre in Paraćin one more time points out in a tragic way that the counterrevolution in Kosovo is a Yugoslav problem.[55]

Although no one was charged at first with helping Kelmendi and no evidence was produced to indicate a conspiracy, *Politika* immediately assumed that Kelmendi had not been acting alone: "Mindless rounds of the murderer Kelmendi, who, everything indicates, did not pull the trigger alone, will not and cannot swing our trust in our army. . . ."[56] The phrase "perfidiously and slyly" was used in this and other articles to describe the manner in which Kelmendi had acted, adducing traits that Serbian folklore attributes to all Albanians. The murders thus became additional proof of the Albanian menace.

When in the wake of the Paraćin Massacre angry Yugoslavs took revenge against Albanians, the more state-aligned Belgrade press downplayed the national element of the attacks. The largest and most conservative Belgrade daily, *Politika,* reported only the occurrence of peaceful protests, while the Yugoslav daily *Borba* admitted only that the gatherings had a "slightly nationalistic tone." Reporting on a demonstration of more than one hundred people in front of a pastry shop in Paraćin, *Borba* wrote: "As we were officially told, apart from the anthem being sung there were no slogans shouted or any other sort of excess behavior."[57]

A Communist Party meeting called to discuss the connotations of such gatherings concluded that the demonstrations were "a kind of protest against the sickening crime in the garrison."[58] The careful language used by the state- and party-aligned media to describe demonstrations against Albanians was much different than that used to describe similar activities undertaken by Albanians. When Albanians protested or wrote graffiti, their actions were seen as paving the way to murder; when Serbs crowded before Albanian shops shouting slogans and destroying property, their actions were simply "protests against the sickening crime."

In marked contrast to the more official reports, the increasingly daring Belgrade weekly *NIN* reported that in the nights following the killing, Albanian shops were damaged all over Serbia, mainly by groups of youth singing Serbian nationalist songs.[59] Similarly, television coverage of the funeral of Srdjan Simić, the soldier from Belgrade, showed an angry mob brandishing Yugoslav national flags and singing the national anthem; some were shouting "murderers" and calling for harsher action against Kosovo Albanians. The press in other republics also tended to be open about the anti-Albanian nature of the responses to the crime. For example, while *Politika* reported that only six hundred people came to the funeral of the victim from Belgrade, the Croatian daily *Slobodna Dalmacija* set the figure around twenty thousand, painting a much more dramatic picture of an embittered crowd shouting against Albanian oppression and crying through the streets of Belgrade.

In the days that followed, media coverage throughout Yugoslavia grew even more stridently anti-Albanian. As the public wondered, "What kind of man could have done this," the press suggested, "an Albanian irredentist." Future articles berated the behavior of the Kelmendi family, teachers and neighbors. The insinuation was the same: all of these people who speak a different language, who hold different customs and who may support a "Kosovo republic" or other Kosovo Albanian political goals are all mass murderers waiting to explode.[60] Kelmendi reportedly belonged to a nationalistic family because his brother had been arrested for writing graffiti with "subversive content," and "in the Kelmendi house [police] found and appropriated subversive propaganda based on Albanian nationalism and separatism."[61]

Police arrested Kelmendi's father for allegedly having an unreported pistol.[62] The press reported that Kelmendi's father had hidden the gun in his wife's *dimije*, the baggy trousers worn by traditional Muslim (and, in some Kosovo villages, non-Muslim) women. *Politika* announced this latest discovery with the headline "Pistol in Dimije," highlighting both the Muslim connection and the supposed supportive role of Albanian women in irredentism.[63]

Kelmendi's entire town, Dušanovo, was blamed for the crime. Desanka Djordjević (the president of the regional branch of SUBNOR—Unity of the Veterans of the People's Liberation Revolution) was quoted as saying that "that suburban place is a lair of separatists, which even before the revolution [WWII] was visited by the Albanian ambassador, who made speeches."[64] *Politika* reported that young Albanians from Dušanovo had sauntered through the streets of Prizren in Albanian peasant costumes. "In this place," *Politika* continued, "hostile slogans were being written, pamphlets were being handed out."[65] Through these allegations, the article subtly equates "hostile activity" with Albanian culture (the peasant costumes), public displays of national identity (the 1981 event in Prizren) and Albanian political speech, drawing a connection between those who participate in these activities and those who murder.

The same article on Dušanovo goes on to state that when a group of "citizens of Serbian and Montenegrin ethnicity" living in the area tried to send a telegram to the family of one of the victims, the post office gave spurious reasons for not accepting it.[66] The allegation has all the attributes of a rumor, as neither the "group of citizens" nor the post office is named, and other details are omitted. This piece of "information" is aimed at showing how cruel and insensitive Albanians are: they are the kind of people who would even refuse to forward condolences to an aggrieved family.

Aleksandar Tijanić, a Serbian journalist writing for the Croatian daily *Danas*, wrote against popular demands to oust the Kelmendi family from their home. Calling for "civilized voices" and the "Serbian sense of democracy," the journalist claimed that Serbs do not need revenge, but only "absolute and undamaged equality of all citizens of Kosovo before the law."[67] Nevertheless, the Belgrade press tended to be sympathetic to attempts to oust the Kelmendi family from their home. In attempts to goad local Kosovo officials (Serbian and Albanian) to take action, the press blasted them for failing to take earlier steps to sanction Kelmendi, questioning why he had been allowed to remain in school after he had been imprisoned for going to Albania illegally. "It is interesting that his absence was not registered in the school record books," *Politika* reported in one sentence, immediately contradicting itself by further observing, "The only thing noted is that he was absent from twenty classes."[68] In addition, the list of those responsible for the crime now included the school system: "All the teachers that lectured to Aziz Kelmendi bear on their souls a part of his crime. . . ."[69]

Kelmendi's place of work, Electroeconomy of Kosovo (Electroprivreda Kosova), was also criticized. It had given training to both Kelmendi and his older brother, although both had been previously "held responsible for hostile activity" (graffiti writing and travel to Albania). The Albanian management of the company was accused of not allowing its Serbian employees to pay tribute to the murdered soldiers; the management allegedly had even "altered the company's bus lines" (that is, its transportation for workers) so as to diminish the number of workers present at funeral services.[70]

Even when Albanians expressed sympathy over the incident, their motives were suspect. When the rector of the Kosovo University, an Albanian, publicly condemned the crime, *Politika* wondered, "Would the rector have condemned the heedless deed had Kelmendi not been their student?"[71] And although the Presidency of Kosovo spoke out against the killing, the press concluded that "they didn't . . . pay a minute of silent tribute to the murdered soldiers," or "they did but it wasn't announced."[72] Any Albanian response to the Paraćin incident was suspicious.

In line with these populist attacks on Albanians, federal authorities began to suggest that the crime was motivated by Albanian nationalist passions. On September 10, 1987, the federal Secretariat for National Defense declared that the following facts had been established about the crime:

Soldier Aziz Kelmendi broke into the official fire-arm cabinet where he found and took ten bullets, 7.62 mm, with which he loaded an automatic rifle that he had for official duty, and then from the living facilities he went towards the guard post.

There he threatened to kill the watchman, Corporal Riza Alibašić, and he took two rounds of ammunition from him. Pointing the weapon at Corporal Alibašić's back, Kelmendi took him back to the living facility. Kelmendi demanded that Alibašić tell him where the soldier Safet Dudaković slept. Alibašić refused to answer. After arriving at the building, Kelmendi ordered Alibašić to step aside and then entered the sleeping room. After finding the soldier Dudaković sleeping, he opened fire and killed him, and then he sprayed shots over the other soldiers, killing Srdjan Simić and Goran Begić and wounding two more soldiers. Immediately after that, he entered the next sleeping room and wantonly sprayed shots, killing the soldier Hasim Dženanović and wounding two more soldiers.

After that, thanks to the chaos in the night, Kelmendi managed to escape from the military base. A chase was organized. Around 8:00 A.M., he was found dead approximately one kilometer away from the base with clear signs of having committed suicide.

The reaction of the military security and the guard in the base were analyzed. The reaction of the guard could have been different, but there had not been a possibility to avoid the bloodshed because of the express determination of the killer.

The killer obviously had planned his actions earlier. He had developed them and within a very short period of time he carried them out.

The unit in which Aziz Kelmendi was serving his military duty did not have any information that would have indicated that he was a sick man or a subversively oriented personality. Conversations with soldiers and officers after the crime indicate that Kelmendi was a loner who had a personal complex because he was ugly and quite nervous. Sometimes he reacted as an explosive person in an aggressive way. He socialized mostly with his compatriots [Albanians]. On two occasions he had a confrontation with the soldier Safet Dudaković.

According to his health records, Kelmendi had applied several times for a medical check-up, mostly because of digestive problems, headaches and once because of the aches in his spine.

An examination of Kelmendi's prior record outside the base shows that

Kelmendi had been punished with fifteen days of prison because he had tried to escape to Albania in 1983 and that he had behaved nationalistically in high school and at the university. He had a record of expressing an aversion toward learning the Serbo-Croatian language.

Discovery of the real motives of this crime as well as other circumstances under which it was performed will come up during the investigation.[73]

The statement suggested that the "real motives" for the shooting — that is, the nationalist conspiracy — would eventually be discovered.[74] Indeed, eight men were soon accused of being accomplices to Kelmendi — Rizah Xhakli, Abdilxhemil Alimani, Afrim Mehmeti, Pajazit Aliu, Shefqet Paqarizi, Enver Beluli, Riza Alibašić and Islam Mahmuti — six Albanians, one ethnic Muslim and one Roma.[75] The military prosecutor, Životije Bojić, emphasized that Kelmendi's act had a nationalistic and subversive background. The accomplices, the Belgrade daily *Novosti* reported at the onset of the military trial, all had given "help to Kelmendi with their incorrect attitude to commit this murder. Some of them did it through their physical activity and others strengthened the execution of this act psychologically by strengthening the will of Kelmendi to act that way."[76]

As in most political trials in Kosovo (and all of Yugoslavia at that time),[77] the evidence relied upon the sworn "confessions" of the accused in which they implicated each other for taking part in the crime.[78] For example, Pajazit Aliu was reported to have stated during the investigation, and to have signed a statement confirming his words, that "Rizah Xhakli told us that we had to help Kelmendi with what he intended to do, because he, Kelmendi, will be a hero for whom a statue will be erected in Prizren."[79] In their pre-trial statements, all of the accused, except for Pajazit Aliu, admitted that they had met with Kelmendi after 9 P.M. on September 2, 1987 (a meeting termed a "consultation") and that Kelmendi had told them there and then that he would kill on that night. During and after the trial, the accused steadfastly contended that they had been grossly mistreated while in custody and that their statements had been coerced. Despite the efforts of their defense attorneys, these claims were flatly rejected.

Much of the trial before the military court in Niš had consisted of the reading of "confessions" that focused not on the actions of the accused but on Kelmendi himself, detailing his extreme nationalist nature. The accusations ranged from Kelmendi's purported support for an independent state of Kosova, to day-to-day prejudice: "Kelmendi objected a lot to Rizah Xhakli for taking a picture with the Macedonian Albanian only because his last name was Selimovic [Serbian spelling] and not Selimi [Albanian]; Kelmendi attacked Xhakli, telling him that he was polluting himself when Xhakli told him that he dated a girl of a Serbian nationality."[80]

The defendants were to have said that Kelmendi was "poisoning" them with nationalism. Afrem Mehmeti, for example, allegedly had testified during the interrogation: "He [Kelmendi] was gloating that he was involved in demonstrations and that after the army he would go to the University and gather his friends to demonstrate again, because Kosovo should become a republic, because then only Albanians would live in Kosovo. [And then] he would go to Albania, because the living is better there than in Kosovo. . . ."[81] "Kelmendi especially hated Serbs and Montenegrins," Islam Mahmuti, another defendant, reportedly confirmed, "He also requested that soldiers of Albanian ethnicity stay together. He loved only his kind. . . . According to my opinion, Kelmendi did not love this country of ours."[82] Awkwardly worded, these "confessions" delivered a clear message apart from the crime at hand: going to national (that is, nationalistic) demonstrations was bad, and the Albanian desire to have a republic was the stuff of nationalist murderers.

Under a barrage of press coverage, all of the accused were convicted. Their alleged deeds ranged from giving Kelmendi ammunition, to knowing that the crime would take place and failing to stop it, to helping him escape. One of the harshest charges was against Rizah Xhakli, whom the Investigative Judge accused of helping Kelmendi by awakening only the Albanian soldiers, so that they could remove themselves from the barracks in which there would be shooting. This charge contradicted earlier press reports (from all over Yugoslavia) that four Albanian soldiers had been sleeping in the rooms in which Kelmendi had raided, and that they had "avoided death only by chance."[83] Nevertheless, the Paraćin Massacre was painted as an Albanian nationalist attack against Yugoslavia. After the trial, the Yugoslav press summarized: "The causes of the murder were according to the opinion of the judges deeply rooted in the upbringing [of the men], where they were taught to hate instead of to love. Those who raised them and guided them taught them nationalism, which means that love for their own nation means hatred for other nations."[84]

Rizah Xhakli and Abdilxhemail Alimani were sentenced to twenty years of imprisonment, Afrem Mehmeti and Pajazit Aliu to thirteen, Shefqet Paqarizi to seven, Enver Beluli to five-and-a-half and Riza Alibašić to fourteen, while Islam Mahmuti's sentence was two years. A set of legal challenges to the proceedings failed. Though review by higher courts was frequently used to reduce the length of sentences in political cases, the Superior Military Court confirmed and actually lengthened the sentences.[85] In addition, the reviewing court rejected the defense attorneys' technical points of appeal, tossing out a challenge to the use of audio and video records from first interrogations, during which the accused did not have access to a lawyer.[86]

Throughout the investigation and trial, the Yugoslav press ran stories touching on the once-taboo theme of Albanian nationalism. The Belgrade daily *Novosti 8* quoted a professor of criminology, Sreten Kovačević, who compared the Paraćin case to the bomb thrown at the Yugoslav embassy in Tirana in 1981, warning of increasing Albanian terrorism.[87] Similarly, *Politika* warned that all Albanians could become future Kelmendis: "[Kelmendi] was writing graffiti and occasionally refusing to speak Serbian, like tens, even hundreds of thousands of dissatisfied young Albanians. His behavior was a straight road to mass murder, and so is theirs."[88]

Numerous stories tracking the plight of the victims of the Paraćin shooting appeared in the Yugoslav press. The Belgrade papers were particularly fond of running stories about the families of victims from other parts of Yugoslavia. In one account published in the Belgrade daily *Večernje novosti*, Ana and Milan Begić, the parents of Goran Begić, one of the four soldiers killed, warned parents to keep their children away from "all nationalists, all warlords, who are attempting to seduce the young ones":

"No, my Milan and I," said Ana Begić, "do not hate all Šiptars [derogatory term for Albanians] because one of their degenerates, one of their criminals, Kelmendi, killed our Goran. . . . We are against all crimes and all criminals no matter where they came from." . . .

"I am Croatian, Yugoslav," said Milan. "Working as a machinist, I have maybe spent as much time in Serbia as in Croatia. In Belgrade, in Paraćin, the same Paraćin where my Goran died, in Svetozarevo, Kraljevo. There was no place where I did not go, in whose houses I did not sleep, and nobody ever asked me who I was, of which religion, of which nationality. . . . I know that there are nationalists both here and there, I know that they would tear apart this country like nobody in the world would. [They would] make children die for some imaginary homelands by tearing apart this real one."[89]

Even this article, which declared itself in parts to be antinationalist, exhibited deep-seated prejudice against Albanians and a larger agenda for Kosovo. The account ended with Ana, a Croat, wondering "why our Croats, if they like Šiptars so much, do not help those people to get civilized? To learn how to live off of their work. Look, there in Kosovo, none of the factories are working. Their children are not going to school, they are raising two fingers in the streets [the V sign, a symbol of freedom for Kosovo Albanians]. They want the illiterate to enter Europe. Traitors are financing demonstrations, they destroyed the lives of so many generations."[90] And Milan commented, "For me even Tito is guilty for the death of my child. Because the Kosovo [problem] should have been resolved in time."[91] All republics, the article thus suggested, should immediately take up the issue of Kosovo.[92]

Serbs, Albanians and members of other groups all grieved for the four young men who were killed and demanded that the culprits be found and held responsible. Yet the ways in which Serbs and Albanians viewed the case differed considerably.

The Truth for many Serbs is that in the Paraćin Massacre a dangerous conspiracy brewing among the sly "Šiptars" was unveiled. Although only a handful of Albanian conspirators were tried, the guilt ran much further—to all Albanian people and to the state that had failed to keep them in their place. The Paraćin case demonstrated for many the failure of Yugoslavia to put down Albanian irredenta once and for all: "Shots in Paraćin, shot from the hideout, cowardly and absurd, show how great can be the price of the aggravation and neglect of such a sensitive and serious problem as counterrevolution in Kosovo."[93] The Paraćin Massacre provided Serbs with a chance to underscore how their minority suffered in Kosovo and to demand that all of Slavic Yugoslavia make Kosovo a matter of concern.

The Truth for more "liberal" Serbs is that Kelmendi was probably a poor soul who had been mistreated in the army and who decided to take revenge. ("We all know how Albanians are treated in the army," more than one Belgrade Serb sighed.)[94] Some Serbs will today express doubt that the men accused as accomplices were actually guilty, and many will speculate that the accused were probably beaten in prison in order to extract statements. But the Kelmendi case has remained taboo, and no one has come forward from the Serbian community to demand the exoneration of the accused accomplices and the release of those still held captive.

The Truth for many Kosovo Albanians is not too far away from that of "liberal" Serbs. Many Albanians accept that Kelmendi committed the crime, speculating that he had been mistreated in the army. *Rilindja*,[95] the Albanian-language newspaper in Kosovo, issued a statement condemning the crime as a tragedy and condemning Kelmendi for the misery and irreplaceable loss that he caused to the families of the deceased and to the JNA, and for worsening the atmosphere of inter-ethnic relations and mutual trust. Even within Kelmendi's hometown area of Prizren and Dušanovo, his neighbors reportedly accepted his guilt by following the old Albanian custom of "boycotting" his family.[96] Nevertheless, most Albanians contend, Kelmendi acted alone and without nationalist motives (and, like many Serbs, Albanians are skeptical that Kelmendi committed suicide). Nearly all Albanians subscribe to the belief that those convicted of being accomplices were framed, "sacrificed in order to quiet the [public's] demand for justice,"[97] and that the only connection between the accused and Kelmendi's act was that they all were Albanians serving at the same military facility. The prosecution, they point out, did not even allege a motivation for the shooting, apart from some desire by Albanians to strike out against the rest of Yugoslavia.

The Truth for other Kosovo Albanians is that the whole incident was manufactured by Serbs to begin with, and that Kelmendi himself was innocent. With hindsight, Kosovo Albanians speculate: "It was too perfect, one person [was] killed from just about every nation." "It was too convenient, [happening] at the time when Serbia was trying to take away [Kosovo's autonomous status]." "It didn't make any sense, he [Kelmendi] was going to be released soon from the army."[98]

The Paraćin case did appear at a particularly auspicious moment for Slobodan Milošević and for Serbian nationalists, for whom the incident was only additional fuel on an already burning fire. Yet apart from the families of the imprisoned "accomplices," few Kosovo Albanians have tried in any sustained fashion to clear either the names of either those imprisoned as accomplices or Kelmendi himself. The Paraćin case made Albanians so intensely unpopular throughout the former Yugoslavia that it became taboo. Even after the outbreak of war in Yugoslavia, Kosovo Albanians did not demand action against what appeared to be the unjust prosecution of the men imprisoned as accomplices.

Following the Truths

The Kelmendi case struck a nerve throughout Yugoslavia, where mass shootings were unheard-of and killings within the army were particularly unusual and offensive. The extensive attention given in the press to the families of the victims in all parts of the former Yugoslavia made Kosovo a Yugoslav problem, not simply a Serbian housekeeping matter. Croats and Slovenes who could previously not relate to the Kosovo problem because it was too far away now had Kosovo in their living rooms on the evening news. In a time when Kosovo Albanians were trying to publicize increasing human rights abuses, coverage of the Paraćin case froze public sentiment against them. For over a year after the case concluded, rumors about the Paraćin shooting continued to abound, ranging from the Sarajevo daily *Oslobodjenje*'s discovery a year after the incident that the Albanian soldiers in Kelmendi's camp had given a "besa" (an oath) to not disclose anything about the crime,[99] to *Politika*'s allegation that Kelmendi's family had received "five kilograms of gold of 'condolences.' "[100] To some extent, the shooting and the subsequent press coverage attracted support for stripping Kosovo of its autonomous status. At the very least, the incident hindered future efforts to attract support within Yugoslavia for Kosovo Albanians when they complained of state-sponsored oppression.

Thus the real power of the Paraćin Massacre then lay in its ability to draw all of the other republics into what was once primarily a matter for the Republic of Serbia. Politicians throughout Yugoslavia, and especially in Serbia, were forced to respond to the uproar over alleged nationalist Albanians in Kosovo. While some leaders tried to quell rising anti-Albanian sentiment, others exploited it.

Slobodan Milošević rode the anti-Albanian tide. Emboldened by the public response to his earlier trip to Kosovo Polje, Milošević manipulated post-Paraćin sentiment on Kosovo to engineer the removal of Serbian politicians who had fallen out of his favor. At the Eighth Session of the Serbian League of Communists' Central Committee in September 1987, Milošević made sure that toughness on Kosovo was a requirement for political sustainability.[101] Those who were said to have grown soft on Kosovo were to see their political careers come crashing to an end. Use of these tactics at the September meeting helped Milošević get rid of his main political competitors — including Belgrade party chief Dragisa Pavlović and his former mentor and friend, Serbian President Ivan Stambolić.[102] Through playing the Kosovo card then, certain opportunistic factions in the League of Communists of Serbia triumphed and Slobodan Milošević emerged firmly as its leader.[103]

Leaders of the Yugoslav National Army (JNA) also did their best to use the Paraćin case to their advantage. To some degree, their reactions were purely defensive, as the military had to explain how such a crime could have occurred in an army barracks. As a public institution emblematic of Yugoslav society, the JNA came under particular scrutiny.[104] The military was supposed to be a stable institution, a protector of the country against both internal and external enemies, not a sitting duck that could be attacked from within. For its very survival, then, the JNA had to root out those responsible and punish them accordingly. The prosecution of Kelmendi's alleged accomplices undoubtedly helped in this regard. Also, since the incident purportedly shed light on "possible irredenta activities," the public was assured that Albanian recruits would be monitored and controlled more carefully. According to both Albanian and Serbian recruits, from this point onward Albanian recruits were increasingly given work in the armed forces as janitors and cooks and denied arms.[105] After the Paraćin shooting, Albanian recruits reported greater harassment in the military; the number of young Albanian soldiers dying under suspicious conditions rose.[106]

The Paraćin shooting, however, had a much deeper impact on the JNA than simply forcing it to make itself safe for recruits. In the atmosphere of uncertainty that followed the Paraćin case and the turmoil within the federal and republic party leadership, JNA leaders presented themselves "as being the only people capable of saving Yugoslavia's current political system, whose slogan of 'Brotherhood and Unity' was, as they saw it, under hostile attack during the 'Paraćin Massacre.' "[107] On September 23, 1987, in a widely reported speech to the league of Communists in the JNA, Admiral Branko Mamula, then the federal Secretary for National Defense, declared: "The problems in our country are growing uncontrollably, to a point which surpasses the leadership's ability to contain them. The crisis is approaching the point at which the integrity of the country and the existing social system may be endangered."[108] At the same meeting, Major-General Djordje Jovičić implicitly threatened a military takeover, warning sternly that "For a long time the Communist party and its leadership have not given us any clear-cut answers to the problems of the people."[109]

The Paraćin Massacre was one of the factors that pushed JNA leaders onto Milošević's bandwagon. From this point onward, the JNA would become increasingly partial towards the policies of Milošević, particularly with respect to Kosovo. This affinity, as Marko Milivojević has noted, "was largely indirectly expressed in the form of not saying anything remotely critical of what was happening in Serbia in relation to Kosovo."[110] While the JNA would sharply criticize other republics' new constitutions (and in particular that of Slovenia), JNA leaders would have little to say about Serbia's constitutional changes stripping Kosovo and Vojvodina of their autonomy.

Other federal and republic leaders and institutions were similarly forced to respond to the Paraćin Massacre. Many Yugoslavs at the time commented that the Kelmendi incident would never have happened if the police had reacted in time to prevent "lunatics and criminals blinded by hate" from influencing the Albanian youth in Kosovo.[111] Even if not seen as an Albanian nationalist, Kelmendi was viewed as the unruly one that got away—due to bureaucratic and police incompetence, a failure of republic and ideological institutions, a decline in lawfulness and certainty. Municipal authorities (which were at that time still comprised heavily of Albanians), including the police and the justice system, were called upon to explain themselves and to take more stringent actions against all forms of "irredentism." This in turned opened the door to the firing of Albanian police, judges, teachers and other civil servants— with a greater cloak of legitimacy this time, as the purges were said to be in the interest not only of Serbia but of Yugoslavia.

The Paraćin shooting, as Branka Magaš has observed, also opened the door for the "orgiastic assault in sections of the Belgrade press on the Albanian population as a whole, an assault which spilled over into actual (and in places seemingly coordinated) violence against Albanian citizens and their property in towns throughout Serbia (similar incidents occurred also in Macedonia and Montenegro)."[112] The Belgrade press ran story after story of victimized Kosovo Serbs.[113] In other parts of Yugoslavia, stories of nationalist-motivated violence in Kosovo served in various ways to prove the demise of Tito's "Brotherhood and Unity" and to open debate on nationalism. For some Yugoslavs, the increasing freedom to talk publicly about nationalism did not necessarily lead to the promulgation of nationalism, or the slander of Albanians or people of any other national or ethnicity. Instead, for some the opening fostered criticism of all forms of nationalism. However, at this point of time, the line between "critical analysis" and "advocacy of nationalism" was paper thin.

By the time 1987 came to a close, the politics of both Yugoslavia and Serbia was entering into a new era. Milošević had arisen as the savior of Serbs, and on this platform he was successfully consolidating power and removing most of the old guard identified with the Titoist regime; anti-Albanian sentiments ran at an all-time high throughout the country, as Kosovo had become a Yugoslav problem; JNA rumblings and attacks against the Communist Party leadership for failing to take action on Kosovo were causing further political shakedowns; intellectuals in Belgrade, and for that matter Zagreb and Ljubljana, were hard at work on plans to overhaul (or overthrow) the Yugoslav system;[114] Kosovo Serbs and their nationalist supporters in Belgrade were encouraged to take radical action to press their agenda; and the press was testing its freedom to write about nationalism and national conflict. The stage was set for the passage of the constitutional amendments that would strip Kosovo of its independence.

Notes

1. "Documents, Petition to the Assembly of the Socialist Federal Republic of Yugoslavia and to the Assembly of the Socialist Republic of Yugoslavia," dated January 21, 1986; reprinted in *The South Slav Journal* 9, nos. 1–2 (spring-summer 1986), 107. All quotations in the next two paragraphs are from this petition, hereafter referred to as the "January 1986 petition."

2. This was again a reference to the call in the Communist bloc since WWII to protect against Serbian domination in Yugoslavia. See chapter two, above, and Wayne S. Vucinich, "Nationalism and Communism," in *Contemporary Yugoslavia: Twenty Years of Socialist Experiment*, ed. Wayne S. Vucinich (Berkeley: University of California Press, 1969), 243.

3. The subject of the second sentence is unclear. Whose objective is an ethnically pure Kosovo *and* "further conquests of Serbian, Macedonian and Montenegrin lands"? Only Albanians? To the extent that an antecedent is provided by the preceding sentence, the subject is not just Albanians but all of non-Serbian Yugoslavia, and perhaps all of the non-Serbian Communist bloc that had been talking about "Serbian hegemonism."

4. Interview with author.

5. Interview with author.

6. Interview with author.

7. Laura Silber and Allan Little, *The Death of Yugoslavia* (London: Penguin Books, BBC Books, 1995), 33–34.

8. An English version of the Memorandum can be found in Kosta Mihailović and Vasilije Krestić, *Memorandum of the Serbian Academy of Sciences and Arts: Answers to Criticisms* (Belgrade: Serbian Academy of Sciences and Arts, 1995) (offering an explanation to the text and then including the original). I use this version of the Memorandum because it is the one presented by the authors as most authentic, and because English-speaking readers may locate this text. (Like nearly all references in this book, it can be found in the Harvard University library system.) All references herein to page numbers for the Memorandum refer to the English version as reprinted and paginated in this volume, and they are given in the form "Memorandum, oo." As this text cannot go

into a full analysis of the Memorandum but rather concentrates on the sections on Kosovo, readers are advised to consult the full text.

9. Mihailo Crnobrnja, *The Yugoslav Drama*, 2d ed. (Montreal: McGill-Queen's University Press, 1996), 97.

10. Philip J. Cohen, "The Complicity of the Serbian Intellectuals in Genocide in the 1990s," in *This Time We Knew: Western Responses to Genocide in Bosnia*, eds. Thomas Cushman and Stjepan G. Meštrović, 39–64 (New York: New York University Press, 1996), 39.

11. See Memorandum, 81–82. Philip Cohen has asserted that the authors included Serbian patriot Vasa Čubrilović (author of the 1937 memorandum on the expulsion of Albanians); Dorbica Ćosić, novelist and essayist (and soon to be president of Yugoslavia); and internationally recognized Serbian philosophers Svetozar Stojanović and Mihailo Marković. See Cohen, "Complicity of the Serbian Intellectuals," 40–41, 51.

12. Memorandum, 76–80.

13. Ibid., 119.

14. Ibid., 95–100.

15. Ibid., 107.

16. Ivo Banac, "The Dissolution of Yugoslav Historiography," in *Beyond Yugoslavia: Politics, Economics, and Culture in a Shattered Community*, eds. Sabrina Petra Ramet and Ljubiša S. Adamovich, 39–65 (Boulder, Colo.: Westview Press, 1995), 55.

17. In their defense of the Memorandum, the authors said: "There is nothing strange in the fact that [Milošević] may have seen some of the problems or solutions in the same or similar light as the document in question. It is more likely that he did not learn about the existence of these problems for the first time in the memorandum, but that he found in it confirmation for some of his personal observations." Memorandum, 80.

18. Memorandum, 117.

19. Memorandum, 117–18 (emphasis added). As the authors have complained about critics quoting the text out of context, I quote this section at length.

20. Memorandum, 125.

21. Memorandum, 127.

22. Ibid.

23. Memorandum, 107, 120–21.

24. Memorandum, 119.

25. Memorandum, 118.

26. Memorandum, 127. The Memorandum uses the term "Kosovo and Metohija," a traditional Serbian name for the Kosovo region.

27. Ibid.

28. Memorandum, 128.

29. Ibid.

30. Memorandum, 130.

31. Memorandum, 133.

32. Memorandum, 138.

33. "Bosniac" is a term for Bosnians which could encompass all nations but

which in reality today refers almost exclusively to Bosnian Muslims. It is now a preferred term, used, for example, in the Dayton Peace Accord, the agreement that ended the war in Bosnia-Herzegovina. See the General Framework Agreement for Peace in Bosnia and Herzegovina, reproduced in UN Doc. A/50/790-S/1995/999 in the form initialed in Dayton on November 21, 1995, and appearing in 35 I.L.M. 89 (1996).

34. For an account on free speech in Yugoslavia written contemporaneously with the Memorandum, see Oskar Gruenwald and Karen Rosenblum-Cale, eds., *Human Rights in Yugoslavia* (New York: Irvington Publishers, 1986)(see in particular the chapters by Nikola R. Pašić, "Political Persecutions in Yugoslavia: A Historical Survey"; Zachary T. Irwin, "Law, Legitimacy and Yugoslav National Dissent: The Dimension of Human Rights"; Aleksa Djilas, "From Dissent to Struggle for Human Rights"; and Michael M. Milenkovitch, "Djilas and Mihajlov: From Revolution to Reform").

35. Memorandum, 15.

36. Ivan Stambolić, *Rasprave o SR Srbiji* (Debates on the Socialist Republic of Serbia) (Zagreb: Globus, 1987), 218–19.

37. Lenard J. Cohen, *Broken Bonds: Yugoslavia's Disintegration and Balkan Politics in Transition,* 2d ed. (Boulder: Westview Press, 1995), 54.

38. Tim Judah reports that Milošević said: "The appearance of the Memorandum of the Serbian Academy of Arts and Sciences represents nothing else but the darkest nationalism. It means the liquidation of the current socialist system of our country, that is the disintegration after which there is no survival for any nation or nationality. . . ." Tim Judah, *The Serbs: History, Myth and the Destruction of Yugoslavia* (New Haven, Conn.: Yale University Press, 1997), 160, quoting *Vreme/ Dossier: From the Memorandum to War* (Belgrade, n.d.).

39. Quoted in Ivo Banac, "Serbia's Deadly Fears," *The New Combat* (autumn 1994), 39.

40. This event is recounted in Crnobrnja, *The Yugoslav Drama,* 101.

41. "Central Committee" refers to the Central Committee of the League of the Communists of Yugoslavia.

42. See Silber and Little, *The Death of Yugoslavia,* 37.

43. *Danas,* April 28, 1987, quoted in Darko Hudelist, *Kosovo, bitka bez iluzija* (Zagreb: Center for Information and Publicity, 1989), 35.

44. *NIN,* May 3, 1987, quoted in Hudelist, *Kosovo, bitka bez iluzija,* 35.

45. U.S. State Department, *Country Reports for Human Rights Practices 1987* (Washington, DC: Government Printing Office, 1988), 1084.

46. In his eyewitness remembrance of the event, *Borba* journalist Slavko Čuruvija recalled a scenario somewhere in between the two reports. Although the police did not charge on command, they did react with violence against the protesters before they began throwing rocks. According to Čuruvija, this was business as usual for the police: "The police officers, Serb and Albanian, unsheathed their batons and, as expected on such occasions, began dealing out blows." Slavko Čuruvija and Ivan Torov, "The March to War (1980–1990)," in *Yugoslavia's Ethnic Nightmare: The Inside Story of Europe's Unfolding Ordeal,* eds. Jasmika Udovički and James Ridgeway (New York: Lawrence Hill Books, 1995), 82.

47. As translated in Silber and Little, *The Death of Yugoslavia*, 37.

48. See Slavoljub Djukić, *Kako se dogodio vodja: borbe za vlast u Srbiji posle Josipa Broza.* (Belgrade: Filip Višnjić, 1992), 124–130. See also Slavoljub Djukić, *Izmedju slave i anateme: Politička biografija Slobodana Miloševića* (Belgrade: Filip Višnjić, 1994).

49. Ćuruvija and Torov, "The March to War," 83.

50. See Hudelist, *Kosovo, bitka bez iluzija*, 36.

51. U.S. State Department, *Country Reports for Human Rights Practices 1986* (Washington, D.C.: U.S. Government Printing Office, 1987), 1095.

52. Pedro Ramet, "Yugoslavia 1987: Stirrings from Below," *The South Slav Journal* 10, no. 3 (autumn 1987), 21.

53. Article 3 of the Changes and Implementations of the Law on Restrictions of the Transactions, published in "Službeni glasnik RS" 28/87. This law was struck down by the decision of the Constitutional Court of Yugoslavia on June 27, 1990. However, Serbia disregarded this decision and re-enacted essentially the same law ("Službeni glasnik RS," 22/1991). See Nekibe Kelmendi, *Kosovo pod bremenom diskriminatorskih zakona Srbije; Činjenice i dokazi* (Priština: n.p., 1992); Dušan Janjić, "National Identity, Movement and Nationalism of Serbs and Albanians," in *Conflict or Dialogue: Serbian-Albanian Relations and the Integration of the Balkans,* eds. Dušan Janjić and Shkelzen Maliqi (Subotica: Open University, 1994), 160n.292.

54. Ramet, "Yugoslavia 1987," 21.

55. Tanjug, "Pucnji u Jugoslaviju" (Shots at Yugoslavia), *Borba*, September 4, 1987. A similar report appears by Tanjug, "Težak zločin u paraćinskoj kasarni" (Heavy Crime in Paraćin Garrison), *Vjesnik*, September 4, 1987.

56. "Keljmendi pucao u Jugoslaviju" (Keljmendi Shot at Yugoslavia), *Politika*, September 4, 1987.

57. "Peaceful Protests of Youngsters," *Borba*, September 11, 1987.

58. Ibid.

59. "Shots That Hit Us," *NIN*, September 11, 1987. The "independence" of *NIN* has shifted over time. At times it has been more aligned with the government than other times. With respect to the Kelmendi shooting, *NIN* was following a line more suitable to those who wanted to play up national differences.

60. See, e.g., "In the Eyes of Truth," *Novosti 8*, September 10, 1987; "The Last Moment," *Politika*, September 8, 1987.

61. Tanjug, "Zločin planiran" (The Crime Planned), *Večernji list*, September 8, 1987.

62. Z. V., "Pokopan Goran Begić" (Goran Begić Buried), *Večernji list*, September 8, 1987.

63. "Dušanovo—leglo nacionalista" (Dušanovo—A Den of Nationalists), *Politika*, September 8, 1987.

64. Tanjug, "Odgovornost za zločin" (Responsibility for the Crime), *Večernji list*, September 8, 1987.

65. "Tragovi vode u Dušanovo" (Traces Lead to Dušanovo), *Politika*, September 7, 1987.

66. Ibid.

67. Aleksandar Tijanić, "Zašto to radimo?" (Why Do We Do That?), *Danas*, September 15, 1987.

68. "Keljmedijevi moraju iz Dušanova" (Kelmendis Must Move Out from Dušanovo,) *Politika*, September 10, 1987.

69. "In Prizren (Disciplinary) Measures Brought against the Former Keljmendi Teacher," *Politika Ekspres*, September 25, 1987.

70. "Who Does Favors to Keljmendi?" *Politika*, September 8, 1987.

71. Ibid.

72. Ibid.

73. Second announcement about the Paraćin murder given by the federal Secretary for the National Defense, printed in *Novosti 8*, September 10, 1987 (direct translation with minor grammatical corrections and clarifications).

74. In their statements to foreign embassies and to the press, Serbian and federal authorities attributed the "real motive" in the Paraćin Massacre to anti-Yugoslav, Albanian nationalist feelings. See U.S. State Department, *Country Reports for Human Rights Practices 1987*, 1080.

75. Tihomir Nesić, "Zločin, organizovano" (The Crime, Organized), *NIN*, January 24, 1988.

76. Miroslav Zarić, "Krivica velika i dokazana" (The Guilt Large and Proven), *Novosti*, January 26, 1988.

77. See Helsinki Watch, *Open Wounds: Human Rights Abuses in Kosovo* (New York: Human Rights Watch/Helsinki Watch, 1994).

78. See, e.g., Miroslav Zarić, "Krivi su drugi" (Others are Guilty), *Večernje novosti*, January 21, 1988; Tanja Tagirov, "Svjedoci o noći strave" (Witnesses of the Night of Horror), *Večernji list*, January 14, 1988.

79. Miroslav Zarić, "Krivi su drugi" (Others are Guilty), *Večernje Novosti*, January 21, 1988.

80. Ibid.

81. V. Tomašević, "Aziz Keljmendi nije voleo ovu našu zemlju" (Aziz Kelmendi Didn't Love This Country of Ours), *Politika*, January 20, 1988.

82. Ibid.

83. See, e.g., "Shots That Hit Us," *NIN*, September 11, 1987. Note that at the time of this article, *NIN* was also printing articles with a decidedly anti-Albanian tone, so it is unlikely the journalist had fabricated it.

84. "Shots That Hit Us," *NIN*, September 11, 1987.

85. See "Povećane kazne za zločin" (Punishments for the Crime Increased), *Vjesnik*, May 8, 1988; N. Spasić, "Posle žalbi—strože kazne" (After Complaints—Harder Punishments), *Borba*, May 9, 1988.

86. "Potvrdjeno 20 godina zatvora" (Twenty Years of Imprisonment—Confirmed), *Večernji list*, November 1988.

87. Momčilo Popović, "Teror po planu" (The Terror According to the Plan), *Novosti 8*, September 10, 1987.

88. "Poslednji trenutak" (The Last Moment), *Politika*, September 8, 1987.

89. "Umrli smo sa njim" (We Died with Him), *Večernje novosti*, September 26, 1990.

90. Ibid.

91. Ibid.

92. Other articles in the Serbian press indicate the Begićs' real attitudes toward Albanians. Another account two days earlier had reported:

Exactly on the day of the third anniversary of the Paraćin murder [September 3, 1990], Albanians, helped by the HDZ [the Croatian Democratic Union, led by Franjo Tudjman], were collecting signatures for their republic and their Constitution in Zagreb in front of the National Theater. The mother of Goran Begić, Ana, was outraged by the fact that Albanians chose to undertake their "dirty actions" in Zagreb on the exact day of the third anniversary of her son's death. She went in front of the Theater and confronted Albanians: "You are not people. . . . Is there anyone to stop this. . . . Why did you kill my child? What human rights are you asking for? I am the one from whom you took a human right. The mother's right to happiness. . . . Go away from here. Go away. . . . This is my Zagreb, my Homeland. Go to your Albania!"

Gordana Brajović, "Suze na zdencu života" (Tears on the Well of Life), *Večernje novosti*, September 24, 1990.

93. Tanjug, "Pucnji u Jugoslaviju" (Shots at Yugoslavia), *Borba*, September 3, 1987.

94. Interview by author.

95. Like the large papers in Belgrade, *Rilindja* had always been at least indirectly influenced by the authorities. It was taken over by the Milošević regime in 1990 and closed. Today a version of the paper is printed abroad.

96. Tanjug, "Pokop zločinca" (The Burial of the Criminal), *Večernji list*, September 6, 1987. Also, the Union of Veterans and the local Socialist Party (mixed Serb and Albanian groups) had reportedly tried to evict Kelmendi's family from their home. Aleksandar Tijanić, "Zašto to radimo?" (Why Are We Doing It?), *Danas*, September 15, 1987.

97. Interview by author.

98. Interviews by author.

99. For an example from Sarajevo, see Djuro Kozar, "Besa i suze" (An Oath and Tears), *Oslobodjenje*, November 20, 1988. The author of the article assumes that Albanian accomplices of Kelmendi gave "besa," an Albanian oath for which one would die if necessary, not to talk and not to admit anything. A more sympathetic article than most, the journalist says that even the conspirators are humans and that they only recently discovered just now how and for what they were used.

100. " 'Condolences' in Gold" ('Saučešće' u zlatu), *Politika*, November 4, 1988.

101. The story of this meeting is brilliantly told in Silber and Little, *The Death of Yugoslavia*, 39–47.

102. "Pokusaj Ivana Stambolića da obmane javnost" (Ivan Stambolić's Attempt to Deceive the Public), *Politika*, December 6, 1987.

103. For more on the downfall of Milošević's rivals, see Sabrina P. Ramet, *Nationalism and Federalism in Yugoslavia, 1962–1991*, 2d ed. (Bloomington, Ind.: Indiana University Press, 1992), 225.

104. For more on changes in the JNA during the time of transition, see James Gow, *Legitimacy and the Military: Yugoslavia in Crisis* (London: Pinter Publishers, 1992); Marko Milivojec, "The Armed Forces of Yugoslavia: Sliding

into War," in *Beyond Yugoslavia: Politics, Economics, and Culture in a Shattered Community*, eds. Sabrina Petra Ramet and Ljubiša S. Adamovich (Boulder, Colo.: Westview Press, 1995), 67–98; Miloš Vasić, "The Yugoslav Army and the Post-Yugoslav Armies," in *Yugoslavia and After: A Study in Fragmentation, Despair and Rebirth*, eds. David A. Dyker and Ivan Vejvoda (New York: Longman, 1996), 116–37.

105. Interview by author.

106. See Helsinki Watch, *Open Wounds*.

107. Marko Milivojević, "The Yugoslav People's Army: Another Jaruzelski on the Way?" *The South Slav Journal* 11, no. 2–3 (summer-autumn 1988), 1.

108. Ibid. Fleet Admiral Branko Mamula took early retirement in May 1988.

109. Ibid.

110. Milivojevic, "The Armed Forces of Yugoslavia," 72.

111. See "Zločin u kasarni" (A Crime in the Garrison), *Danas*, September 8, 1987 (accusing the municipal community of Aziz Kelmendi for not reporting on his deviant behavior and antistate activities).

112. Branka Magaš, *The Destruction of Yugoslavia: Tracking the Break-Up 1980–92* (London: Verso, 1993), 109–10.

113. Allegations ranged from the possible to the fantastical, from cases in which individuals were named to those in which the unknown perpetrators were simply assumed to be Kosovo Albanians. One story that has become legendary among Kosovo Serbs is that of Albanian doctors who were deliberately stunting the growth of Serbian children and killing their Serbian patients. For example, Dušanka Pjevac, a nurse who had worked in the main hospital in Priština before moving to Lazarevac (in Serbia proper), accused a Dr. Mekuli of "destroying [Serbian] children." According to Pjevac, Dr. Mekuli had been taking "bone core" from her little girl for scientific experiments, and, as a result, the girl would not grow to normal height. Dušanka Pjevac, "Special Treatment for the Demonstrators," in *Kosmetski dosije,* Milorad Djoković (Požarevac: Prosveta, 1990), 16.

114. For "rumblings from below" in 1987, see Ramet, "Yugoslavia 1987."

INTERVIEW

Searching for Kelmendi

Earrings and glasses. Even before I open my mouth, earrings and glasses mark me as a foreigner. As we approach police roadblocks, I slip them into my pocket. On the road from Priština to Uroševac [Ferizej on the Kosova Albanian map], as on any trip between two sites of potential conflagration, "automotive safety checks" are a given. Sometimes the officer standing alongside the road motions all cars to pull over, but usually he chooses his prey selectively, often by license plate number. If you don't live in the area, you are expected to have a good reason for being there. If the police ever ask us, we are on the way to or from Kopaonik, the ski resort. I ask my friends why we can't just say that we are visiting family. "Then we would have to give their names," they say.

"The police stop the Albanian cars," my Kosovo Albanian friends claim. I try my best to pick out the Albanian cars, the Albanian drivers, to distinguish Albanians sitting in cars from Serbs sitting in cars. I can tell the humanitarian aid cars by their license plates, the logos stenciled on their doors, by their stops at the UN-run (and UN-customer only) gas station just below Priština. But the other cars all look alike to me. The Albanian cars may come from the same town as the Serbian cars, they may have the same number of passengers, they may be as well or as poorly maintained. "How do the police do it?" I wonder. "They just know," my friends are convinced.

Sometimes the officer will just ask for the drivers' identification, ask a few questions and then motion us along. He may also do some kind of actual auto check. "Turn on the right turn signal. The left. Beep the horn." The main police checkpoint on the road to Uroševac has become such a permanent insti-

tution that the officers have constructed a little wooden shed in which they can keep warm.

In Kosovo, police checkpoints are like visits to the principal's office. We each have our own checkpoint personas, which we slip on for the occasion. Much to her passenger's horror, V. becomes insolent, refusing to speak in Serbian, although she studied medicine at the faculty in Zagreb. She will snap back at the cop in Albanian, English, French or Italian, but, alas, she has forgotten all of her Serbian. In contrast, S. has been known on occasion to correct the young traffic cop's Serbian. Korab just nods his head and obediently does whatever the cop wants him to do. R. acts like he is rushing to an important occasion. And I just hope that no one notices me.

The clouds had yet to clear on the morning in December 1994 when I was to visit the mother of Rizah Xhakli, one of the men jailed eight years earlier as a conspirator in the killing at the Paraćin military base. He had been charged with helping Aziz Kelmendi carry out his crime. He had recently published a letter in Borba, the Belgrade daily, proclaiming his innocence, but nothing came of it. All of the Belgrade human rights groups that I had asked about the Kelmendi case had simply shaken their heads. It was a tragedy, they said. It happened a long time ago. Why would I be interested in resurrecting such a horror? Leave it alone, they warned.

Kosovo Albanians were also less than thrilled that I want to spend time investigating the Kelmendi case. They too feared that the case was too old, too difficult to unravel. There are too many tragedies today, they said. In Uroševac and in the towns throughout Kosovo where relatives of the accused conspirators live, however, the Kelmendi case is not over. For those with enough money to pay the way, Kelmendi now means a monthly trip to the prison to visit their son, nephew, grandson, cousin, brother, uncle. Kelmendi means hiding other male relatives outside the country so that they can avoid their military service and, perhaps, a similar fate. Kelmendi is a lost teenage romance, a broken family, a nightmare, a party for a young man's release.

For "Jev," Kelmendi is another wrong that she works to right. Many of Jev's friends have been beaten and jailed for "subversive activities," but somehow she has escaped scrutiny. While many of the human rights workers in Uroševac have had their passports taken away, Jev remains free to travel. Maybe it is because she is "not political"—that is, she holds no post in the LDK, the Albanian political party. Yet many of the men who are similarly "not political," including young journalists and video-makers, have been either jailed or forced into hiding. Maybe it is because she is a woman. But Uroševac is one place in which Albanian women political leaders have been harassed and jailed.

I visit Jev periodically over three years. Each time we meet, new Albanian political leaders and human rights workers have been harassed or arrested. Jev remains untouched. She can't explain why she is left alone. "I am waiting for my time," she shrugs, "Someday they will come for me." Remembering these words, I am glad to see her again. She is waiting on a street corner with a plastic shopping bag and a thin black backpack.

Jev greets us casually. There has been a "disturbance" at the building they use for human rights meetings, she says, so we should go directly to Rizah's house. Apart from the two main streets running in and out of town and the roads around the city square, most of the roads in Uroševac are unpaved, giving it the look and feel of a large village. Jev directs us through a maze of narrow dirt streets and dusty brown cement walls to a rusty blue metal gate in the middle of a lane. A young man appears out of nowhere and escorts us through the mud to the door of a small white house. A dozen shoes are stacked neatly outside the door. We add ours to the pile and slip inside.

A handful of women greet me: Rizah's mother, a neighbor, a cousin and young activists who are just there to help out. We squeeze into a rectangular room that serves as living room, bedroom, kitchen and dining room. I take a seat on a fuzzy gray sofa. From where I am sitting, I can watch the women on the other side of the room cooking in a wide assortment of metal pots. They are constantly in motion. The older one moves among the others, giving orders. A couple of men from the local human rights group show up, and we try to shoo them away. "She needs to talk to her alone," Jev explains. A bit offended, they agree to wait outside.

A young woman in blue jeans and a black pullover serves us tea. Another young woman passes around cigarettes. Then they both fade away into the kitchen part of the room. Jev explains that one of them, H., a twenty-one-year-old student, was recently sent to prison for thirty days after her youth group organized a party in a private house to honor five young local Albanians who had been killed by police in 1982 and 1984. "She is still very scared," Jev whispers. They picked on her at the police station because she spoke no Serbian. "She's the best girl in Kosovo," Rizah's mother jokes, "because she speaks no Serbian." Later, the student would tell me about the police who threatened to shoot her at the border with Albania, the inspectors who beat her with a stick across her hands and legs, the "bad feeling" she had when they called her an "Albanian whore" and the hopelessness she felt when she heard women screaming in another cell and could do nothing to help them. Her story, she would say, is "nothing special."

Rizah's mother eases her way into a chair across from my sofa. She has hazel eyes; gray hair sticks out of a tan scarf. She begins by apologizing for her ill-health, for her small house, for the bad weather. She knows I am here to talk about her son in prison, but she insists on starting first with her other family members.

I was fifteen years old when I came here [to Uroševac] from Gnji-lane. And now I am alone.

I have five daughters and three sons. I thought I would have a big family and a good life but I am alone. One son was in New York; he died there and they brought back his body. One son is in Holland and one son is in jail. One daughter is in Norway, one daughter in Swe-den, one in Switzerland, and the other two live here in Kosovo.

My son was about twenty years old when he went into the army. I just hoped that he would come back as soon as possible and marry here. I thought good things would happen for him, but things went wrong.

When I heard on TV that something had happened [at the Paraćin military base], I felt very bad. One of my cousins came and told me. He said that something had happened and mentioned the name of Kelmendi. Five days later, my son called and said that he had been called in for informative talks. I asked him, "Are you involved in this?" and he said, "Mother, don't you know me, I'm not involved in anything." He wasn't afraid because he didn't do anything.

The next time he called, he asked me, "Are the children going to school? Are you at home? Did the police take you?" And I asked him again, "Are you involved in that case," and he said, "I am not in-volved. I hope that you will be well."

That was a Wednesday. I went the next Sunday to Niš. He was in prison in Niš.

They stopped me at the prison gates. The guard went to the camp to speak with one of the superiors who was not in uniform. I told him what had happened and that I had raised nine children and no one ever had any problem with them. What had happened? I want to see me son, I said. They told me it wasn't possible. They were polite. There were two guards.

I was pretending that I was not afraid, but I was very much afraid. I was worried that they would take my [male] cousins who were with me.

[The old woman stops suddenly. "Drink your tea," she commands coldly. "I need a break, every time I think about this I get a headache." She stands and disappears.

"We have an agreement to not cry," Jev says, her own eyes dry and angry. "I've seen so many people beaten! Killed! Her husband, you know, was taken many times by the police. He was wounded during the 1981 demonstrations and he died four years later."

"How was he wounded?"

"He was a fireman and he was shot by civilians through the window." Jev says that they never discovered who had shot him. "He could never work after that," she adds.

Mrs. Xhakli returns and, without explanation, begins where she left off.]

I wasn't allowed to see my son. During the first forty-five days, I went to the prison three times and I didn't see him at all. The first time I saw him was five days before the trial.

When I saw him I was shocked. I could tell that he had been treated very, very badly. His lips were turned inside. He was shaking. He was on the other side of the bars and I wanted somehow to touch him. I said, "Give me your finger," and the guard said, "Don't." I said, "Find out who really killed those kids and leave my son alone."

The only thing we spoke about was "How are you?" I told him, "Be brave, you know that we were always accused for no reason."

["Did you talk to a lawyer?" I ask in my best human rights lawyer way, "Did Rizah have a lawyer?"

She becomes confused. A lawyer? A private lawyer? Right before his trial, Rizah saw a lawyer who had been given to him by the court. "We had been skeptical about lawyers," Jev explains, "It didn't seem like a matter of law."

The trial had lasted five weeks. The family came and went throughout the entire trial. There was always a relative in attendance.

"Were you hopeful?" I wonder.

The old woman laughs. No, she never really had any hope.]

When they convicted him, I was very, very tired. I didn't hear when they said fifteen years. My daughter was with me and she started to cry. She said, "They convicted him for fifteen years." I told her, "Don't cry."

After the trial was over, one of those guys convicted with Rizah started to cry. He hugged Rizah. Rizah said, "Don't cry, be a man."

When it was all over, they allowed me to see him. Just me. There was a translator there so they could write down everything we said. When I entered the room, I told him, "You see I am not crying. I am happy you are alive and some day you will tell me what really happened." He said, "Mother, please. . . ." And I said, "Don't please me," because my heart had come to my mouth. I was confused.

He said "mother" once again. He said, "Don't cry for me even if I knew that the soldiers would be killed. But I am telling you that I didn't know."

During the initial investigation, he told the police that he did not do anything. But later he had been tortured so much that he said he did it. At trial then he said that he didn't do anything.

During the time that I saw him, he never said that they were beating him, but later I found out that they were beating him.

Independent human rights groups have expressed concern that those accused of being accomplices to the Paraćin killing were indeed beaten. Albanian defense lawyers have argued that their medical condition in court showed that their prior confessions had been coerced. Proving "what really happened" has become more difficult, since witnesses — the JNA recruits from Slovenia, Croatia, Bosnia-Herzegovina, Macedonia and "Yugoslavia" (Serbia and Montenegro) — now live in what have become separate countries.

Rizah's mother stirs her tea. She likes it strong and sweet. She would like to visit Rizah more often, she says, but it is expensive and she is alone. The International Federation of the Red Cross pays sixty German marks each month to families with one person in prison. She sends her son-in-law to pick up the money. The transportation to and from the prison costs roughly forty-five marks, leaving not enough for sleeping and eating. "When I go," she says, " I come back the same night."

"Three months after the trial some man came here and took Rizah's passport. [He was an Albanian.] I told him, "If I was sure that my son did that, I would burn the passport two times."

Rizah's mother believes that "the Paraćin case was just some kind of camouflage for the mistreatment of Albanians in the army." Like many Kosovar Albanians, she believes that even if Kelmendi did open fire in his barracks, he went berserk due to the mistreatment he had suffered. Her own son, she is sure, has been framed. She forbid her other sons from serving their military service. "When they [the state authorities] wanted them for the army, I told my sons to leave."

"Are you lonely?" I ask.

"Sometimes I remember when they were little. It's like they were here. I think especially about the one who died [the son in America]." Despite her bravado, the old woman begins to cry. "Every time I see him [Rizah], I like

to have something in my mouth because it is difficult to speak. My mouth cramps. I'm with God now. I hope that God will save my mind."

When we leave, I discover that our shoes have been newly polished. Jev notices me noticing. "They are from a village," she says, "they always polish their guests' shoes." We squish though the mud into our awaiting car. Electricity is being rationed, and we have less than an hour of light left. Supposedly there is not enough electricity to go around because of sanctions, but the public secret is that Serbia has been selling electricity to Croatia. Each part of "reduced" Yugoslavia loses electricity each day, for one to eight hours, but the blackouts in Kosovo are among the longest and most frequent.

The next day, we travel to Gnjilane to see Rizah's uncle, his lawyer and a couple of other people concerned with the case. The air is cold and crisp but the sun shines brilliantly and the curving road to Gnjilane is unusually magnificent. The concrete ugliness of Priština ends abruptly and we begin climbing into green rolling hills.

We pass through a small Serbian-populated village and are stuck behind a slow-moving funeral procession. About forty people dressed in black are walking behind a horse pulling a cart. It is bad luck to pass a funeral. Korab dips left into a tiny crossroads and drives like crazy. We wind past a couple homes and the paved road suddenly ends at a pasture. Korab drives across the grass, finds a dirt road, turns again and drives as quickly as possible. Somehow we end up at the main road, about one hundred meters in front of the funeral procession. "And that's not bad luck?" I wonder. Korab shakes his head. Cutting in front of the procession falls within the rules of fate.

Gnjilane is small and unusually quiet. Spared the concrete high rises of Priština, the town boasts a few boutiques stocked with goods from Turkey. On a nice day, the shopping streets look even inviting. We stop at a friend's travel agency, purportedly to use the phone and ask directions, but really the visit is purely social. Our friend is Turkish; he speaks Turkish, Albanian, Serbian, English and some German. With so many Kosovar men traveling abroad to work, travel agencies are a big business in Kosovo, and his agency is doing well. During the holidays, he says, it is almost impossible to get a seat on a plane or bus to Switzerland or Germany, the destinations of choice. Given the sanctions, he says, travel to Turkey has picked up as well; most of the small goods sold in shops come from Turkey or Greece.

Rizah's uncle lives just down the street in a nondescript new apartment building. The gray, damp hallways are lined with an assortment of doors: fancy wooden panel doors, less ornate wooden doors, metal doors, battered doors. The uncle's door opens into a warm, stylish apartment. Rizah's uncle is equally stylish in a white pressed collar shirt, gray vest and blue slacks, using a fancy leather-encased lighter to light his slim cigarettes. He pulls out a folder filled with newspaper clippings and legal papers: his Rizah file. He explains that ever since Rizah's father died, he has tried to be a father to him.

Before Rizah went into the army, I was very afraid for him. At first Rizah was sent to Macedonia, and then he was sent to Serbia two or three weeks later. I had a friend in the army, an Albanian, a captain. When Rizah's mother called and told me where he was, I immediately called my friend. I told him that if it was possible, please help Rizah in any way. I wanted him to make Rizah a driver so he would be less likely to get in trouble. I didn't want Rizah to be around other Albanians because he could have trouble.

[We are interrupted by a phone call; the uncle leaves briefly and then returns. He says his daughter was on the phone.]

It was normal for Albanian soldiers to group together in the same camp, because many of them did not know the language. They were the same so they sought each other out. Officers of the state security work in the army. They are always watching what Albanians are doing. I didn't want Rizah to be any part of that.

My friend said, "Yes, I can help you." After a few days he called and said that Rizah was sent to Paraćin and that he would drive a truck there and that he would be busy all day long. I was very happy about that.

After seven weeks, he came home on vacation. He visited me for about one hour and that was the last time I saw him [before the incident].

About a month later I heard on TV that something had happened in Paraćin. Two weeks from that moment, Rizah was accused. Rizah's mother called me. I was afraid to be interested in the case. I had forever been afraid of these kinds of things. They are always accusing Albanian soldiers.

After the trial I went to see him in Belgrade. Because he doesn't have a father, I have a right to see him like a father. We couldn't say anything to each other because someone was there listening.

After the conviction, the uncle engaged a lawyer, Estram Estaffah. The lawyer was unable to convince the appellate court that Rizah had been coerced into making his confession. When Ćosić was still president of Yugoslavia, the uncle appealed on Rizah's behalf for clemency. "When Rizah found out, he said, if I discover that you wrote an appeal for clemency, I won't allow you to visit me. If you do that, it means I was guilty." The uncle filed a request for clemency anyway, but it was denied.

Unsure what really happened in the Kelmendi case, the uncle nonetheless contends that his nephew is innocent. "My personal opinion," he speculates, "is that one of two things happened. Either this case was directed by the army from the start, or it was directed after the killings."

According to the uncle, on the day of the shootings Aziz Kelmendi's mother and father came to the camp to visit their son. Rizah had acted as their translator [with the guards, who did not speak Albanian]. If Rizah had known something was going to happen, his uncle says, he would have escaped. "The first official statement from the army was that the massacre had been prepared [as a conspiracy]. They said this without any investigation. They had to find someone to blame."

The uncle shows me Rizah's letters from prison, his letter to the press, the court papers. The phone rings again. This time no one is there. Korab is concerned. From the window we can see a police car. The atmosphere in the room has changed. The uncle makes a couple of suggestions about follow-up interviews. One soldier who had been accused was released; perhaps I should talk to him.

Our meeting ends abruptly with a handshake at the door.

For the next month I try to find the soldier who had been released. Either he is truly out of the country or no one wants to help me find him. I keep pressing away at the Kelmendi case, asking questions, following leads. I get nowhere. A couple of months later, an Albanian acquaintance tells me that he heard I should stop investigating Kelmendi. "Move on to another story," he says, "It may be bad for your health."

"Who says this?"

"I don't know," he answers.

I closed the Kelmendi case where I had started. Everyone already had their Truth.

Figure 1. Market day, Prizren, Kosovo. Photograph by Lisa Kahane, 1995.

Figure 2. Buying watermelon, Prizren, Kosovo. Photograph by Lisa Kahane, 1995.

Figure 3. The red roofs of Prizren, Kosovo. Photograph by Lisa Kahane, 1995.

Figure 4. Resourceful transportation, Suva Reka, Kosovo. Photograph by Lisa Kahane, 1995.

Figure 5. School kids, Suva Reka, Kosovo. Photograph by Lisa Kahane, 1995.

Figure 6. Young man on market day, Prizren, Kosovo. Photograph by Lisa Kahane, 1995.

Figure 7. Doing chores, Suva Reka, Kosovo. Photograph by Lisa Kahane, 1995.

Figure 8. Bus stop, Prizren, Kosovo. Photograph by Lisa Kahane, 1995.

Figure 9. Elementary school, Pristina, Kosovo. Photograph by Alice Mead, 1995.

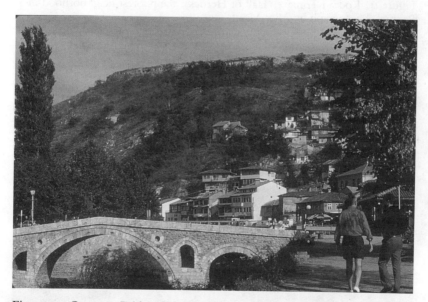

Figure 10. Ottoman Bridge, Prizren, Kosovo. Photograph by Alice Mead, 1995.

Figure 11. Kodra i Trimave (Hall of Heroes), the poorest neighborhood in Pristina. Photograph by Alice Mead, 1995.

Figure 12. Middle-class apartments with satellite dishes, Pristina 1995. Photograph by Alice Mead, 1995.

Figure 13. Highschoolers. Photograph by Alice Mead, 1995.

Figure 14. Prizren mosque. Photograph by Alice Mead, 1995.

Figure 15. Border with Albania (west of Prizren). Photograph by Alice Mead, 1995.

Figure 16. On the outskirts of town, Peć. Photograph by Alice Mead, 1994.

Figure 17. Dirt road in the middle of town, Uroševac. Photography by Julie Mertus, 1994.

Figure 18. Proud hostess, Peć. Photograph by Julie Mertus, 1994.

FOUR

The Alleged Poisoning of Albanian School Children, 1990

Laying the Foundation: 1988–1990

Slobodan Milošević opened 1988 in command of the League of Communists of Serbia.[1] His package for a renewed Serbia included economic reforms, especially the rooting out of bureaucratic waste and inefficiencies (the "anti-bureaucratic revolution");[2] political restructuring, the recentralization of the federal government (at the expense of the autonomy of other republics)[3] and the "unification" of Serbia (through the dissolution or annexation of the autonomous provinces, Kosovo and Vojvodina); and a "national awakening" involving the protection and promotion of the culture and rights of Serbs everywhere, especially in Kosovo. A constitutional change was needed, he contended, in order to give Serbia the kind of control it needed to protect the rights of Serbs to effect economic and political change. His argument, like that of the Memorandum of the Serbian Academy of Sciences and Arts two years earlier, was that the autonomy of the provinces allowed for de facto republics within Serbia, disadvantaging Serbia in relation to other republics and unfairly hindering the ability of Serbia to make reforms.

Milošević crafted his argument against the backdrop of social, political and economic unrest sweeping the country. The economic condition of Yugoslavia had reached a nadir. The World Bank was knocking on Yugoslavia's door, forcing it into a second phase of debt rescheduling, and strict IMF conditions were being placed on the economy. Saddled with austerity measures, Yugoslavia's production plummeted and inflation spiraled, rising from 190 percent in 1986 to 419 percent in 1987 and 1,232 percent in 1988.[4] According to official statistics, salaries in the country dropped by 24 percent in 1988, and with constant shortages and a decline in real purchasing power, living standards fell to those of the mid-1960s.[5]

While many Serbs were concerned about Milošević's demagogic methods and nationalist rhetoric,[6] his platform of economic reforms and a correction of the "inefficiencies" of the 1974 Constitution held broad appeal. Even those who thought of themselves as "liberal intellectuals" were "impressed with his determination to 'right the wrongs' in Kosovo."[7] For many Serbs at the time, "liberalism" meant little more than the protection of the human rights of Serbs.[8] When Milovan Djilas was asked about Milošević in 1989, he responded as would have many of the Serbian intellectuals of the day: "I agree with the policy of sorting out the relations of Serbia with her Province [Kosovo]. I think that he is right in that respect and the mass meetings were a positive thing. At last a Communist has realized that the absurd situation in which the largest nation has yet to win the status that all nationalities enjoy must be put right."[9] Milošević promised something for everyone. Communists were drawn to his traditionally strong position within the party as well as his economic plans, which, although displayed as "mixed" market systems, actually maintained many state functions,[10] and nationalists were attracted to his strong rhetoric on Kosovo and unity for the Serb nation. As independent Serbian journalists have observed, Milošević had "succeeded in tricking both the communists and the nationalists; the communists believed he was only pretending to be a nationalist and the nationalists that he was pretending to be a communist."[11]

The years 1989–90 were, to use Ivo Banac's terminology, the "Yugoslav non-revolution," when a peculiar kind of post-Communism was turning into "post-Yugoslavism."[12] Over these two years, Mirjana Kasapović has explained,

Serbia merged its national populist movement and newly institutionalized Serbian policy with an agreement on a fundamental programmatic point; namely, to reverse the disintegration of Serbia by protecting Serbs in Kosovo and consolidating Serbia into a single sovereign state. The result was an exchange of legitimacy in which the Serbian ethnic social movement actively supported the Serbian party state in order to further the cause of republic consolidation at any price. . . . Essential to this agreement was the understanding that the movement and the party-state depended on each other for support.[13]

The merger of the Serbian social movement with the state-party produced an overwhelming force that, as a matter of state policy, crushed nearly all forms of political differentiation within state and nation.

Milošević was the main beneficiary of this phenomenon; Kosovo was his scapegoat. Milošević emerged as both a "man of the people" and the man of the state. And it was the populist-nationalist campaign over Kosovo that elevated him into the spotlight, winning him the support of the Serbian Orthodox Church and Serbian émigré groups, including foreign Orthodox clergy, and creating the momentum he needed to seize even greater power.[14]

With the blessing of the Serbian state, Serbian populism in 1988 moved from a marginal phenomenon to a dominant one.[15] From July to mid-October 1988 alone, three million people would attend Milošević-sponsored "popular forums" about Kosovo—the so-called "meetings of truth."[16] To orchestrate these momentous gatherings, populist-nationalist organizations emerged, such as the Committee for the Defense of Kosovo Serbs[17] and the Committee for Organizing Departures to the Protest Gatherings Outside the Province.[18] As brutally as Kosovo Albanian protests were shut down, "meetings of truth" were graciously supported by the Belgrade regime. In effect, the power and authority of these Serbian "parallel" organizations far surpassed those of many formal institutions.[19]

The mass rallies over Kosovo were a useful instrument of intraparty struggle. Not surprisingly, then, the Serbian protests spread at the moment "the decomposition of the League of Communists accelerated."[20] Declining support for the party and political spats within the party elite diminished its ability to function. "The growing political vacuum," Branka Magaš has observed, "was being filled with the politics of national chauvinism, especially in Serbia and Macedonia, often systematically fanned by party and state functionaries."[21] When told by the League of Communists in August 1988 to stop his mass demonstrations, Milošević refused, openly flaunting his disrespect for the party's authority and usurping that authority for his own. No one stopped him.

Starting in Kosovo, the demonstrations moved northward. Most of those in attendance were workers who had been paid to attend, but their motives for attending made little difference; on television, a crowd was a crowd. The slogans that emerged were more or less the same everywhere: "Slobodan Milošević, don't let Serbdom down!" "Slobodan, we will march with you to Kosovo!" "Kosovo is ours—don't let Enver [Hoxha, leader of Albania] take it away!" "Serbia asks: when will Slobodan replace Tito?" "Slobodan, we are all yours—only traitors are against you!" "We are all Serbs!" "Only unity can save the Serb!" "Give us arms!"; "Death to Albanians!" "We shall kill [Albanian leader Azem] Vllasi!" "Hang Vllasi and [Fadil] Hoxha [one of the Kosovo Albanian politicians]!"[22]

The rallies were linked directly to specific political agenda of Milošević and his supporters. "What was remarkable about these demonstrations was not just their size and intensity," Marko Milivojevic has observed, "but the fact that they were used by Milošević to topple his Serbian Party rivals in Novi Sad [the capital of Vojvodina] and Titograd [the capital of Montenegro, now Podgorica], and to put immense pressure on his Albanian [party] enemies in Priština, the capital of Kosovo."[23] In the summer of 1988, staged demonstrations in support of the Serbs of Kosovo began in Novi Sad. The demonstrations became more and more militant, with men wearing Chetnik nationalist war mementos demanding the ouster of Albanians, chanting "We want weapons." Demonstrations in Vojvodina began again in the fall of 1988, continuing until the entire Vojvodina party leadership had resigned. In October-November 1988, Milošević engineered the fall of the Kosovo and Montenegrin leaderships.[24] And in January 1989, those who had survived were forced out.[25] In all cases, Milošević supporters filled the vacated seats.

Another aim of the rallies was to draw support for Belgrade taking control of Kosovo, by means of constitutional amendment or otherwise. On November 17, 1988, central Albanian leaders were dismissed from the party and removed from the federal Presidency. In protest, miners from the Trepča mining complex in Kosovska Mitrovica (then Titova Mitrovica) marched fifty-five kilometers from the mine to Priština, where in freezing temperatures they camped out with students in front of the local headquarters of the party. Marchers carried Albanian flags together with Yugoslav ones and hailed the 1974 Constitution. These demonstrations were the last pro-Yugoslav and pro-Tito demonstrations, and the last to end without bloodshed.[26]

Two days later, Serbs in Belgrade held a protest of their own, called Bratstvo i Jedinstvo (Brotherhood and Unity), the "meeting of all meetings." More than a million people turned up, largely workers bused in from other towns.[27] Kosovo was at the heart of Milošević's battle cry.

"We are not afraid," he exhorted. "We enter every battle intending to win. . . . Every nation has a love that eternally warms its heart. For Serbia it is Kosovo."[28] The catchphrase of the day was "the people have happened" or—"the people have become a nation."[29] Serbia's national awakening, which had begun in Kosovo, was now ringing in Belgrade and reverberating throughout Yugoslavia.

The meeting worked. Six days later, the federal Assembly adopted provisions that essentially cleared the way for Serbia to take greater control over Kosovo and Vojvodina. Then, on February 3, 1989, Serbia's national assembly passed amendments to Serbia's constitution that centralized control over some essential functions in Belgrade. From then on, Serbia had more direct control over Kosovo's security, judiciary, finance and social planning.

Kosovo Albanians feared that these measures would only be a step toward the revocation of Kosovo's autonomous status. They were right; the Serbian government was moving rapidly in this direction. Each part of Serbia had only to vote for the changes. The Serbian Assembly would readily agree to centralize control in Belgrade, as would the provincial government of Vojvodina, which was already firmly in Belgrade's grasp. Persuading the Kosovo Assembly to vote itself out of existence was another story. How could Milošević achieve this feat when Albanians were a majority in Kosovo, and when even Milošević's Albanian apparatchiks refused to reduce Kosovo's autonomy below that granted by the 1974 Constitution?

Not only Kosovars but all Yugoslavs looked on with great interest, as the impact of the constitutional change would be felt on the whole of Yugoslavia. Even if they lost their status as provinces in Serbia, Kosovo and Vojvodina would still retain their seats on the federal Presidency. The maneuver would thus give Serbia de facto control over three of the eight seats on the Presidency. With Montenegro safely in Serbia's pocket and Macedonia usually following as well, Yugoslavia would be Serbia's.

Milošević's strategy for winning the constitutional vote was to eliminate all powerful Albanian leaders who could possibly stand in his way. Purges of top Kosovo Albanians from political office culminated by the end of January 1989 with the ousting of top Albanian leaders Kaqusha Jashari, Sinan Hasani and Azem Vllasi. Vllasi's ouster was especially dramatic, given that he was the most important Albanian politician in the Yugoslav Federation and that he had long enjoyed what appeared to be a supportive relationship with Milošević. Vllasi, Jashari and Hasani were replaced with three intensely unpopular "loyal Albanians" (that is, loyal to Milošević). Rahman Morina, the head of the Kosovo secret police, became the head of the League of Communists of Kosovo; Husamedi Azemi became Priština's head of the party; and Ali Shukria became Kosovo's representative in the Central Committee of the League of Communists of Yugoslavia.[30]

A pivotal event, not only for Kosovo but all of Yugoslavia, began on February 20, 1989, when the Trepča miners called another strike. The entire Albanian underground crew of 1,300 men refused to eat or to leave their mine until the three provincial officials imposed by the Serbian party were removed. Work stoppages and demonstrations in support of the miners broke out all over Kosovo. In sensational accounts, the Serbian press warned that the strikes were organized by a "secret committee," quoting the "statute" of the committee as saying that their real goal was "to annex Šiptar regions of Yugoslavia, liberate them and unite them with Albania."[31] The press accused the miners of secretly eating (bananas, some accounts said) and of not really suffering hardship. One account even compared the conditions in a mine to a health resort.[32] In spite of these claims, at least 180 miners were hospitalized during the strike and numerous others received medical treatment afterwards. Morina, Azemi and Shukria were said to have resigned, and the miners gave up their strike, convinced that they had won. As soon as the strike ended, however, the resigned leaders returned to office.[33]

A mass rally was held in Ljubljana, Slovenia, in support of the miners' strike. A parade of speakers condemned Serbian repression in Kosovo. Jože Školc compared Albanians in Yugoslavia to Jews in World War II.[34] This statement, broadcast on Serbian national television, intensely irritated Serbs, who had long seen themselves as the martyrs and drawn parallels between themselves and Jews.[35] But the speaker who really provoked Belgrade was Slovene Communist Party leader Milan Kučan. Kučan told the crowd: "The Trepča miners are defending the rights of citizens and Communists in Kosovo to elect their own leadership. . . . We protest against fanning the psychosis of the state-of-emergency and we have warned that a quiet coup is taking place before our eyes which is changing the face of Yugoslavia."[36]

Kučan's speech aligned Slovenia's struggles with those of Kosovo Albanians. The enemy of both was Serbia, and more specifically Slobodan Milošević. As Susan Woodward has observed, Kučan's challenging Milošević to a duel, allegorically, on the field of Kosovo was "merely a proxy war" (as the Slovene foreign minister after 1990, Dimitrij Rupel, later admitted) over the future of Yugoslavia.[37] Kučan's speech "also played right into the hands of Milošević, whose speeches since April 1987 had attempted to equate the individual rights of Serbs with those of the nation and its unity and to identify Milošević as the protector of the Serb nation against external foes."[38] Ljubljana, like Tirana and Priština and soon Zagreb, could now be said to be conspiring against Serbia.

Serbs watched the pro-Albanian rally in Ljubljana on television and reacted in horror. Why was Slovenia turning against them? Hundreds of thousands of demonstrators gathered in front of the federal Assembly—and this time they weren't all paid to be there. In the middle of downtown Belgrade, they screamed for arms, demanded the arrest of Albanian leaders and threatened to take their mob on to Ljubljana. Milošević waited for twenty-four hours before finally addressing them. He declared: "This rally shows that no-one can destroy the country because the people won't let them, the people are the best guarantee, we are going to get all honest people in Yugoslavia to fight for peace and unity. Nothing can stop the Serb people and leadership from doing what we want. Together we will fight for unity and freedom in Kosovo. We have to change our constitution, and this will mean progress for all people in Yugoslavia. Unity for the Communist Party and the people."[39] Once again Milošević drew together his common themes: the image of the embattled Serbs, victimized but ultimately heroic; the need to unify the Serb nation; the imperative of Kosovo for Serbs and the impending contest there; and the need to change the constitution of Yugoslavia. Milošević's threatening response to Slovenian activists actually aided their cause by encouraging a broad range of anti-Milošević Slovenes to coordinate their activities and to push forward a common agenda.[40]

Milošević's hard stance also encouraged the federal Assembly to take immediate action on Kosovo. In a dramatic discussion of the Kosovo crisis in the federal government, Lazar Mojsov, a member of the Presidency, warned of a conspiracy of Albanian and foreign intelligence networks against the territorial integrity of Yugoslavia.[41] The federal government was persuaded to initiate "emergency measures" in Kosovo, imposing curfews, riot police and administrative detention. Key industries were placed under compulsory work orders, prohibiting strikes, and a large number of federal troops were ordered into Kosovo.[42] It was the fourth such deployment into Kosovo since 1945 (the others being in 1968 and 1981).[43]

Milošević pledged to arrest Vllasi, the man who had always been viewed by Albanians as Milošević's right hand man. Vllasi was complicating Milošević's plans by opposing the constitutional changes. On March 2, 1989, Vllasi was arrested along with fourteen other Albanians accused of being leaders in the February demonstrations. They would be imprisoned for more than five months before being formally charged.[44]

Kosovo's assembly was to vote on the amendments to Serbia's constitution on March 23, with the vote for the Serbian Assembly set for March 28. Secret police "prepared" recalcitrant deputies to vote "correctly."[45] Under extreme pressure, the Kosovo Assembly reportedly voted almost unanimously to accept the amendments, in effect voting itself into oblivion. Some of the Kosovo Albanian delegates later accused Vukašin Jokanović, the President of the Kosovo Assembly, of engineering a fraudulent vote. These delegates described a tumultuous scene in which 400 people crowded the assembly floor; only about 150 were voting members of the assembly. No roll call was taken, and when the vote was taken about 60 persons, many of whom were not entitled to vote, raised their hands in favor (failing to reach the required two-thirds majority vote for constitutional changes); perhaps ten voted to oppose and the rest abstained. Jokanović reported a victory. This account, though described by independent monitors,[46] never received widespread attention. The vote stood.

On March 28, 1989, the Serbian Assembly announced that Serbia was "whole" again—as expected, the amendment had passed. Borisav Jović, the Serbian representative to the federal Presidency, exulted that nothing could be "more natural, more humane, more democratic, for the Serbian people, than, in accordance with their peace-loving traditions, to enter again upon the stage of history and make a demand in the form of the simplest, the most noble formula of justice and equality. . . . [Serbs are] the people who in the modern history of the Balkans made the greatest sacrifices and demonstrated the greatest scope and evidence of its love for freedom and democracy. . . . Serbia is equal now."[47] Belgrade overflowed in joyous celebration while, just a couple of hundred kilometers to the south, military police started to face off against Kosovo Albanians. Massive demonstrations were held in nearly all towns in Kosovo. Federal police used tanks, helicopters, tear gas and automatic weapons against the demonstrators. Twenty-five people were killed, according to official reports, including two police officers; Amnesty International has suggested that as many as a hundred demonstrators may have died.[48]

The federal units that had been sent to Kosovo were ill-prepared for what they would find. Some witnesses say that at times they fired un-

controllably; others say that some units from Slovenia and Croatia refused to shoot; others say that Kosovo Albanian police started to fight
the other police.[49] According to official accounts, the police did not
begin firing until one police officer had been killed by gunfire.[50] Human
rights groups, however, termed the killings of Albanian civilians a "massacre," finding "no justification for firing automatic weapons on the
assembled crowds. The Yugoslav security forces possessed ample crowd
control equipment and troops to prevent riots by other means."[51] Expert
analysis of the wounds of victims in this and other demonstrations suggested that police had used high velocity firearms, shooting many people
in the back as they were running away. Helsinki Watch summarizes one
investigator's findings:

A forensic medical specialist from the Netherlands, Dr. Banard Cohen,
visited Kosovo in 1989 and 1990 on behalf of the U.S.-based Physicians
for Human Rights. He concluded . . . on the basis of interviews with Kosovar medical personnel and reviews of x-rays and photographs that there
was evidence with respect to violence in Kosovo in 1989 and 1990 that at
least two victims had been shot "in the back and/or though the head. . . ."
The sizes and shapes of the entry wounds and exit wounds of the victims
are consistent with high velocity fire arms.[52]

The demonstrations ushered in a new round of crackdowns against
Kosovo Albanians. The government has admitted to hunting down the
participants in the demonstration, bringing misdemeanor charges
against 1,180 and criminal charges against fifty-six.[53] The number of Kosovo Albanians detained, fined, dismissed from their jobs or dismissed
from the party appears to be much higher.[54] An estimated 250 Kosovo
Albanian shopkeepers were put on trial for supporting the demonstration and numerous other persons were charged for verbally supporting
Albanian nationalism.[55]

As part of a measure to counter future demonstrations, police also
subjected 237 Kosovo Albanians to "isolation," not formally placing
them under arrest but rounding them up and holding them in custody,
without charges, for three months, usually without access to attorneys
or their families. According to the U.S. State Department, "The majority
[of the isolated] were held not in Kosovo but in prisons in Serbia, where
they were subject to beatings, cold, inadequate food and harsh interrogations. Isolated prisoners were reportedly detained under the suspicion of belonging to illegal organizations, contact with 'hostile' émigré
groups, illegal arms trafficking, and organizing strikes and demonstra-

tions."[56] The way authorities used "isolation" in these cases was against Yugoslav law, which allowed isolation through house arrest but not imprisonment.

The other Yugoslav republics looked on events in Kosovo with horror, and a handful of journalists began to offer harsh critiques of the actions. In one of the more alarming reports, journalists from the Ljubljana weekly *Mladina* reported operations by Serbian death squads against recalcitrant Albanians.[57]

One month later, on June 28, 1989, a million Serbs from all over Yugoslavia (and, some say, the world) embarked on a pilgrimage to Kosovo Polje to attend the six hundredth anniversary celebration of the Battle of Kosovo. On this flat expense of land just above present-day Priština, Serbian Tsar Lazar was killed by the Ottomans in 1389. A monument marking the spot where he supposedly fell carries the words of Prince Lazar himself, rallying Serbs to their duty to defend Kosovo:

> Let him who fails to join the battle of Kosovo
> Fail in all he undertakes in his fields.
> Let his fields go barren of the good golden wheat,
> Let his vineyards remain without vines or grapes. . . .

Through the years, narratives of the Battle of Kosovo have been preserved through oral poetry, Byzantine frescos and epic ballads.[58] Although scholars have examined this event in excruciating detail, what actually happened has been remembered to suit the conveniences of the day.[59] Tsar Lazar is said to have been given a choice between a reward for surrender or a fight to the death. Lazar, the story goes, refused to betray his nation and died in glory. His defeat was said to usher in five hundred years of Turkish domination over Serbia. In fact, the Ottoman conquest did not occur until seventy years after the Battle of Kosovo;[60] but historical accuracy aside, in Serbian and Montenegrin folklore the event is portrayed as a great defeat of a Christian army by a Muslim army. Michael Sells explains: "In the passion play commemorating the battle of 1389, Lazar is portrayed as a Christ figure with disciples (sometimes explicitly twelve), one of whom is a traitor. The Turks are Christ-killers, and the Judas figure, Vuk Branković, became the ancestral curse of all Slavic Muslims."[61]

The importance of the Kosovo myth to Serbian politics, as Gale Stokes has observed, "lies not in these actual histories but in its selection by the nationalists as the appropriate symbolic universe of Serbianness. It provides a vocabulary of experiences outside of time."[62] In 1989, the "great defeat" served as a reminder of Serbian suffering and the need for Serbs to defend even their motherland, Kosovo. Mention of the Ottoman Empire also triggered the image of the evil Turks—shorthand for all Muslims, including Kosovo Albanians (regardless of their religion) and Yugoslav ("Slavic") Muslims, who were considered to be race traitors for converting to Islam during Ottoman rule.[63]

Milošević had long capitalized on the "vocabulary of experiences" created by the myth of Kosovo. For him, the anniversary extravaganza for the Battle of Kosovo was tailor made. He arrived at the ceremony by helicopter in a display of power and took the place of honor on a stage decorated with the emblems of Serbian nationalism—including an enormous Orthodox Cross encircled by four Cyrillic C's (for the slogan "Only Unity/Harmony Saves the Serbs"). The entire federal leadership was in attendance to hear his warning:

Serbs in their history have never conquered or exploited others. Through two world wars, they liberated themselves and, when they could, they also helped other people to liberate themselves. The Kosovo heroism does not allow us to forget that at one time we were brave and dignified and one of the few who went into battle undefeated.

Six centuries later, again we are in battles and quarrels. They are not armed battles, though such things cannot be excluded yet.[64]

By capitalizing on the greatest myth in Serbian folklore, Milošević pitted Serbs not only against Albanians but also against the other enemy identified by the Kosovo myth: Slavic Muslims.[65] It would be the last time the entire federal leadership would stand on the same stage in unity with Milošević.

Almost simultaneously with his triumph at Kosovo Polje, Milošević unveiled plans to stem the tide of Serbs leaving Kosovo. Unemployed Serbs from the rest of Yugoslavia were told that jobs and accommodations were waiting for them in Kosovo. At the same time, property laws would prohibit Serbs in Kosovo from selling their land or home to Albanians. A law in Serbia (enacted in 1987) restricted the transaction of property between private individuals and nonstate legal bodies in a manner that disadvantaged the ability of Serbs and Albanians to sell land to each other. The transaction would be allowed by the republic's Secretariat for Finances if "the sale did not influence a change in the national structure of the population or emigration of the members of the certain nation or national minority and when that transaction does not cause restlessness or insecurity or inequality with the citizens members of another nation or national minority."[66] Milošević called the plan an effort to boost Serbia's economy. Kosovo Albanians saw it as another wave of recolonization.[67] Indeed, the proclaimed purpose of the law was to prevent moving of Serbs and Montenegrins out of Kosovo, by prohibiting the trade in real estate between Serbs and Montenegrins on one side and Albanians on the other.[68]

On August 28, after being held for six months in prison without an indictment, Azem Vllasi was accused of "counterrevolutionary acts, destruction of brotherhood and unity and destroying the economic base of the country." In addition, although he was in prison during the March demonstrations, he was charged with responsibility for the deaths of Albanian protestors who had been shot by police. Vllasi was the "moral author" of the crime, the prosecutor reasoned, because he had inspired Albanians to protest.[69] Vllasi's trial, which began on October 30, was adjourned and resumed several times but never completed. It was called a "Stalinist show trial" by international human rights observers.[70]

In a sign that Yugoslavia was cracking, intellectuals and politicians from other republics stepped up their criticism of Serbia's increasingly chauvinistic policies. Slovene intellectual Taras Kermauner published "Letters to a Serbian Friend" in 1989, urging his Serbian colleagues to "abandon [their] demands for a united rail system, for a common educational program, for the Kosovization of Yugoslavia, for a unitary Yugoslav official language, for homogeneous society! For everything that the other nations reject! Should you travel with us to Cythera, which is to say Civil Society, you will be able to live as you wish! Nobody will expect you to submit yourself to others, nor will you need to crack the whip over the insubmissive."[71] In protest of Serbia's tactics in Kosovo, first Slovene (on February 4, 1990) and then Croatian (April 4, 1990) police units were recalled from Kosovo. In December 1989, after Slovenia forbid demonstrations in support of Serbia's Kosovo policy, Serbia unilaterally declared a boycott against Slovenia.[72] Similarly, when Croatia refused to go along with political developments in Kosovo, Serbia stepped up support for Serbian separatist groups in Croatia.[73]

By the beginning of 1990, Yugoslavia was at a breaking point. The year began with a disastrous meeting of the Fourteenth Special Congress of the League of Communists of Yugoslavia in Belgrade. After Belgrade remained recalcitrant on its platform on centralization and on Kosovo, the Slovenian and Croatian delegations walked out. The Congress was adjourned indefinitely. As the attention of all republics turned to their own elections, Milošević's putative strategy to restore a more centralized federation evaporated.[74]

Police pressure and martial law continued in Kosovo. On January 24, riot police and military troops used water cannons and tear gas to disperse an otherwise peaceful protest of forty thousand Albanians in Priština. This time, in addition to the release of Azem Vllasi and other political prisoners, the demonstrators were asking for free elections, the release of political prisoners and an end to the state of emergency in Kosovo. The protests grew more violent and, between January 24 and February 3, at least 30 people were killed and 110 wounded.[75] In a move that young Kosovo Albanians will never forget, Belgrade university students countered with their own demonstrations, calling for weapons to be sent to protect fellow Serbs in Kosovo.[76]

A full-fledged state of emergency was declared, and federal troops were sent in again. This time there were fifteen thousand troops, mainly from Niš (Serbia), Skopje (Macedonia) and Titograd (Montenegro), along with two thousand militia troops from Serbia's Internal Affairs Ministry.[77] Demonstrations in Priština, Uroševac, Podujevo and other places in Kosovo were broken up with tear gas and baton-swinging police. Armored police cars (which look like military tanks) and police wearing gas masks moved into Kosovo cities in large numbers, giving Kosovo the feel of a country at war. By March 1990, Kosovo society had grown almost completely segregated. Although Albanians and Serbs worked together and lived in the same neighborhoods, they kept their distance. Even Serbian and Albanian school children were kept apart, with the children attending the same schools in shifts, or at the same time but in different rooms.

In 1990, all of Yugoslavia was having an identity crisis. The unified party system had fallen apart, and across the country multiparty elections were being called on the republic level. Dissent was on the rise, with struggles for power and survival being played out at all levels of society.[78] The conflict in Kosovo provided the tension that temporarily kept the structure together — and eventually pulled it apart.

The Alleged Poisoning of School Children

At the end of March and beginning of April 1990, the Yugoslav press reported that thousands of Albanian school children had mysteriously fallen ill. The first reports suspected some kind of poisoning. The Zagreb daily *Večernji list*, for example, reported that on March 19, in the Podujevo schools Djuro Djaković and November Eighth, a heavy odor caused drowsiness, headaches and faintness among students.[79] The students were helped by their professors to a local health care facility, and from there many were later urgently transferred to the policlinics of the Medical Faculty in Priština. The paper quoted Dr. Muharem Avdiu from the internal ward of the policlinic in Priština as saying that "what's happening is poisoning with neurotoxic effects, and the cases are quite serious." One student who did not suffer any ill effects, Bashrije Berisha, "said that when they sensed the fragrant smell they started to open the windows, but that didn't help, and she saw her classmates falling on the floor."[80]

A teacher from Kosovska Mitrovica similarly testified that "the children started to get sick. It seemed to happen all at once. They were passing out and having problems breathing." She called other adults to help her bring them to the local clinic. One of the doctors who saw them remembered, "They kept coming in, one after the other. We didn't know what was happening with them. We didn't know how to diagnose it. Our main goal was to stabilize them. We gave them sedatives and vitamins."[81] After a brief examination, he told many of the parents to take their children to the hospital.

The hospital in Priština was packed with students and their terrified parents, Albanians said. "It was just horrible," one young doctor recalled. "There was a long line of cars coming down [from Kosovska Mitrovica] to Priština. The patients were just streaming in. Some of them were half-conscious."[82] "We didn't know what to do," an attending physician said, "we weren't sure what had happened."[83] Doctors, teachers and former students throughout Kosovo described the same symptoms: nausea followed by other symptoms such as stomach pain, dizzy spells, problems breathing, coughing, racing of the heart and hallucinations.[84] The next day, *Večernji list* quoted Dean Alush Gashi, the head of the medical center in Priština, as saying that the only symptoms were red eyes and heavy breathing, and that he could not rule out some kind of infection.[85] *Večernji list* set the number of students affected by the symptoms at over one thousand.

On March 22, two thousand parents, teachers and students of Albanian ethnicity gathered at the youth center Boro and Ramiz in Priština and decided to stop sending their children to school until the authorities explained what was happening. *Večernji list* reported that at the same event "it was said" (the article does not say by whom) that the poisoning case was "an act of the destructive forces from Priština to Belgrade, a fascistic act emerging from the ideology of Vuk Drašković [a Serbian nationalist and rival of Milošević]."[86] The same edition of *Večernji list* carried a report by Tanjug, the official Yugoslav press service, stating that young Albanians had started to take revenge for the poisoning.[87] Specifically, a group of young Kosovars in Podujevo had allegedly attacked the Serbian and Montenegrin students, accusing them of poisoning their friends. According to the report, twenty students were injured: "Among the injured ones there was Dragana Nikolić, a student in the third grade of high school, who was beaten up by her Albanian peers because of the accusation that she had kept the poison together with her books in her bag. A similar thing happened to her cousin, Nebojša Djukaić."[88]

Tanjug reported that "[Albanian] nationalists continued with the destruction," breaking some windows and doors on the building of the local committee of the Communist Party and beating up the secretary, Dragan Smigić. Then they tried to penetrate to the Serbian and Montenegrin homes, but the tenants had locked themselves in. "Around 4 P.M., nationalists stopped the train at the train station on the Niš—Priština track. As in a scene from a crime movie, they jumped into the train looking for a man whom they suspected of poisoning the water in Podujevo."[89] According to *Vjesnik*, at least fifty such attacks against Kosovo Serbs occurred within two days of the alleged poisoning.[90]

Meanwhile, the Serbian press and, increasingly, other Yugoslav press reported a far different scenario than that recounted by Albanian physicians. Although Albanian parents and school children were indeed driving to hospitals in droves, the Serbian press told the public that they were not really sick. Writing in *Novosti 8*, Miloš Antić quoted Serbian physicians who said that the Albanian doctors prevented them from seeing the patients and, when they did see the children, their symptoms quickly disappeared. Antić interviewed two hospital patients whom he found outside of the hospital. Sefedin Bajroshi [Albanian or Turkish] was reported to have said:

As soon as they brought those kids it was obvious that there was nothing wrong with them. They were walking through the halls and chatting. At one moment one of the doctors told them in Albanian to go to their beds and be sick because the president of the Executive Committee of Kosovo, Jusuf Zejnulahu, was coming, and they did it. Anyway, until two in the morning I was watching some shameful scenes. In the morning, when one of them would just wash his face with water, [that one] would fall into convulsions and warn others. I drank that water in front of them and I am fine. If there was something wrong with them it was because of nicotine poisoning, because they were smoking all night long, one cigarette after another.[91]

Bajroshi's roommate, Pavle Krstenović [Serb], was also quoted as saying: "After everyone was accommodated suddenly there was a complete chaos at the clinics. Everyone suddenly became healthy, they shouted, sang, chased each other until the morning. When somebody would approach, they ran to their beds and simulated illness. They kicked us out this morning because they are expecting new patients from Suva Reka and Uroševac."[92]

Borba, the influential Serbian daily, similarly analyzed what it found to be contradictions in the treatment of the "poisoned" patients:

For example, in the release list [from the hospital] for the fifteen-year-old Veldete Shala from Podujevo, the diagnose is "neuro-intoxication," but the objective finding contains something that annuls that diagnosis, and that is "she is oriented in space, conscious, and the neurological findings are completely fine." As a therapy for such normal condition a vitamin C infusion was prescribed and the patient was released with the diagnosis "poisoning of the nervous system, which occurred in the school yard or in the classroom." The patient received this therapy only for one day. The other days in the patient's records are empty, but in the [hospital] release report it says that she was released from the hospital after five days.[93]

Borba called for a full investigation into the poisoning and prosecution of the real perpetrators. These and other accounts fueled the belief already prevalent in Serbian communities that the whole episode was a sham concocted by Albanians.

Rumors about the incidents discussed on the streets were reflected in the press. The media wondered why the only victims were Albanians, derisively mocking the notion of a poison that "chooses a nationality."[94] Sporadic accounts of isolated cases of Serbian students who exhibited similar symptoms were used by the mainstream press to prove that the incidents could not have been intentional attacks against Albanians, and by those sympathetic with Albanians to prove that a poisoning had indeed occurred.[95] Although unintended victims were afflicted, Albanians contended, the segregation of school children had made a selective poisoning possible.[96]

The media also speculated as to why no trace of a canister or some other mechanism for delivery of the poison had been found. The Serbian press contended that nothing was found because nothing existed. Some Kosovo Albanians said that at least one suspicious canister had been found that could have contained the poison, but that the Serbian authorities had withheld the information and stopped any investigation.[97] Albanian residents of various towns in Kosovo, including Kosovska Mitrovica and Podujevo, also said that suspicious men had been seen around schools, thus compounding rumors that a deliberate poisoning had occurred and that the (Serbian) authorities were doing nothing to discover and disclose the truth. Serbian authorities, however, denied that any suspects ever existed.[98]

The Croatian daily *Vjesnik* carried an announcement of the presidency of the League of Communists of Kosovo accusing Albanians, speculating that "it is possible that the poisoning of students is a part of a special war . . . the goal [of this special war] is to homogenize Albanians on a nationalist-separatist basis." The author, again Miloš Antić, wrote that the Albanian public is forced to believe the "truth" offered by some of their powerful compatriots, that somebody did it to them on purpose. Antić summarized the rumors surrounding the case:

Albanians suggest that the army did it by using neuro-war poisons. Then that it is an act of the Serbian police. Thirdly accused are Serbs and Montenegrins, who throw poisons in the classrooms and school yards that poison only Albanian children, or who sell poisoned pumpkin seeds to Albanian children. On the other hand, what is not discussed among Albanians is discussed by Serbs and Montenegrins. Based on what was seen and published so far about the entire case, it is claimed [by Serbs and Montenegrins] that the "poisoning" is a joint act of the Albanian separatists, some physicians of Albanian ethnicity, and the powerful Albanian lobby from abroad and their aides, who, one more time, used children for their goals.

"The case of the mysterious 'poisoning' in Kosovo is more complicated than it looks and very useful for various manipulations and misuses," Antić concluded, explaining that "it required the joint action of medical workers, sociologists, lawyers and maybe even experts from other fields." Antić added that "the demystification of the 'mysterious poisoning' " should be done as thoroughly as possible, "because [the allegations] serve to further the aggravation of interethnic conflict in Kosovo."[99]

Federal and Serbian investigators did work quickly to "demystify" the case, promoting one conclusion: no poisoning. The first official report on the case, issued by the Serbian Secretariat of Health late in May

1990, found "no causes which would indicate that the students of Albanian nationality were poisoned."[100] Subsequent studies conducted at the Military Medical Academy in Belgrade (VMA) reached the same conclusion. Doctor Vladimir Vojvodić told the press "that the poisoning allegations were not supported by the results of the analyses of eighty-eight different blood samples and forty-eight urine samples provided by the Medical Faculty in Priština or in the additional twelve blood samples, four urine and one vomit sample provided by the authorities."[101]

The medical department of the Serbian Academy of Sciences and Art (SANU) also agreed with the "no poisoning" thesis. The statement of the Academy, as reprinted in *Politika*, concluded,

Everything is then about the simulated poisoning, the simulation of hysteria, with the neurological reactions induced in order to accuse Serbs and Montenegrins and cause hatred and revolt among Albanians as another contribution to the special war against Serbia and Yugoslavia.

It is obvious that in this deception the Albanian separatists and terrorists abused their own children in carrying out, among other things, an irresponsible attack on their psyche with possible psychological consequences.[102]

If there was no poisoning, how could the carloads of sick children be explained away? Some commentators in Yugoslavia sided with the rumors prevalent in the Kosovo Serb community: an Albanian plot. Many Serbian and Yugoslav journalists accused Albanian separatists and nationalists of using their own children to combat the latest constitutional changes in Kosovo,[103] and they printed story after story of various medical experts who supported this thesis. Professor Dr. Stevan Baljosević, director of the Infectology Clinics, claimed that "the patients are infected by the 'Kosovo-Republic' virus" and he referred them to the neuro-psychiatric ward because "they belong there."[104] Another medical expert, Dr. Duško Bulajić, called the attempts of Albanian doctors to treat the patients with infusions and other medicaments "criminal," because according to Yugoslav law "it is illegal to give medications to healthy people."[105] In the same vein, Dr. Rade Kantić told the press that to the extent that the children had any symptoms, they were brought on not by any poison but by the medicines administered by Albanian doctors.[106]

When additional cases of poisoning were reported, they were also treated with derision by the Serbian and most of the Yugoslav press. In early June 1990, another round of school poisonings was reported in Kosovo. *Politika* claimed in its report that the school teacher rang the school bell as a signal to the Kosovo Albanian school children that they were to "be poisoned" that day.[107] Press reports of Albanian school children being treated in Zagreb in the fall of 1990 for lingering symptoms of poisoning were similarly skeptical.[108]

On top of the many Serbian and Yugoslav reports that no poisoning had occurred, a contradictory thesis emerged: Albanians had poisoned their own children. One journalist who had penned several articles arguing that the poisoning never happened wrote in August 1990 that he had discovered the source of the poisons: an Albanian Catholic church that acted as a hospice had stocked large quantities of the same poison that had infected the school children.

> Special militia units . . . in Uroševac discovered a depot with several hundred kilograms of drugs and sanitation material [gauze, bandages, etc.] in the Catholic church hospice in Uroševac. Most of the drugs are from Switzerland and among them is also "atropine," which can induce the widening of pupils.
>
> Drugs were discovered that mainly cause nausea and headache, exactly the symptoms that were characteristic of the recent "poisoning" of Šiptari in Kosovo and Metohija. This makes it clearer why all of the "poisoned" had the same symptoms. . . .
>
> In March there were dozens of people in white robes in the yard of the hospice and inside, "giving aid" to the "poisoned" who were coming to the hospice for their doze of the "little poison."[109]

No official investigators ever concluded that the poisons in the Albanian church were in fact the same substance detected in the students. Nevertheless, reports of the "discovery of poisons" promoted this version of Truth, that is that Albanians are so inhuman that they poison their own children as a propaganda tool.

Such conspiracy theories caught on quickly throughout Yugoslavia. At least ten years of steady anti-Albanian propaganda had conditioned the Serbian and, perhaps to a lesser extent, the larger Yugoslav public to fear an Albanian conspiracy. The poisoning incidents provided further proof of what many already knew to be the Truth. Many Kosovo Serbs who had witnessed the stream of Albanian parents and children into hospitals in March 1990 say that they "immediately knew" that it was a sham; when asked today to remember their initial response to the alleged poisoning, Kosovo Serbs will often respond, "I thought it was funny."[110] Serbs living in all parts of Yugoslavia were offended by the alleged poisonings because by 1990 their media had conditioned them to think as a unit. Any accusation against the Serbian regime, Kosovo

Serbs, or any other group of Serbs was experienced by many Serbs as a personal attack. Albanians were accusing them *personally* of committing the monstrous deed against the symbol of innocence, children. "I felt sick with anger that they accused *us* of doing this," one Serbian woman said, echoing the sentiments of many, "How could they stoop so low?"[111]

Despite the widespread acceptance of the Albanian conspiracy theory within Serbian circles, many commentators, particularly abroad and in Yugoslav republics other than Serbia and Montenegro, found this notion even more improbable than the poisoning thesis, given the facts. The children were visibly ill, and their symptoms had been documented by Serbian as well as Albanian doctors.[112] Even a loyal and fanatical community would have problems directing one thousand school children to do anything, especially to act out symptoms of illness. Today, those who experienced the symptoms and their doctors convincingly testify about their cases, and not a single person has broken with the original story.[113]

Even if an intentional poisoning was not the culprit, the children could have become ill from natural causes. Some of the Yugoslav and Serbian doctors who investigated the cases concluded that they were probably caused by mass hysteria produced by the atmosphere of hatred and insecurity that permeated Kosovo society. These commentators hypothesized that some of the children may have been ill from a common cause, such as a virus or even dehydration, but then other children fell like dominos. Their symptoms may have been psychological, but in no way were they fabricated.

Although rare, the phenomenon of mass illness caused by hysteria has occurred before in societies in conflict. Mirko Klarin, a *Borba* journalist, pointed to a similar incident in March and April 1983 in an area on the west coast of Jordan that was under Israeli occupation.[114] In that two-month span, more than one thousand Palestinian girls fell ill from a mysterious illness whose symptoms included sudden blindness, headaches, spasms and cyanosis of lower and upper limbs. The girls were moved to a local hospital, and two of them developed complete blindness and were transferred to a hospital in a larger city. All were given oxygen in the local hospital. By the evening their condition had improved and some of the girls were sent home. The next day fifteen additional students from the same school were admitted to the hospital with the same symptoms, and by the fourth day sixty-six students had been hospitalized. On the fifth day the "epidemic" spread from Araba to a small neighboring city and to other towns, and the problem grew exponentially. After sixteen days 943 cases had been registered.

The Arab League accused Israel of using chemical weapons to exterminate the Palestinian people. Israeli authorities (including the army) denied that they had any part in the cases and accused Palestinians of intentionally poisoning their own girls in order to mobilize the masses against Israel. Arab doctors suspected that the girls were poisoned by a gas that induces sterility in women in order to decrease the Palestinian birth rate and change the demographic structure of the occupied territories. Only after Israeli authorities involved international experts whom the Palestinians trusted and those experts confirmed that the girls suffered no biological anomalies did the panic cease.[115]

With respect to Serbia, the mass hysteria thesis was not without detractors. Some adherents to this theory still blamed Albanian leaders for deliberately causing the hysteria or, it was claimed, for fanning the flames of hysteria. Dr. Milan Popović, a professor in Belgrade and a psychiatrist and psychotherapist at the Belgrade Institute for Mental Health, said that "the appearance of the so-called poisoning among young people in Kosovo, according to the possible causes, its massive nature and multiple consequences for the society, exceeded the frames of the medical and even of the psychological-psychiatric problem and represents a socio-pathological phenomenon."[116] Popović found that what was happening in Kosovo was indeed poisoning, "not physical but psycho-nationalistic, that culminates in the explosion of the destructive hatred." The children and their parents were manipulated into "collective hysterical reaction," Popović said, but in addition many cases were simulated. Popović compared the incident to cases of the mass hysteria in Yugoslavia at the end of World War Two, the so-called "partisan disease," in which some soldiers expressed the symptoms of collective hysteria. Their cases ended, Popović reminded, when the soldiers were deprived of special care and status. In other words, the symptoms in Albanian school children and the "symptom" of Albanian nationalism would stop if the international community would stop coddling Albanians.

While some Kosovo Albanians accepted the unintentional poisoning and mass hysteria thesis as their Truth, many adhered to their original theory: poisoning had occurred and Serbs had done it. Kosovar doctors stood by their diagnosis of symptoms of poisoning—wide pupils, dizziness, vomiting, headaches—which, they said, indicated "there has been, by someone, a precisely planned poisoning."[117] Unlike Serbian and federal authorities, however, Albanians could not rely upon their own analyses of blood samples. Serbian authorities had interrupted their laboratory tests, Albanian physicians say, forcing them to send the blood samples to Belgrade.

Without conclusive results of their own, Albanians relied on the analyses of foreign experts. Although most international studies were inconclusive,[118] some foreign researchers have indeed found blood samples of the ill children to contain neuro-toxic gases, typical of those developed for chemical warfare.[119] While most UN observers believed at the time that the incident was a case of mass hysteria, a UN toxicologist did conclude that Sarin or Tabun (poisonous substances used in chemical weapons) were present in blood samples taken from children in Kosovo.[120] The Council for Human Rights of Priština, an Albanian human rights group, has relied particularly heavily on a study that they say was conducted by "A. Heyndricky, Director of International Reference University Laboratories in Belgium." The Council has reproduced a letter signed by "A. Heyndricky," dated February 8, 1992, summarizing the findings "that an organic chemical nerve gas had been used, Sarin and (or) Tabun, listed as a chemical warfare agent."[121] (At the time, the Council suspected that Sarin was being manufactured by Yugoslavia or brought in from another eastern bloc country, such as Czechoslovakia. After the war in Bosnia-Herzegovina, the foreign press reported that Sarin had long been manufactured in Bosnia, thus renewing suspicions that it had been used in Kosovo.)[122]

Yugoslav newspapers reported the existence of such foreign studies but criticized their authors as pro-Albanian.[123] The Sarajevo daily *Oslobodjenje*, for example, reported that an international commission, headed by a Dr. Bernar Benedetti, said to be of Doctors of the World, had determined that there had been a poisoning after all. Benedetti was quoted as saying that "over 3000 young people and children were deliberately poisoned," and "I claim that a mass poisoning was conducted. Of course, only of children of the Albanian origin." Benedetti reportedly based his conclusion on filmed testimonies and videotapes of the victims which had been shot by an Albanian TV crew but banned by Serbian censors. The *Oslobodjenje* journalist concluded that Benedetti's statements "release an odor of political subjectivity."[124] The journalist reasoned that Benedetti's support for Albanian nationalists could be attributed to him being from Corsica, where the "commandos of the liberation army" fight for "freedom and independence" just like Kosovo Albanians.

None of the "conclusions" about the case—whether by Serb, Yugoslav, or foreign experts, or by the people on the street—proved strong enough to put an end to the case. In contrast to the case in Jordan, the international experts trusted by the Kosovo Albanians never found conclusively that poisoning did not occur. Serbian and federal authorities never invited an international investigation or allowed Kosovo Albanian doctors unhindered access to and participation in studies of blood samples. On the contrary, Serbian and federal authorities worked to block local investigations and to hinder treatment of the children.[125] As a result, the competing Truths created by the "poisoning case" have never been settled, nor are they likely ever to reach a mutually acceptable conclusion.

The stories of poisoning only generated additional Truths that further cemented the division between Serbs and Albanians. For example, members of the Serbian Orthodox clergy in Kosovo accused Albanians of physical assault, the burning of property and attempted rape.[126] Serbs also announced that they had uncovered an Albanian plan to poison Serbian and Montenegrin children. The headline on June 27, 1990, in *Politika Ekspres* read: "They Are Preparing a Real Poisoning."

Enemies of Serbia and Yugoslavia from Kosovo, no matter whether from a so-called "democratic alternative" or notorious terrorists, in order to separate the southern Serbian province for some kind of Greater Albania, cannot resist misusing children. First their own, whether displaying them as a protection in front of the bewildered crowd [in the 1981 demonstrations, when Albanian demonstrators allegedly positioned children between demonstrators and the military] or assigning the innocent boys and girls the sad role of being "poisoned" by one-nation poisons, and now they are threatening to the children of Serbs, Montenegrins and Muslims.[127]

At the same time, rumors spread in the Albanian community of Serbian doctors sterilizing and poisoning Albanian children. Some frightened Albanian parents refused to take their children for inoculations, and as a result some of these children have since contracted polio and child paralysis.[128]

Occurring at the time of a political and military crackdown in Kosovo, the Truths of the poisoning sealed what would be the strategy of both Serbs and Albanians for years to come. For Serbian leaders a pattern was set: after a "trouble" (whether of unknown origin or created by Serbs, or by someone else), they would send in the police and military to "protect Serbs" and "establish control." For Albanian leaders, each act of Serbian aggression would be countered with widespread publicity, and the Albanian public would be called upon to don a Ghandi-esque coat of "passive resistance." Serbian brute force would square off against Albanian passivism.

Following the Truths

Looking back, some commentators see the mass poisoning as part of Serbian plan to provoke a military confrontation in the spring of 1990. Shkelzen Maliqi, for example, reasons that a military confrontation in Kosovo "was intended to serve as a pretext for militarization of the 'Serb Question' throughout Yugoslavia, and for the subsequent wars in Croatia and Bosnia." In addition to the poisoning and to "unprovoked massacres," Maliqi says, "the provocation of armed incidents in a number of Albanian villages were all rightly judged to have been attempts to provoke a mass Albanian rebellion which would have served as a *casus belli* and provided the pretext for bombarding Albanian settlements and initiating a mass repression which would have sparked an Albanian exodus." The only problem was that Serbs had waited too long. In 1989, the dominant mood of Albanians had been vengeful and an armed conflict was considered inevitable. But in the spring of 1990, "warriors became unfashionable."[129]

The change in attitude was in part a sign of the times. In 1989, the ticket being sold for change for the oppressed in Central and Eastern Europe was peaceful democracy, not violent conflict. Albanians' friends abroad, especially in the U.S., held out a simple formula: add together free elections, a free press and other democratic institutions, a multiparty government, a free market, a "civil society," and a touch of optimism, mix well and stir. Presto, "instant democracy."[130] And, of course, democracy meant that the will of 10 percent could not rule over a 90 percent majority. Also for Central and Eastern Europeans in 1989, the promise of a united Europe glowed bright. "We are Europeans," many Kosovo Albanians said,[131] longing to belong to that imagined world where borders were increasingly meaningless. It all seemed so simple — and possible.

Within Serbia, anti-Albanian propaganda had gone too far and for too long. For a decade Albanians had been "portrayed as monsters, politically as 'counter-revolutionaries,' 'separatists,' 'irredentists' and the like and as regards their human qualities as 'narrow-minded chauvinists,' 'thugs,' 'people who poison the wells of their Serb neighbors' and so on. . . ."[132] If Albanians were to react to Serbian oppression with vengeance, they would only be promoting the worst accusations against Albanians. A very public campaign of nonviolence helped disprove anti-Albanian propaganda and thus draw sympathy for the Albanian political agenda. Almost overnight, the Albanian political strategy of "passive resistance" took off on the moral high road. This strategy helped to underscore a perception of difference between Albanians and Serbs: Albanians are the peaceful ones, Serbs are violent.[133] True to this formulation, soon after the poisoning incident, Serbia seized control of Kosovo institutions with deceit and the brunt of a gun, and Albanians began constructing their parallel society, complete with their own schools, health care facilities and welfare fund, and with a professed belief in democracy and a new public relations campaign.

Immediately after the alleged poisonings were announced, Serbia took over the police force in Kosovo, purging over 200 Albanian officers from their posts and replacing them with over 2,500 Serbs.[134] This action had a domino effect. The Albanian head of the police resigned, followed by the Kosovo prime minister and six other ministers. Some Albanians resigned in protest, while others were forced out of their positions. In all other parts of society, from businesses to schools to hospitals, Serbs were increasingly taking the place of Albanians.

The rapid transformation was helped along by a series of laws passed by the Assembly of Serbia on March 22, 1990. The main blueprint for Serbia's takeover of Kosovo was outlined in the "Program for Attainment of Peace, Freedom, Equality and Prosperity of the SAP [Socialist Autonomous Province] of Kosovo" and an accompanying ninety-four-point "Operational Plan."[135] The explicit goal of the Program was to ensure that the "injustice" to Serbs and Montenegrins in Kosovo would be made right. Among other measures, the Program promised to create incentives for the return and settling in Kosovo of "all those who wish to live there"; establish a directorate for the promotion of economic and social development, drawing from the funds of Serbia (thus taking over a function that had been coordinated on the federal level); and authorize the Kosovo Assembly, which was in contravention of the Constitution of Serbia. The Operational Plan promised to establish a single body of legislature in Serbia, strengthen the judicial, police and military functions of Serbia, and apply Serbian regulations in the fields of science, culture, information and health care. The plan introduced family planning for Albanians, promised the building of homes for Serbian workers returning to Kosovo, and annulled sales of land by Serbs to Albanians. As part of this policy, numerous laws were passed on "special circumstances" and "emergency measures," which could spring into force and allow the takeover of Kosovo's government as well as the management of the economy, health services, education and other judicial and administrative functions.[136]

In an apparent move toward appeasement, Azem Vllasi and his fourteen codefendants were released on April 24, 1990, along with other, mainly Albanian, political prisoners, including Adem Demaqi, the "Albanian Mandela," who had spent a total of twenty-eight years in prison for nationalist activity and who still had five more years left on his sentence.[137] The same month, at the urging of the federal Presidency, Serbia announced that it would lift emergency measures in Kosovo. In reality, however, police oppression continued and Kosovo steadily fell apart.

By May, all Albanian members of Kosovo's government had resigned in protest. The Kosovo Assembly could no longer function; Serb and Montenegrin delegates routinely walked out when outvoted by Albanians.[138] In June, the Serbian legislature passed a law that effectively extended the emergency measures in Kosovo, allowing Belgrade to exercise considerable control over Kosovo institutions.

A remarkable sequence of events in the summer of 1990 furthered the breakup of Yugoslavia. Once again, Kosovo played a crucial, leading role.

Kosovo Albanians tried one final tactic to use the regular governmental procedures to challenge the new Serbian constitution, which was scheduled for a vote in a referendum on July 1 and 2. On June 20, Albanian delegates from the Kosovo Assembly attempted to block the new constitution by instead proposing a new provincial constitution making Kosovo a republic. Before the matter could come to a vote, Djordje Božović, the (Serbian) president of the assembly, adjourned the session under the agreement that the assembly would reconvene on July 2. He then announced that he had postponed the meeting for July 5 — after the referendum.

On July 2, 114 of the 123 Albanian members of the assembly showed up as originally planned, but Božović had ordered the doors of the assembly to be shut. Since only 111 deputies were needed for a quorum, the delegates called their meeting on the steps of the assembly building. There they unanimously voted on a declaration of self-determination for Kosovo, effectively declaring Kosovo to be independent of Serbia. The delegates also voted to annul the March 1989 decision of the provincial assembly that had diminished Kosovo's autonomy. They issued a declaration describing Albanians as having the status of a "nation"—and not the inferior status of a "national minority" (in Yugoslav constitutional parlance)—and thereby being entitled to their own republic and the right to self-determination.[139]

On the same day that Kosovo Albanian politicians were voting on the steps of their assembly, the Assembly of Slovenia adopted a Declaration on the Sovereignty of the State of Slovenia. Two votes on one day could not be a coincidence, Belgrade argued. The Serbian media accused Slovenia of conspiring with Albanians (the Ljubljana-Priština axis) to destroy Yugoslavia.[140]

Three days later, Serbian authorities dissolved the Assembly of Kosovo and declared the proclamation of the Kosovo Republic illegal. The last remaining Kosovo Albanians in high office in the province, the members of the Kosovo Presidency, resigned, and the Assembly of Serbia used a "special measures" law to enable it to take over the provincial government immediately.

The situation in Kosovo deteriorated rapidly. Almost all Kosovar media were completely suppressed. Local Albanian-language television and radio news broadcasts were halted and, with the exception of *Bujku*, Albanian-language newspapers were taken over by Serbian journalists.[141] *Rilindja*, the most widely read Albanian-language daily, was banned altogether.[142] By the end of the summer, over fifteen thousand Kosovo Albanians holding lower-level public offices would be dismissed,[143] and the managerial positions at leading factories throughout Kosovo would be taken over by Serbs.[144] Albanian gatherings of any kind were disrupted. Even when a peaceful crowd of ten thousand Albanians gathered in Priština to greet a delegation of U.S. senators, police used tear gas, water cannons and clubs to force them to disperse.[145] Police stepped up house-to-house searches for weapons in Albanian villages; in the course of one search in a village near Podujevo, police killed four Albanians.[146]

In the flurry of summer constitutional changes, Croatia adopted its own constitutional revisions on July 25, 1990, defining Croatia as "the national state of the Croatian nation."[147] Meanwhile, on August 19, 1990, Serbs in Krajina, a part of Croatia traditionally settled largely by Serbs but never recognized as a province or as any other official unit, declared their independence at a referendum. On October 1, 1990, the Serbian National Council would declare Krajina autonomous, and in February 1991 Krajina would formally announce its succession from Croatia.[148]

On September 7, 1990, Albanian delegates to the Kosovo assembly, a two-thirds majority, met in secret at Kaqanik in southern Kosovo. There they adopted a constitution for an independent state of Kosovo, declaring that "the Republic of Kosova is a democratic state of the Albanian people and of members of other nations and national minorities who are its citizens: Serbs, Muslims, Montenegrins, Croats, Turks, Romanies and others living in Kosovo."[149] As the "legitimate representatives of Kosova," the delegates "expect[ed] recognition by the federal units of Yugoslavia of the sovereignty of the Republic of Kosova as an equal member of the Yugoslav Community of Nations."[150] Not surprisingly, recognition was not forthcoming. Serbian authorities condemned the "Kaçanik constitution" as a criminal act and sought to arrest all those who had participated. Many of the participants fled to other parts of Yugoslavia; Serbian authorities arrested four delegates and issued arrest warrants for the other 107 who attended the session.[151]

Three weeks later, on September 28, 1990, the new Serbian constitution became official. In sealing Belgrade's takeover of Kosovo, the new constitution merely completed what had already been achieved through force. As legal scholar Vladan Vasilijević has observed, "a semblance of authority was used as a cover for an accomplished act."[152]

Serb government spokesmen praised the new constitution as an advance over the new constitutions passed by other republics because, unlike in Croatia, Slovenia and Macedonia, Serbia was not defined as a "national state" but as a "democratic state of all citizens."[153] Article 49 of the constitution provided that "a citizen shall be guaranteed the freedom to express his national affiliation and culture, and freedom to use his language and alphabet."[154] For Kosovo Albanians, however, this clause was far from sufficient. By failing to address the issue of the status of Albanians in Kosovo, they argued, the constitution perpetuated the old de facto practice and de jure system under which Albanians were relegated to the inferior status of "nationality" or "minority." Moreover, the constitution formally restricted the status of Kosovo and eliminated the possibility of self-determination, declaring instead that "the territory of the Republic of Serbia is a single whole, no part of which may be alienated."[155] Under the new constitution, the provinces were said no longer to have their own constitutions but only provincial statutes, which could not be adopted by the provincial assemblies without the prior consent of the Assembly of Serbia. In addition, the Serbian Constitution abolished the presidencies of the provinces and renamed Kosovo as "Kosovo-Metohija," the Serbian name for Kosovo in use prior to adoption of the 1974 Constitution.[156]

Belgrade had Kosovo firmly within its grasp, but the rest of Yugoslavia was slipping away. Multiparty elections were held in 1990 in each republic. Four of six elections produced non-Communist majorities and governments (although some of those elected included former Communists).[157] Slovenia went first, voting on April 8, 1990, for former Communist leader Milan Kučan as president; DEMOS, an anti-Communist coalition of six parties, won 53 percent of the vote. Croatia held elections on April 22, electing the leader of the Croatian Democratic Union (HDZ), Franjo Tudjman, as president; HDZ received 41.5 percent of the vote and, because of proportional representation, was awarded two-thirds of the parliamentary seats. In voting in Macedonia on November 11, Kiro Gligorov, a former Communist, was elected president; on November 18, Alija Izetbegović became president of Bosnia. Finally, on December 26, 1990, the Socialist Party of Serbia (SPS) won 192 out of 250 seats in the Assembly of Serbia, and Slobodan Milošević was elected president.[158]

The most tumultuous two years in post-War Yugoslav history thus ended with Yugoslavia completely transformed. The trend toward decentralization had continued, pushing power from a decapitated center to the republics. The League of Communists had evaporated and multiparty elections had anointed republic leaders, often on nationalist platforms, who called for greater autonomy, the restructuring of Yugoslavia (into, perhaps, a confederal arrangement) and even separation from Yugoslavia. To various degrees throughout Yugoslavia, national politics were taking the place of the socialist ideals of Brotherhood and Unity. "Without excusing nationalism elsewhere in the former Yugoslavia," as Dragomir Vojnić has written, "it remains a historical fact that, starting with Kosovo, Serbian nationalism initiated and fed all the other nationalisms."[159]

For their part, both Kosovo Albanians and Milošević-supporting Serbs transformed themselves to keep pace with the larger developments within Yugoslavia, with the hope that they could prompt even greater change. The nine years since the 1981 student demonstrations had given both groups a sense of identity, a purpose and a plan. By the end of this period, Kosovo Albanians were for the most part reacting to Serbian repression; Serbs were just beginning their offensive.

Kosovo Albanians had not achieved a single part of their agenda at the 1981 demonstrations, however that agenda could be defined.[160] They had failed not only to achieve a Kosovo Republic but, worse yet, they had lost the rights and autonomy they had once enjoyed under the 1974 Constitution of Yugoslavia. For those who had been youthful protesters on the streets of Priština in 1981, this outcome was almost unfathomable. The two years of relentless usurpation of Kosovo's autonomy and dissolution of Yugoslavia, however, had served as a warning that a change in strategy was needed. Still, until the very last moment of defeat, Albanian Kosovars had hung on to their demand for a Kosovo Republic within Yugoslavia.[161]

Kosovo Albanians boycotted the Serbian election in December 1990, refusing "to dignify Milošević with a vote against him."[162] They swore never again to recognize the legitimacy of Serbia and instead set to building their own parallel society. After the poisoning incident, many parents had taken their children out of school. It would not be long before Kosovo Albanians elected their own illegal government, with their own schools, welfare and health care system. They would shore up their character through "passive resistance" and lay down their rocks and guns — at least until their patience began to crack. (Most Albanians in Kosovo would remain patient throughout the war in Croatia and Bosnia-Herzegovina, with signs of militancy among Kosovo Albanians rising only in 1996.)

While Kosovo Albanians were waiting for better times, Serbian nationalists in 1990 were celebrating their victory and reaching for more. For his part, Milošević, the political opportunist turned nationalist, seemed to have everything he wanted. With his popularity among Serbs boosted by his commanding response to the "Kosovo question," Milošević had achieved the presidency of Serbia. He had solidified his control by pushing through constitutional changes and instituting emergency rule, which gave Serbia iron-clad control over Kosovo and, not incidentally, coercive power over Vojvodina, Montenegro and, it appeared, Macedonia. Milošević was in position to extend the "Kosovo perspective" to events outside Kosovo's borders.[163] Weaned on the historic myth of Kosovo and the present-day Truths of Martinović, Paraćin and the Poisoning, Serbs were conditioned to think of themselves as victims and to fear enemies from inside and outside. To expand his campaign to Croatia and Bosnia-Herzegovina, Milošević had only to add two more ingredients — tighter control over the media and a couple of staged "incidents" in which Serbs were harmed. Then many Serbs would be prepared to fight to unify the Serb nation for their own survival. Kosovo would be just the beginning. Croatia and Bosnia-Herzegovenia would become the site of brutal wars; after Yugoslavia was fully dismembered, Kosovo itself would explode in all-out war in 1998.

Notes

1. For a portrait of Milošević, see Aleksa Djilas, "A Profile of Slobodan Milošević," *Foreign Affairs* 72 (summer 1993), 81–96.

2. See *FBIS-EE*, November 22, 1988, 39.

3. See Sabrina Petra Ramet, *Balkan Babel: The Disintegration of Yugoslavia from the Death of Tito to Ethnic War*, 2d ed. (Boulder, Colo.: Westview Press, 1996), 21.

4. International Monetary Fund, *International Financial Statistics*, vol. 45 (November 1992), 566 and 748–49 (cited in Susan L. Woodward, *Balkan Tragedy: Chaos and Dissolution after the Cold War* (Washington, D.C.: Brookings Institute, 1995), 96n.28).

5. Lenard J. Cohen, *Broken Bonds: Yugoslavia's Disintegration and Balkan Politics in Transition*, 2d ed. (Boulder, Colo.: Westview Press, 1995), 45.

6. For example, Bogdan Bogdanović, the former mayor of Belgrade who has been described by Ivo Banac as "the conscience of the Serbian Left," sent Milošević a letter in August 1988 that read: "Serbia is tired of her fear of abstraction, of higher abstractions, above all, she is tired of her simplified reasoning, of her concretism—the most concrete in the world. . . . Serbia on the East, Serbia on the margins of civilization, tired of the civilization that never really touched her. . . . Serbia is tired of her wrangle with Europe, which she does not know or understand, of her wrangle with Central Europe, which she belittles and disdains, she is tired of her inexplicable and comical Austrophobia . . . , tired of her eastern option, of her mini-Messianist panliberationist obsession. . . ." Ivo Banac, "Serbia's Deadly Fears," in *The New Combat* (autumn 1994), 39.

7. Miranda Vickers, "The Status of Kosovo in Socialist Yugoslavia," *Bradford Studies on South Eastern Europe*, no. 14 (Research Unit on South Eastern Studies, University of Bradford, 1994)(unpaginated version on file with author).

8. Interestingly, at the time one of the key issues for those who identified as liberal intellectuals in Yugoslavia was free speech, which often meant freedom to promulgate nationalist speech. Today, the listings in Helsinki Watch booklets of Yugoslav intellectuals imprisoned in the 1980s for speech and association offenses reads like a who's who of prominent nationalists in the late 1990s. Of course, not all of those listed are nationalists, and in fact some would become prominent antinationalists in the 1990s. See, e.g., Helsinki Watch, *Freedom to Conform* (New York: Human Rights Watch/Helsinki Watch, dated August 1, 1992).

9. Unpublished interview with Milovan Djilas by C. Cirjanić, Belgrade, February 1989 (cited in Vickers, "The Status of Kosovo," n.42).

10. Cohen, *Broken Bonds*, 57.

11. Miloš Vasić, Roksana Ninčić and Tanja Topić, "A Tired Serbia," *Vreme News Digest Agency*, no. 52, September 21, 1992.

12. Ivo Banac, "Post-Communism as Post-Yugoslavism: The Yugoslav

Non-Revolution of 1989–1990," in *Eastern Europe in Revolution*, ed. Ivo Banac (Ithaca, N.Y.: Cornell University Press, 1992), 168–87.

13. Mirjana Kasapović, "The Structure and Dynamics of the Yugoslav Political Environment and Elections in Croatia," in *The Tragedy of Yugoslavia: The Failure of Democratic Transformation*, eds. Jim Seroka and Vukasin Pavlovic, 23–48 (Armonk, N.Y.: M. E. Sharpe, 1992), 30.

14. On Milošević's relations with the Church, see Norman Cigar, *Genocide in Bosnia: The Policy of "Ethnic Cleansing,"* (College Station, Texas: Texas A&M University Press, 1995), 30; Michael A. Sells, *The Bridge Betrayed: Religion and Genocide in Bosnia* (Berkeley: University of California Press, 1997), 58. In 1988, Serb Orthodox bishops in America, New Zealand and Europe published in their religious newsletter a "Declaration of the Bishops of the Serbian Orthodox Church Against the Genocide Inflicted by Albanians on the Indigenous Serbian Population, Together with the Sacrilege of their Cultural Monuments in their Own Country." The document appeared in *Srbobran*, November 2, 1988, and was reprinted in *South Slav Journal* 11, no. 2–3 (summer-autumn 1988), 59–63.

15. See Nebojša Popov, "Srpski populizam; Od marginalne do dominantne pojave," (Serbian Populism: From a Marginal to a Dominant Phenomenon), supplement to *Vreme*, May 24, 1993.

16. Vladimir Goati, "The Challenge of Post-Communism," in *The Tragedy of Yugoslavia*, eds. Seroka and Pavlović, 4.

17. See Veljko Vujačić, "The Crisis in Yugoslavia," in *Dilemmas of Transition in the Soviet Union and Eastern Europe*, ed. George W. Breslauer (Berkeley, Calif.: Berkeley-Stanford Program in Soviet Studies, 1991), 105.

18. Goati, "The Challenge of Post-Communism," 4.

19. Ibid.

20. Branka Magaš, *The Destruction of Yugoslavia: Tracking the Break-Up 1980–92* (London: Verso, 1993), 159.

21. Ibid.

22. Ibid., 169.

23. Marko Milivojević, "Descent into Chaos: Yugoslavia's Worsening Crisis," *South Slav Journal* 12, no. 1–2 (spring-summer 1989).

24. *RFE, SR* 13, no. 42 (December 30, 1988).

25. *RFE, SR* 14, no. 1 (January 17, 1989).

26. See U.S. State Department, *Country Reports for Human Rights Practices 1988* (Washington, D.C.: Government Printing Office, 1989).

27. *RFE, SR* 13, no. 48 (December 30, 1988), 7.

28. Quoted in Laura Silber and Allan Little, *The Death of Yugoslavia* (London: Penguin Books, 1995), 66.

29. Dragomir Vojnić has observed that "the 'Serbian revolution' of 1988 started in Kosovo under the slogan of 'people happening.' . . ." Dragomir Vojnić, "Disparity and Disintegration: The Economic Dimension of Yugoslavia's Demise," in *Yugoslavia: The Former and the Future: Reflections by Scholars from the Region*, eds. Payam Akhavan and Robert Howse (Washington, D.C.: The Brookings Institute, 1995), 75–111.

30. Dijana Pleština, "From 'Democratic Centralism' to Decentralized De-

mocracy? Trials and Tribulations of Yugoslavia's Development," in *Yugoslavia in Transition: Choices and Constraints*, eds. John B. Allcock, John J. Horton and Marko Milivojević (New York: Berg Publishers, 1992), 155.

31. "Who Keeps the Miners Imprisoned?" *Politika*, February 28, 1989. "Šiptar" (shiptar) is a derogatory word for an Albanian. It is highly unlikely that Albanians would use this word in any statement.

32. "The Miners Strike under Safe Conditions," *Politika*, March 4, 1989.

33. *RFE, SR* 14, no. 10 (March 8, 1989). Accounts of the strike vary. Some commentators say the miners gave up voluntarily.

34. Silber and Little, *The Death of Yugoslavia*, 69.

35. Vuk Drašković, for example, compared Serbia to Israel in his speech on September 11, 1911, "Svi Nabukodonosori roda srpskoga" (All the Nebuchadnezzars of Serbian origin). Cited in Cigar, *Genocide in Bosnia*, 76n.61.

36. Silber and Little, *The Death of Yugoslavia*, 69.

37. Woodward, *Balkan Tragedy*, 98.

38. Ibid., 99.

39. Silber and Little, *The Death of Yugoslavia*, 71. The speech can be found in full in the Yugoslav and Serbian press. See "Kosovo i sloga" (Kosovo and Unity), *NIN*, July 2, 1989.

40. Tomaž Mastnak, "Civil Society in Slovenia: From Opposition to Power," in *The Tragedy of Yugoslavia*, eds. Seroka and Pavlovic, 61.

41. Magaš, *The Destruction of Yugoslavia*, 161.

42. Amnesty International, *Yugoslavia: Prisoners of Conscience* (London: Amnesty International, 1982).

43. Marko Milivojević, "The Armed Forces of Yugoslavia: Sliding into War," in *Beyond Yugoslavia: Politics, Economics, and Culture in a Shattered Community*, eds. Sabrina Petra Ramet and Ljubiša S. Adamovich (Boulder, Colo.: Westview Press, 1995), 72.

44. Helsinki Watch and International Helsinki Federation, *Yugoslavia: Crisis in Kosovo*, eds. Julie Mertus and Vlatka Mihelić (New York: Human Rights Watch/Helsinki Watch, 1990), 39–40. Hereafter referred to as "HW and IHF Report."

45. Sabrina Ramet, "The Albanians of Kosovo: The Potential for Destabilization," *The Brown Journal of World Affairs* 3, no. 1 (winter/spring 1996), 359 (citing *The Economist* (London), April 1, 1989, 40).

46. See Michael J. Galligan, Deborah J. Jacobs, Morris J. Panner and Warren R. Stern, "The Kosovo Crisis and Human Rights in Yugoslavia," *The Record of the Association of the Bar of the City of New York* 46, no. 3 (April 1991), 212, 228–30. Hereafter "New York Bar Report."

47. *FBIS*-EE-89–058, March 28, 1989, 54.

48. The first figure is from U.S. State Department, *Country Reports for Human Rights Practices 1989* (Washington, D.C.: Government Printing Office, 1990), 1308; the second is from New York Bar Report, 230.

49. Magaš, *The Destruction of Yugoslavia*, 233.

50. U.S. State Department, *Country Reports for Human Rights Practices 1989*, 1308.

51. HW and IHF Report, 18.

52. HW and IHF Report, 18n.

53. U.S. State Department, *Country Reports for Human Rights Practices 1989*, 1308.

54. At least 1,500 Kosovo Albanians were dismissed from the party in 1989. Ibid., 1310.

55. Helsinki Watch, *Increasing Turbulence: Human Rights Abuses in Yugoslavia* (New York: Human Rights Watch/Helsinki Watch, 1989), 1.

56. U.S. State Department, *Country Reports for Human Rights Practices 1989*, 1305–6. Whether through house arrest or imprisonment, the practice is inconsistent with generally accepted human rights.

57. Magaš, *The Destruction of Yugoslavia*, 161.

58. See Rev. Dr. Krstivoj Kotur, *The Serbian Folk Epic: Its Theology and Anthropology* (New York: Philosophical Library, 1977).

59. See Rade Mihaljčić, ed., *Boj na Kosovu—starija i novija saznanja* (Belgrade: Izdavačka kuća "Književne novine," 1992); Sima Ćirković et al., eds., *Okrugli sto Kosovska bitka u istoriografiji* (Belgrade, 1989); Thomas A. Emmert, *Serbian Golgotha: Kosovo, 1389* (New York: East European Monographs, 1990); Wayne S. Vucinich and Thomas A. Emmert, eds., *Kosovo: Legacy of a Medieval Battle* (Minneapolis: University of Minnesota Press, 1991); Alex Vukadinović, ed., *Kosovo 1389–1989: Special Edition of the Serbian Literary Quarterly on the Occasion of 600 Years since the Battle of Kosovo* (Belgrade: Serbian Literary Quarterly, 1989); Milica Hrgović et al., *The Battle of Kosovo in History and Popular Tradition* (Belgrade: Beogradski Izdavačko-Grafički Zavod, 1989); Duncan Wilson, *The Life and Times of Vuk Stefanović Karadžić: Literacy, Literature and National Independence in Serbia* (Oxford: Oxford University Press, 1970). According to Sabrina Ramet, the theory that the battle was a defeat was a minority view until at least 1940. Ramet, "The Albanians of Kosovo," 358n.20 (citing Ivan Kampus, "Kosovski boj u objavljenim najstarijim i u novijoj Srpskoj historiografiji," in *Historijski Zbornik* (Zagreb periodical) 62, no. 1 (1989)).

60. Ramet, "The Albanians of Kosovo," 358.

61. Michael A. Sells, "Religion, History, and Genocide in Bosnia-Herzegovina," in *Religion and Justice in the War over Bosnia*, ed. G. Scott Davis (New York: Routledge, 1996), 24.

62. Gale Stokes, *The Walls Came Tumbling Down: The Collapse of Communism in Eastern Europe* (New York: Oxford University Press, 1993), 230–31.

63. For accounts on conversion to Islam, see Ivo Banac, *The National Question in Yugoslavia: Origin, History, Politics* (Ithaca, N.Y.: Cornell University Press, 1984), 4; Sells, *The Bridge Betrayed*, 61. Kosovo Albanians are predominately Muslim but also Catholic, atheist and agnostic.

64. Silber and Little, *The Death of Yugoslavia*, 77.

65. See Sells, "Religion, History, and Genocide," 28–30 (analyzing the Lazar legend as depicted in *The Mountain Wreath*, the classic written by Njegoš (Prince-Bishop Petar II) in Montenegro); and H. T. Norris, *Islam in the Balkans: Religion and Society between Europe and the Arab World* (London: Hurst, 1993), 297.

66. Article 3 of the Changes and Implementations of the Law on Restric-

tions of the Transactions, published in "Službeni glasnik RS" 28/1987. This law was struck down by the decision of the Constitutional Court of Yugoslavia on June 27, 1990. However, Serbia disregarded this decision and re-enacted essentially the same law ("Službeni glasnik RS," 22/1991).

67. Christopher Bennett, *Yugoslavia's Bloody Collapse: Causes, Course and Consequences.* (New York: New York University Press, 1995), 214.

68. Nekibe Kelmendi, *Kosovo pod bremenom diskriminatorskih zakona Srbije: Činjenice i dokazi* (Priština: n.p., 1992); Dušan Janjić, "National Identity, Movement and Nationalism of Serbs and Albanians," in *Conflict or Dialogue: Serbian-Albanian Relations and the Integration of the Balkans,* eds. Dušan Janjić and Shkelzen Maliqi (Subotica: Open University 1994), 160n.292.

69. HW and IHF Report, 39. The charge was brought under Article 114 of the federal Criminal Code, which defines as a crime actions which constitute "counterrevolutionary endangering of the social order."

70. Ibid., 40 (citing conclusion of the U.S.-based group Lawyers Committee for Human Rights).

71. Banac, "Serbia's Deadly Fears," 41.

72. "Srbija i Slovenja raskidaju sve veze?" (Are Serbia and Slovenia Breaking All Relations?), *Borba,* December 1, 1989.

73. "Kokarde ponovo marširaju," *Borba,* July 13, 1989. See also Jim Seroka, "Variation in the Evolution of the Yugoslav Communist Parties," in *The Tragedy of Yugoslavia,* eds. Seroka and Pavlovic, 81.

74. Dennison Rusinow has used the term "putative strategy" to describe Milošević's plan for decentralization. Dennison Rusinow, "The Avoidable Catastrophe," in *Beyond Yugoslavia,* eds. S. Ramet and Adamovich, 24.

75. U.S. State Department, *Country Reports for Human Rights Practices 1990* (Washington, D.C.: Government Printing Office, 1991), 1346. Although the use of force in the demonstrations was investigated, the "investigation of police actions [with respect to use of excessive force], conducted by the police themselves, proved to be a whitewash." Ibid.

76. Hugh Poulton, *The Balkans: Minorities and States in Conflict* (London: Minority Rights Publications, 1991), 68.

77. Milivojević, "The Armed Forces of Yugoslavia," 72.

78. For the conflict between Serbia and Slovenia, see Silber and Little, *The Death of Yugoslavia,* 77–86.

79. Sh. Ukaj, "Otrovani učenici albanske narodnosti" (Poisoned Students of Albanian Nationality), *Večernji list,* March 22, 1990.

80. Ibid.

81. Interview by author.

82. Interview by author.

83. Interview by author.

84. Over one hundred people were interviewed independently about the case throughout Kosovo during 1993–1995. For some of the stories of young Kosovo Serbs and Albanians, see the interviews following chapter five.

85. Sh. Ukaj, "Otrovano tisuću učenika" (Poisoned One Thousand Students), *Večernji list,* March 23, 1990.

86. Ibid.

87. "Nacionalisti tuku decu" (Nationalists Beat Children), *Večernji list*, March 23, 1990.

88. Ibid.

89. Ibid.

90. "Trovanja je ipak bilo" (Was There Poisoning After All?), *Vjesnik*, April 4, 1990.

91. Miloš Antić, "I epidemija režirana" (Even the Epidemics Directed), *Novosti 8*, March 28, 1990.

92. Ibid.

93. Miloš Antić, "Istina na videlo što pre" (Out with the Truth as Soon as Possible), *Borba*, April 18, 1990. Arguably *Borba* could be termed the "Yugoslav press," as it was purportedly an all-Yugoslavia publication. However, it was published in Belgrade, and by 1990 it was increasingly Serbian-dominated.

94. M. Antić and R. Barjaktarević, "Otrov 'bira' nacionalnost" (The Poison "Chooses" the Nationality), *Dnevnik*, March 23 1990.

95. "I Srbi otrovani" (Serbs Poisoned Too), *Vjesnik*, March 24, 1990.

96. At that time Serbian and Albanian children were still attending the same schools but they were divided in separate shifts (morning and afternoon).

97. Interview by author.

98. To this day, Kosovar Albanians will swear they spotted a suspect who was never fully investigated by the police. Serbian officials in Kosovo in 1993 and 1994 told the author that no suspects were ever identified.

99. Miloš Antić, "Djelo separatista" (Act of Separatists), *Vjesnik*, March 24, 1990.

100. R. I., "Opsjednute bolnice, protestni štrajkovi" (Hospitals Besieged, Strikes of Discontent), *Vjesnik*, March 24, 1990.

101. M. Urošević, "Osam provera za istinu" (Eight Checkups for the Truth), *Borba*, April 1, 1990.

102. "Albanski lekari su izdali lekarsku etiku" (Albanian Doctors Betrayed Medical Ethics), *Politika*, May 6, 1990.

103. Miloš Antić, "I epidemija režirana" (Even the Epidemics Directed), *Novosti 8*, March 28, 1990.

104. "Trovanja je ipak bilo?" *Vjesnik*, April 4, 1990.

105. Ibid.

106. Ibid.

107. "Opet histerija 'trovanja' " (Again the Hysteria of "Poisoning"), *Politika*, June 10, 1990.

108. In November 1990, the parents of seven Albanian girls, aged eleven to sixteen, who were still allegedly suffering from symptoms of poisoning, brought them from Kosovo to the hospital in Zagreb. The children reportedly felt cramps around their eyes and were having spasms and losing their consciousness. Dr. Duško Mardešić, an attending physician at the Rebro Clinic in Zagreb, told the press that "the children were brought to the hospital with the story that they suffer from symptoms displayed through spasms, body convulsions, breathing problems and changes in the skin color. When they came, the three girls really had such attacks and their appearance was worrisome, but all of that quickly changed without any special interventions." Mladen Smrekar, "Nova 'epidemija' " (New 'Epidemics'), *Vjesnik*, November 8, 1990.

109. M. Vujović, "Magacin otrovčića u konaku" (Depot of "Little Poisons" in the Hospice), *Politika*, August 8, 1990.

110. See interviews that follow.

111. Interview by author.

112. The author interviewed two Serbian physicians who said that they had treated patients with the same symptoms. According to their opinion, the very real symptoms could have been psychosomatic. See the interviews following for one of the doctors' testimony (names omitted upon request).

113. The author interviewed at least seventy people about the incident throughout Kosovo during 1993–1995.

114. Mirko Klarin, "Sve je počelo 23. marta ali 1983" (Everything Started on March 21, but in 1983), *Borba*, March 28, 1990.

115. Ibid.

116. Bojana Popović, "Histerija u pakovanju nacionalizma" (Hysteria Packaged by Nationalism), *Borba,* April 4, 1990.

117. "Trovanja je ipak bilo?," *Vjesnik*, April 4, 1990.

118. See Jasna Zanić-Nardini, "Zdravstvena panika" (Health Care Panic), *Vjesnik*, March 29, 1990.

119. Nenad Novaković and Mensur Čamo, "Repriza generalne probe" (Replay of the Dress Rehearsal), *Oslobodjenje*, April 1, 1990.

120. Noel Malcolm, *Bosnia: A Short History* (New York: New York University Press, 1998), 345.

121. Photocopy of letter on file with author and reproduced in *The Frozen Smiles: Violence against Children in Kosova* (publication of the Council for Human Rights of Priština, dated October 31, 1992). According the Council, the letter is authentic. The U.S. State Department frequently quotes the Council in its annual country reports on human rights as an authoritative source. The author has found that the Council is usually accurate about the occurrence of human rights events, although their fact-gathering techniques are often less than perfect. For example, at times they may print information before checking the accuracy of the allegations. Nevertheless, the standards of the Council have been steadily improving.

122. See *OMRI Daily Digest,* 27 November 1995. In December 1995, the Kosovo Information Center, an information agency sympathetic to Kosovo Albanians, announced that it had "linked the mysterious poisonings in Kosovo in 1990 to reports about Sarin nerve gas production in rump Yugoslavia and Serb-held territory in Bosnia." *OMRI Daily Digest,* 12 December 1995.

123. "Trovanja je ipak bilo?," *Vjesnik*, April 4, 1990.

124. See M. Pudar, "Optužbe doktora Benedettija" (Dr. Benedetti's Accusations), *Oslobodjenje*, September 15, 1990.

125. For example, a number of the ill children had been taken to the hospital of the Roman Catholic Covenant of Binica, where they continued to suffer cramps and other symptoms long after the poisoning. Nuns at the convent told the International Helsinki Federation that police detained them and forced them to send away the children. HW and IHF Report, 23. See also U.S. State Department, *Country Reports for Human Rights Practices 1990*, 1346.

126. U.S. State Department, *Country Reports for Human Rights Practices 1990*, 1356. No charges were brought in these cases. In the past, Serbs always

said that charges were not brought in such cases because Albanian officials refused to bring them, but by mid-1990 the police were firmly in Serbia's control.

127. "Pripremaju pravo trovanje" (They Are Preparing a Real Poisoning), *Politika Ekspres*, June 27, 1990.

128. Interview by author.

129. Shkelzen Maliqi, "Albanian Self-Understanding through Non-Violence: The Construction of National Identity in Opposition to the Serbs," *Journal of Area Studies,* no. 3 (1993), 121–22.

130. See, e.g., David Chapman, *Instant Democracy: Constitutional Proposals for Emerging Democracies* (London: Institute for Social Inventions, 1990).

131. Interview by author.

132. Maliqi, "Albanian Self-Understanding," 122. See also results of survey on stereotypes of Serbs and Hungarians toward Albanians in Appendix B.

133. Ibid.

134. Poulton, *The Balkans,* 68.

135. The Program and Plan are published in "Službeni glasnik," 15/1990 (*The Official Gazette of the Socialist Republic of Serbia*).

136. See "The Law on Actions of the Republican Bodies in Extraordinary Circumstances," "Službeni glasnik," 30/1990 (*The Official Gazette of the Socialist Republic of Serbia*).

137. U.S. State Department, *Country Reports for Human Rights Practices 1990,* 1343 (reporting that Vllasi was acquitted)

138. Minority Rights Group, *Kosovo: The Oppression of Ethnic Albanians* (London: Minority Rights Group, n.d.), 5.

139. Cohen, *Broken Bonds,* 122.

140. Cohen, *Broken Bonds,* 124. See also M. Andrejevich, "Kosovo and Slovenia Declare their Sovereignty," *RFE-EE,* July 27, 1990.

141. Although not taken over, *Bujku* would be subject to other forms of harassment, including measures that would increase printing costs. Albanian journalists had long been subjected to censorship and harassment. Thirty journalists from the Albanian-language daily *Rilindja* had already been suspended for reporting on the miners' strike in February 1989, and a succession of four *Rilindja* editors had been sacked or pressured out. Poulton, *The Balkans,* 70.

142. See "Threats to Press Freedoms: A Report Prepared for the Free Media Seminar, Commission on Security and Cooperation in Europe," *Helsinki Watch Reports* 5, no. 21 (November 1993), 40; International Federation of Journalists and International Federation of Newspaper Publishers, *Information under Control: The Media Crisis in Montenegro and Kosovo,* Report of the IFJ/FIEJ mission, November 21–25, 1993; Les Cahiers de L'Organisation Internationale des Journalistes, *Reporters et Medias en ex-Yougoslavie* (Paris: Mondiapress, 1993). In September 1990, the police harassed even foreign journalists. An American and a Yugoslav correspondent were detained while covering the general strike in September. Police threatened them with beatings and expulsion before releasing them.

143. U.S. State Department, *Country Reports for Human Rights Practices 1990,* 1348.

144. Although all the factories in Kosovo were the property of the state, under the "national key" system, they were managed primarily by Albanians (as Albanians were at least 80 percent of the population under the official census).

145. U.S. State Department, *Country Reports for Human Rights Practices 1990*, 1347.

146. Ibid.

147. See Robert M. Hayden, "Constitutional Nationalism in the Former Yugoslav Republics," *The Slavic Review* 51 (1992), 657.

148. Stokes, *The Walls Came Tumbling Down*, 246.

149. Poulton, *The Balkans*, 70.

150. Statement of the delegates at Kačanik, September 7, 1990, printed in Ibrahim Berisha et al., eds., *Albanian Democratic Movement in Former Yugoslavia: Documents 1990–1993* (Priština, 1993).

151. U.S. State Department, *Country Reports for Human Rights Practices 1990*, 1354.

152. Vladan A. Vasilijević, "Kosovo: Exercise and Protection of Human Rights," in *Conflict or Dialogue*, eds. Janjić and Maliqi, 85.

153. Janusz Bugajski, *Ethnic Politics in Eastern Europe*, (Armonk, N.Y.: M. E. Sharpe, 1995), 139n.7.

154. *The Constitution of the Republic of Serbia* (Belgrade: Secretariat for Information of the Republic of Serbia, 1990), translated by Boško Milosavljević, Margot Milosavljević and Djurica Krstić.

155. Ibid., Article 4.

156. The Constitution set forth the limited functioning of the province governments in Articles 108–112. Significantly, the last article of this section provides in full: "If an agency of an autonomous province, despite a warning of the corresponding republic agency, fails to execute a decision or a general enactment of the autonomous province, the republic agency may provide for its direct execution."

157. See Steven L. Burg, "Nationalism and Democratization in Yugoslavia," *The Washington Quarterly* 14, no. 4 (autumn 1991).

158. For a summary of election results and for active political parties (and especially a listing of nationalist parties), see Bugajski, *Ethnic Politics in Eastern Europe*, 3–192.

159. Vojnić, "Disparity and Disintegration," in *Yugoslavia: The Former and the Future*, eds. Akhavan and Howse, 98–99.

160. See interviews in chapter one.

161. In his memoir of his service as America's last Ambassador to Yugoslavia, Warren Zimmerman remarks that as late as the end of January 1990, Kosovo Albanians still supported a Kosovo republic or another solution within Yugoslavia. Warren Zimmerman, *Origins of a Catastrophe* (New York: Random House, 1996), 61.

162. Interview by author.

163. Kasapović, "The Structure and Dynamics," 30.

Young People Remember
the Alleged Poisoning

These are some of over seventy interviews conducted on this subject in 1994 and 1995. In order to encourage people to speak freely about the incident, half of the young Serbs were questioned by a young Serbian journalist from Priština, and half of the young Albanians were questioned by a young Albanian journalist from Priština. The author conducted the remaining interviews. Among the questions asked: What were you doing at the time of the poisoning of Albanian school children? What do you think happened? Do you think it was a poisoning?

Serbs

WOMAN, AGE 21 IN 1990, BORN
IN PRIŠTINA, LIVING IN PRIŠTINA

During the time of "poisoning" we were living more or less normally. There weren't really any problems around here. I never saw them [the poisoned Albanians] personally, I was not out there [on the street], but I saw it on TV. I think that it was only a way to attract attention. It was a bad way. If they had been poisoned, we [Serbian schoolchildren] would have been poisoned in the same way. I don't want to comment on that. It was another disappointment [for me in Albanians].

214

MAN, AGE 28 IN 1990, BORN
IN PRIŠTINA, LIVING IN PRIŠTINA

I was out on the street early in the morning. I saw the cars running. Those were not official cars, but private. The police did not stop them or fine them for speeding, but they allowed them to go to the hospital and create a scam. On that occasion I realized that, even though we know that something is white, the media and propaganda are able to prove to the rest of the world that it is actually black. This was a poorly created scam made [by Albanians] for good publicity in the world. I was not surprised by it.

WOMAN, AGE 25 IN 1990, BORN
IN PRIŠTINA, LIVING IN BELGRADE

I was still going to school when the "poisoning" happened, but I didn't see it because my school was not involved. I was astonished to see how far they [Albanians] can go with their games. They set up the whole thing. Sometimes you could clearly see that the events were fabricated. . . . I remember the children who were lying still in the hospital, and as soon as the cameras started to show them they started to have spasms.[1] I never changed my opinion about that. Everything was absolutely faked. That taught me how powerful propaganda can be and how it can present a distorted picture to those who believe in it.

MAN, AGE 34 IN 1990, BORN
IN PRIŠTINA, LIVING IN PRIŠTINA

I remember that poisoning. It was not only schoolchildren but also the adults. I saw a lot of things—Albanians falling and rolling, and people watching them and wondering what was going on The whole thing was like a cheap cabaret performance. . . . I was participating as a neutral observer. I found the whole thing very funny, but those events had a much more serious background. It was a good maneuver [for Albanians]. People saw through the whole thing but no westerners said it aloud. Americans would be very interested in that "one nationality" poison. Many Albanians today are probably ashamed of the whole thing, but the ends justified the means [for them].

The phrase "cabaret performance" and the like had been used extensively by the Serbian media.

MAN, AGE 38 IN 1990, BORN IN KOSOVSKA MITROVICA, LIVING IN NOVI SAD

The "poisoning" case was stupid and funny. I didn't see it personally, because everything happened in the hospital, but I talked a lot about that with other people. If they wanted to attract some public attention, they should not have gone about it so naively. I couldn't believe that anybody would take it seriously. What kind of tap water is it that poisons only Albanians and does not have any effects on Serbs? What happened was that they invited foreign journalists and performed a typical drill of "civil protection." The foreign "humanitarian" agencies were paying a lot to the best actors, those who screamed the most. . . . I think that this [incident] is forgotten today, but we should talk about it more because human rights [claims] are equally manipulated today.

The claim that foreign agencies paid the Albanian school children is rather unique. Most assertions to this effect were that Albanians were paying foreign journalists, or that the children had themselves been paid by their leaders. By "humanitarian agencies" he may mean human rights groups; in interviews, some people tended to mix up the two kinds of organizations.

WOMAN, AGE 24 IN 1990, BORN IN PRIŠTINA, LIVING IN PRIŠTINA

I heard about the "poisoning" on the news. It was obvious from the TV report that everything was acting. The whole thing is practically impossible. If the water was poisoned, not only Albanians would be poisoned. Unfortunately, I think that the paid foreign journalists took it for granted and a wrong picture went out to the world. I knew what was happening then, but only now am I aware of the media impact of that story. At that time I thought that nobody would believe it. This enabled me to see how many lies there are in the Albanian request for the republic. I was thinking about their "moral correctness" and the "moral correctness" of their struggle. I don't understand how they could lie so terribly.

MAN, AGE 26 IN 1990, BORN
IN PRIŠTINA, LIVING IN PRIŠTINA

That poisoning was a comedy. I don't remember that there was a big fuss around the city but I saw ambulance cars. I heard about the spasms and fainting. When I was poisoned I didn't have time to get up from the toilet bowl and certainly not to perform around the city. I was very amused by the whole thing. . . . I think that they [Albanians] are a little ashamed of it.

MAN, AGE 26 IN 1990, BORN
IN PRIŠTINA, LIVING IN PRIŠTINA

I was a student in the time of poisoning. I saw it on TV. I saw how the "poisoned," who were playing in the hospital hall, ran back to their beds whenever the camera came close. . . . I thought that it was funny. The whole thing was a game for the public and for [Albanians] the publicity had positive reactions in the world.

MAN, AGE 26 IN 1990, BORN
IN PRIŠTINA, LIVING IN PRIŠTINA

I was in Skopje during that time. I was working part time as a translator for TV Skopje. They showed some clips on the Skopje TV made by hidden camera of how the children acted and had fun at the same time. I wanted never to go back to my town like many others did. Everything was clear to me at that time. I knew that Albanians were leading a nationalistic political campaign and that their leaders had a clear and explicit goal—an ethnically clean Kosovo—and that they have influential friends in the rich Western countries. I still have the same opinion, but now I am more disappointed with the destiny of Serbian people in the Balkans. This event evoked stubbornness in me. I wanted to [but couldn't] explain to my Albanian neighbors with love and understanding that this does not lead anywhere and that we should open towards the world.

MAN, AGE 28 IN 1990, BORN
IN PRIŠTINA, LIVING IN PRIŠTINA

I was a student at that time. I saw the actors of this event go to the hospital in a theatrical way. I was worried because the

Albanian side was trying by all means (using the methods of Goeb-
bels) to convince the world public of the rightness of their goals. . . .
The poisoning was an organized event by the Albanian movement. I
know it.

WOMAN, AGE 19 IN 1990, BORN
IN PRIŠTINA, LIVING IN PRIŠTINA

I was going normally to school at the time. It happened
in my school too. It was amusing. There were rumors at the school
that they [Albanians] had been paid to pretend that they were poisoned. When I heard about that I felt stupid. I couldn't understand it
then and I don't understand it now. Why did they do it? . . . The
whole thing was forgotten really quickly. It was not convincing.

*Although many Serbs interviewed said that the event was "forgotten quickly,"
the incident seemed to be fresh on the minds of Kosovo Albanians.*

WOMAN, AGE 25 IN 1990, BORN
IN PRIŠTINA, LIVING IN BELGRADE

I don't remember the "poisoning" case well. I was in
Uroševac at that time visiting my grandmother. I think that several
children got poisoned by eating burek [a kind of pie] and then somebody misused it. I didn't know what happened, but now I know that
the whole thing has been blown out of proportions for political pur-
poses.

WOMAN, AGE 25 IN 1990, BORN
IN PRIŠTINA, LIVING IN PRIŠTINA

I was a student at the time. I saw it on TV. I didn't
have any particular feelings about it. I was more pissed off because of
the foreign agencies [journalists and human rights groups] who accepted those lies because it was so obvious that the whole thing was a
setup. . . . This was another attempt of [Albanians to] manipulate
people. . . . It was fruitless because it is natural that illness cannot
choose the nationality [of its victims].

MAN, AGE 25 IN 1990, BORN
IN PRIZREN, LIVING IN PRIZREN

I was in the army at the time and we joked about it. It was really funny. The whole thing had a political background, and I was familiar with the situation [in Kosovo] so it was not very hard for me to figure out what it was about. This [event] never influenced me very much except for showing me that they [Albanians] are ready for anything.

WOMAN, AGE 29 IN 1990, BORN
IN PRIŠTINA, LIVING IN PRIŠTINA

It didn't happen so long ago, but to me it seems that it happened in another life. I am glad that they [Albanians] stopped with stupid things like that. I was hurt. Serbian people never poisoned other people's children. I have never forgiven them for that. That was a horrible accusation and nobody ever apologized for it to this state. I don't know that anybody was ever punished for it. I always knew that the whole thing was a scam, and it was shameful. It made me even more bitter.

WOMAN, AGE 30 IN 1990, BORN
IN PRIŠTINA, LIVING IN PRIŠTINA

I was in Belgrade at that time and I saw it on TV. Of course I didn't feel well. Four days later, I went to the clinics, where the situation was totally unclear. [She is a doctor.] Opinions were divided. It was not clear to me what had happened but it was out of my power to find out. I still feel puzzled and I would love if somebody would explain to me what happened. I had patients for months after that who were having a psychological reaction to the whole thing. But there were cases [of patients] with unexplainable symptoms [and] I was not sure that they were related to this case. . . . I was unsatisfied that some of the [medical] analysis was not performed in a correct way. I was also hurt by my colleagues of one nationality avoiding colleagues of the other [nationality]. Another separation among people. It was never officially said what had really happened.

WOMAN, AGE 26 IN 1990, BORN
IN LIPLJAN, LIVING IN LIPLJAN

I was just about to leave for Priština when [the people I was supposed to see] called and said that there was some kind of trouble in town so I didn't go. I saw the whole thing on TV. I saw children in hospital beds but it was not very convincing. I don't think that there was any poisoning. I felt stupid when I heard about it. I think they used it to start their boycott of the state.

WOMAN, AGE 21 IN 1990, BORN
IN PRIŠTINA, LIVING IN BELGRADE

I saw several cars heading for the hospital and listened to the news on the radio about the alleged poisoning. I felt that something stupid, impossible and incomprehensible was happening. . . . I thought of it then as a manipulation [by Albanians] and I still think of it in the same way.

WOMAN, AGE 27 IN 1990, BORN
IN VUČITRN, LIVING IN KRAGUJEVAC

I was working then and I didn't see it, but everyone was talking about it. I felt rage. . . . Our Albanian colleagues believed it and they didn't want to talk or drink coffee with us. There were some huge arguments. . . . Of course I didn't believe in the poisoning. It was impossible. After that event I had more problems with some of my Albanian colleagues.

MAN, AGE 25 IN 1990, BORN
IN PRIŠTINA, LIVING IN PRIŠTINA

I saw the crowd in the city and later those clips on TV, how they [Albanians] were running away from cameras and how they were being carried into the hospital. I thought that the whole thing was a little funny. I was already used to looking at such things with scorn. The whole thing was forced too much. Bad directing. I don't think that they achieved what they wanted. They achieved something else: the focusing of public attention to happenings in Kosovo.

The media frequently alluded to "directing" and "Hollywood."

Kosovo Albanians

MAN, ABOUT 23 IN 1990, BORN IN A VILLAGE NEAR PODUJEVO, LIVING IN PODUJEVO

I was working in my garden that day. A friend came running and said, "Come quickly, the children are poisoned." My father came and said, "Something terrible is going on, your sister got sick in school and she is in Priština [at the hospital]." We brought four [other sick children] with us to Priština. There were plenty of cars filled with children going toward Priština and empty cars going back [towards Podujevo]. . . . I went to look for my sister in the hospital. It was terrible. [Some of the children were having] hysterical attacks. When I was there, I saw some doctors taking blood samples. Someone came and said that the blood could only be taken by the military academy doctors. . . .When the state police came to the hospital, the volunteer doctors had to hide. . . . I stayed with my sister for five days in that clinic, and then for two weeks they did therapy here [in Podujevo]. During those two weeks, she had four attacks, and before the end of the year she had another two [attacks].

This was one of the most disturbing things for me in my life. I think that this was the way [for Serbs] of showing [their] barbarism by poisoning the Albanian kids.

WOMAN, AGE 24 IN 1990, BORN IN PRIŠTINA, LIVING IN PRIŠTINA

I was a student at the time of poisoning. It was very shocking. There were many crying adults carrying children from cars into the hospital. Some of the children were half-conscious. . . . I was very afraid because I knew that it could happen to me. I think that it was a terrible thing done by this regime.

WOMAN, AGE 18 IN 1990, BORN IN PODUJEVO, LIVING IN PRIŠTINA

I can't forget what happened. We were beginning the school day and all of a sudden I couldn't breathe. My throat was tight and I felt strange, like my head was light. There were kids everywhere around me who were sick too. Some of them were passing out. The teacher ran to get help and we were brought to the clinic and then to Priština to the hospital. There were so many children there. And some were having fits and people were crying. I will never forget that. . . . They didn't find out what happened but they said it was poisoning. Still today I sometimes feel sick. I have a hard time concentrating.

MAN, AGE 29 IN 1990, BORN IN PODUJEVO, LIVING IN PRIŠTINA

I was helping transport the kids from Podujevo to the hospital in Priština. Everyone was helping if they could. There were so many [sick children]. I was very shocked and upset to see those victims and I never felt more close to my people. I felt that we are unbreakable and that they [Serbs] were committing genocide against Albanians. They wanted to scare us to make us leave.

Both Kosovo Serbs and Kosovo Albanians use the word "genocide" to describe what is happening to "their people" in Kosovo.

WOMAN, AGE 26 IN 1990, BORN IN PRIŠTINA, LIVING IN PRIŠTINA

I saw the poisoned kids. The streets were full of people. Cars from Podujevo were going to the hospitals. Everyone in the city was in a panic. The citizens were out in the streets crying. . . . I don't know how it happened but of course we all do [know what happened]. The poisoning existed and it was done by Serbs and I can never forgive them.

WOMAN, AGE 30 IN 1990, BORN IN PRIŠTINA, LIVING IN PRIŠTINA

I never saw any cases, but I was so scared that it could happen to me. I think that everyone was hysterical. I am not sure if they were really poisoned but I know they were sick.

WOMAN, AGE 20 IN 1990, BORN IN VILLAGE NEAR PRIZREN, LIVING IN PRIZREN

Some kids in my class started to get sick and no one knew what was happening. They started to take the kids to the hospital and we all started to follow them or go home. I was walking home when suddenly I couldn't see and I fell down. I had cramps in my hands and throat and felt weak in the knees. I lost consciousness. I was with my friends and one of them stopped a car and they brought me to the hospital. . . .When I got to the hospital, I could see that there were many cases, and much worse cases. . . . Some people could not move any part of their bodies. We stayed for a night [in the hospital]; the next day the police didn't allow any of us to stay there. . . .

When the attack begins, my muscles get tight, I become tired and I can't stand and my heart beats fast. The last time I had an attack was last year. In the beginning, I had [the attacks] more often. . . . I think they [Serbs] did this just to terrify people. There were some rumors that they wanted to sterilize [Albanians], but I don't know. The problem is for my parents—they never know if I am OK.

MAN, AGE 24 IN 1990, BORN IN PEĆ, LIVING IN PRIŠTINA

I was not here when the poisoning happened, but when I heard I was very disappointed. I think that the poisoning happened and then there was a cover-up. . . . I think that the poisoning is just another proof of discrimination against Albanians.

MAN, AGE 25 IN 1990, BORN IN PRIŠTINA, LIVING IN PRIŠTINA

I was a student and I saw the cases of poisoned people in hospital, the convoy of cars taking the kids to the hospital. I felt powerless. . . . I think that the poisoning existed. How could it not exist? I saw it.

WOMAN, AGE 26 IN 1990, BORN IN PODUJEVO, LIVING IN PRIŠTINA

At the time of the poisoning I was confused. It was really hectic and I didn't know what was going on. . . . I think that the poisoning happened. . . . I had a neighbor [who is a Serb] and we talked every day. After the poisoning, we didn't speak anymore. I am very sad about everything.

MAN, AGE 33 IN 1990, BORN
IN PRIŠTINA, LIVING IN PRIŠTINA

I transported the blood of the poisoned people out of the country, to France [for tests by independent experts]. I was in shock. I kept asking myself, how could they do this? . . . I am one hundred percent sure that the poisoning happened.

MAN, AGE 32 IN 1990, BORN
IN PODUJEVO, LIVING IN PODUJEVO

The poisoning existed. I took kids from Podujevo to the hospital with my car. They had come to get me to help. I don't know what was wrong but I could see the kids were very sick. There were so many of them, and so many cars. . . . I felt very bad, worse then ever. . . . I could see what Serbia was doing to us.

WOMAN, AGE 30 IN 1990, BORN
IN PRIŠTINA, LIVING IN PRIŠTINA

The poisoning was the most terrible thing in my life. The kid of my neighbor was poisoned and I cannot describe what I saw happening to him. I cannot describe the pain he was going through. . . . This was a means for the Serbian destruction of Albanians.

MAN, AGE 27 IN 1990, BORN
IN PRIŠTINA, LIVING IN PRIŠTINA

I was a student and I saw the poisoning cases. It was so disturbing. At that time I felt ready to fight against Serbia because they had harmed our children. . . . Yes, that was a real poisoning. I am totally disappointed by Serbs.

MAN, AGE 31 IN 1990, BORN
IN PRIŠTINA, LIVING IN PRIŠTINA

I saw cases of poisoned kids. I took them from Podu-
jevo to the Priština hospital myself. I don't doubt that it was a poisoning. I saw it myself. . . . This affected my life—I hated Serbs more
than ever. At that time I felt I wanted to destroy them because of
what they were doing to us.

MAN, AGE 30 IN 1990, BORN
IN PRIŠTINA, LIVING IN PRIŠTINA

I was a student at that time and I saw everything that
happened. I knew people who were poisoned. It wasn't an act and I
was upset to hear that Serbs said it was. . . . I was shocked and powerless. . . . I believe that it instigated more hatred [against Serbs] in my
people. Things were bad before, but after the poisoning it got worse.

MAN, AGE 27 IN 1990, BORN
IN PRIŠTINA, LIVING IN PRIŠTINA

I saw cases of poisoning. I was working at the hospital
at that time. I can swear that they had symptoms that were not psychological [like some people said]. . . . It was something that I will
never forget. I am not sure how it happened. The doctors [at the hospital in Priština] had a meeting of the whole staff and they made a
text in which they called [the cause of the illness] a "mysterious poison." The next day, the main news in Belgrade opened with the sentence from the text, that it was some kind of "mysterious poison." I
think that what really happened was the poisoning of relations between people, in preparation for the final poisoning.

MAN, ABOUT 36 IN 1990, BORN
IN PODUJEVO, LIVING IN PODUJEVO

The day before [the poisoning], I saw on TV something
about the conflict between Romanians and Hungarians in Romania.
The next day, when the poisoning happened and the state police and
police from Kosovo came here and no one did anything, I thought it
was like the beginning of a war. It smelled like war. . . . There were

plenty of strange cars with Belgrade registration here. Some [Albanian] citizens found someone hiding [in some apartments under construction] and they were trying to beat him. We didn't allow them to beat him; we brought [the man] to the police. . . . After that, the person left Podujevo and never came back. I think that he had something to do with the poisoning. The police stations here, and all over [Kosovo], were taken from the Albanians and the Serbian [police] came. After the Serbian police came, they took over the [government of the] municipality.

MAN, AGE 31 IN 1990, BORN
IN PRIŠTINA, LIVING IN PRIŠTINA

I heard about the poisoning on the TV. I felt bad and I thought that nobody else could do this except for people of the regime. . . . I had some Serbian friends and I didn't blame them. I don't think they knew [what would happen].

MAN, AGE 26 IN 1990, BORN
IN PRIŠTINA, LIVING IN PRIŠTINA

When the kids started to arrive at the hospital there was a lot of pain on their faces. People were crying. I was there as a volunteer, helping. I was very afraid and I think no one knew what was happening. . . . I am 99 percent convinced that the poisoning existed. I was there. The consequences of the poisoning still exist.

Note

1. Newspaper accounts reported that children "acted" for the cameras. See Miloš Antić, "I epidemija režirana" (Even the Epidemics Directed), *Novosti 8*, March 28, 1990.

FIVE

Step One for NGOs:
The Root Cause of Conflict

"I think your name was in the Notebook. I would be careful, you know," the young American "peace worker" whispered as soon as we rounded the corner toward Studentski Park, the small spot of green in the center of Belgrade.

I stopped, alarmed by her tone. "What Notebook?"

"You haven't heard? P. [an American who was working with a non-governmental organization in Kosovo] was called into the police station in Priština for questioning. When she went to the station, she brought her knapsack with her notebook. It was full of all the names and addresses of . . ."

I tried to make sense of it, "So they picked her off the street and she had the book on her?"

"No, she went back home to get her bag."

I groaned. I could imagine the Notebook, full of lists of women's groups, peace groups, human rights activists. I knew how easily "conspiracy" cases can be constructed in Kosovo.

"They xeroxed the entire Notebook," my friend sighed.

I could imagine the police officer carefully lining up each page on the antique Xerox machine. The copies would be clear enough to read the names.

The police had given P. forty-eight hours to leave the country. But within months, "MIR,"[1] the organization supporting P., had returned, giving rise to Kosovo Albanian suspicions that MIR had been cooperating with Serbian officials all along. After the Notebook incident, no one trusted the group.

It was 1995. At that time, a handful of foreign nongovernmental organizations (NGOs) were working openly in Kosovo on humanitarian aid projects.[2] Most of them had initially entered Kosovo on official trips organized by the Serbian Red Cross or another Serbian government institution. Not all of them were viewed as collaborators with the Serbian regime. Kosovo Albanians were well aware that in order to operate openly in Kosovo, all foreign groups need the approval of the Serbian and/or Yugoslav government, if only to obtain entry visas and the proper permits for bringing in equipment and establishing an office. The NGOs that Kosovo Albanians trusted delivered tangible services and responded to concrete problems. MIR suffered from a particularly acute identity problem. Representatives of the NGO could never explain its plans beyond "promoting peace."

P.'s mistakes endangered the work of others, locals and foreigners alike. One Kosovar Serb featured prominently in page after page of P.'s notebook was trailed by police for months. Two Americans whose names were in the notebook were harassed, their phones tapped and flats searched. Police began questioning their acquaintances about their activities. The Kosovo Albanian activists featured in the book waited for the same treatment. A few of them were denied reissuance of their passports, and their phones were tapped and houses monitored. Although the connection to the Notebook was far from clear, for months P. was the source of blame for any police activity against anyone who could have appeared in the Notebook.

MIR provides only the most egregious illustration of failed NGO activity in Kosovo, the land that remains tenuously part of "new Yugoslavia" (Serbia and Montenegro). But similar examples can be found in many forms throughout the world. Kosovo has long been a magnet for human rights and conflict resolution specialists. While many NGOs were much more effective than MIR, they did not prevent war. Why? The difficult conditions that they face in Kosovo illustrate many of the challenges found in any society divided by ethno-national conflict:

- Firmly entrenched ethno-national groups are fighting for control—here, ethnic Albanians and ethnic Serbs.

- The most populous group (ethnic Albanians, 90 percent of the population) is physically dominated by the least populous group (ethnic Serbs, 10 percent of the population), which maintains control over the police and military.

- The two groups live almost entirely separate from one another; neither side understands what each other wants, needs and fears.

- The dispute concerns competing notions of borders, history, language and culture. According to Serbs in power, Kosovo is an integral part of Serbia and Kosovo Albanians who seek autonomy are simply irredentists.[3] According to the majority of Albanians who live in Kosovo, Albanians were the first to populate the area, they comprise the vast majority of the population, and as the Tito-era Yugoslavia no longer exists, the status of all territories within that area are up for reconsideration, including Kosovo.

- The competing narratives are played out graphically through brutal police oppression and structural violence as social and economic conditions deteriorate. Although all people living in the region suffer under such conditions, today the terror of police harassment, false arrest and torture in prison is reserved for one group (the Kosovo Albanians).

- The targets of state oppression have established their own form of resistance as a matter of survival—in this case, a Kosovo Albanian–run parallel structure complete with its own government, economic and social programs and schools.[4]

- The long stalemate pushed some groups to greater militancy. Serbs have long claimed that Kosovo Albanians are armed and dangerous, and Kosovo Albanians have long denied these assertions. For the most part, Kosovo Albanians have successfully carried out a campaign of "passive resistance." However, in late 1997 an armed Kosovo Albanian resistance emerged, the Kosovo Liberation Army (KLA).

- The conflict has been heavily influenced by outside forces, including a neighboring war (in Bosnia-Herzegovina and Croatia, now quiet), an active diaspora and regional and international power brokers which have made various promises and threats to the parties throughout the years, leading to what could be false hopes.

- Tension between the two groups has a complicated historical background and few outsiders fully understand the complexity and depth of mistrust.

- Animosity between the two groups has become almost a part of their cultures; individual and group identities are constructed against the mirror of their enemy "other."

In all areas in conflict, these conditions are shrouded by Truths—that is, the "hidden transcripts"[5] of conflict, the storytelling that serves to define the competing identities of the parties in conflict, propelling and intensifying animosities. NGOs that work in areas of ethno-national conflict are hindered by their lack of awareness of such Truths. While no outside NGO can ever hope to fully understand or resolve the Truths that have become part of the identities of competing groups, NGOs cannot afford to ignore the existence of hidden transcripts. Without even attempting to probe hidden transcripts and to examine National Truths, NGOs cannot begin to understand the root cause of the conflict, and thus they cannot begin to address it.

This book has attempted to unravel some of the Truths that have led to the building of Serbian and Kosovo Albanian nationalisms, turning Serbian fears and suspicions into chauvinist aggression and Kosovo Albanian victimization into a passive martyrdom that could have only lasted so long before exploding. NGOs at work in Kosovo must realize that when sitting down to talk with Serbs and Albanians, when developing joint plans for a health care clinic, when providing resources for water purification, when providing refugee aid—when doing anything at all—people are not thinking only of the project at hand but also about the stains of the 1981 student demonstrations, the Martinović "impaling," the Paraćin massacre, the poisoning of school children, the purported rapes of Serbian women, the high natality rate of Albanian women and the other Truths that dominate their oppositional lives. NGO efforts constructed without knowledge of such hidden transcripts are bound to fail—that is, if success is defined by meeting the needs of local people as they actually exist, and not as imagined by the outsider NGOs.

As in other areas faced with similar problems, nearly every NGO that has attempted to work in Kosovo has had limited success. The problems vary from a basic misunderstanding of the core nature of the problem, to inappropriate and unrealistic goals and strategies, to poor execution of even the best plans. Many foreign NGO interventions have had unintended results, at times creating new conflicts, legitimizing new power structures or indirectly reinforcing an oppressive status quo. At the same time, the people of Kosovo continue to seek assistance with a wide range of development, humanitarian and human rights initiatives. NGOs alone cannot solve the problems of Kosovo, but after the fighting stops they can play a more active and productive role. This means more aid for Kosovo, not less. But all assistance should be better crafted to suit local needs; this means greater awareness of National Truths and hidden transcripts.

Through its examination of NGO activities in Kosovo, this chapter offers concrete suggestions for NGOs who would like to improve their current performance in areas in conflict such as Kosovo and/or start new projects, and information for private and governmental funders who seek better results from their investments. Information was collected through scores of interviews conducted between 1993 and 1996 with Kosovo Albanians and Serbs in over twenty cities and villages in Kosovo and Serbia proper; interviews with government officials and representatives of foreign NGOs in Serbia proper, Kosovo, Geneva, Vienna, New York and Washington; observations of the operations of local and foreign NGOs in Kosovo; and through documentation, training materials and other publications provided by the NGOs themselves.

Analyzing NGO performance anywhere is tricky. Often, those with the most information work with NGOs that depend upon the same small pool of government or private foundation funding. Understandably, they do not want to bite the hand that feeds them. Many would-be critics reason that some NGO work in the region, however misdirected, is better than none at all. Any negative comments, they fear, would result in the withdrawal of NGO funds altogether. Although some commentators have begun to criticize the activities of funders in other parts of the former Yugoslavia,[6] the analysis has not reached the level of thorough, constructive criticism.[7] And no one has breathed a word about Kosovo.

The chapter begins with a summary of the root cause of conflict in Kosovo, proceeds with a general analysis of NGO activities in Kosovo, and continues with closer examination of NGO work in the area of "conflict resolution." It then concludes with a list of recommendations tailored most closely to NGOs working on conflict resolution in Kosovo, but applicable to other NGO interventions in Kosovo and to many areas in conflict. Ultimately, this chapter seeks to encourage NGOs and funders to take steps to improve their current work in Kosovo and other areas in conflict, and/or begin new programs that could help establish conditions for peace with justice.

The Root Cause of Conflict in Kosovo: A Summary

The root cause of conflict in Kosovo is two-pronged. On one level, conflict has been prompted by power struggles among elites, that is, states or quasi-states. On another level, conflict has been propelled by historically conflicting national identities, human development needs, misunderstandings among the general populace, and a culture of failing to accept responsibility for social problems. Structural violence, including institutionalized poverty and institutionalized discrimination against Kosovo Albanians, only perpetuates and widens divisions.[8]

On the level of the state or quasi-state, one leader—Slobodan Milošević—has used Serbian claims over Kosovo and virulent anti-Albanian sentiments to build his power base. The struggle for power was not only for power over Kosovo but for control over all of Yugoslavia. Milošević would like the struggle over Kosovo to seem like one between Serbs and Albanians over scarce resources. According to this picture, Serbs want Kosovo to be part of Serbia and Albanians, led by Ibrahim Rugova, want Kosovo to be independent.[9] A more complete understanding of Milošević's rise to power shows greater complexities. When opportune for Serbian power brokers, Kosovo is much more than a dispute over land; Kosovo is the image of Serbianity which Serbs must protect. To the extent that the question pits Milošević and his supporters against Rugova and his supporters, the political elites on each side understand each other perfectly well—only their immediate and long-term agendas directly conflict.

In their struggle for power, political elites exploit the disturbances that already exist in the general populace and, when desirable and feasible, they create new disturbances. (Although Serbian and Albanian elites both may engage in such behavior, Serbian elites presently have more power to do so.) Disturbances also stem from the national identities of each group, which are defined in opposition to each other: stereotypically, Serbs see themselves as "cultured" compared to the "primitive" Albanians, while Kosovo Albanians today see themselves as "peaceful" compared to the "aggressive" Serbs. Serbian nationalism is wrapped in the story of Serb victimization, the need to fight and defend the "motherland" whose heart is Kosovo, the glorious struggle for Orthodox purity against the primitive, traitorous other, the Albanian, the Slavic Muslim and so forth. Kosovo Albanian nationalism stems also from a narrative of victimization, but a more recent and historical victimization at the hands of Serbs.

In discussions over nationalisms, cause and effect are often debated.[10] Do politicians create nationalisms, or do existing nationalisms shape the political power struggles? The answer with respect to Kosovo is "both." Serbian and Albanian nationalisms have some degree of autonomy that precedes and shapes the political struggles of today. At the same time, however, Serbian and Albanian leaders have used nationalism as a theory of political legitimacy to justify the political reality.[11] To recognize this complexity is to reject *both* the notion that politics is the cause of everything and that nationalism has nothing to do with it, *and* the notion that conflict is simply the result of age-old, primal Balkan hatreds and thus there is nothing anyone can do until those people get tired of killing each other.[12] Moreover, to recognize the complexity does not entail equalizing blame or absolving Serbian leaders and their followers for moral responsibility for gross and continuous human rights violations against Kosovo Albanians. Rather, an understanding that Serbian and Albanians nationalisms exist and predate the current conflict explains why Milošević's appropriation of the Kosovo myth and other nationalist leaders' ploys were so successful: there was something there to be manipulated.

This phenomenon exists and has been played out in different ways throughout time in most societies in the world and is in no way a particular Balkan (read: primitive, uncivilized, backward, historically fated) mode of behavior. Recognizing the nearly universal dimension of the conflict helps one to see the other level on which the conflict is played, that of everyday social life.

On the second level, the conflict stems not only from oppositional national identities but from the ways in which these identities play out in everyday life. In particular, conflict in Kosovo, as in other places, has been influenced by "the quality of the relationship between peoples and how these relationships either promote or thwart the satisfaction of basic human needs of development."[13] Societies in which human development needs are threatened are ripe for conflict. These needs include the need to belong to a group from which one's identity is derived; the need to feel a sense of security and esteem in the expression of one's identity; and the need to have one's identity recognized and acknowledged.[14] In the contested terrain of Kosovar society, the very identities of Serbs and Kosovo Albanians are under attack.

In addition, Serbs and Kosovo Albanians grossly misunderstand each other's needs and desires. As we have seen in the discussion of National Truths, gross stereotypes of the "other" are perpetuated in the state and party controlled media. Equating the other with the agenda of their leaders, each side fails to recognize the shared interests and common ground between them. Stories about human rights violations, documented and imagined alike, spread fear among the general population, adding to their belief that their identity is threatened. When the other becomes de-humanized, violent conflict against even one's own neighbor becomes possible.

The culture of both Serbia proper and Kosovo has not been conducive to accepting individual and group responsibility for social problems and for taking action to effect change. Rather, whenever possible every problem is blamed on the state (or the rulers, whoever they may be). In turn, every solution must come from the state or the party. Individual attempts to address social problems are generally regarded as futile. Both Serbs and Kosovo Albanians demonstrate a particular unwillingness to accept responsibility for what they see as "political issues"—that is, official relations between the two groups and the ultimate solution for Kosovo. Of course, the two groups' failure to act should not be equated. As the lever of power bends far in the direction of Serbs, Serbs generally have greater ability to act and to effect social change. However, the general unwillingness of most Albanians to act has had a detrimental effect on resolution of the conflict as well.

Political elites deliberately perpetuate and exploit conflict between the general populace. Social and economic institutions and structures that perpetuate poverty and injustice further ensure that human development needs remain unmet. The Serbian-run institutions in Kosovo discriminate against Albanians in particular and have a great detrimental impact on the quality of life of all residents of Kosovo. These institutions are themselves a form of structural violence against both Serbs and Albanians, serving to divide and prepare both sides for war.

As discussed more fully below, many NGOs at work in Kosovo seek to address one or several of these underlying root causes of conflict. The success of NGOs ultimately depends on working together to develop a multifaceted approach that touches on both the levels of the elites and the level of everyday social life.

NGO Interventions in Kosovo

A small but considerable number of foreign NGOs attempted to intervene in Kosovo prior to the outbreak of war in 1998. The largest efforts addressed humanitarian concerns and development, providing general aid to hospitals and schools as well as creating specific problem-based projects, such as literacy programs in villages, a women's and children's helath center and clean water projects. Periodic attention was also paid to human rights, mainly the monitoring and reporting of human rights violations, with less attention paid to training and supporting the efforts of local NGOs to do the same. NGOs also claimed to be working to develop "civil society"—loosely defined as the sphere of life outside both state and family—including aid to and training of the independent media, support of youth clubs and camps, and the training and support of local NGOs. Finally, NGOs cast their interventions as conflict resolution or conflict management, conflict transformation, citizen diplomacy. These efforts often involved publications, trainings and workshops aimed at promoting interpersonal communication skills and issue awareness, and meetings designed to resolve particular inter- and intragroup conflicts among a target population.[15]

All of these interventions continue to be needed in Kosovo. Some of the best projects cross categories and combine types of intervention. For example, once the fighting ceases one can envision foreign NGO support of a local NGO designed to help disabled Serbs and Kosovo Albanians by setting up small businesses in which at least half the jobs could be performed by disabled people. Such a project turns short-term humanitarian aid for the disabled into a longer-term development plan that supports civil society and promotes human rights. By bringing together Serbs and Kosovo Albanians on the same project, the plan is also an example of conflict resolution through deeds and not mere words.

Analysis of particular NGO projects depends greatly upon specifics such as personnel and interpersonal relations; the relationship of the NGO with Serbian and Kosovo Albanian political leaders and their constituents; and timing, location and exact method of implementation. Above all, the exact nature of NGO efforts will be influenced by the outcome of the war that began in 1998. Nevertheless, lessons can be drawn from earlier efforts in Kosovo. This chapter does not predict any political solution for Kosovo division, autonomy, or independence. Instead, it offers broad suggestions for NGO improvements under any political arrangement. This chapter first examines foreign NGO performance according to the organization's relationship with local NGOs and individuals, and then focuses on the problems faced by those attempting one particular type of project, conflict resolution.

GENERAL OBSTACLES
TO NGO INTERVENTIONS

Foreign NGOs face an array of obstacles according to their perceived relationship with local NGOs and individuals. Regardless of the foreigners' self-categorization, local NGOs may experience their foreign guests as one of four general types: war tourists; flag planters; seed planters; or nearly invisible hands. NGOs rarely fit perfectly within these categories. Even the same activities may be perceived differently by different people. Nevertheless, the categories provide a useful framework for examination of obstacles to NGO interventions. Below, each category is discussed with particular reference to Kosovo, although NGOs face similar issues elsewhere.

War Tourists. Many foreign NGOs send delegations or individuals to travel around Kosovo, observe and report back on the situation. While fact-finding may play an integral role in the activities of many NGOs, the "war tourists" are not sufficiently trained in gathering factual information, weighing its credibility and cross-checking its content. Nor do they seek out information from varied sources on all sides and in many geographic locales. They often travel to the big cities or one exoticized village, quickly becoming experts. They have few plans for using the information they obtain, and little concept of continuity of contact with the region. Once they have come and seen the situation, they are on to something else. They tend to make quick comparisons between the situation in Kosovo and other areas in conflict without taking the time to try to understand the complex and particular nature of the conflict between Serbs and Kosovo Albanians. To the extent that such NGOs write reports on their travels or undertake any follow-up activity, such as writing protest letters to governments, they often fail to share them with the local people who provided the hospitality that made their trip possible.

War tourists usually visit only Kosovo Albanians. Although Kosovo Albanians tend to be hospitable with all foreign visitors who show an interest in their cause, their patience has worn thin. "We used to think that everyone who came was going to help us," said X., a member of the Council for Human Rights, a Priština-based human rights group. "But now we think they are writing in their notepads, 'Mother I'm so bored, mother I'm so bored.' "[16]

Although local NGOs still remain helpful to foreigners, the visitors quickly fall into disfavor once they fail to deliver as promised. NGOs can try to avoid the label of war tourist by limiting the aims of their mission to those they can realistically reach, by communicating those aims to local NGOs during their mission, and then by communicating again with the local NGOs after their mission about any subsequent steps taken.

NGOs that are not equipped to gather factual information should not undertake what are purported to be fact-finding missions. Ill-prepared and incomplete fact-finding trips only waste the time of local individuals and disrupt the efforts of properly prepared fact-finding missions. In particular, war tourists can interfere with the collection of testimony from witnesses and survivors of human rights violations. By interviewing these witnesses first, the tourists unwittingly participate in the preparation of their story. Once the fact-finding team arrives, the rendition sounds rehearsed—it has lost some of its authenticity, as the witnesses or survivor begins to repeat what the earlier foreigner seemed to like to hear. As a result, the fact-finder cannot weigh the credibility of the witness or survivor.

Flag Planters. Some foreign NGOs have an institutional and/or programmatic need to establish an open presence in every country in which they work. When sanctions remained against Serbia and Montenegro, only a handful of foreign humanitarian aid NGOs (and the ill-fated MIR organization) attempted to open an office in Kosovo. Today, more organizations are considering this option. In doing so, they should be aware that in Kosovo an institutional presence entails both advantages and drawbacks.

For the foreign NGO, a local presence can help facilitate operations, enabling them to assess and address local needs and to tailor programs on the ground to any sudden changes. Some humanitarian aid organizations find that a local presence can enhance their control over programs, facilitate aid delivery and help to ensure that local programs are in line with the overall philosophy of the parent office. For the people of Kosovo, the main advantage of a foreign office is the very presence of foreigners. As long as the foreign staff open their eyes and ears (which optimally would entail learning both Albanian and Serbian), they can observe what is happening around them. Although their mandate may not entail monitoring human rights violations, they become valuable witnesses.

The main drawback to establishing an institutional presence in Kosovo is common to NGO work in many places. To succeed, NGOs must wade through political quagmires and reams of red tape. Obtaining and maintaining visas for foreign staff, receiving permission to build or lease an office and to purchase or import equipment and supplies, avoiding harassment from police and receiving protection from threatening local groups—the day-to-day grind of life on the ground can take time away from programmatic aims. Moreover, an NGO with a local office must tread gently with Serbian authorities. Individuals and organizations that are too active, too critical, too effective at delivering services to the needy or training to local NGOs, risk eviction. Ultimately, a local office may require more programmatic compromises than the parent office is willing to concede.

In addition to the general problem of working with authorities, NGOs at work in Kosovo have faced the specific problem of "dual authorities." NGOs often declare themselves to be agents of "civil society" without clarifying their exact role vis-à-vis the state in which they "operate."[17] Most foreign NGOs in Kosovo made the same initial mistake: they forget that two de facto governments exist in Kosovo.[18] This situation may change if the status of Kosovo changes, but as of this writing international organizations desiring to work on humanitarian projects and other concerns in Kosovo must deal with both governments. This rule applies to all NGOs, but those desiring to open an office face the worst long-term results for failing to jockey their way through both governments.

The Serbian government remains the "official" government. For foreigners, government control involves issuing and denying visas and granting or denying permission to work in Kosovo. Through this mechanism it also controls the content and method of operations of foreign organizations, ensuring that all foreign projects come to some benefit for Serbs. For Kosovo Albanians, Serbia controls through the brute force of the military and police, the courts and the law.

The Kosovo Albanian government, unrecognized by any country except Albania, is branded illegal by the Serbian regime. Still, it has great power over both Kosovo Albanians and foreign institutions wishing to work in Kosovo.[19] It controls through moral authority, demanding the strict solidarity of the Kosovo Albanian people. For example, the Kosovo Albanian government has a very strong influence over whether and when Kosovo Albanians will attend NGO-sponsored activities or take advantage of NGO services. While "non-governmental" organizations purportedly exist in Kosovo, nearly all are tied in some way to the Kosovo Albanian government and are dependent upon it for their ability to exist. Just as the Kosovo Albanian government can shut down an international organization, it can do the same to a local Kosovo Albanian organization.

An organization that does not follow the rules set by the Serbian government cannot get into the country. At the same time, an organization that does not pay its respects to the Kosovo Albanian government cannot effectively serve the Kosovo Albanian population. Foreign organizations that visit Kosovo on official trips, usually planned by the Serbian Red Cross, do not see the real Kosovo Albanian-run projects. Failure to make a parallel trip planned by the Kosovo Albanian government, by Kosovo Albanian health organizations, is fatal to both identifying the problems of the region and fashioning solutions.

Groups that want to establish an institutional presence should realize that part of the price of their office is this dance between Serbian and Kosovo Albanian authorities. NGOs that fail to recognize both sets of authorities are forever haunted by their mistakes. Rarely will both sides be satisfied. The groups that have established offices in Kosovo are generally perceived to be too pro-Serbian by Kosovo Albanians and too pro-Albanian by Serbs. Moreover, although branch offices of foreign NGOs can be quite supportive of locally designed initiatives, often local people view branch offices as imposing foreign plans. Especially in such cases, there is a danger that the foreign outsider—individual and/or organization—could become scapegoated for everything that goes wrong. Attention can became focused on the foreign imposition and/or on the personality of the foreigner, instead of problems with the project itself.

Seed Planters. Organizations that do not have an institutional mandate to establish a local office have more options. Instead of spending time courting local authorities for permission to raise their flag, they can devote their energies to more programmatic goals. While these groups may travel around the region gathering information, unlike those perceived as war tourists they also deliver information and respond to local needs. Through informal or formalized meetings— billed as workshops, trainings or meetings—the seed planters offer information to local NGOs and individuals on such matters as developing education programs, communication skills (often as part of conflict resolution; see below) and small businesses.

Local participants view the experience of seed planters and the information they receive with varying degrees of utility. For example, although many local NGOs in Kosovo want help with writing grant proposals, few of them have found local workshops to be of much practical use. Information on small businesses has been highly valued, but participants complain that they are shown no ways to obtain the equipment and other resources needed to start the business. Communication skills workshops are seen as fun but of little practical utility. On the other hand, local NGOs tend to value workshops and trainings involving education and the media.

Above all, the idea is to plant seeds for local initiatives. At times the seeds do indeed take root, resulting in local media networks, education programs, book projects and follow-up meetings. The foreign NGO continues to maintain some involvement throughout the process, although additional foreign and local NGOs may be brought in as well, both as collaborators on substantive issues and as sources of funding. Ideally, the roles of the initial foreign NGO and the local actors become reversed. The initiative for activity begins with the foreign NGO planting seeds, but realization of any long-term plan depends on the local NGO cultivating the seeds.

The seeding process does not always go as smoothly in practice. Often the roles are never reversed and the foreign NGO always maintains the initiative. The foreign NGO may see itself as prodding local groups into action; the local groups may experience the outsiders as pushing their own agenda. Local participants complain (to each other, not to the foreign NGO) that they have little time to think about the ideas suggested by outsiders before making a commitment to a new project. Despite promises to the contrary, locals say, the foreigners are rarely open to substantive input. The "seeds" come as fully grown plants—and the locals can take them or leave them. For fear that the foreign NGO will abandon them, the participants cannot help but say yes to almost any suggestions. In states such as Croatia, which is flooded with foreign interventions, members of local NGOs are more bold in their feedback to foreigners. But in places like Kosovo, where few foreign NGOs have paid much attention, few local NGOs can afford to be so open.

This dilemma leads to problems in implementation. Some local individuals will "adjust" foreign plans on their own, without communicating the changes to the foreign NGO—for fear that "they would be upset" or that "they might not come again."[20] As a result, foreign NGOs will continue to operate under the assumption that they are working on the original project when in fact the plan has changed substantially. Foreign NGOs can minimize these problems by honestly assessing their agenda before they begin: Would they be open to substantial changes? Would they feel hurt if local individuals rejected their original plan? Could they support an entirely new plan? If they can adjust to make themselves more flexible, they should do so before they arrive in-country. If they cannot, they should communicate the limitations clearly to local participants.

The problem is not just a matter of personal feelings. Often the foreign NGO has already received substantial funding for a particular project and thus cannot add local suggestions, unless the new ideas only slightly change the already conceived plan. A foreign NGO caught in such a bind should explain the existing funding limitations and not pretend to be open to any local ideas. If a foreign NGO would be willing to attempt additional fundraising to support new suggestions, they should make clear that the funding is not guaranteed. They should also encourage local groups to apply elsewhere for such funding and, if possible, facilitate such applications. Foreign NGOs that underestimate their local partners' capacity to understand such matters come across as patronizing; foreign NGOs that continue to pretend that they can respond to every local need can be perceived as disingenuous or worse.

Foreign NGOs that attempt to bring in local NGOs as partners in the seeding process face additional problems. Lines of authority and responsibility between locals and foreigners are not always clearly delineated, leading to substantial interpersonal problems and interfering with implementation of the project. One common dilemma is that the local participants may see the foreign NGO as working for them—as their source of funding and resources—while foreign participants may see the locals as working for *them*—as the personnel on the ground implementing a project. Alternatively, the sides may see each other as equal partners with no clear understanding of what such "equality" means. One bone of contention along these lines is salaries. A foreign expert may receive $250–$350 per day for work for which locals are either expected to volunteer or for which they receive $150–250 per month. Another set of problems arises when the foreign NGO says that it is up to the local participants to implement the project in whatever way they see fit. Usually, in reality, many restrictions exist on how the local participants should proceed.

These kinds of problems can be minimized by clearer communication and through the development of anonymous mechanisms for feedback. Above all, however, foreign NGOs should come to terms with the reality: although foreign and local groups may be equal in terms of valuable knowledge and expertise, they are rarely equal in terms of power and control. "Seeded" projects begin with the outsider's initiative. They then often continue to depend on foreign funding and other technical assistance. Members of the foreign NGO come and go as they please, often as part of their job. The local NGO has fewer options. Few of its members can leave and often it is their lives, not their jobs, that are at stake. If seed-planting NGOs face these realities and improve their feedback mechanisms, they can avoid conflict with local partners or more easily resolve problems once they arise.

Nearly Invisible Hands. NGOs that do not have to have any presence in the region can act as "nearly invisible hands" supporting local initiatives. These NGOs may enter the field, either through their own representatives or surrogates, in order to gather information about local projects and/or to monitor projects that they have already supported. Alternatively, they may hear about local initiatives from personal networks, publications and other sources and then contact the local NGO and support its work from afar. Nearly Invisible Hands seek to support the locally inspired plan, not to bring in an outside idea or to promote an outside group. Some NGOs that operate as flag planters or seed planters quietly become invisible hands as well.

NGOs have two main motivations for becoming Nearly Invisible Hands: to reward local initiative and avoid meddling in locally designed projects, and to circumvent government controls that would deny or restrict such projects. In Kosovo, only a few foreign NGOs, such as OXFAM and the parent office of the Soros Foundation, have been willing to accept and support local NGO plans. In addition, another organization, a flag bearer that will remain anonymous in order to protect its operations, has extended its mission in Kosovo by quietly undertaking substantial support of local humanitarian initiatives. Nearly Invisible Hands can circumvent Serbian controls which have a tendency to skim off medicines in distribution and "tax" (or simply take) donations to NGOs.

Still, Nearly Invisible Hands pay a high price for their methods. Often NGOs cannot afford such quiet support, as it means forsaking the publicity that could lead to more funding. In addition, many NGOs are institutionally opposed to less than transparent operations. Moreover, NGOs that become Nearly Invisible Hands do not have the same control over the projects they support. However, when the NGO knows and trusts the local recipient, the relationship can be mutually beneficial.

Obstacles to "Conflict Resolution" NGOs

Foreign NGO often announce their work as conflict resolution, conflict mediation, conflict management, conflict transformation, preventative diplomacy or the like.[21] Dr. Eftiha Voutira and Shaun Whishaw Brown, of the Refugees Studies Program at the University of Oxford, have analyzed conflict resolution NGOs in three general categories that are applicable here:[22]

Model A NGOs:
– address conflicts at the top level;
– use UN vocabulary (conflict management, conflict resolution, conflict transformation, training, preventative diplomacy);
– rely on funding from government sources and international bodies;
– undertake field missions to collect information, network, solicit invitations;
– organize high profile conferences; and
– assume that conflicts are generated by basic misunderstandings between the parties.

Model T NGOs:
– aim at influencing public opinion;
– use "development" vocabulary (education, conflict mitigation, conflict mediation, citizen diplomacy, peace and development);
– rely on funding from membership, public, church and some government sources;
– undertake independent field research at all levels of society;
– encourage citizen diplomacy and grassroots awareness, as well as attempting to influence leaders; and
– assume that conflicts are generated from the lack of free flow of information to all parties involved.

Model B NGOs:
– address conflicts at the level of everyday social life;
– use peace activist vocabulary (justice, tolerance, education, nonviolence action, empowerment, fellowship, human rights);
– rely on funding from membership and private foundations;
– make use of methods and techniques selected from the other two models;
– rely on the information gathered from the grassroots level; and
– assume that conflicts are the result of human rights violations and aim at the promotion of peace.

All three of these models were present in Kosovo. Although few NGOs fell neatly within these categories, the generalizations offer a useful framework for analysis. Each model encounters its own set of problems. This section discusses problems encountered by NGOs at work in Kosovo prior to the outbreak of war. Lessons learned can be applied to NGOs working in post-war Kosovo.

PROBLEMS ENCOUNTERED BY MODEL A NGOS

Audience. Model A NGOs are dependent both upon access to top-level decision makers and upon those decision-makers having the authority to compromise. This leads to several limitations. In Kosovo, for example, although top-level decision makers would meet with NGOs, the meetings were largely a show for the media, since the local participants had not been authorized to compromise about the underlying political dispute. Serbian President Slobodan Milošević would argue that Kosovo was an internal matter of Serbia and Yugoslavia and that Kosovo should not be allowed to separate from Serbia. Kosovo Albanian leader Ibrahim Rugova would contend that Kosovo must be autonomous from Serbia. Until there is some space for compromise, Model A NGOs will achieve little progress apart from bringing public attention to the issue, a useful contribution but not sufficient to end the conflict.

Carrots or sticks are needed to prod political leaders into action. NGOs alone cannot offer top-level decision makers the carrots they need to create grounds for compromise. For this step, governmental involvement is needed. Model A NGOs can, however, turn their attention to other top-level decision makers—the U.S. government, the United Nations and the European Community—and pressure them to offer substantial economic incentives to make negotiation worthwhile.

Funding Sources. Model A NGOs are often hamstrung by the limitations set by their funders, usually government sources and large international bodies. The rigidity of bureaucracies prevented the kind of flexibility that work in Kosovo demanded. Also, government funders feared being viewed as "taking a side" in the question of autonomy for the Albanian state of Kosova. They did not want to do anything that would signal recognition of the Albanian Kosovar government. However, as explained above, the Kosovo Albanian government, regardless of its legality, has power over roughly two million people. Nearly every Kosovo Albanian NGO in Kosovo is connected to the Kosovo Albanian government in some way, if only for implicit permission to exist. NGOs could not work in Kosovo without respecting the Kosovo Albanian leaders, but this did not necessarily mean recognition of Kosova's autonomy.

Model A NGOs that accept funding from government sources are rarely critical of their own government's actions with respect to Kosovo. The government-funding game forces them to justify their existence. In other words, these NGOs must somehow preserve the need for "foreign experts." This task can cloud programmatic goals. The NGOs can seldom afford to implement a program which would fully establish the self-sufficiency of local organizations.

Sources of Information. Model A NGOs have two primary sources of information: academic sources and information gathered in large group field missions. Both sources may be narrow and limited. Early warning information from academic sources is often divorced from the reality on the ground. Early warning information on Kosovo tended to rely heavily on those who command conflict and not those who hold the guns.[23] At the same time, information gathered in "field missions" was likely to be incomplete as field missions undertaken by high-profile Model A organizations were easily controlled by the Serbian government. To the extent that an independent Kosovo Albanian leg to the trip was permitted, it was just as likely to be controlled by the Kosovo Albanian government.

By their very nature, field missions face additional limitations. Field missions often fail to gather important information because they are too rigidly structured and, thus, fact-finders have little flexibility to respond to new information discovered during the trip. Even the best designed mission depends heavily upon the skills and interests of the individual participants. In many cases, participants in Model A field missions are chosen for their notoriety, not for their particular substantive knowledge about the region or human rights issue in question. Thus, while Model A organizations are excellent for interviewing witnesses about a particular human rights violation and for recording the comments of high-level officials to such violations, they tend to be poor choices for assessing public opinion or determining long-term trends.

Output. High profile conferences and reports of Model A organizations can be extremely useful for turning public attention to a conflict area. However, the people of Kosovo (including many of those who attended Model A conferences and contributed to their reports) demanded more concrete and consistent actions. For a long time no public, ongoing high-level meetings existed on Kosovo. The meetings that did occur reinvented the wheel each time, usually with a

lack of focus and with little thought—or great thought but no resources—to concrete output.

The reports and conferences of Model A organizations may not always address local needs. Model A NGOs often position themselves
to become "invited" into a region to facilitate conflict resolution sessions or to conduct a report. As with seed planting NGOs, it is unclear
how free the invitation is in practice. The Model A NGO may think
that it has planted a seed for a conflict resolution seminar, but the local
NGO may think that it had no choice but to accept the idea. Often
the local NGO accepts the conflict resolution training based on
its own, hidden agenda, and/or with the hope that the training will
lead to something else, such as funding for a completely different local
project.

Assumptions on Nature of Conflict. As discussed above, in
Kosovo the conflict between top-level leaders was not generated by
misunderstandings among decision makers, as Model A organizations
tend to believe. The parties understood each other quite well: Rugova
wanted Kosovo to be independent from Serbia, while Milošević
wanted Kosovo to be part of Serbia. Both sides wanted power and
resources. For these leaders, the stakes were clear in a zero-sum game.

Misunderstandings are a factor in the conflict in Kosovo, but they
are a factor among lower-level actors, not the power elites addressed
by Model A NGOs. Top-level decision makers competing for power
and resources in Kosovo only fuel their conflict by promoting and
exploiting divisions and insecurities among their constituents. They
know that few individuals will speak out or accept responsibility should
full-scale conflict arise. A steady and intense propaganda campaign
against the "other" has promoted fear and anxiety. Fear spreads with
the help of social and economic institutions and structures that perpetuate poverty and injustice, themselves forms of structural violence.

Addressing the misunderstandings that exist among the general populace is no easy task. Both Kosovar Serbs and Kosovo Albanians have
become conditioned to leading two-act lives, the public act and the
private act. For most, the first act is a well-guarded performance, designed to please members of their own group and to stay out of serious
trouble with authorities. In the second act, their feelings are played out
in hidden transcripts of anger, aggression and disguised discourses of
dignity, the modes whereby groups can act out the feelings they or-
dinarily must conceal, such as through gossip, rumor and creation of

autonomous, private spaces for assertion of dignity.[24] Serbians and Kosovo Albanians are not privy to each others' hidden transcripts, nor could they understand each others' transcripts if they could gain access.

Should NGOs choose to address the issue of misunderstandings between Serbs and Kosovo Albanians, they must take the time to research both acts of Kosovar life and begin to understand the hidden transcripts. Only then can they begin to measure the true divide. For example, until recently few Kosovo Albanians would ever speak negatively about their leaders, especially the LDK. Still, in their private lives, through gossip and anger directed at individual LDK members, they often told of their disenchantment. Today, more Kosovo Albanians will speak openly against the LDK, but only in the second act of their lives, the private sphere.

PROBLEMS ENCOUNTERED BY MODEL T NGOs

Audience. The focus of Model T NGOs on public opinion and the media is extremely important, as public opinion can influence both decision-makers and the general population.[25] Until recently, few independent media groups in Kosovo or Serbia proper worked publicly to influence their leaders or the general public to support a peaceful solution in Kosovo. This inaction could be explained in part by the difficulty of the task: silence on Kosovo was deep-rooted in both Serbia proper and Kosovo, and the reach of the independent media was extremely limited.

In Belgrade, fear of authorities only partially explained most NGOs' public silence on Kosovo. The same NGOs that were too afraid to speak out on Kosovo continually addressed controversial issues concerning Bosnia and Croatia. Nor can a lack of information provide an explanation. Even after receiving information about human rights abuses in Kosovo, many groups remained quiet. Nor can social inertia, that is, the general unwillingness in the population to accept responsibility. After all, these are the few people who do accept responsibility on other matters. The inaction can be explained only by deeply imbedded prejudices and fear of Kosovo Albanians as well as great personal insecurity.

Among Kosovo Albanians, the silence stemmed from personal insecurity, group solidarity, and an unwillingness to accept responsibility for what are seen as "political issues" — Kosovo Albanians would rather leave the final solution on Kosovo to their leaders. For years there was little space in Kosovo society for discussion of a solution that did not fit the strategy of passive resistance undertaken by the ruling LDK. When space for divergent opinions opened in 1996–1997, the new voices called for a more militant strategy instead of passive resistance.

Model T NGOs have limited options in working with the media in Kosovo and Serbia proper. The influence of the independent media in both Serbia proper and Kosovo remains weak, as it reaches a very small, urban population. Most Serbs still rely on state-controlled television and radio for information. Although more Kosovo Albanians have satellite dishes that beam in foreign stations such as Sky TV, CNN and Italian, Turkish and Albanian TV, they similarly rely heavily upon media controlled by the governing Kosovo Albanian party. The international media that include voices of independent Serbian and Kosovo Albanian journalists are read by only a handful of local residents. To the extent that the local independent media has any power, it rarely uses it to influence public opinion toward peaceful resolution of the conflict in Kosovo. The independent Serbian media seldom runs any positive images about Kosovo Albanians; the independent Kosovo Albanian media seldom runs positive images of Serbs.

Funding. Funding for Model T projects tends to be extremely limited. With the exception of the Soros Foundation, which single-handedly supported most of the independent press in Kosovo, most funders were more interested in sponsoring foreign-run workshops than paying for locally produced independent magazines or other media related projects. Although media workshops are crucial for training independent journalists and improving their efforts, more resources need to be allocated for media operations and, in particular, the broadcast media.

Sources of Information. Few groups that tried to influence public opinion in Kosovo had adequate resources to undertake independent field research at all levels. Foreign NGOs could improve their information on public opinion by conducting more joint research projects with independent journalists and local NGOs.

Output. Model T NGOs are most useful in aiding the production of independent magazines and in holding conferences on public opinion. As long as the independent media in the region remains weak, however, these actions alone do little to promote "citizen diplomacy." Nevertheless, foreign support could help spur change.

Assumptions on the Nature of Conflict. To some degree, the conflict between lower-level Kosovo Albanians and Serbs was generated by a lack of information, as Model T NGOs tend to assume. As discussed earlier, the media has often presented partial Truths in its effort to build the larger National Truths. A public-opinion survey by the author (in conjunction with independent Kosovo Albanian journalists and the Belgrade-based group Argument) found that Serbs and Kosovo Albanians do not even know what each other wants. For example, 65 percent of Kosovo Albanian respondents felt the Serbian people want Kosovo Albanians to leave Kosovo "for some other place," while only nine percent of the Serbian respondents said that this was the goal of the Serbian people.[26] Keeping the Kosovo Albanian and Serbian peoples ignorant of each other reinforced fear and reliance on a top-down political solution for Kosovo. The lack of ongoing dialogue hid shared interests and common ground between Serbs and Kosovo Albanians.

Still, the conflict cannot be completely explained away by a lack of information. Alternative sources of information, produced locally and outside the region, have always been available, albeit often only in urban centers and, with respect to the print media, at a high monetary cost. Serbs in Serbia proper have the best access to alternative information. Nevertheless, members of both sides tend to believe what they are prepared to believe. Even members of opposition groups seek out and emphasize media accounts which reconfirm their original opinion toward the other.

Information alone does not prompt willingness to accept responsibility for social problems. Many residents of old Yugoslavia (like much of Central and Eastern Europe) have been conditioned since childhood to follow the group and to avoid responsibility for their own lives.[27] The heavy hand of the party-state is to blame for every problem, not individuals within society. To the extent that individuals feel a sense of obligation to respond to social injustice, they have little incentive to act — individual action in the face of the state is deemed to be futile.

In this context, Serbs who hear about Serbian police abuses against Kosovo Albanians will likely refuse to do anything if they can diffuse responsibility or reflect it elsewhere.[28] They may reason that the Ko- sovo Albanian probably "deserved it." State-supported propaganda campaigns against Kosovo Albanians have dehumanized them as "evil," "irredentists," and "terrorists"; few Serbs have ever seen a positive media image of an Albanian. "Feelings of responsibility are subverted by excluding certain people from the realm of humanity or defining them as dangers to oneself and one's way of life and values."[29] Al- though opening channels of communication is a worthy goal to which NGOs can contribute, such efforts alone will not solve the conflict. Other interventions are needed to encourage individuals to confront their own prejudices toward the other and to accept responsibility.

PROBLEMS ENCOUNTERED BY MODEL B NGOS

Audience. The conflict in Kosovo stemmed both from power grabs at the state or quasi-state level and a level, and from unmet human needs, of misunderstandings and lack of responsibility at a level below the state. By working with grassroots organizations, Model B NGOs attempt to thwart attempts of political elites to take advantages of fears among the general populace.

Very few groups worked on the grassroots level in Kosovo. Gen- erally, those that made any attempt reached only urban elites, the very people who had already been discussing conflict resolution in Kosovo. A small circle of Serbs and Kosovo Albanians met with each other regularly, particularly at international conferences. Contacts were de- veloped between human rights groups in Kosovo (such as the Human Rights Council and the Kosova Helsinki Committee) and Belgrade (such as the Humanitarian Law Fund, the Belgrade Helsinki Com- mittee, the Anti-War Center and the conflict resolution group "Most" [Bridge]) and a number of Kosovo Albanian and Serbian women's groups developed contacts with each other. Meetings between these groups were generally cordial and, although rarely resolving anything in their societies, the parties usually parted on good terms. But these intellectuals/activists had little control over their government's policy (especially in the case of Serbian intellectuals who would speak about peaceful solutions in Kosovo), nor did they have much of an impact on the rest of the populace.

Conflict resolution efforts that work on the grassroots level contrib- ute the most if they address unmet human needs for identity. On the other hand, they contribute little if they focus on the ultimate question of Kosovo's future political status, a question perceived to be beyond the control of grassroots initiatives. "I don't want to talk about politics, I want to leave that up to politicians," many Serbs and Kosovo Albanians are likely to say. Instead, NGOs working on the grassroots level can try to teach communication skills and work with homogeneous groups on examining deep-rooted fears and prejudices toward the other. Serbian scapegoating of Kosovo Albanians has long been an important tactic to divert attention from other pressing social and political issues. "Finding a scapegoat makes people believe their problems can be predicted and controlled; it eliminates one's own responsibility, thus diminishing guilt and enhancing self-esteem."[30] Properly trained facilitators can help homogeneous groups examine how their prejudices of their other relate to their own ontological needs.

The language barrier poses a considerable problem for work that would be truly at the grassroots level. Foreign NGOs have not taken the time or resources to train local Kosovo Albanians or Serbians to work within their own communities. Nor do they directly support the local people who are already able and willing to do the work. (The few exceptions are the seed planters, discussed above.)

Funding Sources. Few foundations have any interest in funding truly grassroots work. The work is less glamorous; there are no major conferences or publications; progress is slow and subtle. Even fewer foundations are willing to provide support directly to the local groups or local trainers who are desperately needed to surmount language and cultural barriers when working in rural areas.

Output. Measuring the output of Model B NGOs is exceedingly difficult, as they are eclectic in approach. The relationship between individual self-awareness and change in Kosovo is impossible to quantify. In general, the output of these groups could improve if their work were to be linked to the creation of local NGO projects, such as local village literacy programs and magazines. Exceptional literacy/ women's empowerment programs presently exist in Kosovo in which the sponsoring NGO funds local trainers directly.

Sources of Information. The few grassroots NGOs working in Kosovo do not undertake their own field research as they are too underfunded. Instead, they rely upon the information of others and that which they gather anecdotally.

Assumptions on the Nature of Conflict. Conflict in Kosovo was propelled by human rights violations, as Model B NGOs assume, but it did not arise from human rights violations alone. Rather, as explained above, the root causes of conflict in Kosovo were political power games (in particular the attempted appropriation of Kosovo by Milošević and others to gain power over not only Kosovo but all of Yugoslavia).

Human rights violations have long been an ugly tool in the Kosovo conflict. Political elites use real and imagined human rights violations to push their own power struggles before the international community. As we have seen in proceeding chapters, the discourse of human rights abuses has been appropriated by Slobodan Milošević. According to Milošević and his followers, Kosovo Albanians committed human rights violations against Serbs and led irredentist movements to separate illegally from Yugoslavia, thereby justifying the militarization of Kosovo and mass arrests of Kosovo Albanians. On the other hand, according to Ibrahim Rugova and his followers, Serbian human rights violations against Kosovo Albanians have made it impossible for Kosovo to stay part of Serbia. Despite the very real suffering of the people of Kosovo, both leaders can twist the human rights situation to suit their own agendas.

Stories about human rights violations, well-documented and imagined alike, also spread fear among the general population, adding to their belief that their very identity is threatened by the other. Those who have suffered human rights abuses themselves play a peculiar role in the story telling process. Although they may not wish to speak about their own torture, their identity becomes the "former political prisoner," the "torture survivor." In Elaine Scarry's words: "What is remembered in the body is remembered well."[31] In Kosovo, the "remembering" is done by those who speak on behalf of the tortured. Teller and listener become the victims. The violations become "shared traumas" that can even be transmitted from one generation to the next.[32] Strong national identities take root in these shared traumas and generations of people define themselves in opposition to the torturer.[33]

The telling of stories of human rights violations in a safe and non-judgmental environment (such as a homogeneous group led by a trained and informed facilitator) can be an important step in unraveling the traumas, in examining their origins and addressing the anxiety they have caused.[34] Human right violations should be stopped immediately and the telling of human rights abuses should begin now, but this alone would not end the divisions between peoples or answer the political questions on Kosovo.

Recommendations

Some kind of "conflict resolution" efforts were and are needed in Kosovo. However, outsiders must surmount considerable obstacles if their efforts are to effect even the smallest change. Although the following recommendations for NGO effectiveness are written with respect to Kosovo, they can be applied to nearly any conflict situation.

1. UNDERSTAND THE ROOT CAUSE OF THE CONFLICT

"Any intervention that does not take into account the original conditions which give rise to the conflict will be necessarily palliative and short-term."[35] As stated earlier, the root cause of conflict in Kosovo is two-pronged. On the one hand, conflict has been prompted by power struggles among elites; in particular, Slobodan Milošević used a virulent form of anti-Albanian Serbian nationalism to build his power base and to set the terms of debate for politicians in the future. On the other hand, conflict has been propelled and perpetuated at the level of the general populace by historically conflicting national identities, unmet human development needs, misunderstandings and a culture of failing to accept responsibility for social problems. Social and economic institutions and structures that perpetuate poverty and injustice ensure that human development needs remain unmet and that conflict continues.

NGOs at work in Kosovo rarely acknowledge Kosovo's larger role as the punching bag for Serbian nationalists struggling for power. NGOs at work in Kosovo also often fail to see the role of competition for resources, power and control, as well as the contribution that insecurity and crises in identity have on the populations' readiness for conflict. Nor do they directly address the role of structural violence.

Multifaceted conflict resolution strategies must be crafted on both of the level of the political elite and the level of the general populace. International pressure — carrots and sticks — must be used to force Milošević and Rugova to reach an agreement on their competing and adversarial interests.[36] At the same time, a different set of techniques can be used to help members of both populations analyze their unmet human development needs.[37] Such techniques can develop "new norms of interaction . . . which could potentially transform the relationship to one where both parties are free to develop and flourish as human beings, without threat to their existence."[38] For either of these techniques to succeed, however, malfunctioning (or well-functioning, if their mission is to create injustice) social and economic institutions and endemic poverty must be addressed.

Few if any NGOs are equipped to address all levels. Nor can they offer all the needed interventions. Thus, NGOs should view their activities as falling within the spectrum of needed responses and should endeavor to complement the efforts of other NGOs and government actors.

2. UNDERSTAND THAT FEW LOCAL NGOS AND INDIVIDUALS SEEK "PEACE AND HARMONY"

Foreign NGOs which seek only peace and harmony should understand that they have little support from either side in Kosovo. "Peace and harmony" can be an ideology of oppression, introduced to consolidate gains and maintain domination, as for example in Serbia proper, where there may be peace but no justice.[39] "In fact, celebrating harmony as a virtue, over complaining or disputing, amounts to trading justice for harmony."[40] The ultimate goal for many in Kosovo is not peace and harmony if the cost of peace is too high. Rather, the goal is peace with justice. Justice does not mean the elimination of all complaints or disputes, but rather the creation of fair conditions in which disputes can be heard and decided, without violence or devaluing the other.

3. DO NOT PRETEND TO BE NEUTRAL

NGOs should not pretend to be neutral because they cannot be neutral. NGOs decide with whom to work, which voices to magnify, which long-term local projects to support. All of these decisions may unwittingly place the NGO more in one corner than the other. In Kosovo, as in most areas in conflict, the parties do not have equal power. Under these conditions, the intervention of "neutrals" would only serve to cement the status quo. Until power is equally distributed, NGOs tend to act as facilitators instead of mediators. Many NGOs take an active role in laying the conditions for conflict resolution, which at times means giving voice to the more disempowered group, so that its concerns can be heard and addressed.

NGOs would not accept just any solution on Kosovo. Few if any NGOs would accept human rights violations as part of a compromise on Kosovo. NGOs do not simply accept each party's word that his or her side does not engage in human rights violations and then simply let each side slug it out at the bargaining table with the NGO acting as a neutral middleman. Rather, NGOs undertake their own assessment of evidence on human rights violations, at times establishing their own monitoring systems. In demanding adherence to human rights principles, NGOs cannot be said to be neutral. They lean toward whatever side is more respectful of such principles.

NGOs also would not agree to compromise individual ontological needs. Fundamental human needs of development (identity, belonging, security and recognition) are not negotiable.[41] As Donna Hicks has noted, "Political strategies designed to overcome with force, individuals or groups who react, violently if necessary, to having those needs met, are inherently flawed. The strategies are flawed because human beings cannot be socialized out of these developmental needs. It is like trying to stop a child from learning to walk. The fulfillment of these needs is a developmental imperative. Their inherent force is greater than any external power that attempts to control them."[42]

The NGO may strive to create the conditions where human needs can flourish without threat to their existence. They may also seek fulfillment of such needs on their own, without reference to and devaluing of an other.[43] Regardless of the exact approach used, the NGO should not value one group's needs over those of another. The NGO cannot accept plans that would negotiate away developmental needs.

4. CHOOSE CLEAR AND REALISTIC GOALS AND OBJECTIVES

NGOs should separate their long- and short-term goals from their specific objectives. Both should be as realistic as possible. The NGO's goal should not be resolving the conflict in Kosovo, because many additional interventions will be needed for ultimate resolution. Nor should the goal be resolving competing versions of history, because competing versions of history have become deeply internalized in the cultures and individual and social identities. For some, changing conceptions of history means changing their very self. For this reason, although competing versions of history must be heard, they cannot be simply "resolved."

A more realistic goal would be helping to "establish the conditions for resolving conflict," to help "transform" the conflict, to reduce it to more manageable proportions.[44] NGOs should try to be as specific as possible, while retaining flexibility. A more specific approach would be to state that the goal is to hold three media workshops. The objectives of the workshop should be stated in behavioral terms: having taken the workshop, participants should be able to critique an article; write an op-ed and a factual account on the same story; outline the goals for a new independent magazine. Although objectives can evolve over time, they should be in line with the overall goals and philosophy of the NGO, and at all times communicated to local participants.

5. APPRECIATE THAT WORK ON INDIVIDUAL ATTITUDES REQUIRES BABY STEPS

Although the root cause of conflict rests in large part with power struggles between elites, as explained above, conflict also is perpetuated through unmet human needs and misunderstandings among the general populace and a general unwillingness to accept responsibility. While top-level decision makers can make sudden political concessions, the attitudes of the people will not change overnight. Serbs' and Kosovo Albanians' attitudes toward each other are particularly hard to change as these attitudes have become an integral part of individual and group identities. For some, to be a Kosovo Albanian means to be in a struggle with Serbs; to be a Serb means to fight for the Serbian Jerusalem, Kosovo.[45] Those who have grown up with identities formed as a mirror to the threatening other must begin by turning the mirror on themselves. As Adam Curle has observed, survival with an enemy entails a game of wearing masks and wading through mirages.[46] The view of the enemy becomes tied to the view of oneself and vice versa. In order to change the view of the enemy, one must first change one's view toward oneself.

In Serbia proper and Kosovo, a victim mentality has taken over. The identity of most Kosovo Albanians and Serbians is that of the suffering victim: Kosovo Albanians suffer at the hands of Serbs; Serbs have been misunderstood throughout history by the entire world. To change their attitudes toward each other, Serbs and Kosovo Albanians must first change this view of themselves. But altering a deeply embedded sense of self takes time. A foreign NGO cannot accomplish the task in a handful of workshops.

The problem in Kosovo is particularly complex where threats to identity come from all sides. The cost of both Serbian and Kosovo Albanian identities has been the loss of other identities. For example, a good Kosovo Albanian is first an Albanian and anything else—woman, Catholic, Muslim, Protestant, nonbeliever, student, lawyer, doctor—after. Kosovo Albanians must examine their needs for identity and security vis-à-vis Serbs and also vis-à-vis other Albanians and themselves. Conversely, Serbians also must examine their needs vis-à-vis other Serbs and themselves.

NGOs that focus on changing the individual through rational or emotional arguments miss the full dynamics of identity. Rational or emotional arguments have little impact on individuals where, as in Kosovo, the issue is one for the collective. Kosovo Albanians experience oppression as part of a collective (and only second as individuals) and they represent the collective. When X speaks at a meeting, she speaks first as a Kosovo Albanian, second as a woman, third as a journalist. At the same time, X's personal relationship with Y—her envy, admiration, prior history, etc.—influence her behavior as well.

So far, no NGOs have grappled with the full extent of these complexities in Kosovo. Those who do are advised to take baby steps, such as convening homogeneous consciousness-raising groups, self-reflective drama and poetry, interactive educational programs and so forth, within a single local group, a single city, single village. Heterogeneous groups traveling together to an international conference, applying together for an education program, establishing a joint youth project[47]—all of these small steps are important for long-term change.

6. DO NOT SIDESTEP CORE ISSUES

Being clear and realistic and taking baby steps does not mean sidestepping core issues. Even the most narrowly-crafted program must deal with core issues as they arise, that is, issues relating to root causes of the underlying conflict. For example, an NGO teaching a homogeneous group about social relationship skills might focus on specific learning objectives — teaching the participants to be active listeners and to argue both sides of a case. In doing so, the NGO cannot avoid the moral, legal and political problems that arise in the course of discussion. In Kosovo, social relationships are defined as moral issues, the self-definition of individuals and groups is related to moral and political problems, and legal problems can be divorced from neither politics nor morality.

NGOs should be aware of where they are. One NGO trainer in Belgrade attempted to conduct a training about mediating conflict within groups. The audience included mostly Serbs but also a handful of Croats and Kosovo Albanians. When larger issues arose as to the war in Croatia or Serbian police abuse of Kosovo Albanians, the trainer was wholly unprepared to deal with the topic and she attempted to turn the topic back to intergroup relations. But intergroup relations depend upon the identity of members of the group, and in the former Yugoslavia today these identities have much to do with war and police oppression. In this particular case, the group could not rush to a conclusion about all Croats or all Kosovo Albanians because a few Croats and Kosovo Albanians were present and willing to speak. Had these members not been present, however, the trainer, who had already lost control, would have had no way to avoid what could have been disastrous stereotypical conclusions, propelled by "group think," the process by which the group takes on a life of its own, pushing its members toward forced and premature consensus.[48] Although all trainers need not address all issues, they cannot side-step core issues once they arise. Trainers with little familiarity of the nature of the conflict should not lead the group.

7. ENGAGE IN LONG-TERM PROJECTS THAT MOBILIZE AND BUILD LOCAL RESOURCES

Short-term projects become the dabbling of war tourists. In particular, one-shot conferences should be avoided, as they rarely lead to any concrete results. However, long-term projects can create over-reliance upon the intervening NGO. There must be a balance between parachuting in for a quick fix and having local NGOs become dependent on long-term support. One intermediate solution is to support local efforts and to build their capacity so that NGOs can eventually pull out, leaving functioning organizations behind. For example, one NGO has attempted to establish a women's media project in Kosovo and, as part of its work, it has trained women in grant writing. With follow-up, this program could foster a long-term local project with diversified forms of support.

Few international NGOs work with existing foreign or local networks and projects. These can be an important resource. The need in Kosovo is great enough to absorb all well-designed NGO plans, but cooperation can also avoid duplication of efforts. For example, while programs for journalists have become fashionable, long-term efforts for educational reform for school children are neglected. The issue of education has been deeply tied to political issues which many NGOs wish to side-step. As long as Kosovo Albanian children have been attending "parallel" schools (schools run by Albanians without the sanction of the state), NGOs working on educational programs cannot avoid supporting the parallel Albanian system, implicitly or explicitly. Not wanting to fall out of favor with Serbian authorities, many NGOs have avoided entering the education arena at all.

8. DO NOT UNDERESTIMATE LOCAL PARTNERS

No NGO deliberately underestimates local partners. Nevertheless, many local NGOs and individuals complain that their skills and intelligence are indeed undervalued. One foreign NGO worker, for example, established a hygiene program for Kosovar village women. Her first step was to show women the steps of proper hand-washing. Deeply insulted by the low level of information in the hygiene program, women in Kosovo have been talking about the "hand-washing incident" for months. But, of course, they have not complained to the NGO directly. NGOs should strive to open lines of communication so that local participants can contribute to the content of programs in advance and offer constructive criticism afterwards. Trust is needed between any working partners so that disclosures such as this can occur. Yet the need for professionalism and open lines of communication becomes more complex between peoples of different cultures and experiences.

The world of Kosovo is small. As in many societies in conflict, a foreign NGO cannot do anything in Kosovo without all of Kosovo knowing. NGOs should be aware that their reputation throughout Kosovo is made daily through each contact. One particular problem arises when foreign NGOs must make selections for activities and resources.

The basis for such selections and the basis for choosing the person responsible for the decisions should be made transparent. Otherwise, rumors will circulate. In addition, NGOs that work in the region over the long-term should devise a system for anonymous complaints. All of this may sound trivial, but embittered locals can pull the brakes on even the best NGO project.

Finally, NGOs should not pretend that their relationship is one between friends. Although intense personal relationships can develop, the representative of the foreign NGO is perceived as holding the purse strings (regardless of the reality). The kind of information foreigners receive from locals may be influenced by their impression that they could be a source of funding for their own activities. With foreign aid in short supply, the tendency of locals to be guarded or to "perform" before foreign NGOs is understandable. This dynamic will remain until a foreigner makes clear that she has no access to funding for local NGOs, or until he/she establishes lines of trust that run beyond money.

9. TURN CONFLICT RESOLUTION INTO DEEDS, NOT JUST WORDS

In the Balkans, the words "conflict resolution" can only *create* conflict and drive away those who wish to avoid it. For example, when one NGO announced a conflict resolution workshop for Serbs and Kosovo Albanians in Kosovo last year, only the Serbs participated. But at the same time, a dozen Serbs and a dozen Kosovo Albanians active in the humanist movement met in Budapest, where they authored a joint statement on the crisis in Kosovo. The humanists did not dare call their meeting "conflict resolution" or "dialogue." Few people like thinking of themselves solely in terms of conflict. The Palestinian-Israeli talks began as economic discussion in Oslo. The Carter Center's work in Estonia steers away from the label "conflict resolution," terming its meetings instead as workshops on ethnicity, nationalism and political change. So too, any meaningful work in Kosovo will have to find alternative terminology.

Above all, NGOs should link talk to action. Even if a group of Kosovo Albanians and Serbs sat down at a table and agreed to something, the meeting has little importance apart from the deeds it inspires. A joint health care project, independent news chapter or education campaign would ensure continued contact over a specific project. Humanitarian aid efforts directed at both Serbs and Kosovo Albanians, education programs that happen to involve teachers and students from all groups, women's meetings over common concerns — all such efforts can serve to break down the wall between opposing groups, dismantle stereotypes and, in doing so, manage or resolve the conflict. Certainly, working together on common tasks will not be sufficient to address the trauma, hurt and resentment of victims of atrocities. However, in many cases, it is a necessary beginning.

The conflict resolution groups that do not mention the words "conflict resolution" — those that engage in deeds that help establish the conditions necessary for resolving conflict and not just in the words of the experts — usually have a more positive relationship with local individuals and NGOs and more positive, long-term results. Similarly, NGOs focusing on meetings with top-level decision makers should also link talk to action. For example, a Model A NGO brokering a discussion between decision makers could help ensure future cooperation between the parties by persuading them to agree to a joint program, such as one in the field of health, education or economics.

10. MONITOR FOR UNINTENDED RESULTS

All NGO projects can have unintended results. In particular, foreign interventions may serve to create new power structures and new competition over scarce resources, including the scarce resource of the foreigners' very attention. In doing so, conflict resolution projects may incite new conflict. For example, conflict resolution efforts among Kosovo Albanian women in the past created new intragroup conflicts when differences among group members came to light. Some of these conflicts were at a personal level: "She needs power"; "She [an American] uses us"; "She is too uneducated to understand." Other conflicts were directed at a more political level (although the motive may well have been personal): "She cooperates with Serbs," "She is against the LDK." Most of these differences were communicated in the local language, so the foreign trainers had little idea what had occurred. When the foreign trainer left the new conflicts exploded. No plans existed to "resolve" these conflicts. Foreign NGOs should be attuned to such possibilities, scheduling time to work on new conflicts and creating follow-up meetings.

Conclusion

The root cause of conflict in Kosovo is far from simple. We cannot get off easily, saying it is just the result of "ancient hatreds." Rather, the conflict was propelled through media propaganda and political hate speech. These orchestrated efforts were successful at instilling a sense of fear and victimization. From there, Kosovo played a large role in the rise of Serbian nationalism and the larger conflicts in the Balkans. The conflict has been created over time by power struggles among elites, oppositional national identities, misunderstandings and failure to take responsibility, and unmet human development needs of the general populace. Economic and social institutions that only perpetuate poverty and injustice (themselves structural violence) served to complete the equation for conflict.

NGO interventions are needed that address all levels of the conflict. NGOs and government actors can use economic incentives to induce decision-makers to the bargaining table. Media projects can open information on Kosovo and development of local NGOs and youth projects can help encourage people to take responsibility. Long-term work with individuals and groups can help them discover ways to meet their need for identity without devaluing the other. And substantial development programs can strike at the root of structural violence.

Many people in Kosovo seek help with transforming their society from one in conflict to one in which all individuals enjoy peace and freedom. They seek humanitarian aid of all types and assistance with building their own "civil society." The creation of civil society is particularly complex in Kosovo, where two parallel societies have long existed and local and foreign relations to the government(s) are unclear. Still, NGOs and governments cannot afford to avoid this task. The building of institutions of a "civil sphere" outside the control of either Serbian or Albanian leaders can help promote peace with justice by creating a "society of enablement." A society which supports "the capacity [of individuals and groups] to choose and fulfill 'reasonable' goals" and which enhances individuals' stake in their community, Ervin Staub has observed, "goes a long way toward increasing personal satisfaction and the perception of justice."[49] Through their work, newly created local NGOs teach "pro-social values,"[50] values of connectiveness, care and responsibility. While never *resolving* Truths, NGOs can influence the production of Truths so that they are less likely to lead to feelings of insecurity, victimization and despair. NGOs can help create the conditions in which disabling Truths diminish in importance and alternative, constructive Truths can take root.

Notes

1. The names of all NGOs and individuals in this paper have been changed in order to protect their anonymity, with the exception of NGOs who work openly in Kosovo and only when the comments reflect positively upon their work.

2. "Foreign NGO" is used throughout to signify any NGO that is not local to Serbia proper or Kosovo. Local branches of organizations based in another country are referred to as "local office of a foreign NGO."

3. This official opinion differs greatly from the sentiments of many Serbs who live in Serbia proper. Many Serbs, especially urban residents in Belgrade or other parts of northern Serbia, are apathetic toward Kosovo. "I wouldn't care if it just floated away," many people can be heard to say, "just as long as it does not get us in another war."

4. In September 1996, Serbian President Slobodan Milošević and Ibrahim Rugova, the elected president of the Kosovar Albanians, signed an agreement on education. The vague document promises a compromise on schooling, but its terms have yet to be implemented. Kosovar Albanians had begun boycotting schools more than five years before, after the Milošević regime seized control over the school curriculum and began firing Albanian teachers, often for refusing to profess their loyalty to the state of Serbia.

5. This term is developed by James C. Scott in *Domination and the Arts of Resistance: Hidden Transcripts* (New Haven: Yale University Press, 1990), 198.

6. D. Samuels, "At Play in the Field of Oppression: A Government-Funded Agency Pretends to Export Democracy," *Harper's,* March 1995, 47–54.

7. This chapter assumes that NGOs and funders who are serious about working in Kosovo and in other areas in conflict will not be stymied by critical analysis. On the contrary, with more feedback on work in the field, NGOs and funders should become increasingly willing to undertake new projects in Kosovo. This chapter has been motivated by the NGOs, funders and government agencies who have requested more precise information on NGO work in areas in conflict. It thus seeks to begin a long overdue discussion. As such, it steers clear of any practices that would close discussion, such as the drawing of absolute conclusions or criticizing NGOs by name for any current work. I do want to acknowledge at the outset, however, that some groups have been sponsoring some excellent projects in Kosovo; in particular, I am familiar with the good work of Mercy Corps International, the Soros Foundation, OXFAM and Médicins sans Frontières.

8. For a discussion of "structural violence," see W. Eckhardt and G. Kohler, "Structural and Armed Violence in the 20th Century: Magnitudes and Trends," *International Interactions* 6, no. 4 (1980); J. Galtung, "Paper Violence and Peace," in *A Reader in Peace Studies,* eds. Paul Smoker, Ruth Davis and Barbara Munske (New York: Pergamon Press, 1990).

9. Ibrahim Rugova is the popularly elected president of the state of Kosova, which is unrecognized by all countries except for Albania.

10. The literature on nationalism is bountiful. Compare Montserrat Guibernau, *Nationalisms: The Nation-State and Nationalism in the Twentieth Century* (London: Polity Press, 1996); Mary Kaldor, "Cosmopolitanism versus Nationalism: The New Divide?" in *Europe's New Nationalism: States and Minorities in Conflict*, eds. Richard Caplan and John Feffer (Oxford, England: Oxford University Press, 1996), 42–58; Thomas M. Franck, "Clan and Superclan: Identity and Community in Law and Practice," *American Journal of International Law* 90 (July 1996), 359; Lea Brilmayer, "Propter Honoris Respectum: The Moral Significance of Nationalism," *Notre Dame Law Review* 71, no. 7 (1995); John Hall, "Nationalisms, Classified and Explained," in *Notions of Nationalism*, ed. Sukumar Periwal (Budapest: Central European University Press, 1995), 8–33; David Miller, *On Nationality* (Oxford, England: Oxford University Press, 1995); Anthony D. Smith, *Nations and Nationalism in a Global Era* (Cambridge, England: Polity Press, 1995); Nathaniel Berman, "But the Alternative Is Despair: European Nationalism and the Modernist Renewal of International Law," *Harvard Law Review* 106 (1993), 1792; John Breuilly, *Nationalism and the State*, 2d ed. (Chicago: University of Chicago Press, 1994); Paul Brass, *Ethnicity and Nationalism* (New Delhi: Sage Publications, 1991); Eric Hobsbawm, *Nations and Nationalism Since 1780* (Cambridge, England: Cambridge University Press, 1990); Peter Alter, *Nationalism* (London: Edward Arnold, 1985); Benedict Anderson, *Imagined Communities: Reflections on the Origin and Spread of Nationalism* (London: Verso Books, 1983); Ernest Gellner, *Nations and Nationalism* (Oxford, England: Blackwell, 1983).

11. See Gellner, *Nations and Nationalism.*

12. This thesis is commonly attributed to Robert Kaplan's *Balkan Ghosts: A Journey through History* (New York: Vintage Books, 1993). The author overheard a member of the United Nations Protection Force for the Former Yugoslavia (UNPROFOR) uttering a similar remark in Zagreb.

13. Donna Hicks, "Conflict Resolution and Human Rights Education: Broadening the Agenda," in *Human Rights Education for the Twentieth Century*, ed. George J. Andreopoulos and Richard Pierre Claude (Philadelphia: University of Pennsylvania Press, 1997).

14. John Burton, ed. *Conflict: Human Needs Theory* (London: Macmillan Press, 1990).

15. Given the unstable situation in Kosovo and the lack of the rule of law or institutions capable of enforcing justice fairly (see Helsinki Watch, *Open Wounds: Human Rights Abuses in Kosovo* (New York: Human Rights Watch/ Helsinki Watch, 1994)), Kosovo has not been the target of the "rule of law" and "democratization" projects prevalent in the rest of Central and Eastern Europe. Nevertheless, the steps taken by most governmental and nongovern-

mental organizations have been in line with the goals of promoting partici-patory democracy, privatization and a free-market economy. For example, hu-manitarian aid for hospitals tries to steer clear of (re)establishing reliance on state-run, centralized health care. Similarly, workshops for the independent media rarely contemplate mandatory state support of independent media, and American-sponsored workshops rarely sanction content-based controls on speech (such as prohibitions against hate speech), as such controls would in-terfere with the "free marketplace of ideas."

16. Author's interview, Macedonia, May 1995.

17. E. Voutira and S. Whishaw Brown, *Conflict Resolution: A Review of Some Non-Governmental Practices: A Cautionary Tale* (Uppsala, Sweden: The Nordic Africa Institute, 1995), 5.

18. Even if a compromise can be reached on Kosovo, the authority of Ko-sovo Albanian leaders over their people is so strong that this phenomenon of "dual authorities" is likely to exist for some time.

19. For a statement in accord, see Tim Judah, *The Serbs: History, Myth and the Destruction of Yugoslavia* (New Haven, Conn.: Yale University Press, 1997), 305–6.

20. Quotes drawn from remarks made to author after NGO interventions in Kosovo, 1994.

21. Some of the organizations who use these terms in their literature and grant applications do not in fact perform "conflict resolution" when it comes to reality. The term has become a trendy way for some NGOs to obtain money.

22. Voutira and Whishaw Brown, *Conflict Resolution*.

23. See Israel W. Charny, "Early Warning, Intervention, and Prevention of Genocide," in *Genocide in Our Time: An Annotated Bibliography with Analytical Introductions*, eds., Michael N. Dobkowski and Isidor Walliman (Ann Arbor, Mich.: Pieran Press, 1992).

24. Scott, *Domination and the Arts of Resistance*, 198.

25. See Jacques Ellul, *Propaganda: The Formation of Men's Attitudes* (New York: Vintage, 1973).

26. Ibid.

27. See Erich Fromm, *Escape from Freedom* (New York: Avon Books, 1954).

28. Ervin Staub, *Positive Social Behavior and Morality,* vol. 1, *Social and Per-sonal Influences;* vol. 2, *Socialization and Development* (New York: Academic Press, 1978–79); M. Scott Peck, *People of the Lie: The Hope of Healing Human Evil* (New York: Simon and Schuster, 1982).

29. Ervin Staub, *The Roots of Evil: The Origins of Genocide and Other Group Violence* (New York: Cambridge University Press, 1989), 83. See also Leo Ku-per, *Genocide: Its Political Use in the Twentieth Century* (New Haven, Conn.: Yale University Press, 1981), 86.

30. Staub, *The Roots of Evil*, 48.

31. Elaine Scarry, *The Body in Pain: The Making and Unmaking of the World* (New York: Oxford, 1985), 109.

32. Vamik Volkan, "The Transgenerational Transmission of Traumatized Self-Representations and Its Consequences: From Clinical Observations to Re-

search on Large-Group Psychology," paper presented at the Sixth International Psychoanalytical Association Conference on Psychoanalytic Research, 1995. See also Vamik Volkan, "Intergenerational Transmission and 'Chosen' Traumas: A Link between the Psychology of the Individual and That of the Ethnic Group," in *Psychoanalysis at the Political Border: Essays in Honor of Rafael Moses*, eds. Leo Rangell and Rena Moses-Hrushovski (Madison, Conn.: International Universities Press, 1996), 251–76.

33. Mack, "Nationalism and the Self," *Psychoanalytic Review* 2 (1983), 44–69.

34. Donna Hicks, "Conflict Resolution and Human Rights Education."

35. Voutira and Whishaw Brown, *Conflict Resolution*, 6.

36. For a discussion of "power politics," see Andrew Bard Schmookler, *The Parable of the Tribes: The Problem of Power in Social Evolution* (Berkeley: University of California Press, 1984); Kenneth Waltz, *Theory of International Politics* (Reading, Mass.: Addison Wesley, 1979).

37. John Burton, ed., *Conflict: Human Needs Theory*.

38. Donna Hicks, "Conflict Resolution and Human Rights Education."

39. Paul E. Salem, "In Theory: A Critique of Western Conflict Resolution from a Non-Western Perspective," *Negotiation Journal* 9, no. 4 (October 1993), 361–69.

40. Laura Nadar, "From Legal Processing to Mind Processing," *Family and Conciliation Courts Review* 30, no. 4 (1992), 469–73.

41. H. C. Kelman and S. P. Cohen, "The Problem-Solving Workshop: A Social-Psychological Contribution to the Resolution of International Conflicts," *Journal of Peace Research* 13 (1990), 79–90.

42. Hicks, "Conflict Resolution and Human Rights Education," 85–86.

43. A full discussion of ways to proceed with regards to learning is beyond the scope of this paper. Voutira and Whishaw Brown have explained the existence of two general schools: behavior modification or humanistic. "Psychological interventions in changing people's behavior involve making someone 'x.' For instance, non-racist, non-xenophobic, cooperative rather than competitive, or honest. Cognitive interventions focus on making someone appreciative of being 'x.' They allow, however, for the possibility of someone being appreciative of honesty, yet remaining honest. Behavioral interventions allow for someone becoming honest as a result of a learning experience without allowing for appreciation of honesty per se." Voutira and Whishaw Brown, *Conflict Resolution*, 28.

44. Ted Robert Gurr, "Transforming Ethno-political Conflicts: Exit, Autonomy or Access," in *Conflict Transformation*, ed. Kumar Rupesinghe (New York: St. Martins Press, 1995), 1–30.

45. This part of Serb identity is much weaker for urban Serbs in Serbia proper. In addition, by conducting identity workshops with diverse groups throughout Serbia and Kosovo, the author has discovered that "the oppressive Serb" plays a larger role in Kosovo Albanian identity than the "oppressive Albanian" does in the identity of Serbs in Serbia proper.

46. Adam Curle, *Mystics and Militants: A Study of Awareness, Identity and Social Action* (London: Tavistock Publications, 1972); Adam Curle, *True Justice:*

Quaker Peace Makers and Peace Making (London : Quaker Home Service, 1981). See also Tom Woodhouse, ed., *Peacemaking in a Troubled World* (Oxford: Berg Publications, 1991).

47. Homogeneous youth groups, such as "Green clubs" (concerned with the environment) or cultural clubs, would serve the goals of awarding the initiative and taking responsibility for one's community. In addition, such clubs may provide an opportunity for facilitated discussion of prejudices and stereotypes, and promote a positive, secure self-identity that does not depend upon the other. Heterogeneous groups should be approached with caution as Serbian and Albanian youth have had little contact with each other for a long time and fear of the other is extremely high. One initiative run by the Belgrade-based NGO Most involves a mixture of Serb and Albanian adult facilitators working with Albanian youth. So far, the young participants have decided not to expand to include Serbian youth.

48. Irving Lester Janis, *Victims of Groupthink: A Psychological Study of Foreign-Policy Decisions and Fiascoes* (Boston: Houghton Mifflin, 1983).

49. Staub, *The Roots of Evil*, 267.

50. Ervin Staub, "The Learning and Unlearning of Aggression: The Role of Anxiety, Empathy, Efficacy and Prosocial Values," in *The Control of Aggression and Violence: Cognitive and Physiological Factors*, ed. Jerome Singer (New York: Academic Press, 1971).

Postscript, 1997:
A Wall of Silence

Albanian-Serbian relations in reduced Yugoslavia simmer, as tamed as an untapped geyser. The slightest shifting of ground could cause an explosion. No one wants war. But a wall of silence between Albanians and Serbs has created deep misunderstandings, and the policies of both Albanian and Serbian leaders have only reinforced division. An extensive survey of the region shows that Albanians and Serbs disagree on nearly everything—even on what the other wants. Each side believes in extremely different national Truths. Until the wall is broken, the divide cannot be bridged and these neighbors cannot begin to live in peace.

After the Serbian Constitution of 1990 revoked the autonomous status of Kosovo, Albanians protested the changes as illegal acts, arguing further that since the old Yugoslavia no longer existed, Kosovars could choose their fate. In 1991, in a popular referendum not recognized by Serbia, Kosovars voted to separate from Serbia. Ibrahim Rugova was elected president of an independent Kosova, but the elections were branded illegal by the Serbian regime and went unrecognized by any government other than Albania's.

Today, life in Kosovo has many of the attributes of a war zone. Parents fear sending their children out to play. Serbian police raids on marketplaces, homes and villages, often under the pretext of searching for arms, still occur on a daily basis. Courts are political bodies and the police an arm of the Belgrade regime. The rule of law is nonexistent. Kosovar Albanians have no recourse against being held without charges, beaten into signing confessions, and ultimately imprisoned for "endangering the territorial integrity of Yugoslavia." Never a nation of suicidal martyrs, Kosovar Albanians have chosen a path of "peaceful resistance," withdrawing from Serbian society, establishing a half-functioning "shadow" government, and waiting for autonomy.

After years of waiting, only social conditions in Kosovo have changed—from bad to worse. The infrastructure has collapsed. Fetid garbage lines unpaved city streets. Mines and factories are closed. The unemployment rate in Kosovo is the highest in Europe. The rate of maternal morbidity and mortality has soared; the average life expectancy has fallen. Nearly half the population are students, but the parallel schools for Kosovar Albanians offer only rudimentary education and little hope. Life in Kosovo is entirely segregated: each side has its own schools, hospitals and cafés. However, poverty does not discriminate between Serbs and Kosovar Albanians, and both populations are deeply afraid.

Building the Wall

While police violence against Albanians continued, a parallel Albanian society took root, withdrawing from the larger Kosovar society. Today Albanians and Serbs live as separate lives as possible. While some Albanians and Serbs still work side by side in government and private enterprises, most do not socialize together. Cafés and restaurants, the mainstays of urban Kosovar life, are segregated. The few young Albanians who venture into Serbian clubs—usually because they stay open longer—find themselves justifying their actions to their friends. Mixed tables of Serbs and Albanians cause stares; the mere speaking of Serbian in an Albanian establishment turns heads.

Life in villages is even more segregated. In villages that are one hundred percent Albanian, children can grow up without ever meeting a Serb, apart from the local policeman. Where villages are mixed, the groups tend to keep to themselves. In villages with a lopsided Serbian or Albanian majority, those in the minority may survive because of their close relationship with a family in the majority group; yet because this relationship is seen as exceptional, it fails to dismantle stereotypes. A Serbian woman living in one of two Serbian households in a village of fourteen houses can praise her Albanian neighbors' generosity, attesting that she would "live and die" for them, while continuing to cast the most vile slurs against Albanians.

The parallel Albanian society only finished the construction of the wall between Serbs and Albanians. As we have seen, Serbian leaders laid the foundation soon after Tito's death. With the Serbian media painting a picture of dangerous, rock-throwing Albanian separatists, most Serbs supported the influx of police and military forces into Kosovo and the mass arrests of Albanian activists. Throughout the 1980s, the media pumped out stories of Albanian atrocities: Albanians poisoning Serbian wells, raping Serbian women, driving Serbs from their land. Slobodan Milošević, then a rising star in the Communist Party, built the wall shoulder-high when he visited Kosovo in 1989 and gave credence to these stories, declaring to a cheering Serbian audience, "No one must beat these people."

Albanians have supported the wall through strict mores governing life in their parallel society. Albanian leaders are quick to say that all ethno-national groups are welcome in Kosovo, pointing out that Albanian-run health clinics are open to Serbs, although few actually go. Still, contact between Serbs and Albanians is actively discouraged. Only a few elite Albanian intellectuals can appear publicly on panel discussions with Serbs without fear of public censure from Albanian leaders. Other Albanians have reported receiving warnings from the League for Democratic Freedom (LDK), the ruling Albanian party, to stay away from anything resembling dialogue with Serbs. Public contact with Serbs within Kosovo is off limits, and the LDK has the power to shut anyone down who violates this unspoken rule. Not all Albanians are members of the LDK, and not all LDK members support such a rigid prohibition, but most Albanians (like most Serbs) would rather leave the establishment of contacts to their political leaders.

"For the moment," one Albanian said on the condition of anonymity, "the wall serves both Albanians and Serbs." At the very least, by keeping the Albanian and Serbian peoples ignorant of each other, the wall reinforces fear and supports reliance on a top-down political solution in Kosovo. Enforced ignorance hides agreement between Serbs and Albanians where it exists, and buries the deep misunderstandings that beg for a hearing. The wall thus perpetuates the mistake common throughout ex-Yugoslavia: the belief that "politics" — including contact with the "other" — is the province of politicians alone.

Against a Refugee Crisis: Surveying Opinions

In August 1995, over one hundred thousand ethnic Serbian refugees from Krajina, which had been a Serbian stronghold in Croatia, poured into Serbia. This sudden flood of immigration had a profound impact on Serbs. Nearly everyone in Serbia knew someone who came from Krajina. Serbian officials settled over seven thousand of these refugees in Kosovo, often against their will and in defiance of warnings from the international community that the newcomers could provoke Albanians. Against this backdrop, I developed a questionnaire on Kosovo generally. I sought to reach a representative sample of two hundred adults in Serbia proper and Vojvodina and two hundred in Kosovo. As both populations were likely to respond differently to an outsider, local groups administered the survey in the local languages. The results are given in tables in Appendix B.

MIXED SIGNALS: ALBANIAN
AND NON-ALBANIAN RESPONDENTS

In general, Albanians are more pessimistic than Serbs about the possibility of the two groups living in peace, more pessimistic about negotiations and more fearful about the impact of settling Krajina refugees in Kosovo. At the same time, however, they are more optimistic about avoiding war. Opinions on who would make concessions at the bargaining table are diametrically opposed: 91 percent of Albanians say Milošević would have to give in, while 88 percent of non-Albanians say the conciliatory party would be either Rugova alone or both Rugova and Milošević.

Both sides misread each other's goals. While no Albanians think Serbs want them to be part of Serbia and subject to the same laws, most non-Albanians (62 percent) name this outcome as the goal of the Serbian people. Over 65 percent of Albanians contend that Serbs want "Albanians to leave Kosovo for some other place," but only 17 percent of non-Albanians say that Serbs want to kick out Albanians. As far as their own goals are concerned, Albanians are split between joining Albania or creating their own state, with slightly more respondents favoring the latter. Even though non-Albanians also identify these as Albanians' top choices, a minority (12 percent) still hold hope that Albanians seek to

POSTSCRIPT, 1997

become an autonomous region within existing Yugoslavia. In one-to-one interviews, many Albanians say they would have accepted this outcome in the past, and some would even allow it as interim solution, but not a single Albanian respondent identifies staying with Yugoslavia as today's goal.

Only a minuscule percentage of Albanians think the heavy police presence is justified ("to protect us from the Krajina Serbs," one woman joked), compared to a majority of non-Albanian respondents (65 percent). The surprise lies in how many non-Albanians find the police presence unjustified—21 percent—and how many non-Albanians support the right of Albanian children to education in the Albanian language—81.5 percent

SURPRISING OPTIMISTS AND PESSIMISTS: SERBIAN-LANGUAGE RESPONDENTS

The Serbian media paints Serbian families who have left Kosovo as a desperate lot who were chased off their land by dangerous Albanians. Contrary to what one might expect, then, families in Serbia who had lived in Kosovo (11 percent of respondents) were far *less* pessimistic about the fate of Kosovo. Nearly 68 percent say war is unlikely in Kosovo, compared with 46 percent of the non-Albanian respondents who had not lived in Kosovo. Serbs with closer ties to Kosovo are also optimistic about Albanians' desired solution for Kosovo. Nearly 24 percent of the respondents whose families had previously lived in Kosovo, twice the percentage of other non-Albanian respondents, think Albanians want autonomy within Yugoslavia.

Respondents with relatives from Krajina form an even more distinct opinion group. They are almost twice as likely as others to answer yes to the question, "Do you think that the solution of the crisis in our country is on the horizon?" They also see a much greater need for negotiations on Kosovo than other non-Albanian respondents (86 percent to 63 percent). At the same time, they are more pessimistic about the possibility of Serbs and Albanians living together (57 percent to 37 percent), the chances for war (64 percent to 38 percent) and the detrimental impact of settling Krajina refugees in Kosovo (36 percent to 22 percent).

Respondents who listed their ethnicity as "Hungarian" or "other" (ethno-national minorities) are more optimistic than other non-Albanian respondents about negotiations, the possibility of life in a common state, and the possibility that Albanians would want to stay within

Yugoslavia. Far fewer of the ethno-national minorities think the goal of Serbs is to kick Albanians out of Kosovo (4.5 percent to 18.5 percent), or that the heavy police presence in Kosovo is justified (45.5 percent to 68 percent). Ethno-national minorities are more likely to recognize that the human rights of both Albanians and Serbs are violated in Kosovo (32 percent to 22 percent).

Women, young people and the highly educated are more pessimistic about the possibilities for war in Kosovo. These results indicate that the underlying reasons for hopelessness among these groups—discrimination, poor educational opportunities, unemployment, the decay of culture—must be addressed.

DISMANTLING THE WALL

The Serbian-language survey included one question that was not in the Albanian-language version: "Is the solution of the crisis in the country on the horizon?" Those who answered yes were far less likely to predict war in Kosovo (28 percent to 60 percent) and far more likely to think that Serbs and Albanians could live in peace in a common state (66 percent to 36 percent). These results confirm that optimism spreads. But so does fear and ignorance. Dismantling the wall will involve listening to national Truths. The Truths will never be *resolved*, but their mere telling could be transformative. Conflicts do not arise because people hold different collective Truths, but "because one people belittles, disrespects, and disparages the myth of another."[1] The goal then will be to encourage conditions in which both Serbs and Albanians can tell their own Truths *and* listen to the others' Truth without becoming disparaging, and without folding up in a state of fear or victimization. Breaking the wall of silence between Serbs and Albanians will not magically cause agreement, but it will force both groups to have a good look at each other—and at themselves.

Note

---

1. Traian Stoianovich, *Balkan Worlds: The First and Last Europe* (Armonk, N.Y.: M. E. Sharpe, 1994), 305.

Postscript, 1998:
Kosovo in Conflict

The following essays were written in Sarajevo and Washington, D.C., in June and July of 1998, following a fact-finding mission to Kosovo.[1] The situation in Kosovo was grim, with the territory engulfed in violence and a political solution nowhere in sight. What we had said would happen had happened. The Truths outlined in this book set the charge for a reverberating explosion.

In the summer of 1998, the conflict remained within Kosovo, and military analysts predicted that it was unlikely to spill across borders into Albania or Macedonia. The number killed was nowhere near those in Bosnia, and absent a wider "theater of war" the international community was unlikely to intervene. But for those who care about the people of Kosovo, Serbs and Albanians alike, continued inaction on the part of the international community was immoral and inexcusable. So was continued ignorance of the history of Kosovo. U.S. politicians were attempting to force Albanians to the bargaining table under a framework that ignored the pattern of Serbian abuse against Albanians.

Many of the same people working on human rights issues in Kosovo had lived and worked in Bosnia-Herzegovina and Croatia during or after the wars there. The stories of refugees and displaced people from those conflicts are hauntingly similar to those told by Kosovars. "I am physically sick when I hear about Kosovo," one Bosniac told me. She herself was uprooted from her home in Srebrenica and, in the summer of 1998, lived in a divided Mostar. Along with a friend in Sarajevo, she was planning an aid drive for Kosovo Albanians. "It won't be much," she said, "but it would be symbolic." The cycle of brutality and international ineptitude witnessed in Bosnia continues in Kosovo.

I have kept these pieces in the present tense in order to give the reader a sense of the urgency that many people felt over Kosovo in the summer of 1998. They are short and to the point, reflecting my own sense of frustration over the inability of policymakers, the original audience for these essays, to understand Kosovo. Unlike other parts of this book, they are prescriptive. In turn, they review the humanitarian situation, the political situation and the military situation, making concrete suggestions for action.

One hopes that by the time this book is published the situation will have improved for all people in the Balkans. Meanwhile, lived history continues. Stories are experienced, remembered, told and retold. "Truths" shape new generations. Perhaps they will find a way to live in peace with justice. So far we have failed.

The Humanitarian Situation: How to Aid Kosovo

In one of the walled gardens in Priština, the provincial capital of Kosovo, Flora sits patiently on a stone bench fiddling with a picture book. The five-year-old's left leg is propped up with a large pillow; two wooden bars prevent her from moving her knee. A piece of a grenade has been in her knee for over a month. Her doctor cautioned that movement might cause the metal to sever her nerve permanently.

Flora, along with some 120,000 ethnic Albanians over the last four months, was driven out of her home by Serbian forces in Kosovo. The local hospital would not treat her, but a private surgeon offered to do what he could for free. It was not enough. The shrapnel remains. He recommended another surgeon in Macedonia, but the road to Macedonia is blocked by fighting militia. Her face pale with pain, Flora waits for someone to tell her what will come next.

The girl's thirty-one-year-old mother, Hedije, and fifty-five-year-old grandmother, Hajrije, take care of the other children in a small basement room: the newborn who arrived after the family had fled their home in Decan and who sits in a corner swaddled in borrowed blankets, and the vivacious two-and-a-half-year-old girl who keeps the entire family awake with her nightmares. Hajrije apologizes for the children's old clothes.

"We had everything before," she says. "I had bought the baby such beautiful new things and we left them all behind." They left in the night in their slippers when Serbs began shelling their home. "We had three stores on the main street," the woman sighs, "and now they are completely gone." When asked about the young men in the family, she says they have gone back to look after the livestock, but everyone knows they stayed to fight. No one has heard from them in over two months.

Hedije's eyes are red from tears and exhaustion. She was nine months pregnant when she fled on foot from Decan to the village of Ismiq. It was there that five Serbian policemen gave her a ride to the hospital in Peja (Peć) to give birth. While she was in the delivery room, another group of police beat up her husband in the waiting room, accusing him of lying about his wife's pregnancy. Within minutes of giving birth, with the placenta still attached, Hedije was wheeled into the hospital waiting room to prove to the police that she had indeed been pregnant; only then did the police stop beating her husband.

The next day, she returned to the village, and it was there that she heard Flora's piercing scream that "just would not stop." Hedije is apologetic: "I didn't know she was hit, I thought she was only afraid. But then I saw the blood." Hedije made a makeshift tourniquet to stop the bleeding and waited for some neighbors to bring a doctor. Flora had her first surgery on the floor of a house in Ismiq. "We thought it was done. We didn't know why she still had pain. We didn't know there was more inside her knee and that it could move to her nerve. . . ." The family used a horse cart to move the children to Priština, with the women walking alongside it.

Hedije is quick to point out that they are among the lucky ones because they have a safe place to live now, with a nice host family. While many displaced Kosovo Albanians live with relatives, even more, like this family, are dependent on others for shelter. Priština is the family's third place of refuge in three months. They had to leave the first two because of Serb shelling; both of those villages, previously one hundred percent ethnic Albanian, are now uninhabitable and controlled by Serbs. They had first stayed in Priština in the apartment of Hedije's sister, a student at the private (and officially illegal) Kosovo Albanian university. But that was a tiny apartment across the street from the police station in the city center, and Hedije spent all her time trying to hush the children. She was afraid to open the windows lest the neighbors hear their cries. The Center for the Protection of Women and Children, a Kosovo Albanian nongovernmental humanitarian organization where she sought medical care, suggested a room with a host family. The host family itself depends upon aid from the Kosovo Albanian solidarity fund to get by from month to month, so it can offer little except space and moral support.

Apart from Flora's trip to the surgeon, none of the family members move outside the walls of the courtyard. They fear that police will harass or even kill them. Perhaps their fear is justified: Serb forces have massacred entire families, especially those coming from places known to harbor the Kosova Liberation Army. While police in Priština routinely stop ethnic Albanian men, women and children can usually walk the street without police harassment. Nonetheless, this family, like thousands of others hidden in Priština and other cities and villages throughout Kosovo, is terrified. Only the gravest health concerns could persuade them to leave their shelter. The host family is afraid as well, for they too could be a target of police for harboring families from "enemy" villages.

Hedije is breastfeeding her newborn, and she relies on handouts from a Kosovo Albanian women's group to feed the rest of the family. All of her daughters need diapers: the two-and-a-half-year-old forgot her toilet training after the shelling began, and five-year old Flora cannot move without help, which she is sometimes too embarrassed to ask for. Kosovo Albanian nurses have come by to examine the children, and local merchants have donated clothes. Given the extremely high percentage of women working in positions of authority at Kosovo Albanian humanitarian groups, the aid that does come to Hedije specifically addresses the health needs of women, including the provision of sanitary pads and postnatal vitamins. Her greatest need at the present time is to find someone to transport Flora safely to Macedonia or some other third country for her operation.

While international groups debate whether the conflict in Kosovo has risen to the status of an "emergency," this war has marked each day of Flora's life. At first, it was a low-intensity war, one that the international community could easily overlook. Kosovo Albanians carried out a largely nonviolent campaign for restoration of political and cultural rights while Serbian police and military raided their villages, detaining, harassing and torturing Kosovo Albanians. Children like Flora grew up with substandard education, medical care and nutrition.

In the winter of 1998 the conflict in Kosovo erupted into all-out combat. It became harder for the international community to ignore. Serbian forces shell ethnic Albanian homes in the middle of the night, driving out entire villages. But international groups still managed to deny that a war was raging in Kosovo. Many of the same humanitarian groups who were active in Bosnia and Croatia have turned their backs on Kosovo.

Some governments and humanitarian organizations withhold meaningful aid from Kosovo Albanians in the hope of exerting pressure for a political solution. Using innocent civilians like Flora as bargaining chips in political games violates international humanitarian norms and basic standards of human decency.

International groups attempt to justify their inaction by repeating the Serbian mantra that Kosovo is an "internal problem." Invocations of state sovereignty to justify gross human rights abuses is unequivocally contrary to international law. Moreover, in 1989 Serbian politicians illegally stripped Kosovo of its autonomous status in old Yugoslavia, shortly before that country was torn apart. This history calls the legal status of Kosovo within Serbia into question and exposes the fallacy of claims that it is an internal Serbian problem.

Internationals on the ground offering aid point to an array of access-related difficulties. Belgrade denies visas to many internationals and blocks the delivery of aid to conflict-ridden areas by locals and internationals alike. Even when aid does get through the uprooted families are hard to reach, because they, like Flora, are hidden in private homes.

Meanwhile, the conflict rages on and a health crisis mounts. The needs of the displaced population, which come from the most impoverished parts of Kosovo, are acute. Most families have one pregnant or nursing woman; many of the children are malnourished; some of the women report being sexually assaulted by Serbian forces.

It is the duty of the international community to demand immediate access by local and international humanitarian aid groups to the populations affected by the conflict. Given the widespread impact of the conflict in Kosovo, this means access must be afforded to the entire territory. A key component of such a plan would involve the placement of international monitors in Kosovo to observe aid delivery and compliance with human rights standards. Humanitarian corridors like those organized in Bosnia may help to secure access as long as measures are put into place to ensure that such corridors are not politically manipulated. As of this writing, such steps have not been taken.

One of the lessons of the war in Bosnia was that the entire population required aid. Families that played host to the displaced were among those most in need. This lesson should be applied in Kosovo, where humanitarian aid groups can work by delivering aid directly to the families playing "host" to the uprooted. Collective centers would not work for the Albanians displaced in Kosovo, as they fear detection from police.

Above all, in order to be effective international humanitarian groups need to learn about the capacities of local humanitarian groups and work through them. During the past seven years, Kosovo Albanians developed an intricate network of delivery channels to reach needy families. The Albanian humanitarian organization "Mother Theresa" has over one hundred clinics throughout Kosovo and thousands of volunteers. For eight years, Mother Theresa has been the lifeline for hundreds of thousands of Kosovo families that depend on it for medical care, food and other material assistance. Other groups actively aiding displaced populations include the Center for the Protection of Women and Children, the Albanian Woman's League and the women's rights group Helena. The Albanian Woman's League, for example, has published and distributed ten thousand copies of the Red Cross Emergency Aid Instructions. Instead of creating ineffective parallel mechanisms, internationals are most effective when they tap into the aid delivery structure that already exists.

Reaching Flora will not be easy. Impossible it is not.

Sarajevo, June 1998

The Political Situation:
How to Resolve the Status of Kosovo

American negotiators are attempting to push Kosovo Albanians to the bargaining table with Serbs. The threshold requirement, American diplomats say, is that Kosovo Albanians give up their fight for independence and accept living within Serbia forever. Kosovo Albanians refuse. Of course. Given all that has happened in Kosovo, the only tenable solutions are independence or division.

Imagine a marriage that begins on bad terms and grows worse over time. The husband restricts his wife's freedoms, forbidding her from seeing her friends, from wearing the clothing of her choice, from reading the books she loves. He begins to beat her, at first because the dinner is sometimes cold and later with no reason at all. At times the beatings are so bad that she cannot even walk.

The wife seeks help from outsiders. During the early years, she hopes to remain in the marriage and retain her dignity and independence. But then the husband starts to beat the children as well. The wife can see no possible resolution apart from a separation. She has nowhere to go and no means by which to get there. She again turns to outside counselors for help, and they tell her to be patient. The abuse escalates. The wife sells everything she has for a gun. When her husband tries to beat her children again, she threatens him with the weapon. He grabs it from her and shoots her in the neck.

A marriage counselor visits the wife in the hospital. "I've talked to your husband," he says. "He will take you back." The counselor tells her she must live with him forever. Outrageous? Such is the case of the Kosovo Albanians. Newspaper accounts call Kosovo Albanians separatists, but they are only fighting for freedom from an already destroyed marriage.

Under the 1974 Constitution of Yugoslavia, Kosovo was an autonomous province of Serbia within Yugoslavia. This meant that Kosovo was almost like a republic, complete with its own governing authorities, independent schools, Albanian-language university, hospitals and banks. It even had its own seat on the collective Presidency of the federal government of Yugoslavia. Kosovo Albanians had the expectation that they would always be able to enjoy such autonomy.

In 1989, the backers of Slobodan Milošević used illegal measures to strip Kosovo of its autonomous status. Police detained and harassed Albanian leaders, and Milošević's men installed puppet Albanian politicians who would pay obeisance to Belgrade's command. Eventually, police even chained the doors of the provincial government to prevent Kosovars from meeting. Similar illegal actions were taken in Vojvodina, the other autonomous province of Serbia.

Despite losing their provincial autonomy, Kosovo and Vojvodina retained their seats on the collective Presidency of Yugoslavia, and Milošević hand-picked the people who held those seats. He controlled the leadership of Montenegro as well, and with these four automatic votes on the Presidency, Milošević wielded great control over the future of Yugoslavia. Abuses against Kosovo Albanians intensified, Milošević seized greater power, and Yugoslavia was torn apart.

What is the status of Kosovo today? It was unconstitutionally denied autonomy in the framework of a country that no longer exists. Kosovo Albanians voted in their own government, but the international community has refused to recognize it. The best we can say about the legal status of Kosovo is that it is ambiguous.

How can the status of Kosovo be resolved? The long history of Serbian abuse of Kosovo Albanians rules out the possibility that this marriage can survive. That Kosovo Albanians have taken up arms to fight for freedom makes reconciliation all the more untenable. To tell Kosovo Albanians that they must stay within Serbia or reduced Yugoslavia (Serbia and Montenegro) would be to tell them to return to their tormentor.

As of this writing, the only workable options for Kosovo are independence or division. Both would require that ethnic minorities be accorded human rights and that international monitors be positioned to assure compliance with international standards. Given that Kosovo is 90 percent ethnic Albanian, an even territorial division would be impossible. Still, Kosovo is rich in natural resources, and Serbs may be satisfied if they can retain a small northern sliver of the territory.

Perhaps a less drastic solution would have been possible had the international community answered Albanians' earlier cries for help. Now it is too late.

Washington, D.C., July 1998

The Military Situation: Bosnia Redux

The international community has promised the same kind of response to Kosovo as to Bosnia. In nearby Sarajevo, Bosnians cannot bear to listen. They know what this means. Kosovo Albanians are in for a long, lonely fight.

What exactly does it mean for the international community to give Kosovo the same treatment it gave Bosnia?

It means flying NATO warplanes and other international aircraft far overhead in grand displays of force while the butchery of civilians continues on the ground. As in Bosnia, the United States would wait for over half the population of Kosovo to be uprooted from their homes before finally beginning strategic air strikes inside Kosovo.

It means enforcing an arms embargo to block military shipments to Kosovo Albanians. This would aid Serbian forces, who would once again be fighting with vastly superior military resources. After years of bloody war, the United States would step in to arm and train Kosovo Albanians, just as they are belatedly equipping the Bosnian Federation army.

It means sending in UN troops to freeze the "status quo." This would prevent Kosovo Albanians from retaking land in the Drenica region, the area devastated by Serbian forces in the earliest days of fighting this year. Serbian forces seized nearly all of the land they presently control in Bosnia during the early days of that war, and UN forces effectively prevented Bosnian troops from taking back the ground. Kosovo Albanians would have to relinquish the land they once lived in near the Albanian border. As in Bosnia, very few of the original residents of that land are willing to give up so easily.

It means setting up "safe areas" for Kosovo Albanians to be guarded by international troops. The international troops would run from the safe areas at the hint of combat, wholly failing to offer any real safety to civilians. As in Srebenica, Serbian forces would invade the safe areas and kill every living man they can find. Kosovo Albanians, like the Bosnians supposedly protected by "safe areas," would lose all faith in the international community.

It means using international troops to block Kosovo Albanians from returning home to fight, while at the same time using international transport to truck people out of areas under siege. When the fighting ended, the international community would plead with refugees to return to their destroyed homeland. Already Germany and Switzerland want to return Kosovo Albanians; the pressure for forced and early repatriation after a bloody war in Kosovo would be overwhelming.

Treating Kosovo like Bosnia means waiting until after the destruction of lives and communities to begin serious third-party-facilitated talks. It means spending billions of dollars and deploying thousands of international soldiers after the war ends in a futile attempt to rebuild what once was. It means an entire population never forgetting the horror of war. Kosovo Albanians are in trouble if the international community responds in the same way it did in Bosnia.

Inaction by the international community has already served to radicalize the ethnic Albanian population in Kosovo. Albanians who one year ago would have accepted some kind of autonomous Kosovo within existing Yugoslavia are now vowing to fight to the death for an independent state. Given their determination, the only feasible solution is international mediation leading to independence of all or at least part of the Kosovo territory. Any compromise short of this would only prolong a long and bloody guerrilla war.

Out of a population of two million in Kosovo, over one hundred thousand people are already internally displaced, and perhaps an equal number have fled to Albania, Macedonia, Bosnia, Germany, Slovakia, Switzerland, anywhere they can get in. The war in Kosovo has begun. The longer it continues, the greater the international intervention that will be needed to stop it.

The international community can show it learned something from Bosnia, or it can follow the old pattern and give up on the people of Kosovo. No wonder Sarajevans turn the channel when news of Kosovo comes on. They know.

Sarajevo, June 1998

Note

1. The first of these essays draws from a report written by the author for the Women's Commission for Refugee Women and Children. The author is grateful to the Women's Commission and the Halle Center for International Affairs at Emory University for supporting her research in 1998.

Select Chronology:
Kosovo and Yugoslavia,
1918–October 1998[1]

1918

A new state is created: The Kingdom of Serbs, Croats and Slovenes. The new state is the most ethnically heterogeneous in Europe, with the exception of the Soviet Union.[2] Serbs are the largest nation in the Kingdom, forming 39 percent of the postwar population. Government authorities shut down all Albanian-language schools in Kosovo and attempt to force Albanians to assimilate. Armed uprisings in Kosovo begin in 1918 and continue until 1920.[3]

Over the next twenty years, the Yugoslav government exerts pressure on the Kosovo Albanian population to emigrate or assimilate, forcing them to add Serbian suffixes to their names and mandating that all official business be conducted in Serbo-Croatian.[4] Migration figures differ wildly, but some commentators believe that as many as half a million Albanians emigrate from Yugoslavia during this period;[5] others set the figure as low as thirty-five thousand.[6] Emigrating Turks and Albanians are soon replaced by Serbian and Montenegrin settlers brought from Montenegro, Herzegovina and Lika. The settlers receive special privileges and, "under the vague pretext of agrarian reform, land which was 'abandoned' or deliberately described as such, is liberally distributed to Serb and Montenegrin colonists."[7] According to some Serbian researchers, as many as six hundred thousand Serbs and other Slavs arrive during this time.[8]

1921

The Constitution of the Kingdom of the Serbs, Croats and Slovenes—the Vidovdan Constitution—attempts to unify and centralize Yugoslavia.[9] Tension centers mainly on conflicting national ideologies, with the two strongest nations—Serbs and Croats—pitted against one another.[10]

1926

An agreement is reached for the borders of Albania (which had been granted independence in 1913 despite disagreements about borders). Half a million Albanians are left inside the territory of Yugoslavia in an area called *Kosovo and Metohija* (or "Kosmet") by Slavs and *Kosova* by Albanians.[11]

1929

The Serbian King Aleksandar I abolishes the Constitution of the Kingdom and imposes a dictatorship, renaming the country Yugoslavia—the Kingdom of South Slavs.[12] Forced assimilation of Kosovo Albanians continues. A document of the Ministry of Interior Affairs states that "there are no minorities in our southern regions."[13]

1931

The Constitution of 1931 establishes a quasi-parliamentary system subject to the king. Tensions remain between nations. Serbian leaders support the notion of a centralist or unitary state and Croatian leaders prefer a dualistic or federal system.[14]

1937

Vasa Čubrilović, a member of the Serbian Academy of Arts and Sciences, publishes a Memorandum on the Expulsion of the Albanians, arguing that the "brute force of [the] organized state" should be used to expel Albanians from Kosovo. He argues: "At a time when Germany can expel tens of thousands of Jews and Russia can shift millions of people from one part of the continent to another, the shifting of a few hundred thousand Albanians will not lead to the outbreak of a world war."[15]

1939

The centralist structure of the state of Yugoslavia is revised to give autonomous status to Croatia in the form of a separate *banovina* (province)

WORLD WAR TWO

Germany and its allies invade Yugoslavia in 1941 and quickly take control. The Axis powers divide up the country; Kosovo becomes part of "greater Albania" and is placed under Italian control.[16] While some Kosovo Albanians fight with Tito's Partisans against the Axis occupation, the majority of Kosovars experience the occupiers as liberators.[17] The occupiers encourage the establishment of Albanian schools and media and give Kosovo Albanians the right to bear arms. Kosovo Albanians take revenge on Slavs, harassing and driving out Slavic families—again, estimates of emigration vary widely, from ten thousand to one hundred thousand.[18] Some Kosovo Albanians are said to not only collaborate with the Axis occupation but also join fascist terrorist groups.[19]

1944–45

After WWII, Kosovo Albanians are under the impression that the Yugoslav Communist Party has promised that they can secede from Yugoslavia and join with Albania.[20] However, "Tito realize[s] that only by retaining Kosovo within Serbia's borders [can] he hope to win the Serbs over to communism."[21] The Partisans launch a military campaign in Kosovo in order to consolidate their rule and to root out those who had collaborated with the Axis occupation. Albanians resist in a popular uprising. In February 1945, the Yugoslav government declares martial law and a military force is sent in to take control over Kosovo. Albanian sources estimate that about thirty-six thousand Albanian victims perished through systematic mass executions, "disarming," "pacification," "rehabilitation" programs and other forms of violence condoned by the party.[22] For years to follow, Kosovo Albanians will be "treated with deep mistrust because of their wartime support of the occupying forces."[23]

1946

The first postwar Yugoslav Constitution is adopted, centralizing power after the Soviet federal model. "As a result, the Yugoslav national question [is] transformed from the prewar conflict of opposing national ideologies into a conflict over the structure and composition of the Yugoslav federation."[24]

Yugoslavia is defined as a federal state of six sovereign republics. The republics are defined partially according to national principles and partially according to history. A special compromise is created in the Republic of Serbia: two "provinces" are given a degree of autonomy. Vojvodina, with a sizable Hungarian population, is proclaimed to be an "Autonomous Province" and allowed its own governmental structure, with independent decision-making responsibility and its own Supreme Court. In contrast, Kosovo-Metohija is called an "Autonomous Region." Local administrative units there are denied any independent decision-making authority. Both provinces are allowed to send representatives to a chamber of the federal legislature, but their internal affairs (for example, their systems of education, their specific rights and degrees of autonomy) are to be defined by the Republic of Serbia, not by the federal government.

At this time, Yugoslavia is divided into two categories—in Zoran Pajić's terms, the "hosts and the historical guests."[25] The hosts, or nations (*narod*), are Serbs, Croats, Slovenes, Macedonians and Montenegrins. The guests are called "national minorities," and they include all other groups. Within the federal government, a Council of Nations represents the interests of the republics and the provinces. The 1946 Constitution declares "four equalities": (1) all Yugoslav citizens have equal rights and duties; (2) all of the republics are equal; (3) all of the nations of Yugoslavia are equal; and (4) all nations are said to have had contributed equally to the struggle for national liberation.

1948

Tito's regime is expelled from the communist bloc (the "Cominform break"). The government of Albania in Tirana breaks off relations with Yugoslavia.

During the period from 1948 to 1966, border clashes break out along the Kosovo-Albania border. The Yugoslav security police, under the direction of Aleksandar Ranković (who is also the vice-president of Yugoslavia), heighten persecution of the Albanian population in Kosovo.[26] Thousands of Kosovars emigrate to Turkey.[27] At the same time, Serbs begin to migrate from Kosovo for economic reasons and because of alleged Albanian persecution and harassment. Many Kosovars are arrested and tried for political offenses and other alleged crimes. Between 1960 and 1964, the first groups of Kosovar Marxist-oriented intellectuals are arrested.[28]

1953

The constitutional law of 1953 radically changes the 1946 Yugoslav Constitution (so much so that the document is recognized by many as almost a new constitution). The most radical change is the abandonment of the Soviet constitutional model. The law defines Yugoslavia as a community of people whose "socialist consciousness" supersedes national consciousness. The working people of Yugoslavia are to create a united Yugoslav national consciousness that will supplant all other national identities. In a move toward greater centralization, the constitutional law of 1953 abolishes the Council of Nations. The constitutional powers of Vojvodina and Kosovo are delegated to the Republic of Serbia. Neither the republics nor the provinces have much autonomy at this time, as Yugoslavia is controlled by a strong centralist administration.

1956

The classification of "national minorities" is upgraded to "nationalities" (*narodnosti*) because use of the word "minority" is perceived to be demeaning.

In July, a group of Kosovo Albanians is tried and convicted in Prizren on charges of espionage.[29]

1961

The "Muslims" become the last group to be given the status of a "nation," having been allowed the appellation on the federal census in 1961.[30] Although Albanians living in Yugoslavia also seek to gain the status of a "nation," they are still considered a "national minority."

1963

New Yugoslav and Serbian constitutions are adopted. Both documents increase Serbia's control over the provinces by conditioning the provinces' autonomy on the will of the Serbian government. The province's representatives to the federal Assembly are to sit as part of the Serbian delegation, not as separate provincial delegations.

The 1963 statute of Kosovo-Metohija changes the "Regional Council" into a "Provincial Assembly," thus upgrading it to the status of Vojvodina.

1966

Police pressure against Kosovo Albanians eases in 1966 when Aleksandar Ranković is dismissed from his state and party functions. The Sixth Plenum of the Serbian Party Central Committee issues a condemnation of "certain sections of the State Security apparatus for discriminatory and illegal practices entirely contrary to the League of Communists of Yugoslavia's program and the Yugoslav Constitution."[31] Discrimination against Albanians is specifically condemned.

1968

In February, the Kosovar Albanians who had been convicted in Prizren of espionage in 1956 are rehabilitated on the grounds that the state security police had rigged the proceedings.[32]

In the summer and fall, various party bodies discuss whether Kosovo should be reconstituted as a republic.[33] The provincial party decides to press instead for giving the province more autonomy (without republic status).

In October, the first Kosovar student demonstrations are reported in at least three towns in Kosovo.[34]

On November 27, the eve of the Albanian National Independence Day and Kosovar Liberation Day, rioting breaks out throughout Kosovo, leaving at least one person dead and more than two dozen badly injured. The demonstrations demand that Kosovo be recognized as a separate republic. Federal and Serbian authorities make several concessions, including the establishment (in 1969) of an Albanian-language university, the University of Priština, the creation of Albanian cultural institutions and renewed cultural and educational ties between Albania and Kosovo.

Between 1968 and 1974, amendments to the federal Yugoslav and Serbian constitutions further augment the independent authority of Kosovo and Vojvodina. The provinces are allowed to promulgate their own laws, provided such laws conform to the federal and Serbian constitutions. Kosovo and Vojvodina again are allowed to participate in the federal government as separate delegations representing their respective provinces. Kosovars win a symbolic victory as the name for the region officially changes from Kosovo-Metohija to Kosovo. The reforms in Kosovo take place against rising Croatian nationalism and a steady emigration of Slavs from Kosovo.

1971

The "Croatian spring" is crushed. A series of antiliberal purges follows that only serves to strengthen nationalism.[35]

1974

A new Yugoslav Constitution codifies the changes that had already been taking place with respect to the autonomy of the provinces and republics.[36] First, with respect to the provinces, the 1974 Constitution formally defines the autonomous provinces as constituent members of the federation. Kosovo and Vojvodina are granted the de facto status of sovereign republics in almost all respects, differing from the other six Yugoslav republics insofar as they are not granted the right to secede from the federation. Both Vojvodina and Kosovo are given seats in the federal Assembly and the federal constitutional court. (Note that the federal constitution only regulated Kosovo's and Vojvodina's constitutional status in *federal* affairs; it did not explicate the authority Kosovo and Vojvodina would have within Serbia—that was left to the Serbian government. In 1974, the new Serbian constitution incorporated the principles set forth in the amendments to the 1963 constitution, thus granting both Kosovo and Vojvodina a large degree of autonomy, but at the same time retaining the right to regulate the political status of the two provinces.)

The 1974 Constitution may be said to be a turning point in which national difference became "constitutionally enshrined."[37] Article 1 of the Constitution defines Yugoslavia as "a federal state having the form of a state community of voluntarily united nations and their Socialist Republics."[38] The possessive construction of this provision is important: the republics belong to the nations. Power under the 1974 Constitution is further decentralized from the federal to the republic level. Each of Yugoslavia's six republics and two provinces has a central bank as well as separate police, educational and judicial systems. Important economic and political perks are divvied out on the subfederal level, that is, among the six republics and two provinces. These units, with the exception of Bosnia and Herzegovina, are organized largely around national identity, based on the majority nation of that region. Thus, rewards are in fact made based on national status. Through such arrangements, "ethnicity [national status], which had seemingly been buried by the 1971 intervention [Tito's squelching of nationalist movements in Croatia], returns by the back door."[39]

1976

The first attempt by Serbian politicians to change the 1974 Constitution occurs when Professor Najdan Pašić presents to the Yugoslav party leadership a document referred to as "the Blue Book."[40] Tito rejects the Blue Book without public discussion.

Kosovo Albanians make enormous cultural and educational achievements during the 1970s. At the same time, their disappointment in not being granted the status of a "nation" or being granted a republic continues to grow. Sporadic demonstrations and arrests of Kosovo Albanians continue. Emigration of Serbs and Montenegrins from Kosovo increases; many of those leaving complain that they were driven out by Albanians.

1980

Josip Broz Tito dies in May.

1981

March 11: Two thousand ethnic Albanian students demand better food in school cafeteria and improved living conditions in the dormitories.

March 23–25: Student protests begin in Prizren and two days later in Priština. Some of the protesters begin calling for a "Kosovo Republic" within Yugoslavia. Seventy-five Serbians and Montenegrins from Kosovo sign the first protest petition against human rights violations committed by Kosovo Albanians.

April 1 and 2: Six Kosovo cities erupt in mass revolt, bringing tens of thousands of ethnic Albanians into the streets. While most of the protesters carry placards calling for a "Kosovo Republic," some hold pro-Tirana signs, demanding the unity of Kosovo with Albania.

April 3: The demonstrations spread to Kosovska Mitrovica, Vučitrn and Uroševac, and from there to nearly every municipality within Kosovo. The Yugoslav press reports that by the end of April eleven civilians have been killed by police; Amnesty International reports that the number may have been as high as three hundred;[41] some Kosovars claim that almost one thousand were killed.[42]

1982

February 3: The Provincial Secretary of Internal Affairs, Mehmet Maliqi, claims to have uncovered thirty-three illegal groups, describing the support of Albanians for even the most radical groups as "massive."[43] Some 3,344 Kosovo Albanians are jailed between 1981 and 1985 for "nationalistic offenses."

By July, some one thousand Albanian members of the League of Communists of Kosovo (LCK) are expelled and some basic units of the LCK are dissolved altogether.

September: Serbian politicians make another attempt to change the 1974 Constitution. The rotating Presidency sets up a special commission to investigate the matter. (In September 1983, the commission presents its initial findings, which support some kind of constitutional change, but there is no consensus on the reform and the project dissipates.)[44]

1983

Aleksandar Ranković, the former Yugoslav internal affairs minister and vice-president of Yugoslavia from 1945 to 1966, dies. His funeral becomes a display of Serbian nationalism.[45]

Kosovo Serbs demand the protection of Serbian and federal authorities from Albanians who they say are violating their human rights. According to Serbian sources, in the 1980s up to thirty thousand Serbs and Montenegrins leave Kosovo.[46]

1985

April 13: Enver Hoxha, longtime dictator of Albania, dies. Albania ends its isolationist stance.

May 1: Yugoslav daily newspapers report that a Serbian peasant, fifty-six-year-old Djordje Martinović, was attacked on his field by two unknown Albanian men who tied him down, mistreated him and forced a bottle in his rectum. In time, the same papers report that Martinović had confessed to injuring himself, and then that his confession had been forced. No one is ever arrested in connection with the case.

October: Kosovo Serbs create another petition to the Assemblies of Serbia and Yugoslavia. This time the petition is signed by two thousand people.

1986

In January, two hundred Belgrade intellectuals submit a petition on Kosovo to the Assemblies of Serbia and Yugoslavia, demanding immediate action. The Committee of Serbs and Montenegrins (a Kosovo protest group) collects fifty thousand signatures on yet another protest petition, demanding greater rights for Serbs and Montenegrins in Kosovo.

In September, the Memorandum of the Serbian Academy of Sciences and Arts is leaked to the press. The Memorandum will soon be called the platform for Serbian nationalism, and even a "blueprint for war." Alleged human rights violations against Serbs in Kosovo feature prominently in the Memorandum, as does the 1974 Yugoslav Constitution's granting of greater autonomy to the provinces.

Slobodan Milošević, the newly appointed leader of the League of Communists of Serbia, is one of the few party leaders who does not castigate the writers of the Memorandum. Instead, in a speech in Kragujevac, Milošević repeats some of the basic concepts of the Memorandum.

1987

At the beginning of the year, Milošević addresses a rally near Belgrade, calling for a reduction in the autonomy of Kosovo and

Vojvodina. In April, he travels to Kosovo to hear the complaints of Kosovo Serbs. At a Kosovo Serb demonstration, he says "No one shall beat these people!" That line is considered to be Milošević's promise to protect Serbs.

On June 16, Milošević calls a special meeting of the Yugoslav Communist Party to discuss the unrest in Kosovo. Three thousand Serbs from Kosovo come to Belgrade to protest in front of the federal Assembly in downtown Belgrade.

On September 3, Aziz Kelmendi, a young Albanian soldier of the Yugoslav Army, opens fire in his army barracks in the Serbian town of Paraćin, killing four soldiers and wounding five others. The military reports that he then committed suicide. Eventually, eight Albanian soldiers would be convicted of helping Kelmendi in the attack.

1988

Milošević proposes several measures and constitutional amendments that would effectively revoke the autonomous status of Vojvodina and Kosovo. In response, Albanian demands for secession from Serbia increase.

From July to October, three million people attend Milošević-sponsored "popular forums," so-called "meetings of truth." The meetings are often followed by political purges.

On November 17, central ethnic Albanian leaders are dismissed from the party and removed from the Presidency. In protest, ethnic Albanian miners from the Trepča mining complex in Kosovska Mitrovica march fifty-five kilometers from the mine to Priština, where they, together with the Albanian students, camp in front of the local party headquarters.

One million people attend a Bratstvo i Jedinstvo (brotherhood and unity) protest in Belgrade on November 19.

1989

February 3: Serbia's national assembly passes amendments to Serbia's constitution which centralize in Belgrade control over essential functions.

February 20: Trepča miners call another strike. They refuse to eat or leave their mine until the three provincial officials imposed by the Serbian party are removed. A mass rally is held in Ljubljana, Slovenia, in support of the miners' strike. Angered by the Ljubljana protest, thousands of Serbs take to the streets in Belgrade.

The federal government initiates "emergency measures" in Kosovo, imposing curfews, riot police and administrative detention. Key industries are placed under compulsory work orders (thus prohibiting strikes) and a large number of federal troops are ordered into Kosovo.[47] It is the fourth such deployment into Kosovo since 1945 (the others being in 1968 and 1981).[48]

March 2: Albanian political leader Azem Vllasi is arrested along with fourteen other Albanians accused of being leaders in the February demonstrations.

March 23: The Kosovo Assembly (the local government of the province), acting under extreme pressure, votes nearly unanimously to accept the constitutional amendments that strip Kosovo of its autonomy. Street violence erupts. The official death toll is twenty-one; commentators say it may be as high as one hundred.

March 28: The constitutional amendments pass the Serbian Assembly. Serbian officials announce that Serbia is "whole" again. While Belgrade celebrates, violence breaks out in Kosovo. According to the official reports, twenty-five people are killed in face-offs with police.

A million Serbs from all over Yugoslavia gather on Kosovo Polje on June 28 for the six-hundredth anniversary of the Battle of Kosovo. Milošević uses the event to solidify his populist movement.

In December, after Slovenia forbids demonstrations in support of Serbia's Kosovo policy, Serbia unilaterally declares a boycott against Slovenia.

1990

January 20–22: The Fourteenth Special Congress of the League of Communists of Yugoslavia (LCY) takes place in Belgrade. This culminates in the decision of the Slovenian and Croatian delegations to leave the Congress. The end of the Congress is indefinitely postponed.

January 24: Demonstrations commence in Kosovo. Forty thousand Albanians demand the lifting of emergency measures, the dismissal of Azem Vllasi's trial and the proclamation of an "Albanian Republic of Kosovo." A full-fledged state of emergency is declared and federal police troops are sent to Kosovo. At least ten people die in police clashes. In disagreement with Serbia's tactics in Kosovo, first Slovene (on February 4) and then Croat (April 4) federal police units are recalled from Kosovo.

February: Yugoslavia sends troops, tanks, war planes and two thousand more police to Kosovo. By the end of the month more than twenty people have been killed and a curfew imposed.

March 21: Reports of "poisoning" of school children in Kosovo begin.

March 22: The Serbian Assembly passes the "Program for Attainment of Peace, Freedom, Equality and Prosperity in Kosovo." The plan is designed to promote the status of Serbs in Kosovo.

April: The federal Yugoslav authorities lift the special measures in Kosovo and remove most of the federal police, leaving matters to the Serbian government and its republican security forces.

April 24: Azem Vllasi and his fourteen codefendants are released, as well as other political prisoners, mainly Albanian, including Adem Demaqi, the "Albanian Mandela," who spent a total of twenty-eight years in prison.

June: The Serbian legislature passes a law that effectively extends the emergency measures in Kosovo. The law leads to the closing of the Kosovo Academy of Arts and Sciences and the dismissal of many thousand state employees.

July 2: The Assembly of Slovenia adopts the Declaration on the Sovereignty of the State of Slovenia.

Albanian members of the Assembly of Kosovo gather in front of the assembly building in Priština (which had been locked to them) and adopt a constitutional declaration proclaiming the Kosova Republic.

July 5: The Assembly of the Socialist Republic of Serbia officially dissolves the Assembly of Kosovo and declares the proclamation of the Kosovo Republic illegal.

September 7: At a secret meeting in Kačanik, Albanian representatives of the officially dissolved Assembly of Kosovo pass the Constitution of the Republic of Kosova. The "parallel" Kosovar Albanian State begins.

September 28: The Assembly of Serbia passes the new Constitution of Serbia. Vojvodina and Kosovo are deprived of their autonomous status. Serbia keeps three seats on the federal Presidency (the Serbian seat and the ones allocated for Kosovo and Vojvodina).

December 9: Elections take place in Serbia and Montenegro. Kosovar Albanians boycott the elections. In Montenegro, the candidates of the League of Communists win the greatest number of representatives on the first ballot. The second ballot takes place in Serbia on December 26, and the Socialist Party of Serbia (SPS) wins 192 out of 250 seats in the Assembly of Serbia. Slobodan Milošević is elected President of Serbia.

December 23: In Slovenia 88.5 percent of the voters cast their ballots in favor of sovereignty and independence of Slovenia.

1991

January 25: The Assembly of Macedonia adopts a Declaration of Independence as well as a platform for negotiations about the future of Yugoslavia.

January 31: The Assembly of Slovenia adopts a charter announcing that it will initiate the procedure of disassociating from Yugoslavia.

February 20: The Assembly of Slovenia adopts amendments to the Constitution of the Republic according to which Slovenia is defined as an independent state that will, as one of the successors to the Socialist Federal Republic of Yugoslavia (SFRY), regulate its relations with other states on the basis of international law.

February 22: Slobodan Milošević, president of the Republic of Serbia, and Momir Bulatović, president of the Presidency of Montenegro, submit a common draft on principles of constitutional organization of Yugoslavia as a democratic federation.

March 9: Opposition parties stage mass demonstrations in Belgrade against the authorities in Serbia. Harsh conflicts occur between demonstrators and the militia. At least two persons are killed and several wounded.

March 19: The National Assembly of Serbia forces Riza Sapunxhiu from the federal Presidency and assumes authority for the dissolved Kosovo Assembly.

March 20: The National Assembly of Serbia appoints Sejdo Bajramović as the federal Presidency member from Kosovo.

March 31: Armed conflict occurs in Plitvice, Croatia, between Croatian police and Krajina Serbian paramilitary units. At an extraordinary session, the federal Presidency calls for a cease-fire and orders increased combat readiness of the JNA.

April 6: Armed clashes break out in Sarajevo and other places throughout Bosnia-Herzegovina. Sarajevo citizens demonstrate against national conflicts.

May 2: Armed conflicts breaks out between Croatian police and Serbs in Borovo Selo.

May 8: The Assembly of the Republic of Slovenia gives the federal Assembly a Declaration on Dissociation from Yugoslavia, scheduled to take place by 26 June 1991 at the latest.

May 10: The joint session of both chambers of the federal Assembly is interrupted after delegates from Croatia and Slovenia, along with seventeen Kosovo Albanian delegates, claim that the appointment of Sejdo Bajramović as a new federal Presidency member from Kosovo was illegitimate and against the federal constitution, since the Kosovo Assembly had been dissolved.

May 19: In a vote on separation from Yugoslavia, 83 percent of the Croatian electorate shows up at the polls. 94.17 percent of them vote in favor of an independent and sovereign state of Croatia. Most ethnic Serbs living in Krajina boycott the referendum.

May 29: The Assembly of the Republic of Slovenia adopts a Resolution on Consensual Dissociation from SFRY.

June 25: The Assembly of the Republic of Croatia unanimously adopts a declaration on proclamation of an independent and sovereign Republic of Croatia and starts the process of dissociation from Yugoslavia. The Assembly of Slovenia adopts documents on separation from SFRY and declaration of independence. Serb representatives adopt the decision to form the Serbian Autonomous Region of Slavonia, Baranja and West Srem.

June 26: The Yugoslav federal government, using the votes of the puppet representatives from Kosovo and Vojvodina in Belgrade's favor, finds that the votes for independence in Slovenia and Croatia were illegal. Delegates from Slovenia and Croatia leave the Yugoslav Federal Assembly.

June 27–28: Conflicts breaks out between JNA units and the Territorial Defense force of Slovenia.

September 7: The Conference on Yugoslavia opens in the Hague with the participation of the representatives of the SFRY Presidency, the federal government, presidents of the Yugoslav republics, the Council of the European Community and representatives of EC member states and of the European Commission. A series of foreign-mediated conflict negotiation sessions are held throughout the year, all without representation from Kosovo.

September 25: The United Nations Security Council adopts Resolution on Yugoslavia no. 713. It notes that the development of the situation in Yugoslavia constitutes a threat to peace and security in the world. On the basis of Article 41 of the UN Charter, the Council decides to enforce an embargo on all deliveries of weapons and military equipment to Yugoslavia.

September 26: Branko Kostić calls a session of the federal Presidency.

From then on the sessions of the Presidency are attended only by representatives of Serbia, Vojvodina, Kosovo (the Belgrade-approved representative) and Montenegro.

October 8: The Assembly of Croatia severs state and legal bonds with SFRY and declares independence. The Assembly of Slovenia similarly declares its independence.

November 20: After completely destroying the city, the JNA takes over the town of Vukovar (in Croatia).

December 20: Federal Prime Minister Ante Marković resigns.

December 23: Germany officially recognizes the independence and sovereignty of Slovenia and Croatia, to become effective as from 15 January 1992. The Slovenian Assembly adopts a new constitution proclaiming Slovenia as a sovereign and independent state.

1992

January 2: Cyrus Vance, personal envoy of the UN Secretary General, informs the public that a general agreement has been reached on the Plan of Peace Operations in Yugoslavia (the Vance Peace Plan).

January 9: The UN Security Council adopts Resolution no. 727, supporting the proposal of the UN Secretary General to send to Yugoslavia fifty officers to monitor the cease-fire and make initial preparations for possible arrival of some ten thousand UN troops.

March 1: A referendum in Montenegro draws a 66.04 percent response from voters, of whom 95.94 percent vote that Montenegro as a sovereign state enter into the common state of Yugoslavia. Muslims, Albanians and some opposition parties boycott the referendum.

March 22: At the session of the Council on Security and Cooperation in Europe (CSCE; now known as the Organization for Security and Cooperation in Europe) Ministerial Council, Slovenia and Croatia are admitted to full-fledged membership in the CSCE.

April 6: In Luxembourg, the Ministerial Council of the EC adopts a Declaration on Yugoslavia stating that the Community and its members decide to recognize Bosnia-Herzegovina within the present borders. Armed clashes continue in Sarajevo and other places throughout Bosnia-Herzegovina.

May 11: The Ministerial Council of the European Community at its session in Brussels adopts a Declaration on Bosnia-Herzegovina in which the EC demands the commitment of Belgrade to respect the integrity of the borders, to observe the rights of minorities, including

Vojvodina and Kosovo, and to work on concluding an agreement on the special status of Kosovo. The EC and its member states decide to recall their ambassadors in Belgrade and to demand suspension of the Yugoslav delegation from decisionmaking in CSCE.

May 20: A new Declaration on Yugoslavia is adopted at the meeting of the Committee of Senior CSCE Officials in Helsinki. The Committee express its concern for the further deterioration of the situation in the former SFRY. It demands that all sides in conflict ensure opening of the Sarajevo airport for delivery of humanitarian aid, supports efforts of the international community for solution of the refugee problem, and decides to send to Yugoslavia two special missions to examine the situation in Kosovo.

May 22: At the plenary session of the UN General Assembly, Slovenia, Bosnia-Herzegovina and Croatia are admitted to the membership of the United Nations.

May 24: Parliamentary and presidential elections deemed illegal by the Serbian authorities are held in Kosovo. Out of 821,588 registered voters, 721,534, almost exclusively of Albanian nationality, vote. With more than 95 percent of the vote, Ibrahim Rugova is elected president of the Republic of Kosova. Rugova's party, the Democratic Alliance of Kosovo (LDK or DLK), wins a reported 99.5 percent of the votes. In the elections for Parliament, out of one hundred single-constituency seats, ninety-six are won by the LDK, one by the Party of Democratic Action, one by the Parliamentary Party of Kosovo, and two by independents who were members of the LDK. In addition, forty-two seats are distributed on the basis of proportional representation.

May 27: In downtown Sarajevo a line of people waiting to buy bread is hit by shellfire. Sixteen are killed and more than 140 wounded. Fighting continues.

May 30: The UN Security Council adopts Resolution no. 757, which imposes economic sanctions on Yugoslavia (that is, Serbia and Montenegro).

May 31: Elections are held in the Federal Republic of Yugoslavia for the federal Assembly and for provincial and local government bodies. Kosovo Albanians do not take part in the elections. In Serbia, the Socialist Party of Serbia takes 43.44 percent of the vote.

June 15: Deputies of the federal Assembly elect Dobrica Ćosić as president of the Federal Republic of Yugoslavia.

June 27: The summit of heads of states or governments of the European Community finishes in Lisbon with the adoption of a Declaration on Yugoslavia. Among other matters, the declaration states that it expects the Serbian leadership to stop the reprisals in Kosovo and establish a serious dialogue with the representatives of Albanians from that province.

July 10: The federal Assembly elects the government of the Federal Republic of Yugoslavia (Serbia and Montenegro). Serbian-American businessman Milan Panić is elected prime minister.

August 2: Presidential and parliamentary elections take place in Croatia. Franjo Tudjman is re-elected president of the republic, winning 56.2 percent of the vote.

August 13: At its session in Prague, the Committee of High Officials of the CSCE adopts the report of the mission on the situation in Kosovo, Sandžak (an area in Serbia with a large Muslim population) and Vojvodina. The CSCE proposes a permanent mission to Kosovo.

August 18: The United States establishes diplomatic relations with Croatia, Slovenia and Bosnia-Herzegovina.

September 23: The UN General Assembly adopts Resolution no. 777 of the Security Council, suspending Yugoslavia from the General Assembly.

September 28: Co-Chairmen of the Conference on Yugoslavia Cyrus Vance and David Owen meet with Slobodan Milošević and, among other issues, talk about the problems in Kosovo.

September 30: Kosovars vote in a referendum to declare Kosova a "sovereign and independent state."

October 2: George Bush, president of the United States, announces that the USA may become more engaged in the Yugoslav conflict in all actions of offering assistance and protection of humanitarian convoys for Bosnia, possibly including military involvement. He advocates securing the presence of foreign observers in Kosovo.

October 6: The UN Security Council adopts Resolution no. 780 on setting up an unbiased international commission of experts who would investigate war crimes committed in the former Yugoslavia.

October 12: Demonstrations are held in almost all towns in Kosovo. The protesters present five demands: immediate opening of schools for Albanians, abolition of emergency and forced measures in student dormitories, recovery of financial resources, cessation of repression and accountability for all who participated in the destruction of the educational system in Kosovo. The next day police forces in Priština prevent new attempts of Albanians to gather in large numbers.

October 14: Two-day talks between Serbs and Albanians on the problems of education in Albanian language end in Priština without success.

October 15: Federal Prime Minister Milan Panić visits Kosovo. After talks with representatives of Serbs and Montenegrins, he meets with Ibrahim Rugova. According to official Serb sources, they agree on the establishment of joint task forces to deal with legislation, education and the provision of information in the Albanian language. According to Rugova, Panić is attempting to strike a deal in order to entice Albanians to vote in the next federal elections.

October 29: David Owen and Cyrus Vance, together with Prime Minister Panić, visit Priština. The Serbian media features Lord Owen stating at the press conference that "Kosovo should have a special status or autonomy, but only within Serbia."

Tadeusz Mazowiecki, special envoy of the UN Secretary General, submits a report to the UN Commission on Violation of Human Rights in the former Yugoslavia. The report includes violations in Kosovo.

December 11: The UN Security Council adopts Resolution no. 795, by which it approves the deployment in Macedonia of the United Nations Protection Force (UNPROFOR), consisting of seven hundred soldiers, thirty-five military monitors and twenty-six members of civil police.

December 17: The NATO Ministerial Council in Brussels adopts the Declaration on Yugoslavia, expressing concern over the deteriorating situation in the former Yugoslavia. They stress that NATO is ready to undertake appropriate measures at the request of the UN Security Council.

December 18: The UN General Assembly adopts a new resolution on the situation in Bosnia-Herzegovina that provides that if Serbia and Montenegro continue to fail to fulfill all relevant Security Council resolutions, Chapter VII of the UN Charter (which stipulates the use of military force) may be invoked.

The UN Security Council adopts Resolution no. 798, in which it expresses concern over the reports of massive, organized and systematic detention and rape of women, in particular Muslim women, in Bosnia-Herzegovina.

December 20: Federal, republican and provincial parliamentary and local elections, as well as elections for the presidencies of Serbia and Montenegro, are held in Yugoslavia. Once again, Kosovar Albanians do not participate in the elections. Slobodan Milošević is elected president of Serbia in the first round, winning 2,515,047 votes (56 percent of those who voted); the second-ranked candidate, Milan Panić, wins 1,516,693 votes (34.02 percent).

December 29: Deputies of both chambers of the federal Assembly cast a vote of no confidence in Prime Minister Milan Panić. This time the vote passes.

1993

Unsuccessful peace talks are held throughout the year. Kosovo is rarely included on the agenda. Intense fighting in Bosnia continues throughout the year.

February 22: The UN Security Council adopts Resolution no. 808, establishing an international tribunal for the prosecution of persons responsible for serious violations of international humanitarian law committed in the territory of the former Yugoslavia since 1991.

April 8: UN General Assembly admits the Republic of Macedonia to its membership, under the name of the Former Yugoslav Republic of Macedonia.

April 12: Fighter bombers and interceptors from the U.S., French and Dutch air forces fly from NATO bases in northern Italy into Bosnian airspace, beginning the flight control operation in Bosnia-Herzegovina.

April 16: Despite a cease-fire, armed conflict between the Serbian and Muslim forces breaks out in Srebrenica. Over fifty persons are killed.

May 25: Vitaly Churkin, deputy foreign minister of the Russian Federation, meets Albanian leaders in Priština. The Belgrade press reports that Churkin says at a press conference that human rights in Kosovo must be respected, but that the world powers do not support ethnic Albanians' declaration on the province's independence.

The UN Security Council adopts Resolution no. 827, establishing an international tribunal for the sole purpose of prosecuting persons responsible for serious violations of international humanitarian law committed in the territory of the former Yugoslavia between 1 January 1991 and a date to be determined by the Security Council upon the restoration of peace.

June 11: At the session of foreign ministers of sixteen NATO countries and twenty-two Eastern European countries, a decision is passed that NATO would provide air support to UNPROFOR after the UN so requests.

The government of the Former Yugoslav Republic of Macedonia accepts the UN proposal to deploy a contingent of three hundred U.S. soldiers in its territory.

June 25: The federal Assembly of Yugoslavia elects Zoran Lilić as president.

July 2: The government of Yugoslavia refuses to extend the mandate of the CSCE monitoring missions in Kosovo, Vojvodina and Sandžak. The CSCE is effectively kicked out of the country.

August 3: NATO declares that it is ready to take severe measures, including air raids against the responsible parties, the Bosnian Serbs and others, if they continue to lay siege to Sarajevo and other areas.

The UN Security Council adopts a resolution demanding that the Government of Yugoslavia enable the observers of the CSCE to keep working in Kosovo, Sandžak and Vojvodina.

August 20: The UN subcommittee for protection of minority rights adopts in Geneva a Resolution on Kosovo, condemning Yugoslavia for discriminatory measures and violation of the human rights of the ethnic Albanians in Kosovo.

Throughout the rest of the year, fighting continues amid new sets of negotiations. Serbia tries unsuccessfully to have the economic sanctions imposed against it lifted.

November 17: The first session of the International Court for War Crimes Committed on the Territory of the Former Yugoslavia takes place in the Hague.

November 30–December 1: The two-day meeting of the ministers of foreign affairs of the fifty-three member countries of the CSCE takes place in Rome. Representatives of Yugoslavia do not participate in the meeting. In the final document of the conference the ministers call on the warring parties in Bosnia-Herzegovina to "take initiative based on the EU action plan, presented in Geneva" and among other matters, to allow the international observers to resume their missions in Kosovo, Vojvodina and Sandžak.

December 19: Early elections are held in Serbia for 250 deputies of the Assembly of Serbia. Most Albanians do not participate. The Socialist Party of Serbia wins the greatest number of votes and seats.

1994

NATO and the UN continue to issue threats. The UN and NATO eventually respond to protect "safe areas" and to safeguard UN positions. Negotiations continue as well as fighting. Bosnian Serbs and Croats reach an agreement on a joint federation, the Federation of Bosnia-Herzegovina. International human rights investigators document widespread and systematic Serbian police abuse against ethnic Albanians in Kosovo, including random raids on villages, abuse in detention, street beatings and harassment of merchants.

1995

Fighting continues in Bosnia throughout the year, along with negotiations. Police harassment continues in Kosovo and there is little attention to the unrest there.

July: A Serbian court sentences sixty-eight ethnic Albanians to up to eight years in prison for allegedly setting up a parallel police force.

August: Serbian authorities settle several hundred Serb refugees from Croatia in Kosovo, drawing protests from ethnic Albanian leaders. Tensions mount in Kosovo; police abuse of ethnic Albanians continues.

November 20: After twenty days of talks in Dayton, Ohio, the peace negotiations on Bosnia are completed by initializing the General Framework Agreement for Peace in Bosnia and Herzegovina.

November 22: The UN Security Council adopts Resolution no. 1022, suspending sanctions against Yugoslavia. The Council also adopts Resolution no. 1021 on gradual lifting of the embargo on arms delivery to the states created in the territory of the former Yugoslavia. As provided by resolution, the embargo on arms and military equipment should be lifted after Bosnia-Herzegovina, Croatia and Yugoslavia have officially signed the peace agreement and it is to be implemented according to a set schedule.

November 23: The leaderships of Yugoslavia and Republika Srpska, the Serb-controlled section of Bosnia, meet in Belgrade. Republika Srpska states that it accepts the Dayton Agreement.

November 29–30: Deputies of the (Muslim) Assembly of Bosnia and Herzegovina support the decision made by the delegation of Bosnia-Herzegovina to initialize the Dayton General Framework Agreement on Peace in Bosnia and Herzegovina. They authorize the delegation to sign the agreement in Paris on 20 December 1995.

November 30: The government of Slovenia recognizes the Federal Republic of Yugoslavia.

December 4: In accordance with UN Security Council Resolution no. 1022 of 22 November 1995, the European Union suspends sanctions against Yugoslavia under the conditions prescribed by Resolution no. 1022.

December 14: The General Framework Agreement for Peace in Bosnia and Herzegovina and the 12 Annexes are signed in the Elysée Palace in Paris by Slobodan Milošević, Franjo Tudjman and Alija Izetbegović.

December 15: The UN Security Council adopts Resolution no. 1033, giving IFOR—the new international forces under aegis of NATO—a year mandate to make possible implementation of the General Framework Agreement for Peace in Bosnia and Herzegovina and the 12 Annexes, signed in Paris. The Security Council also ratifies the designation of Carl Bildt as High Representative of the Peace Implementation.

December 20: At the joint closed session of the Chamber of Citizens and Chamber of Republics of the Assembly of Yugoslavia, deputies accept the report of federal Minister for Foreign Affairs Milan Milutinović on the results achieved at the Peace Implementation Conference in London and the Conference in Paris, at which was signed the General Framework Agreement for Peace in Bosnia and Herzegovina. IFOR officially takes over command from UNPROFOR in Bosnia.

December 28: President Bill Clinton signs a decree on suspension of all sanctions imposed against Yugoslavia by the U.S. The decree becomes effective on December 28, 1995.

1996

Serbia signs a deal with ethnic Albanian leaders to return Albanian students to mainstream education after a six-year boycott of state schools and colleges. The agreement is not implemented.

The clandestine separatist group Kosovo Liberation Army (KLA) emerges for the first time, claiming responsibility for a series of bomb attacks against Serbs.

Disputes among the Kosovo Albanian movement grow more public as militant ethnic Albanian leaders question Rugova's strategy of "passive resistance."

1997

January: The Serb rector of the University of Priština is badly injured by a car bomb. A suspected leader of the outlawed KLA is killed in a gun battle with police.

March: Four people are injured when a bomb explodes in the center of Priština.

September: Armed men stage simultaneous night attacks on police stations in ten Kosovo towns and villages. As the number of guerrilla incidents increases, clashes also continue sporadically between police and peaceful protesters.

October–December: A grenade and machine-gun raid is made on a Serb refugee camp, but there are no casualties. Members of the KLA claim to have shot down a Yugoslav Airlines training aircraft.

1998

January: An ethnic Serb politician is killed in apparent retaliation for the reported killing of an ethnic Albanian by the police.

February–March: Dozens are killed in Serbian police operations against suspected Albanian separatists in the Drenica region of Kosovo. Houses are burned and villages evacuated. Tens of thousands protest in Priština against the violence, and street clashes erupt. Kosovo Albanian leader Ibrahim Rugova, disregarding Western calls for compromise, demands outright independence for Kosovo. Ethnic Albanians vote for a president and assembly in elections that are considered illegal by Belgrade. Rugova is elected again, but tensions deepen among Kosovo Albanian leaders.

April: In a referendum, 95 percent of Serbs vote against international intervention in Kosovo. The Contact Group for the Former Yugoslavia agrees, with the exception of Russia, to impose new sanctions against Yugoslavia over Kosovo. The sanctions are never effectively implemented.

May: U.S. envoy Richard Holbrooke begins a round of shuttle diplomacy that results in Yugoslav President Milošević inviting Ibrahim Rugova for peace talks without the presence of a third-party negotiator. Ethnic Albanian and Serb negotiators start talks in Priština as fighting continues.

June: UN Secretary General Kofi Annan warns NATO that it must seek a Security Council mandate for any military intervention in the Serbian province. Hundreds of ethnic Albanians flee their village homes after Serb police and military and paramilitary troops attack in the middle of the night.

July: France and Britain draft a UN Security Council resolution to try to bring about a cease-fire. The number of displaced people in Kosovo reaches at least one hundred thousand. The KLA claims to hold one-third of the territory of Kosovo. Human rights monitors report that Serbs are deliberately targeting civilians.

August: A massive month-long offensive severely weakens the KLA.

A significant stronghold, the village of Junik, falls into Serb hands on the sixteenth of the month. The KLA loses territory. The UN calls for a cease-fire. The number of displaced people now is estimated at three to five hundred thousand (out of a population of 2.5 million). Human rights monitors continue to document mass executions and abuses against civilians.

September: The Yugoslav army continues to attack villages in the Drenica region of Kosovo, and at the same time widens the offensive to regions surrounding Uroševac and Priština. The UN Security Council votes in favor of a resolution calling for a cease-fire in Kosovo and warning the Yugoslav government of "additional measures" if it fails to comply. NATO takes the first formal steps toward military intervention in Kosovo. Serbian Prime Minister Mirko Marjanović announces the defeat of the Albanian separatists and the withdrawal of government forces from Kosovo. Heavy fighting continues despite Serbian assurances that the offensive is over. Humanitarian groups report that thousands of ethnic Albanians are still hiding in the woods in Kosovo: many, they fear, will freeze to death in the approaching winter.

Mid-October: NATO threatens military action against Serbia. Milošević agrees to pull Yugoslav troops out of Kosovo and to permit monitoring by international observers. Early reports from the field are that Serbian police and military are openly flouting the agreement.

Notes

1. Sources for the chronology include the time line prepared by Ivana Nizich for Helsinki Watch, published in Helsinki Watch, *Yugoslavia: Human Rights Abuses in Kosovo 1990–1992* (New York: Human Rights Watch/Helsinki Watch, October 1992), the chronologies by Yugoslavia and Law, found at /www.yugoslavia.com/Society_and_Law/Chronology/default.html.

2. Veljko Vujačić, "The Crisis in Yugoslavia," in *Dilemmas of Transition in the Soviet Union and Eastern Europe,* ed. George W. Breslauer (Berkeley, Calif.: Berkeley-Stanford Program in Soviet Studies), 95.

3. Sabrina Ramet, "The Albanians of Kosovo: The Potential for Destabilization," *The Brown Journal of World Affairs* 3, no. 1 (winter/spring 1996), 355.

4. Miranda Vickers, "The Status of Kosovo in Socialist Yugoslavia," *Bradford Studies on South Eastern Europe,* no. 1 (1994), 7.

5. Dimitrije Bogdanović, *Knjiga o Kosovu,* 3d ed. (Belgrade: Srpska akademija nauka i umetnosti, 1996), 8.

6. See Alex N. Draganich and Slavko Todorovich, *The Saga of Kosovo: Focus*

on Serbian-Albanian Relations (Boulder, Colo.: Eastern European Monographs, 1994), 120.

7. Ibid. Dimitrije Bogdanović says that the colonists "mainly took over vacant and often infertile land," but that the agrarian form and colonization program was an "ill-advised action" which "only created bad blood." Bogdanović, *Knjiga o Kosovu*, 291–92.

8. Estimates vary widely. This figure is according to Bogdanović, *Knjiga o Kosovu*, 291.

9. For the Constitution of the Kingdom of the Serbs, Croats and Slovenes, adopted June 28, 1921, see Shiva Rao, *Select Constitutions of the World* (Madras: Madras Law Journal Press, 1934).

10. For more on the interwar period and the question of nationalities, see Barbara Jelavich, *History of the Balkans: Twentieth Century* (Cambridge, England: Cambridge University Press, 1983), 143–57; see generally Ivo Banac, *The National Question in Yugoslavia: Origin, History, Politics* (Ithaca, N.Y.: Cornell University Press, 1984).

11. Bejtulah Destani, "Albania: A History of Border Changes," *WarReport* (February 1994), 5.

12. Janusz Bugajski, *Ethnic Politics in Eastern Europe* (Armonk, N.Y.: M.E. Sharpe, 1995), 134.

13. Banac, *The National Question in Yugoslavia*, 298.

14. Ibid.

15. Copy of memorandum on file with author.

16. Aleksa Djilas, *The Contested Country: Yugoslav Unity and Communist Revolution, 1919–1953* (Cambridge, Mass.: Harvard University Press, 1991), 13.

17. See Reginald Hibbert, *Albania's National Liberation: The Bitter Victory* (London: Pinter, 1991).

18. Tim Judah, *The Serbs: History, Myth and the Destruction of Yugoslavia* (New Haven, Conn.: Yale University Press, 1997), 131. In his study on population losses during WWII, Vladimir Žerjavić has set the total demographic losses in Kosovo at 51,000. Out of that number, 24,000 were "war victims" and the rest were "demographic victims." Vladimir Žerjavić, *Gubici jugoslovenskog stanovništva u Drugom svetskom ratu* (Zagreb: Jugoslovensko viktimološko društvo, 1989), 69. For alternative accounts of this time, see Bogdanović, *Knjiga o Kosovu*, 291–92; Branko Horvat, *Kosovsko pitanje* (Zagreb: Globus, 1989), 74.

19. Vickers, "The Status of Kosovo," 7. Sami Repishti has written that some of the Kosovar Albanians accused of collaborating with the fascist occupiers were really German or Italian troops wearing Albanian peasant dress. Sami Repishti, "Human Rights and the Albanian Nationality in Yugoslavia," in *Human Rights in Yugoslavia*, eds. Oskar Gruenwald and Karen Rosenblum-Cale (New York: Irvington Publishers, 1986), 235. For more on WWII, see Jozo Tomasevich, "Yugoslavia During the Second World War," in *Contemporary Yugoslavia: Twenty Years of Socialist Experiment*, ed. Wayne S. Vucinich (Berkeley: University of California Press, 1969), 59–118.

20. Derek Hall, *Albania and the Albanians* (London and New York: Pinter Reference, 1994), 204. According to Bogdan Denitch: "The first pre-War Ser-

bian Marxists believed that the Albanian majority had a right to self-determination and that Kosovo had been unjustly conquered in 1912. . . . The views of Serbian socialists, however, were not taken seriously by either the Serbian or Yugoslav interwar governments." Bogdan Denitch, *Ethnic Nationalism: The Tragic Death of Yugoslavia* (Minneapolis: University of Minnesota Press, 1994), 118.

21. Vickers, "The Status of Kosovo," 10.

22. Repishti, "Human Rights and the Albanian Nationality in Yugoslavia," 238.

23. Djilas, *The Contested Country*, 169. See also Paul Shoup, *Communism and the Yugoslav National Question* (New York: Columbia University Press, 1968), 104.

24. Ivo Banac, "Post-Communism as Post-Yugoslavism: The Yugoslav Non-Revolution of 1989–1990," in *Eastern Europe in Revolution*, ed. Ivo Banac. (Ithaca, N.Y.: Cornell University Press, 1992), 171.

25. Zoran Paijić, "Bosnia and Herzegovina: From Multiethnic Coexistence to 'Apartheid' and Back," in *Yugoslavia: The Former and the Future: Reflections by Scholars from the Region,* ed. Payam Akhavan and Robert Howse (Washington, D.C.: The Brookings Institute, 1995), 162.

26. For the experience of Kosovars during this period, see Ivo Banac, *With Stalin Against Tito: Cominformist Splits in Yugoslav Communism* (Ithaca, N.Y.: Cornell University Press, 1988), 214–16.

27. Vickers, "The Status of Kosovo," 18. For a higher estimate (230,000), see Anton Logoreci, "A Clash between Two Nationalisms in Kosova," in *Studies on Kosova*, eds. Arshi Pipa and Sami Repishti (Boulder, Colo.: Eastern European Monographs, 1984), 188.

28. Shoup, *Communism and the Yugoslav National Question*, 218.

29. Until 1988, the trial was widely believed to be an anti-Albanian ploy. Beginning in 1988, however, Serbian scholars have started to suggest that the trial was justified. See Sabrina P. Ramet, *Nationalism and Federalism in Yugoslavia, 1962–1991*, 2d ed. (Bloomington: Indiana University Press, 1992), 188.

30. See Fritz Hondius, *The Yugoslav Community of Nations* (The Hague: Mouton, 1968).

31. Ibid., 19.

32. Ramet, *Nationalism and Federalism in Yugoslavia*, 190.

33. Ibid.

34. See Peter Prifti, *Kosovo in Ferment* (Cambridge, Mass.: MIT Center for International Studies, 1969), 9.

35. R. J. Crampton, *Eastern Europe in the Twentieth Century* (New York and London: Routledge, 1994), 351.

36. *The Constitution of the Socialist Federal Republic of Yugoslavia* (Ustav Socijalistčke Federativne Republike Jugoslavije) (Belgrade: Dopisna Delavska Univerza, 1974). For one of the most concise analyses of the 1974 Constitution and its contribution to the collapse of Yugoslavia, see Vojin Dimitrijević, "The 1974 Constitution and Constitutional Process as a Factor in the Collapse of Yugoslavia," in *Yugoslavia: The Former and the Future: Reflections by Scholars from the Region*, eds. Payam Akhavan and Robert Howse (Washington, D.C.:

The Brookings Institute, 1995), 45–74, and for a thorough examination of the constitution's framework for negotiating conflict, see Steven Burg, *Conflict and Cohesion in Socialist Yugoslavia* (Princeton: Princeton University Press, 1983), 242–300.

37. The term is used by Katherine Verdery in "Nationalism and National Sentiment in Post-Socialist Romania," *Slavic Review* 52, no. 2 (summer 1993), 179–203; and Mary Kaldor, "Cosmopolitanism versus Nationalism: The New Divide?" in *Europe's New Nationalism: States and Minorities in Conflict*, eds. Richard Caplan and John Feffer (Oxford, England: Oxford University Press, 1996), 42–58.

38. *Ustav Socijalisticke Federativne Republike Jugoslavije.*

39. George Schopflin, "The Rise and Fall of Yugoslavia," in *The Politics of Ethnic Conflict Regulation: Case Studies of Protracted Ethnic Conflicts*, eds. John McGarry and Brendan O'Leary (London: Routledge, 1993), 190.

40. See Zdenko Antić, "Serbian Problems," *The South Slav Journal* 11, no. 4 (winter 1988/89), 16–17.

41. Amnesty International, *Yugoslav Prisoners of Conscience* (London: Amnesty International, 1985), 12.

42. Miranda Vickers, *The Albanians: A Modern History* (London: I. B. Tauris, 1995), 205.

43. Branka Magaš, *The Destruction of Yugoslavia: Tracking the Break-Up 1980–92* (London: Verso Press, 1993), 12–13.

44. These attempts are discussed in Antić, "Serbian Problems," 16–17.

45. See Slavoljub Djukić, *Izmedju slave i anateme — Politička biografija Slobodana Miloševića* (Belgrade: Filip Višnjić, 1994), 36.

46. See chapter two, note 78, for various estimates of the number of Serbians who left Kosovo during this period.

47. Amnesty International, *Yugoslavia: Prisoners of Conscience* (London: Amnesty International, 1982)(Index EUR 48/18/92).

48. Marko Milivojević, "The Armed Forces of Yugoslavia: Sliding into War," in *Beyond Yugoslavia: Politics, Economics, and Culture in a Shattered Community*, eds. Sabrina Petra Ramet and Ljubiša S. Adamovich (Boulder, Colo.: Westview Press, 1995), 72.

APPENDIX A

Demographics

Prior to the establishment of concept of nations, early population counts of the region known today as Kosovo were based on confession. The data in table 5, based on the notes of Dr. Joseph Müller, a German traveler, show that in three districts that are now part of Kosovo, Muslims outnumbered Christians, although the population of the groups was close.

Table 5 *Confessional Population Count, 1838*

District	Muslims		Christians		Total
	Population	*%*	*Population*	*%*	*Population*
Peć	34,000	52	31,000	48	65,000
Djakovica	31,000	60	21,000	40	52,000
Prizren	49,000	63	29,000	27	78,000
All districts	114,000	58	81,000	42	195,000

SOURCE: Radovan Samardžić et al. *Kosovo i Metohija u srpskoj istoriji* (Beograd: Srpska književna zadruga, 1989), 190–91, as cited in Milan Vučković and Goran Nikolić, *Stanovništvo Kosova u razdoblju od 1918. do 1991. godine* (Munich: Slavica Verlag, 1996), 53.

Early counts of the population of the region can be found in district-by-district calculations. The data in table 6 are taken from a census of the entire number of houses and citizens, according to the official facts of the regent in 1905, of the districts of Peć, Prizren and Priština in the Raša-Prizren eparchy. These estimates are complicated by the categories used for the respondents. Note in particular the large number of people listed as "Albanized Muslim Serbs."

Table 6 *Census of Districts, 1905*

	Number of houses	Population
Orthodox Serbs	10,346	206,920
Albanized Muslim Serbs	15,600	390,010
Catholic Serbs	108	1,750
Muslim Serbs from Bosnia	50	1,200
Protestant Serbs	0	1
Catholic Albanians	260	1,560
Albanians	1,000	20,000
Turks	270	3,230
Jews	50	300
Total	27,684	624,971

SOURCE: Radovan Samardžić et al., *Kosovo i Metohija u srpskoj istoriji* (Belgrade: Srpska književna zadruga, 1989), 246, as cited in Milan Vučković and Goran Nikolić, *Stanovništvo Kosova u razdoblju od 1918. do 1991. godine* (Munich: Slavica Verlag, 1996), 59.

In the earliest population census for Kosovo, conducted in 1921, data were collected on religion and mother tongue (see table 7). Subsequent population estimates from the censuses in 1931 and 1939 indicate a decline in the percentage of Albanians and an increase in Serbs and Montenegrins. Milan Vučković and Goran Nikolić, the authors of a recent book analyzing Kosovo's population, attribute this population shift not to birth rates but to the increased emigration of Albanians, Turks and Muslims and immigration of Serbs, Montenegrins and Croats.[1]

Note

1. Milan Vučković and Goran Nikolić, *Stanovničtvo Kosova u razdoblju od 1918. do 1991. godine* (Munich: Slavica Verlag, 1996).

Table 7 *Kosovo Census Data: 1921, 1931, 1939*

	1921		1931		1939	
	Population	*%*	*Population*	*%*	*Population*	*%*
Albanians	288,900	65.8	331,549	60.1	350,946	54.4
Serbs and Montenegrins	92,490	21.1	148,809	26.9	213,746	33.1
Muslims	13,630	3.1	24,760	4.5	26,215	4.0
Turks	27,920	6.3	23,698	4.3	24,946	3.8
Roma	11,000	2.5	14,014	2.5	15,221	2.3
Croats	2,700	0.6	5,555	1.0	7,998	1.2
Others	2,360	0.5	3,679	0.7	5,940	0.9
Total	439,000	100	552,064	100	645,012	100

SOURCE: *Statistički godišnjak Kraljevine Jugoslavije za 1938/39* (Belgrade: Opšta državna statistika, 1939), as cited in Milan Vučković and Goran Nikolić, *Stanovništvo Kosova u razdoblju od 1918. do 1991. godine* (Munich: Slavica Verlag, 1996), 80.

Table 8 *Kosovo Census Data: 1948, 1953, 1961, 1971, 1981, 1991*

	1948		1953		1961		1971		1981		1991	
	Population	*%*	*Population*	*%*	*Population*	*%*	*Population*	*%*	*Population*	*%*	*Population*	*%*
Albanians	498,242	68.5	524,559	64.9	646,805	67.2	916,168	73.7	1,226,736	77.4	1,607,690*	82.2
Serbs	171,911	23.6	189,869	23.5	227,016	23.6	228,264	18.4	209,498	13.2	195,301	9.9
Montenegrins	28,050	3.9	31,343	3.9	37,588	3.9	31,555	2.5	27,028	1.7	20,045	1.0
Muslims	9,679	1.3	6,241	0.8	8,026	0.8	26,357	2.1	58,562	3.7	57,408	2.9
Gypsies	11,230	1.5	11,904	1.5	3,202	0.3	14,593	1.2	34,126	2.2	42,806	2.2
Turks	1,315	0.2	34,583	4.3	25,784	2.7	12,244	1.0	12,513	0.8	10,838	0.5
Croats	5,290	0.7	6,201	0.7	7,251	0.8	8,264	0.7	8,717	0.6	8,161	0.4
Others	2,103	0.3	3,541	0.3	8,316	0.7	6,248	0.4	7,260	0.4	12,498	0.7
Total	727,820	100.0	808,141	100.0	963,988	100.0	1,243,693	100.0	1,584,441	100.0	1,954,747	100.0

*Estimate of the Federal Institute for Statistics, based on the data on the natural augmentation and migrations during the previous period (1981–1990)

SOURCE: "Jugoslavija 1918–1988, statistički godišnjak" (1989), 42–43; "Statistički godišnjak Jugoslavije za 1992. godinu" (1992), 62–63; as cited in Milan Vučković and Goran Nikolić, *Stanovništvo Kosova u razdoblju od 1918. do 1991. godine* (Munich: Slavica Verlag, 1996), 108–9.

APPENDIX B

Attitudinal Surveys

Ethnic Distance: Attitudes of Young Serbs and Hungarians Toward Other Nations

In 1987, 160 seventeen-year-old ethnic Serbian and ethnic Hungarian high school students in Serbia were asked a series of questions about their ability to accept other nations and nationalities. From their answers, a composite was drawn regarding the "degree of acceptance" (see table 9).

The same study addressed various stereotypes of different nations and nationalities. Out of fifty proposed attributes, positive and negative, students chose the ones they considered characteristic of each nation. Table 10 shows the characteristics that Serb and Hungarian respondents most commonly attributed to Albanians.

Attitudinal Survey of Serbs and Albanians on Kosovo

The following tables give the results of the survey discussed in "Postscript, 1997" above. In September 1995, the Belgrade-based independent research firm "Argument" administered the Serbian-language questionnaire by telephone with adults chosen randomly from the telephone book, in eight areas representing each part of Serbia proper and Vojvodina (Belgrade, Zrenjanin, Kragujevac, Leskovac, Niš, Novi Sad, Smederevo and Užice). The sample controlled for gender, urban/rural area, age, education and ethno-national identity to ensure that the respondents were representative. In addition, respondents were asked whether

Table 9 *Serbian and Hungarian High-School Students' Acceptance of Other Nationalities*

Serbs	%	Hungarians	%
Hungarians	61.2	Serbs	90.0
Slovaks	60.0	Croats	62.5
Croats	57.5	Slovaks	56.2
Romanians	46.2	Romanians	56.2
Albanians	27.5	Albanians	27.5

SOURCE: V. Mićović, Graduate Thesis, "Socijalna distanca i etničke stereotipije kod srednjoškolaca madjarske i srpske nacionalnosti" (Belgrade: Filozofski fakultet, 1986), as cited in Srdja Popović et al., eds., *Kosovski čvor: Drešiti ili seći?* (Belgrade: Kronos, 1990), 135.

Table 10 *Stereotypical Characteristics of Albanians, According to High-School Students of Serbian and Hungarian Nationality*

Serbs	%	Hungarians	%
undeveloped [uncivilized]	76.2	uncultured	56.0
don't like other nations	55.0	don't like other nations	53.0
sly	55.0	arguers	48.0
aggressive	50.0	undeveloped [uncivilized]	46.0
uncultured	50.0	aggressive	40.0
united	45.0	proud	33.8
like to rule	42.5	courageous	31.2
dirty	41.2	hostile	31.2
backwards	38.8	crude	31.0
introverts [closed]	37.5	obnoxious	29.2
insolent	36.2		
arguers	33.8		

SOURCE: V. Mićović, Graduate Thesis, "Socijalna distanca i etničke stereotipije kod srednjoškolaca madjarske i srpske nacionalnosti" (Belgrade: Filozofski fakultet, 1986), as cited in Srdja Popović et al., eds., *Kosovski čvor: Drešiti ili seći?* (Belgrade: Kronos, 1990), 135.

anyone in their family had ever lived in Kosovo and whether any of their relatives are refugees from Krajina.

The same month, I worked with independent Albanian and Serbian journalists in Kosovo on a companion survey. We could not use the telephone, as it was impossible to identify the language of residents by their phone numbers, and no one trusted the privacy of their telephone line. Instead, the Kosovar Albanian team gave the survey in person at health clinics, apartment complexes and workplaces in Priština, one smaller city and two villages. Although they controlled for age, gender and education, due to the inadequacy of the sampling method, they could not guarantee a representative sample by rural/urban divide.

The Serbian team in Kosovo was too afraid to approach strangers, for fear that they would report them to the police. For this reason, their findings are skewed and are not included here. I note, however, that the answers of Serbs in Kosovo were most similar to those in Serbia proper who had once lived in Kosovo.

Table 11 *Attitudes toward Serb–Albanian Relations and the Kosovo Question*

	Respondents to Serbian-language survey (percentage)	Respondents to Albanian-language survey (percentage)
1. Do you think it is possible for Serbs and ethnic Albanians to live in a common state?		
Yes	54.5	19.0
No	40.0	65.0
No answer/Don't know	5.5	16.0
2. In your opinion, how do Albanians in Kosovo want to solve their national and state question?		
By joining Albania	22.5	43.0
By creating their own state	30.0	57.0
By becoming an autonomous region within the existing Yugoslavia	12.0	0.0
Something else	23.5	0.0
No answer	12.0	0.0
3. In your opinion, what do Serbian people want?		
For Kosovo to be part of Serbia, with Albanians subject to the same laws as all Serbs	62.0	3.0
For Kosovo to be part of Serbia, with special laws for Albanians	4.5	28.0

Table II (continued)

	Respondents to Serbian-language survey (percentage)	Respondents to Albanian-language survey (percentage)
For Albanians to leave Kosovo for some other place	17.0	65.0
Something else	9.0	3.0
No answer	7.5	1.0

4. Do you think Albanian children in Kosovo have a right to education in the Albanian language?

Yes	81.5	100.0
No	16.0	0.0
No answer	2.5	0.0

5. Do you think that heavy police presence in Kosovo is justified?

Yes	65.5	6.0
No	21.0	89.0
No answer	13.5	5.0

6. In your opinion whose human rights are violated in Kosovo: Serbs' or Albanians'?

Serbs' rights	52.0	0.0
Albanians' rights	1.5	91.0
The rights of both groups	23.0	7.0
Neither	17.0	0.0
No answer	6.5	2.0

7. Do you think war is likely in Kosovo?

Yes	42.0	17.0
No	49.0	37.0
No answer/Don't know	9.0	46.0

8. Who would cause the war?

Albanians	45.1	9.0
Serbs	4.8	71.0
Foreigners	28.6	15.0
Somebody else	17.9	5.0
No answer/Don't know	3.6	0.0

Table II *(continued)*

	Respondents to Serbian-language survey (percentage)	Respondents to Albanian-language survey (percentage)
9. Do you think that settling refugees from Krajina in Kosovo is more likely to start a war there?		
Yes, more likely	23.5	45.0
No, not more likely	59.5	16.0
No impact on chances for war	6.5	33.0
No answer	10.5	6.0
10. In your opinion, are negotiations between President Milošević and Mr. Ibrahim Rugova necessary?		
Yes	66.5	72.0
No	25.5	7.0
No answer	8.0	21.0
11. Who would make concessions?		
President Milošević	9.0	91.0
Mr. Ibrahim Rugova	30.8	0.0
Both of them	57.2	9.0
No answer	3.0	0.0

Table 12 *Cross-Tabulation of the Serbian Responses by Geographic Region (in Percentages)*

1. Kosovo has been for several years one of the most serious problems in Serbia. Do you think it is possible for Serbs and ethnic Albanians to live in a common state?

	Belgrade	Zrenjanin	Kragujevac	Leskovac	Niš	Novi Sad	Smederevo	Užice
Yes	43.6	68.2	53.6	47.1	61.9	51.7	50.0	66.7
No	56.4	27.3	39.3	52.9	38.1	31.0	40.0	29.2
No answer	0.0	4.5	7.1	0.0	0.0	17.3	10.0	4.1

2. In your opinion, how do Albanians in Kosovo want to solve their national and state question?

	Belgrade	Zrenjanin	Kragujevac	Leskovac	Niš	Novi Sad	Smederevo	Užice
A	25.6	31.8	21.4	11.8	23.8	20.7	15.0	25.0
B	28.2	27.3	42.9	52.9	9.5	20.7	35.0	29.2
C	17.9	0.0	10.7	11.8	19.0	17.2	5.0	8.3
D	28.2	9.1	25.0	11.8	28.6	20.7	30.0	29.2
No answer	0.0	31.8	0.0	11.8	19.0	20.7	15.0	8.3

A—By joining Albania

B—By creating their own state

C—By becoming an autonomous region within the existing Yugoslavia

D—Something else

3. In your opinion, what do Serbian people want?

	Belgrade	Zrenjanin	Kragujevac	Leskovac	Niš	Novi Sad	Smederevo	Užice
A	71.8	77.3	60.7	47.1	52.4	51.7	60.0	66.7
B	5.1	0.0	3.6	0.0	4.8	13.8	0.0	4.2
C	23.1	13.6	21.4	23.5	19.0	3.4	20.0	12.5
D	0.0	4.5	14.3	17.6	4.8	17.2	5.0	12.5
No answer	0.0	4.5	0.0	11.8	19.0	13.8	15.0	4.2

A—For Kosovo to be part of Serbia, with Albanians subject to the same laws as all Serbs

B—For Kosovo to be part of Serbia, with special laws for Albanians

C—For Albanians to leave Kosovo for some other place

D—Something else

4. Do you think Albanian children in Kosovo have a right to education in the Albanian language?

	Belgrade	Zrenjanin	Kragujevac	Leskovac	Niš	Novi Sad	Smederevo	Užice
Yes	76.9	90.9	85.7	76.5	71.4	79.3	80.0	91.7
No	20.5	4.5	14.3	23.5	28.6	17.2	10.0	8.3
No answer	2.6	4.5	0.0	0.0	0.0	3.4	10.0	0.0

5. Do you think that heavy police presence in Kosovo is justified?

	Belgrade	Zrenjanin	Kragujevac	Leskovac	Niš	Novi Sad	Smederevo	Užice
Yes	74.4	54.5	67.9	64.7	66.7	69.0	65.0	54.2
No	20.5	36.4	14.3	23.5	28.6	13.8	15.0	20.8
No answer	5.1	9.1	17.9	11.8	4.8	17.2	20.0	25.0

Table 12 *(continued)*

6. In your opinion whose human rights are violated in Kosovo, Serbs' or Albanians'?

	Belgrade	Zrenjanin	Kragujevac	Leskovac	Niš	Novi Sad	Smederevo	Užice
Serbs	59.0	40.9	46.4	70.6	33.3	58.6	55.0	50.0
Albanians	2.6	4.5	0.0	0.0	0.0	0.0	5.0	0.0
Both	20.5	9.1	35.7	5.9	42.9	17.2	20.0	29.2
Neither	12.8	27.3	14.3	23.5	19.0	17.2	5.0	20.8
No answer	5.1	18.2	3.6	0.0	4.8	6.9	15.0	0.0

7. Do you think war is likely in Kosovo?

	Belgrade	Zrenjanin	Kragujevac	Leskovac	Niš	Novi Sad	Smederevo	Užice
Yes	48.7	36.4	35.7	29.4	42.9	48.3	40.0	45.8
No	46.2	45.5	60.7	52.9	47.6	44.8	45.0	50.0
No answer	5.1	18.2	3.6	17.6	9.5	6.9	15.0	4.2

8. Who would cause the war?

	Belgrade	Zrenjanin	Kragujevac	Leskovac	Niš	Novi Sad	Smederevo	Užice
Albanians	31.6	37.5	70.0	40.0	22.2	64.3	37.5	54.5
Serbs	5.3	0.0	0.0	0.0	11.1	0.0	12.5	9.1
Foreigners	31.6	25.0	10.0	40.0	44.4	28.6	25.0	27.3
Somebody else	31.6	12.5	20.0	20.0	11.1	7.1	25.0	9.1
No answer	0.0	25.0	0.0	0.0	11.1	0.0	0.0	0.0

9. Do you think that settling refugees from Krajina in Kosovo is more likely to start a war there?

	Belgrade	Zrenjanin	Kragujevac	Leskovac	Niš	Novi Sad	Smederevo	Užice
Yes	35.9	31.8	14.3	29.4	9.5	34.5	5.0	16.7
No	53.8	59.1	75.0	52.9	71.4	41.4	55.0	70.8
No impact	10.3	9.1	3.6	0.0	4.8	3.4	10.0	8.3
No answer	0.0	0.0	7.1	17.6	14.3	20.7	30.0	4.2

10. In your opinion, are negotiations between President Milošević and Mr. Ibrahim Rugova necessary?

	Belgrade	Zrenjanin	Kragujevac	Leskovac	Niš	Novi Sad	Smederevo	Užice
Yes	61.5	68.2	67.9	58.8	66.7	72.4	75.0	62.5
No	30.8	27.3	21.4	35.3	28.6	13.8	15.0	33.3
No answer	7.7	4.5	10.7	5.9	4.8	13.8	10.0	4.2

11. Who would make concessions?

	Belgrade	Zrenjanin	Kragujevac	Leskovac	Niš	Novi Sad	Smederevo	Užice
Milošević	8.3	13.3	5.3	20.0	0.0	4.8	13.3	13.3
Rugova	25.0	20.0	42.1	30.0	35.7	28.6	60.0	6.7
Both	66.7	60.0	52.6	50.0	57.1	61.9	26.7	73.3
No answer	0.0	6.7	0.0	0.0	7.1	4.8	0.0	6.7

12. Do you think that the solution of the crisis in our country is on the horizon?

	Belgrade	Zrenjanin	Kragujevac	Leskovac	Niš	Novi Sad	Smederevo	Užice
Yes	46.2	59.1	57.1	47.1	71.4	44.8	60.0	58.3
No	53.8	27.3	35.7	35.3	28.6	55.2	30.0	37.5
No answer	0.0	13.6	7.1	17.6	0.0	0.0	10.0	4.2

Table 13 *Selected Breakdowns of Serbian Responses (in Percentages)*

1. Gender by "possible life in common state"

	No answer	Yes	No
Male	0.0	67.9	32.1
Female	9.2	45.4	45.4

2. Age by "possible solution of crisis"

	No answer	Yes	No
18–30	7.4	33.3	59.3
31–45	3.7	55.6	40.7
46–60	6.3	64.6	29.2
Over 60	4.5	68.2	27.3

3. Age by "possible life in common state"

	No answer	Yes	No
18–30	5.6	38.9	55.6
31–45	3.7	55.6	40.7
46–60	8.3	54.2	37.5
Over 60	4.5	72.7	22.7

4. Age by "heavy police presence is justified"

	No answer	Yes	No
18–30	7.4	64.8	27.8
31–45	16.7	61.1	22.2
46–60	8.3	72.9	18.8
Over 60	22.7	63.6	13.6

Table 13 *(continued)*

5. Education by "whose human rights are violated in Kosovo"

	Serbs'	Albanians'	Both groups'	Neither	No answer
Up to elementary school	58.7	1.6	14.3	11.1	14.3
High school	52.5	1.0	25.3	18.2	3.0
University degree	37.8	2.7	32.4	24.3	2.7
No answer	100.0	0.0	0.0	0.0	0.0

6. Education by "possibility of war in Kosovo"

	Yes	No	No answer
Up to elementary school	28.6	52.4	19.0
High school	47.5	48.5	4.0
University degree	51.4	43.2	5.4
No answer	0.0	100.0	0.0

7. Education by "who would cause the war in Kosovo"

	Albanians	Serbs	Foreigners	Somebody else	No answer
Up to elementary school	50.0	11.1	27.8	5.6	5.6
High school	55.3	2.1	23.4	17.0	2.1
University degree	15.8	5.3	42.1	31.6	5.3

8. "Previously lived in Kosovo" by "How Albanians want to solve their national and state problem"

	Join Albania	Create their own state	Autonomy within Yugoslavia	Something else	No answer
Yes	19.0	23.8	23.8	23.8	9.5
No	22.9	30.7	10.6	23.5	12.3

Table 13 *(continued)*

9. "Previously lived in Kosovo" by "war likely in Kosovo"

	War likely	War not likely	No answer
Yes	33.3	66.7	0.0
No	43.0	46.9	10.1

10. Nationality by "possible life in common state"

	Yes	No	No answer
Serbs and Montenegrins	52.2	42.7	5.1
Hungarians, undeclared and others	72.7	18.2	9.1

11. Nationality by "How Albanians want to solve their national and state problem"

	Join Albania	Create their own state	Autonomy within Yugoslavia	Others	No answer
Serbs and Montenegrins	23.0	32.6	11.2	24.2	9.0
Hungarians, undeclared and others	18.2	9.1	18.2	18.2	36.4

12. Nationality by "heavy police presence in Kosovo is justified"

	Yes	No	No answer
Serbs and Montenegrins	68.0	21.3	10.7
Hungarians, undeclared and others	45.5	18.2	36.4

13. Nationality by "whose human rights are violated in Kosovo"

	Serbs'	Albanians'	Both groups'	Neither	No answer
Serbs and Montenegrins	53.9	1.1	21.9	18.0	5.1
Hungarians, undeclared and others	36.4	4.5	31.8	9.1	18.2

Table 13 *(continued)*

14. Nationality by "negotiations between Milošević and Rugova are necessary"

	Yes	No	No answer
Serbs and Montenegrins	65.2	27.5	7.3
Hungarians, undeclared and others	77.3	9.1	13.6

15. Nationality by "who would make concessions"

	Milošević	Rugova	Both of them	No answer
Serbs and Montenegrins	7.8	33.6	55.2	3.4
Hungarians, undeclared and others	17.6	11.8	70.6	0.0

References

Nearly all the references are available at the Harvard University libraries. Because of the large number of articles cited, the individual titles of articles from newspaper and periodicals of the region are not included in this reference list.

Newspapers and Periodicals from the Region

Borba (Belgrade daily, formerly the Yugoslav voice of the Party, now influenced by the Milošević regime)
Bujku (Albanian-language daily)
Danas (Zagreb weekly)
Dnevnik (Novi Sad daily newspaper)
Duga (Belgrade weekly)
FBIS and *FBIS-EE* (Foreign Broadcasting Information Service, Eastern Europe Service)
Feral Tribune (Split-based Croatian weekly)
Illustrovana Politika (Belgrade weekly magazine)
Illyria (The Albanian-American Newspaper)
Intervju (Belgrade weekly)
Jedinstvo (Kosovo Serbian daily)
Koha (Independent Kosovo Albanian-language weekly)
Koha English Digests (Condensed English version of *Koha*)
OMRI (Open Media Research Institute Reports)
Naša Borba (Independent Belgrade Weekly—a split from *Borba*)
NIN (Belgrade weekly magazine)
Novosti 8 (Belgrade weekly magazine)
Oslobodjenje (Sarajevo daily newspaper)

Politika (Belgrade daily, very instrumental in promoting the policies of Slobodan Milošević)

Politika Express (Belgrade daily owned by Politika)

Politika Svet (Belgrade weekly)

Pravoslavlje (Serbian Orthodox publication in Belgrade)

Republika (Belgrade independent publication)

RFE-RFL Reports (Reports of Radio Free Europe/Radio Free Liberty)

RFE, SR (Radio Free Europe daily)

Rilindja (Albanian-language press, formerly published in Kosovo, now an "émigré press")

Slobodna Dalmacija (Split daily newspaper)

Srbobran (Orthodox Religious Newsletter)

Sveske (Sarajevo publication)

Tanjug (Official News Agency in Belgrade)

Večernji list (Zagreb daily)

Večernje Novosti (Belgrade daily)

Vjesnik (Zagreb daily)

Vreme (Independent Belgrade weekly)

Vreme English Digest (Condensed English reports from *Vreme*)

Zeri i Popullit (Tirana daily, formerly the organ of the Communist Party)

Books and Articles

About the Events in Kosova: Articles from "Zeri i Popullit" and Other Press Organs. 1981. Tirana: The 8 Nentori Publishing House.

Agani, Fehmi. 1994. "Nation, National Minority and Self-Determination." In *Conflict or Dialogue: Serbian-Albanian Relations and the Integration of the Balkans,* eds. Dušan Janjić and Shkelzen Maliqi, 205–25. Subotica: Open University.

Ahmeti, Sevdie. 1994. "Forms of Apartheid in Kosovo." In *Conflict or Dialogue: Serbian-Albanian Relations and the Integration of the Balkans,* eds. Dušan Janjić and Shkelzen Maliqi, 108–16. Subotica: Open University.

Akhavan, Payam, and Robert Howse, eds. 1995. *Yugoslavia: The Former and the Future: Reflections by Scholars from the Region.* Washington, D.C.: The Brookings Institute.

Ali, Rabia, and Lawrence Lifschultz, eds. 1993. *Why Bosnia? Writings on the Balkan War.* Stony Creek, Conn.: Pamphleteer's Press.

Allcock, John B., John J. Horton, and Marko Milivojević, eds. 1992. *Yugoslavia in Transition: Choices and Constraints.* New York: Berg Publishers.

Almond, Mark L. 1994. *Europe's Backyard War: The War in the Balkans.* London: Heinemann.

Alter, Peter. 1985. *Nationalism.* London: Edward Arnold.

Amnesty International. 1982. *Yugoslavia: Prisoners of Conscience.* London: Amnesty International.

———. 1992. *Yugoslavia: Ethnic Albanians—Victims of Torture and Ill-Treatment by Police.* New York: Amnesty International.

————. 1994. *Yugoslavia: Ethnic Albanians: Trial by Truncheon*. New York: Amnesty International.

————. 1994. *Yugoslavia: Police Violence in Kosovo Province: The Victims*. New York: Amnesty International.

Anderson, Benedict. 1991. *Imagined Communities: Reflections on the Origin and Spread of Nationalism*. London: Verso Books.

Andrić, Ivo. 1959. *The Bridge on the Drina*. New York: Macmillan.

Anthias, Floya, and Nira Yuval-Davis. 1992. *Racialized Boundaries: Race, Nation, Gender, Colour and Class and the Anti-Racist Struggle*. New York: Routledge.

Antić, Zdenko. 1988/89. "Serbian Problems." *The South Slav Journal* 11, no. 4 (winter).

Arendt, Hannah. 1951. *The Origins of Totalitarianism*. New York: Harcourt Brace.

————. 1954. *Between Past and Future: Eight Exercises in Political Thought*. New York: Penguin Books.

Armstrong, Hamilton Fish. 1951. *Tito and Goliath*. New York: Macmillan.

Avramov, Dragan, et al. 1988. *Demografski razvoj i populaciona politika SAP Kosova*. Belgrade: Institut drustvenih nauka, Centar za demografska istrazivanja.

Bajraktari, Jusuf, et al., eds. 1996. *The Kosova Issue: A Historic and Current Problem*. Tirana: Institute of History.

Balibar, Etienne, and Immanuel Wallerstein. 1991. *Race, Nation, Class: Ambiguous Identities*. Translated by Chris Turner. New York: Verso.

Banac, Ivo. 1984. *The National Question in Yugoslavia: Origins, History, Politics*. Ithaca, N.Y.: Cornell University Press.

————. 1988. *With Stalin Against Tito: Cominformist Splits in Yugoslav Communism*. Ithaca, N.Y.: Cornell University Press.

————. 1992. "Post-Communism as Post-Yugoslavism: The Yugoslav Non-Revolution of 1989–1990." In *Eastern Europe in Revolution*, ed. Ivo Banac, 168–87. Ithaca, N.Y.: Cornell University Press.

————. 1994. "Serbia's Deadly Fears." *The New Combat* (autumn), 36–43.

————. 1995. "The Dissolution of Yugoslav Historiography." In *Beyond Yugoslavia: Politics, Economics, and Culture in a Shattered Community*, eds. Sabrina Petra Ramet and Ljubiša A. Adamović, 39–66. Boulder, Colo.: Westview Press.

————. 1995. "Nationalism in Serbia." In *Balkans: A Mirror of the New International Order*, eds. Gunay Goksu Ozdogan and Kelmali Saybasili, 133–52. Istanbul: Muhittin Salin EREN.

————. 1995. "Nationalism in Southeastern Europe." In *Nationalisms and Nationalities in the New Europe.*, ed. Charles A. Kupchan, 107–21. Ithaca, N.Y.: Cornell University Press.

Banks, Marcus. 1996. *Ethnicity: Anthropological Constructions*. London: Routledge.

Bataković, Dušan T. 1992. *The Kosovo Chronicles*. Translated by Dragana Vulićević. Belgrade: Plato.

Behlull, Beqaj. 1996. *Ethnicity in Post-Communism: The Albanians in the Post-*

Communist Transformation of Yugoslavia. Belgrade: Institute of Social Sciences.

Bell-Fialkoff, Andrew. 1996. *Ethnic Cleansing*. New York: St. Martin's Press.

Bennett, Christopher. 1995. *Yugoslavia's Bloody Collapse: Causes, Course and Consequences*. New York: New York University Press.

Berisha, Ibrahim, et al., eds. 1993. *Albanian Democratic Movement in Former Yugoslavia: Documents 1990–1993*. Priština: Kosova Information Center.

———. 1993. *Serbian Colonialization and Ethnic Cleansing of Kosova*. Priština: Kosova Information Center.

Berisha, Isuf. 1994. "Pristina's One-Party Rule." *Balkan War Report* (February).

Berman, Nathaniel. 1993. "But the Alternative Is Despair: European Nationalism and the Modernist Renewal of International Law." *Harvard Law Review* 106, 1792.

Bhabha, Homi. 1994. *The Location of Culture*. New York: Routledge.

Bianchini, Stefano, and Paul Shoup, eds. 1995. *The Yugoslav War, Europe and the Balkans—How to Achieve Security?* Ravenna: Longo.

Biberaj, Elez. 1982. "Kosovo, The Struggle for Recognition." *Conflict Studies*, no. 137. London: Institute for the Study of Conflict.

———. 1993. "Kosova: The Balkan Powder Keg." *Conflict Studies*, no. 258. London: Institute for the Study of Conflict.

Biserko, Sonja, ed. 1993. *Yugoslavia: Collapse, War, Crimes*. Belgrade: Centre for Anti-War Action and Belgrade Circle.

Blagojević, Marina. 1991. "Serbian Migrations from Kosovo from the End of the '60s: Social Factors." Reprinted from *Serbs and Albanians in the 20th Century* (academic conferences of the Serbian Academy of Sciences and Arts, vol. 61, Department of Historical Sciences, no. 20). Belgrade: Srpska akademija nauka i umetnosti.

Bogdanović, Dimitrije. 1986. *Knjiga o Kosovu*. 3d ed. Belgrade: Srpska akademija nauka i umetnosti. English summary published in same volume as "The Kosovo Question: Past and Present."

Bogosavljević, Srdjan. 1994. "A Statistical Picture of Serbian-Albanian Relations." In *Conflict or Dialogue: Serbian-Albanian Relations and the Integration of the Balkans,* eds. Dušan Janjić and Shkelzen Maliqi, 17–29. Subotica: Open University.

———. 1994. "A Statistical Picture of Serbo-Albanian Relations." *Republika* 6, special issue 9 (February). Published also in Serbian as "Statistička slika srpsko albanskih odnosa."

Bojičić, Vesna. 1996. "The Disintegration of Yugoslavia: Causes and Consequences of Dynamic Inefficiency in Semi-Command Economies." In *Yugoslavia and After: A Study in Fragmentation, Despair and Rebirth*, eds. David A. Dyker and Ivan Vejvoda, 28–47. New York: Longman.

Bok, Sissela. 1979. *Lying: Moral Choice in Public and Private Life*. New York: Vintage Books.

Brass, Paul. 1991. *Ethnicity and Nationalism*. New Delhi: Sage Publications.

Breslauer, George W., ed. 1991. *Dilemmas of Transition in the Soviet Union and Eastern Europe*. Berkeley, Calif.: Berkeley-Stanford Program in Soviet Studies.

Breuilly, John. 1994. *Nationalism and the State*. 2d ed. Chicago: University of Chicago Press.

Brilmayer, Lea. 1995. "Propter Honoris Respectum: The Moral Significance of Nationalism." *Notre Dame Law Review* 71, no. 7.

Brubaker, Rogers. 1996. *Nationalism Reframed: Nationhood and the National Question in the New Europe*. Cambridge: Cambridge University Press.

Bugajski, Janusz. 1995. *Ethnic Politics in Eastern Europe*. Armonk, N.Y.: M. E. Sharpe.

Burg, Steven. 1983. *Conflict and Cohesion in Socialist Yugoslavia*. Princeton: Princeton University Press.

———. 1991. "Nationalism and Democratization in Yugoslavia." *The Washington Quarterly* 14, no. 4 (autumn).

Burton, John, ed. 1987. *Resolving Deep-Rooted Conflict: A Hand Book*. Lantham, Md.: University Press of America.

———. 1990. *Conflict: Human Needs Theory*. London: Macmillan Press.

Les Cahiers de l'Organisation Internationale des Journalistes. 1993. *Reporters et médias en ex-Yougoslavie*. Paris: Mondiapress.

Cani, Bahri, and Cvijetin Milivojević, eds. 1996. *Kosmet ili Kosova*. Belgrade: NEA.

Cerović, Vuksan. 1989. *Kosovo: Kontrare volucija koja teče*. Belgrade and Priština: Nova Knjiga, Jedinstvo.

Chapman, David. 1990. *Instant Democracy: Constitutional Proposals for Emerging Democracies*. London: Institute for Social Inventions.

Charny, Israel W. 1992. "Early Warning, Intervention, and Prevention of Genocide." In *Genocide in Our Time: An Annotated Bibliography with Analytical Introductions*, eds. Michael N. Dobkowski and Isidor Walliman, 149–57. Ann Arbor, Mich.: Piernan Press.

Chatterjee, Partha. 1993. *Nationalist Thought and the Colonial World*. Minneapolis: University of Minnesota Press.

Cigar, Norman. 1995. *Genocide in Bosnia: The Policy of "Ethnic Cleansing."* College Station, Texas: Texas A&M University Press.

Ćirković, Sima., et al., eds. 1989. *Okrugli sto Kosovska bitka u istoriografiji*. Belgrade.

Cocks, Joan. 1989. *The Oppositional Imagination: Feminism, Critique and Political Theory*. New York: Routledge.

Cohen, Lenard J. 1995. *Broken Bonds: Yugoslavia's Disintegration and Balkan Politics in Transition*. 2d ed. Boulder, Colo.: Westview Press.

Cohen, Paul A. 1997. *History in Three Keys: The Boxers as Event, Experience and Myth*. New York: Columbia University Press.

Cohen, Philip J. 1996. "The Complicity of the Serbian Intellectuals in Genocide in the 1990s." In *This Time We Knew: Western Responses to Genocide in Bosnia*, eds. Thomas Cushman and Stjepan G. Meštrović, 39–64. New York: New York University Press.

Conference in Ljubljana. 1989. "Kosovo-Serbien-Jugoslawien." Report on file with author.

The Constitution of the Federal People's Republic of Yugoslavia. 1946. Washington, D.C.: Information Officer, Embassy of the Federal People's Republic of Yugoslavia.

The Constitution of the Kingdom of the Serbs, Croats and Slovenes [adopted June 28, 1921]. 1934. In *Select Constitutions of the World*, ed. Shiva Rao. Madras: Madras Law Journal Press.

The Constitution of the Republic of Serbia. 1990. Belgrade: Secretariat for Information of the Republic of Serbia. Translated by Boško Milosavljević, Margot Milosavljević, and Durica Krstić from *The Official Gazette of the Republic of Serbia*, no. 1, 1990.

The Constitution of the Socialist Federal Republic of Yugoslavia. 1963. Belgrade: Secretariat of Information of the Federal Assembly.

The Constitution of the Socialist Federal Republic of Yugoslavia (Ustav Socijalis-tičke Federativne Republike Jugoslavije). 1974. Translated by Dragoljub Djurović. Belgrade: Dopisna Delavska Univerza.

Council for Human Rights of Priština. 1992. *The Frozen Smiles: Violence Against Children in Kosova.* Priština: The Council for Human Rights.

Crampton, R. J. 1994. *Eastern Europe in the Twentieth Century.* New York and London: Routledge.

Crnobrnja, Mihailo. 1996. *The Yugoslav Drama.* Montreal and Kingston: Mc-Gill-Queen's University Press.

Čubrilović, Vasa. 1937. "The Expulsion of Albanians by the Serbs." Memorandum; n.p. On file with author.

Cukić, Dragan. *Kosovo: Znamenitosti i Lepote.* Priština: Turisticki Savez SAP Kosovo.

Curle, Adam. 1972. *Mystics and Militants: A Study of Awareness, Identity and Social Action.* London: Tavistock Publications.

———. 1978. *Peace Making: Public and Private.* Kingston, Ontario: Queen's University.

———. 1981. *True Justice: Quaker Peace Makers and Peace Making.* London: Quaker Home Service.

Čuruvija, Slavko, and Ivan Torov. 1995. "The March to War (1980–1990)." In *Yugoslavia's Ethnic Nightmare: The Inside Story of Europe's Unfolding Ordeal*, eds. Jasmika Udovički and James Ridgeway, 73–104. New York: Lawrence Hill Books.

Cvijić, Christopher. 1991. *Remaking the Balkans.* London: Pinter Publishers.

Demaçi, Adem. 1990. *Republika e Kosovës është Shpallur në zemrën e popullit tim.* Priština: n.p.

Denich, Bette. 1994. "Dismembering Yugoslavia: National Ideologies and the Symbolic Revival of Genocide." *American Ethnologist* 21, no. 2 (May), 367–90.

Denitch, Bogdan. 1994. *Ethnic Nationalism: The Tragic Death of Yugoslavia.* Minneapolis: University of Minnesota Press.

Destani, Bejtulah. 1994. "Albania: A History of Border Changes." *WarReport* (February), 5.

Dimitrijević, Vojin. 1992. "Nationalities and Minorities in the Yugoslav Federation." In *The Protection of Minorities and Human Rights*, eds. Y. Dinstein and M. Tabory. Dordrecht: Martinus Nijhoff Publishers.

———. 1995. "The 1974 Constitution and Constitutional Process as a Factor in the Collapse of Yugoslavia." In *Yugoslavia: The Former and the Future:*

Reflections by Scholars from the Region, eds. Payam Akhavan and Robert Howse, 45–74. Washington, D.C.: The Brookings Institute.

Djilas, Aleksa. 1991. *The Contested Country: Yugoslav Unity and Communist Revolution, 1919–1953*. Cambridge, Mass.: Harvard University Press.

———. 1993. "A Profile of Slobodan Milošević." *Foreign Affairs* 72 (summer), 81–96.

———. 1995. "Fear Thy Neighbor: The Breakup of Yugoslavia." In *Nationalisms and Nationalities in the New Europe*, ed. Charles A. Kupchan, 85–106. Ithaca, N.Y.: Cornell University Press.

Djilas, Milovan. 1980. *Tito: The Story from the Inside*. New York: Harcourt Brace Jovanovich.

Djoković, Milorad, ed. 1990. *Kosmetski dosije*. Požarevac: Prosveta.

Djukić, Slavoljub. 1992. *Kako se dogodio vodja: borbe za vlast u Srbiji posle Josipa Broza*. Belgrade: Filip Višnjić.

———. 1994. *Izmedju slave i anateme—Politička biografija Slobodana Miloševića*. Belgrade: Filip Višnjić.

"Documents, Petition to the Assembly of the Socialist Federal Republic of Yugoslavia and to the Assembly of the Socialist Republic of Yugoslavia." Dated January 21, 1986; reprinted in *The South Slav Journal* 9, nos. 1–2 (spring-summer 1986), 107.

Draganich, Alex. 1995. *Yugoslavia's Disintegration and the Struggle for Truth*. Boulder, Colo.: East European Monographs.

Draganich, Alex N., and Slavko Todorovich. 1984. *The Saga of Kosovo: Focus on Serbian-Albanian Relations*. Boulder, Colo.: East European Monographs.

Duhaček, Daša. 1993. "Women's Time in the Former Yugoslavia." In *Gender Politics and Post-Communism: Reflections from Eastern Europe and the Former Soviet Union*, ed. Nanette Funk and Magda Mueller, 131–37. New York: Routledge.

Durham, Edith. 1909. *High Albania*. London: E. Arnold.

Dyker, David. 1990. *Yugoslavia: Socialism, Development and Debt*. London: Routledge.

Dyker, David A., and Ivan Vejvoda, eds. 1996. *Yugoslavia and After: A Study in Fragmentation, Despair and Rebirth*. New York: Longman.

Eckhardt, W., and G. Kohler. 1980. "Structural and Armed Violence in the 20th Century: Magnitudes and Trends." *International Interactions* 6, no. 4.

Ellul, Jacques. 1973. *Propaganda: The Formation of Men's Attitudes*. Trans. Konrad Kellen and Jean Lerner. New York: Vintage.

Elsie, Robert, ed. 1997. *Kosovo, in the Heart of the Powder Keg*. New York: Columbia University Press.

Emmert, Thomas A. 1990. *Serbian Golgotha: Kosovo, 1389*. New York: East European Monographs.

Esman, Milton J. and Shibley Telhami, eds. 1995. *International Organizations and Ethnic Conflict*. Ithaca: Cornell University Press.

Forging War: The Media in Serbia, Croatia and Bosnia. 1994. London: Article 19.

Foucault, Michel. 1980. *Power/Knowledge: Selected Interviews and Other Writings 1972–1997*. Trans. Colin Gordon. New York: Pantheon.

Franck, Thomas M. 1996. "Clan and Superclan: Identity and Community in Law and Practice." *American Journal of International Law* 90 (July), 359.

Fromm, Erich. 1954. *Escape from Freedom*. New York: Avon Books.

Funk, Nanette, and Magda Mueller, eds. 1993. *Gender Politics and Post-Communism: Reflections from Eastern Europe and the Former Soviet Union*. New York: Routledge.

Galligan, Michael J., Deborah J. Jacobs, Morris J. Panner, and Warren R. Stern. 1991. "The Kosovo Crisis and Human Rights in Yugoslavia." *The Record of the Association of the Bar of the City of New York* 46, no. 3 (April), 212–30.

Galtung, J. 1990. "Paper Violence and Peace. " In *A Reader in Peace Studies*, eds. Paul Smoker, Ruth Davis, and Barbara Munske. New York: Pergamon Press.

Gasparini, Alberto, and Vladimir Yadov, eds. 1995. *Social Actors and the Designing of the Civil Society of Eastern Europe*. Greenwich, Conn.: JAI Press.

Gellner, Ernest. 1983. *Nations and Nationalism*. Oxford, England: Blackwell.

Giddens, Anthony. 1991. *The Consequences of Modernity*. Cambridge: Polity Press.

Glazer, Nathan, and Daniel P. Moynihan, eds. 1975. *Ethnicity: Theory and Experience*. Cambridge, Mass.: Harvard University Press.

Goati, Vladimir. 1992. "The Challenge of Post-Communism." In *The Tragedy of Yugoslavia: The Failure of Democratic Transformation*, eds. Jim Seroka and Vukasin Pavlovic, 3–22. Armonk, N.Y.: M. E. Sharpe.

Golubovic, Zagorka. 1993. "Nationalism and Democracy: The Yugoslav Case." *Journal of Area Studies*, no. 3, 65–77.

Gow, James. 1992. *Legitimacy and the Military: Yugoslavia in Crisis*. London: Pinter Publishers.

Greenfield, Liah. 1992. *Nationalism: Five Roads to Modernity*. Cambridge, Mass.: Harvard University Press.

Grudin, Robert. 1996. *On Dialogue: An Essay in Free Thought*. New York: Houghton Mifflin.

Gruenwald, Oskar. 1986. "Yugoslavia's Gulag Archipelago and Human Rights." In *Human Rights in Yugoslavia*, eds. Oskar Gruenwald and Karen Rosenblum-Cale, 3–48. New York: Irvington Publishers.

Gruenwald, Oskar, and Karen Rosenblum-Cale, eds. 1986. *Human Rights in Yugoslavia*. New York: Irvington Publishers.

Guibernau, Montserrat. 1996. *Nationalisms: The Nation-State and Nationalism in the Twentieth Century*. London: Polity Press.

Gurr, Ted Robert. 1993. *Minorities at Risk: A Global View of Ethnopolitical Conflict*. Washington, D.C.: U.S. Institute for Peace Press.

———. 1995. "Transforming Ethno-political Conflicts: Exit, Autonomy or Access." In *Conflict Transformation*, ed. Kumar Rupesinghe, 1–30. New York: St. Martin's Press.

Gurr, Ted, and Barbarat Harff. 1994. *Ethnic Conflict in World Politics*. Boulder, Colo.: Westview Press.

Hall, Derek. 1994. *Albania and the Albanians.* London and New York: Pinter Reference.

———. 1996. "Albanian Identity and Balkan Roles." In *Reconstructing the Balkans: A Geography of the New Southeast Europe,* eds. Derek Hall and Darrick Danta, 119–33. New York: John Wiley & Sons.

Hall, Derek, and Darrick Danta, eds. 1996. *Reconstructing the Balkans: A Geography of the New Southeast Europe.* New York: John Wiley & Sons.

Hall, John. 1995. "Nationalisms, Classified and Explained." In *Notions of Nationalism,* ed. Sukumar Periwal, 8–33. Budapest: Central European University Press.

Hampson, Françoise J. 1993. "Responsibility of and for the Media in the Conflicts in the Former Yugoslavia." In *Yugoslavia: Collapse, War, Crimes,* ed. Sonja Biserko, 79–113. Belgrade: Centre for Anti-War Action and Belgrade Circle.

Hann, Chris, and Elizabeth Dunn. 1996. *Civil Society: Challenging Western Models.* New York: Routledge.

Hayden, Robert M. 1992. "Constitutional Nationalism in the Former Yugoslav Republics." *The Slavic Review* 51, no. 4, 654–73.

Helsinki Watch. 1989. *Increasing Turbulence: Human Rights Abuses in Yugoslavia.* New York: Human Rights Watch/Helsinki Watch.

———. 1991. *Freedom to Conform.* New York: Human Rights Watch/Helsinki Watch.

———. 1992. *Human Rights Abuses in Kosovo 1990–1992.* New York: Human Rights Watch/Helsinki Watch.

———. 1992. *War Crimes in Bosnia-Hercegovina, Volume I.* New York: Human Rights Watch/Helsinki Watch.

———. 1992. *Yugoslavia: Human Rights Abuses in Kosovo 1990–1992.* New York: Human Rights Watch/Helsinki Watch.

———. 1993. *Abuses Continue in the Former Yugoslavia: Serbia, Montenegro and Bosnia-Hercegovina.* New York: Human Rights Watch/Helsinki Watch.

———. 1993. "Threats to Press Freedoms: A Report Prepared for the Free Media Seminar, Commission on Security and Cooperation in Europe." *Helsinki Watch Reports* 5, no. 21 (November). New York: Human Rights Watch/Helsinki Watch.

———. 1993. *War Crimes in Bosnia-Hercegovina, Volume II.* New York: Human Rights Watch/Helsinki Watch.

———. 1994. *Open Wounds: Human Rights Abuses in Kosovo.* New York: Human Rights Watch/Helsinki Watch.

———. 1996. *Yugoslavia (Serbia and Montenegro): Persecution Persists: Human Rights Violations in Kosovo.* New York: Human Rights Watch/Helsinki Watch.

Helsinki Watch and International Helsinki Foundation. 1990. *Yugoslavia: Crisis in Kosovo.* Eds. Julie Mertus and Vlatka Mihelić. New York: Human Rights Watch/Helsinki Watch.

Hibbert, Reginald. 1991. *Albania's National Liberation: The Bitter Victory.* London: Pinter.

Hicks, Donna. 1997. "Conflict Resolution and Human Rights Education:

Broadening the Agenda." In *Human Rights Education for the Twentieth Century*, eds. George J. Andreopoulos and Richard Pierre Claude. Philadelphia: University of Pennsylvania Press.

Hobsbawm, Eric. 1990. *Nations and Nationalism Since 1780*. Cambridge, England: Cambridge University Press.

Hondius, Fritz. 1968. *The Yugoslav Community of Nations*. The Hague: Mouton.

Horowitz, Donald. 1985. *Ethnic Groups in Conflict*. Berkeley: University of California Press.

Horvat, Branko. 1989. *Kosovo pitanje*. Zagreb: Globus.

Hrgović, Milica, Vesna Bjelogrlić-Goldsworthy, John White, and Ružica White. 1989. *The Battle of Kosovo in History and Popular Tradition*. Belgrade: Beogradski Izdavačko-Grafički Zavod.

Hudelist, Darko. 1989. *Kosovo, bitka bez iluzija*. Zagreb: Centar za informacije i publictet.

Huntington, Samuel P. 1996. *The Clash of Civilizations and the Remaking of World Order*. New York : Simon & Schuster.

Hutchinson, John, and Anthony D. Smith, eds. 1996. *Ethnicity*. New York: Oxford University Press.

Igić, Živorad. 1992. *Kosovo i Metohija (1981–1991): Uvod u jugoslovensku krizu*. Priština, Podgorica: Jedinstvo, Oktoih.

International Crisis Group. 1998 (March). *Kosovo Spring: International Crisis Group Report on Kosovo*. Sarajevo: International Crisis Group.

———. 1998 (May). *Again, the Visible Hand: Slobodan Milosevic's Manipulation of the Kosovo Dispute*. Belgrade: International Crisis Group.

International Federation of Journalists and International Federation of Newspaper Publishers. 1993. *Information under Control: The Media Crisis in Montenegro and Kosovo*. Report of the IFJ/FIEJ mission, November 21–25.

International Helsinki Federation for Human Rights. 1993. *From Autonomy to Colonization: Human Rights in Kosovo 1989–1993*. Vienna: International Helsinki Federation.

Irwin, Zachary T. 1986. "Law, Legitimacy and Yugoslav National Dissent: The Dimension of Human Rights." In *Human Rights in Yugoslavia*, eds. Oskar Gruenwald and Karen Rosenblum-Cale, 169–210. New York: Irvington Publishers.

Islami, Hivzi. 1994. "Demographic Reality in Kosova." In *Conflict or Dialogue: Serbian-Albanian Relations and the Integration of the Balkans*, eds. Dušan Janjić and Shkelzen Maliqi. Subotica: Open University, 30–53.

———. 1996. "Demographic Problems of Kosova and Other Ethnic Albanian Territories." In *The Kosova Issue: A Historic and Current Problem*, ed. Jusuf Bajraktari et al., 139–45. Tirana: Institute of History.

Ismajli, Rexhep. n.d. *Kosovo and the Albanians in Former Yugoslavia*. Kosovo: Kosova Information Center.

Janis, Irving Lester. 1983. *Victims of Groupthink: A Psychological Study of Foreign-Policy Decisions and Fiascoes*. Boston: Houghton Mifflin.

Janjić, Dušan. 1993. "Socialism, Federalism and Nationalism in (the Former) Yugoslavia: Lessons to Be Learned." *Journal of Area Studies*, no. 3 (1993), 102–19.

————. 1994. "National Identity, Movement and Nationalism of Serbs and Albanians." In *Conflict or Dialogue: Serbian-Albanian Relations and the Integration of the Balkans,* eds. Dušan Janjić and Shkelzen Maliqi, 117–76. Subotica: Open University.

————. 1995. "Resurgence of Ethnic Conflict in Yugoslavia: The Demise of Communism and the Rise of the 'New Elites' of Nationalism." In *Yugoslavia: The Former and the Future: Reflections by Scholars from the Region,* eds. Payam Akhavan and Robert Howse, 19–44. Washington, D.C.: The Brookings Institute.

Janjić, Dušan, and Shkelzen Maliqi, eds. 1994. *Conflict or Dialogue: Serbian-Albanian Relations and the Integration of the Balkans.* Subotica: Open University.

Janke, Peter. 1994. *Ethnic and Religious Conflicts: Europe and Asia.* Brookfield, Vt.: Dartmouth University Press.

Jelavich, Barbara. 1983. *History of the Balkans: Twentieth Century.* Cambridge, England: Cambridge University Press.

Jevavich, Charles and Barbara. 1977. *The Establishment of the Balkan National States, 1804–1920.* Seattle: University of Washington Press.

Jerković, Nebojša, ed. 1995. *Kosovo and Metohija and Integral Parts of the Republic of Serbia and FR of Yugoslavia: Documents and Facts.* Belgrade: Review of International Affairs.

Jevtić, Djordje. 1995. *Bitka za Kosovo, šest vekova posle I.* Priština: Novi Svet.

Judah, Tim. 1997. *The Serbs: History, Myth and the Destruction of Yugoslavia.* New Haven, Conn.: Yale University Press.

Juka, S. S. [Safete Sophie]. 1984. *Kosova: The Albanians in Yugoslavia in Light of Historical Documents.* New York: Waldon Press.

Kadare, Ismail. 1997. "The Wedding Procession Turned to Ice, 1981–1983." In *Kosovo, in the Heart of the Powder Keg,* ed. Robert Elsie, 105–94. Boulder, Colo.: East European Monographs.

Kaldor, Mary. 1996. "Cosmopolitanism versus Nationalism: The New Divide?" In *Europe's New Nationalism: States and Minorities in Conflict,* eds. Richard Caplan and John Feffer, 42–58. Oxford, England: Oxford University Press.

Kandić, Nataša, ed. 1996. *Spotlight on: Human Rights in Serbia and Montenegro.* Belgrade: Humanitarian Law Center.

Kaplan, Robert D. 1993. *Balkan Ghosts: A Journey Through History.* New York: Vintage Books.

Kasapović, Mirjana. 1992. "The Structure and Dynamics of the Yugoslav Political Environment and Elections in Croatia." In *The Tragedy of Yugoslavia: The Failure of Democratic Transformation,* eds. Jim Seroka and Vukasin Pavlovic, 23–48. Armonk, N.Y.: M. E. Sharpe.

Kaufman, Chaim. 1996. "Possible and Impossible Solutions to Ethnic Civil Wars." *International Security* 20, no. 4, 141.

Keane, John Jr. 1988. *Democracy and Civil Society.* London: Verso.

Kelman, H. C., and S. P. Cohen. 1990. "The Problem-Solving Workshop: A Social-Psychological Contribution to the Resolution of International Conflicts." *Journal of Peace Research* 13, 79–90.

Kelmendi, Nekibe. 1992. *Kosovo pod bremenom diskriminatorskih zakona Srbije: Činjenice i dokazi.* Priština: n.p.

Kiš, Danilo. 1993. "On Nationalism." In *Why Bosnia? Writings on the Balkan War,* eds. Rabia Ali and Lawrence Lifschultz. Stony Creek, Conn.: Pamphleteer's Press.

Kohl, Christine von. 1992. *Kosovo: Gordischer Knoten des Balkan.* Vienna and Zurich: Europaverlag.

Kohl, Christine von, and Wolfgang Libal. 1992. "Kosovo, the Gordian Knot of the Balkans." In *Kosovo, in the Heart of the Powder Keg,* ed. Robert Elsie, 3–104. Boulder, Colo.: East European Monographs.

Komnenić, Milan. 1989. "The Kosovo Cataclysm." In *Kosovo 1389–1989: Special Edition of the Serbian Literary Quarterly on the Occasion of 600 Years since the Battle of Kosovo,* ed. Alex Vukadinović, 141–50. Belgrade: Serbian Literary Quarterly.

Kotur, Rev. Dr. Krstivoj. 1977. *The Serbian Folk Epic: Its Theology and Anthropology.* New York: Philosophical Library.

Kristeva, Julia. 1991. *Strangers to Ourselves.* New York: Columbia University Press.

———. 1993. *Nations without Nationalism.* New York: Columbia University Press.

Krstić, Branislav. 1994. *Kosovo izmedju istorijskog i etničkog prava.* Belgrade: Kuća Vid.

Kullashi, Muhamedin. 1994. "Kosovo and the Disintegration of Yugoslavia." In *Conflict or Dialogue: Serbian-Albanian Relations and the Integration of the Balkans,* eds. Dušan Janjić and Shkelzen Maliqi, 177–88. Subotica: Open University.

Kupchan, Charles A., ed. 1995. *Nationalism and Nationalities in the New Europe.* Ithaca and London: Cornell University Press.

Kuper, Leo. 1981. *Genocide: Its Political Use in the Twentieth Century.* New Haven, Conn.: Yale University Press.

Kuzmanović, Jasmina. 1995. "The Media: The Extension of Politics by Other Means." In *Beyond Yugoslavia: Politics, Economics, and Culture in a Shattered Community,* eds. Sabrina Petra Ramet and Ljubiša A. Adamović, 83–100. Boulder, Colo.: Westview Press.

Kymlicka, Will. 1995. *Multicultural Citizenship: A Liberal Theory of Minority Rights.* Oxford, England: Oxford University Press.

Lazić et al. 1994. *Razaranje društva.* Belgrade: Filip Višnjić.

Letica, Slaven. 1996. "The Genesis of the Current Balkan War." In *Genocide after Emotion: The Postemotional Balkan War,* ed. Stjepan G. Meštrović, 91–112. New York: Routledge.

Logoreci, Anton. 1984. "A Clash between Two Nationalisms in Kosova." In *Studies on Kosova,* eds. Arshi Pipa and Sami Repishti, 185–94. Boulder, Colo.: East European Monographs.

Magaš, Branka. 1993. *The Destruction of Yugoslavia: Tracking the Break-Up 1980–92.* London: Verso.

Malcolm, Noel. 1994. *Bosnia: A Short History.* New York: New York University Press.

————. 1998. *Kosovo: A Short History*. New York: New York University Press.

Maletic, Mihajlo. 1973. *Kosovo, Yesterday and Today*. Belgrade: n.p.

Maliqi, Shkelzen. 1993. "Albanian Self-Understanding Through Non-Violence: The Construction of National Identity in Opposition to the Serbs." *Journal of Area Studies*, no. 3, 120–128.

————. 1994. "Štampa na Kosovu." *Horizonti: Časopis za komunikaciju kultura* (September), 46.

————. 1996. "The Albanian Movement in Kosova." In *Yugoslavia and After: A Study in Fragmentation, Despair and Rebirth*, eds. David A. Dyker and Ivan Vejvoda, 138–54. New York: Longman.

Marmullaku, Ramadan. 1975. *Albania and the History of Albanians*. London: Hurst.

Mastnak, Tomaž. 1992. "Civil Society in Slovenia: From Opposition to Power." In *The Tragedy of Yugoslavia: The Failure of Democratic Transformation*, eds. Jim Seroka and Vukasin Pavlovic, 49–66. Armonk, N.Y.: M. E. Sharpe.

Mayall, James. 1990. *Nationalism and International Society*. Cambridge: Cambridge University Press.

McClintock, Anne. 1991. "No Longer a Future in Heaven: Women and Nationalism in South Africa." *Transition* 1, no. 51, 104.

McGarry, John, and Brendan O'Leary. 1993. *The Politics of Ethnic Conflict Regulation: Case Studies of Protracted Ethnic Conflicts*. New York: Routledge, 1993.

Mertus, Julie. 1994. " 'Woman' in the Service of National Identity." *Hastings Women's Law Journal* 4, no. 1.

————. 1995. "Remember Kosovo?" *Uncaptive Minds* 8, nos. 3–4 (fall-winter).

————. 1996. "Gender in the Service of Nation: Female Citizenship in Kosovar Society." *Social Politics: International Studies in Gender, State and Society* 3, no. 2/3 (summer/fall).

————. 1996. "A Wall of Silence Divides Serbian and Albanian Opinion on Kosovo." *Transition* 2, no. 6, 48–51.

Mertus, Julie, Jasmina Tešanović, Habiba Metikos, and Rada Borić, eds. 1997. *The Suitcase: Refugee Voices from Bosnia and Croatia* (Berkeley: University of California Press).

Meštrović, Stjepan. 1994. *The Balkanization of the West: The Confluence of Postmodernism and Postcommunism*. London and New York: Routledge.

————, ed. 1996. *Genocide after Emotion: The Postemotional Balkan War*. New York: Routledge.

Mihailović, Kosta, and Vasilije Krestić. 1995. *Memorandum of the Serbian Academy of Sciences and Arts: Answers to Criticisms*. Belgrade: Serbian Academy of Sciences and Arts.

Mihajlović, Živorad. 1989. *Podzemni rat na Kosovu i Metohiji, 1389–1989*. Belgrade: Jugoslovenska Estrada.

Mihaljčić, Rade, ed. 1992. *Boj na Kosovu—starija i novija saznanja*. Belgrade: Izdavačka kuća "Književne novine."

Milivojević, Marko. 1984. "The Uneven Impact of Economic Adjustment in Yugoslavia." *South Slav Journal* 7, no. 3/4 (autumn-winter).

———. 1988. "The Yugoslav People's Army: Another Jaruzelski on the Way?" *The South Slav Journal* 11, no. 2–3 (summer-autumn).

———. 1989. "Descent into Chaos: Yugoslavia's Worsening Crisis." *The South Slav Journal* 12, no. 1–2 (spring-summer).

———. 1995. "The Armed Forces of Yugoslavia: Sliding into War." In *Beyond Yugoslavia: Politics, Economics, and Culture in a Shattered Community*, eds. Sabrina Petra Ramet and Ljubiša A. Adamović, 67–82. Boulder, Colo.: Westview Press.

Miller, David. 1995. *On Nationality*. Oxford, England: Oxford University Press.

Milošević, Slobodan. 1989. *Godine Raspleta*. Belgrade: BIGZ.

Mišović, Miloš. 1987. *Ko je tra'io Republiku: Kosovo 1945–1985*. Belgrade: Narodna Knjiga.

Mladenović, Marko. 1989. "Counter-Revolution in Kosovo, Demographic Policy and Family Planning." In *Kosovo 1389–1989: Special Edition of the Serbian Literary Quarterly on the Occasion of 600 Years since the Battle of Kosovo*, ed. Alex Vukadinović, 141–50. Belgrade: Serbian Literary Quarterly.

Mojzes, Paul. 1994. *Yugoslavian Inferno*. New York: Continuum.

Moljević, Stevan. 1981. "Homogena Srbija." *Zbornik dokumenata i podataka o narodnooslobodilačkom ratu naroda Jugoslavije* 14, no. 2, 1–10.

Moore, Barrington. 1978. *Injustice: The Social Bases of Obedience and Revolt*. White Plains, NY: M.E. Sharpe.

Nadar, Laura. 1992. "From Legal Processing to Mind Processing." *Family and Conciliation Courts Review* 30, no. 4, 469–73.

Norris, H. T. 1993. *Islam in the Balkans: Religion and Society between Europe and the Arab World*. London: Hurst.

Oklobdžija, Mira. 1993. "The Creation of Active Xenophobia in What Was Yugoslavia." *Journal of Area Studies*, no. 3.

Paijić, Zoran. 1995. "Bosnia and Herzegovina: From Multiethnic Coexistence to 'Apartheid' and Back." In *Yugoslavia: The Former and the Future: Reflections by Scholars from the Region*, eds. Payam Akhavan and Robert Howse, 152–63. Washington, D.C.: The Brookings Institute.

Pantić, D. 1990. "Vrednosti mladih u vreme krize." In *Deca krize,* ed. Mihailović et al. Belgrade: IDN, Centar za politikološka istraživanja i javno mnjenje.

Parekh, Bhikhu. 1995. "The Concept of National Identity." *New Community* 21, no. 2, 255–68.

Parin, Paul. 1994. "Open Wounds: Ethnopsychoanalytic Reflections on the War in the Former Yugoslavia." In *Mass Rape: The War against Women in Bosnia-Herzegovina*, ed. Alexandra Stiglmayer, 35–53. Lincoln: University of Nebraska Press.

Parker, Andrew, et al., eds. 1992. *Nationalisms and Sexualities*. New York: Routledge.

Pašić, Nikola R. 1986. "Political Persecutions in Yugoslavia: A Historical Survey." In *Human Rights in Yugoslavia*, eds. Oskar Gruenwald and Karen Rosenblum-Cale, 49–106. New York: Irvington Publishers.

Pavlowitch, Steven K. 1982. "Kosovo: An Analysis of Yugoslavia's Albanian Problem." *Conflict Studies*, no. 138. London: Institute for the Study of Conflict.

———. 1988. *The Improbable Survivor: Yugoslavia and Its Problems: 1918–1988.* London: Hurst.

———. 1992. *Tito—Yugoslavia's Great Dictator: A Reassessment.* London: C. Hurst & Company.

Peck, M. Scott. 1982. *People of the Lie: The Hope of Healing Human Evil.* New York: Simon and Schuster.

Periwal, Sukumar, ed. 1995. *Notions of Nationalism.* Budapest: Central European University Press.

Perunčić, B. 1985. *Pisma srpskih konzula iz Prištine, 1890–1910.* Belgrade: Narodna Knjiga, 1985.

Pešić, Vesna. 1996. "Serbian Nationalism and the Origins of the Yugoslav Crisis." Paper prepared for the U.S. Institute for Peace. Available on the internet at http://www.usip.org/oc/sr/pesic/pesic.html#exp.

Petković, Ranko. 1994. "Relations of Yugoslavia and Albania since the end of World War I to the so-called Yugoslav Crisis." In *Conflict or Dialogue: Serbian-Albanian Relations and the Integration of the Balkans,* eds. Dušan Janjić and Shkelzen Maliqi, 253–65. Subotica: Open University.

Petrović, Radovan. 1982. "Kontrarevolucionarne akcije nacionalista i iredentista na Kosovu—Napad na bratstvo-jedinstvo i integritet SFRJ." *Bezbednost* (Belgrade) 1–2 (1982), 191.

Petrović, Ruža. 1987. *Migracije u Jugoslaviji.* Belgrade: Istraživačko izdavački Centar SSO Srbije.

Petrović, Ruža, and Marina Blagojević. 1989. *Migracije Srba i Crnogoraca sa Kosova i Metohije.* Belgrade: SANU.

Petrovich, Micahel Boro. 1976. *A History of Modern Serbia.* New York: Harcourt Brace Jovanovich.

Physicians for Human Rights and the Johannes Wier Foundation. 1991. *Yugoslav Mistreatment of Ethnic Albanians.* The Hague: Johannes Wier Foundation.

Pipa, Arshi. 1985. "The Other Albania: A Balkan Perspective." *The South Slav Journal* 8, nos. 1–2 (spring-summer).

Pipa, Arshi, and Sami Repishti, eds. 1984. *Studies on Kosova.* Boulder, Colo.: East European Monographs.

Pleština, Dijana. 1992. "From 'Democratic Centralism' to Decentralized Democracy? Trials and Tribulations of Yugoslavia's Development." In *Yugoslavia in Transition: Choices and Constraints,* eds. John B. Allcock, John J. Horton and Marko Milivojević, 125–55. New York: Berg Publishers.

———. 1992. *Regional Development in Communist Yugoslavia: Success, Failure and Consequences.* Boulder, Colo.: Westview Press.

Popović, Janićije. 1987. *Život Srba na Kosovu: 1812–1912.* Belgrade: NIRO Književne novine.

Popović, Srdja, Dejan Janča, and Tanja Petrovar, eds. 1990. *Kosovski čvor: Drešiti ili seći?* Belgrade: Kronos.

Poulton, Hugh. 1991. *The Balkans: Minorities and States in Conflict.* London: Minority Rights Publications.

Poulton, Hugh, and Miranda Vickers. 1997. "The Kosovo Albanians: Ethnic Conflict with the Slav State." In *Muslim Identity and the Balkan State,* eds. Hugh Poulton and Suha Taji-Farouki, 139–69. New York: New York University Press.

Prasnikar, J., J. Svejnar, and M. Klinedinst. 1990. "Structural Adjustment Policies and Productive Efficiency of Socialist Enterprises." *European Economic Review* 36, no. 1, 179–201.

Prifti, K., et al., eds. 1993. *The Truth on Kosova.* Tirana: n.p.

Prifti, Peter. 1969. *Kosovo in Ferment.* Cambridge, Mass.: MIT Center for International Studies.

———. 1972. *The Kosovo.* Cambridge, Mass.: MIT Center for International Studies.

———. 1984. "Kosova's Economy: Problems and Prospects." In *Studies on Kosova,* eds. Arshi Pipa and Sami Repishti, 125–65. Boulder, Colo.: East European Monographs.

Pusić, Vesna, "The Rulers and the Managers: A Possible Transition Team?" In *The Tragedy of Yugoslavia: The Failure of Democratic Transformation,* eds. Jim Seroka and Vukasin Pavlovic, 89–104. Armonk, N.Y.: M. E. Sharpe.

Qosja, Rexhep. 1997. "The Albanian Question and Its Solution." In *Kosovo, in the Heart of the Powder Keg,* ed. Robert Elsie, 207–32. New York: Columbia University Press.

Ramet, Sabrina Petra [Pedro]. 1982. "Yugoslavia 1982: Political Ritual, Political Drift, and the Fetishization of the Past." *The South Slav Journal* 5, no. 3 (autumn), 13–21.

———. 1987. "Yugoslavia 1987: Stirrings from Below." *The South Slav Journal* 10, no. 3 (autumn), 21.

———. 1990. "Primordial Ethnicity or Modern Nationalism: The Case of Yugoslavia's Muslims Reconsidered." *The South Slav Journal* 13, nos. 47–48 (spring-summer), 1–20.

———. 1991. *Social Currents in Eastern Europe: The Sources and Meaning of the Great Transformation.* Durham, N.C.: Duke University Press.

———. 1992. *Nationalism and Federalism in Yugoslavia, 1962–1991.* 2d ed. Bloomington, Ind.: Indiana University Press.

———. 1995. *Social Currents in Eastern Europe: The Sources and Consequences of the Great Transformation.* 2d ed. Durham, N.C.: Duke University Press.

———. 1996. "The Albanians of Kosovo: The Potential for Destabilization." *The Brown Journal of World Affairs* 3, no. 1 (winter/spring), 353–72.

———. 1996. *Balkan Babel: The Disintegration of Yugoslavia from the Death of Tito to Ethnic War.* 2d ed. Boulder, Colo.: Westview Press.

———. 1998. *Nihil Obstat: Religion, Politics and Social Change in East-Central Europe and Russia.* Durham, N.C.: Duke University Press.

Ramet, Sabrina Petra, and Ljubiša A. Adamović, eds. 1995. *Beyond Yugoslavia: Politics, Economics, and Culture in a Shattered Community.* Boulder, Colo.: Westview Press.

Rau, Zbigniew, ed. 1991. *The Reemergence of Civil Society in Eastern Europe and the Soviet Union.* Boulder, Colo.: Westview Press.

Repishti, Sami. 1984. "The Evolution of Kosova's Autonomy within the Yugoslav Constitutional Framework." In *Studies on Kosova*, eds. Arshi Pipa and Sami Repishti, 195–231. Boulder, Colo.: East European Monographs.

———. 1986. "Human Rights and the Albanian Nationality in Yugoslavia." In *Human Rights in Yugoslavia*, eds. Oskar Gruenwald and Karen Rosenblum-Cale, 227–81. New York: Irvington Publishers.

Ridley, Jasper Godwin. 1994. *Tito*. London: Constable.

Roux, Michel. 1992. *Les Albanais en Yougoslavie: Minorite nationale, territorie et développement*. Paris: Maison des Sciences de l'Homme.

Rubin, Barnett R., ed. 1996. *Towards Comprehensive Peace in Southeast Europe: Conflict Prevention in the South Balkans*. New York: The Twentieth Century Fund Press.

Rugova, Ibrahim. 1994. *La Question du Kosovo*. Paris: Fayard.

Rupesinghe, Kumar, and Valery A. Tishkov, eds. *Ethnicity and Power in the Contemporary World*. Tokyo and New York: United Nations University Press, 1996.

Rusinow, Dennison. 1977. *The Yugoslav Experiment: 1948–1974*. Berkeley: University of California Press.

———. 1988. *Yugoslavia: A Fractured Federalism*. Washington, D.C.: Wilson Center Press.

———. 1995. "The Avoidable Catastrophe." In *Beyond Yugoslavia: Politics, Economics, and Culture in a Shattered Community*, eds. Sabrina Petra Ramet and Ljubiša A. Adamović, 13–38. Boulder, Colo.: Westview Press.

Said, Edward. 1978. *Orientalism*. New York: Vintage.

Salecl, Renata. 1993. "Nationalism, Anti-Semitism, and Anti-Feminism in Eastern Europe." In *Journal of Area Studies*, no. 3, 78–90.

———. 1994. *The Spoils of Freedom: Psychoanalysis and Feminism after the Fall of Socialism*. New York: Routledge.

Salem, Paul E. 1993. "In Theory: A Critique of Western Conflict Resolution from a Non-Western Perspective." *Negotiation Journal* 9, no. 4 (October 1993), 361–69.

Salihu, Kurtesh. 1982. *The Origin, Position, and Development of the Socialist Autonomous Province of Kosova*. Priština: Center for Marxist Studies.

Samardžić, Radovan, et al. 1989. *Kosovo i Metohija u srpskoj istoriji*. Belgrade: Srpska književna zadruga.

Samary, Catherine. 1995. *Yugoslavia Dismembered*. Translated by Peter Drucker. New York: Monthly Review Press.

Samuels, D. 1995. "At Play in the Field of Oppression: A Government-Funded Agency Pretends to Export Democracy." *Harper's Magazine*, March, 47–54.

Scarry, Elaine. 1985. *The Body in Pain: The Making and Unmaking of the World*. New York: Oxford.

Schmookler, Andrew Bard. 1984. *The Parable of the Tribes: The Problem of Power in Social Evolution*. Berkeley: University of California Press.

Schopflin, George. 1993. "The Rise and Fall of Yugoslavia." In *The Politics of Ethnic Conflict Regulation: Case Studies of Protracted Ethnic Conflicts*, eds. John McGarry and Brendan O'Leary. London: Routledge.

————. 1995. "Nationalism and Ethnicity in Europe, East and West." In *Nationalisms and Nationalities in the New Europe*, ed. Charles A. Krupchan, 37–65. Ithaca, N.Y.: Cornell University Press.

Scott, James C. 1990. *Domination and the Arts of Resistance: Hidden Transcripts*. New Haven: Yale University Press.

Sekelj, Laslo. 1993. *Yugoslavia: The Process of Disintegration*. Trans. Vera Vukelić. Boulder, Colo.: Social Science Monographs.

Sells, Michael A. 1996. "Religion, History, and Genocide in Bosnia-Herzegovina." In *Religion and Justice in the War over Bosnia*, ed. G. Scott Davis, 23–43. New York: Routledge.

————. 1997. *The Bridge Betrayed: Religion and Genocide in Bosnia*. Berkeley: University of California Press.

Seroka, Jim. 1993. "Yugoslavia and Its Successor States." In *Developments in East European Politics*, eds. Stephen White et al., 98–123. Durham, N.C.: Duke University Press.

Seroka, Jim, and Vukasin Pavlovic, eds. 1992. *The Tragedy of Yugoslavia: The Failure of Democratic Transformation*. Armonk, N.Y.: M. E. Sharpe.

Shoup, Paul. 1968. *Communism and the Yugoslav National Question*. New York: Columbia University Press.

Silber, Laura, and Allan Little. 1995. *The Death of Yugoslavia*. London: Penguin Books, BBC Books.

Singleton, Fred. 1985. *A Short History of the Yugoslav People*. New York: Cambridge University Press.

Slijepčević, Djoko. 1982/83. "Concerning the Albanization of the Serbs." *The South Slav Journal* 5, no. 4 (winter).

Smith, Anthony D. 1986. *The Ethnic Origins of Nations*. Oxford: Blackwell.

————. 1995. *Nations and Nationalism in a Global Era*. Cambridge, England: Polity Press.

Spasojević, S. 1986. *Slučaj Martinović*. Belgrade: n.p.

Stambolić, Ivan. 1987. *Rasprave o SR Srbiji* (Debates on the Socialist Republic of Serbia). Zagreb: Globus.

Starova, Gzime. 1993. "The Religion of the Albanians in the Balkan European Context." *Balkan Forum* (Skopje) 1, no. 4 (September).

Staub, Ervin. 1971. "The Learning and Unlearning of Aggression: The Role of Anxiety, Empathy, Efficacy and Prosocial Values." In *The Control of Aggression and Violence: Cognitive and Physiological Factors*, ed. Jerome Singer. New York: Academic Press.

————. 1978–79. *Positive Social Behavior and Morality*. Vol. 1, *Social and Personal Influences*. Vol. 2, *Socialization and Development*. New York: Academic Press.

————. 1989. *The Roots of Evil: The Origins of Genocide and Other Group Violence*. New York: Cambridge University Press.

Stiglmayer, Alexandra. ed. 1994. *Mass Rape: The War Against Women in Bosnia-Herzegovina*. Lincoln: University of Nebraska Press.

Stoianovich, Traian. 1994. *Balkan Worlds: The First and Last Europe*. Armonk, N.Y.: M. E. Sharpe.

Stojanović, Radosav. *Živeti s' genocidom: Hronika kosovskog bešćašća, 1981–1989*. Belgrade: Sfairos.

Stojković, Ljubiša, and Miloš Martić. 1952. *National Minorities in Yugoslavia.* Belgrade: Jugoslavija Publishing and Editing.

Stokes, Gale. 1993. *The Walls Came Tumbling Down: The Collapse of Communism in Eastern Europe.* New York: Oxford University Press.

Surčulija, Živko. 1995. "Nationalism and Post-Communism: The Role of Nationalism in Destroying Former Socialist Federations with Particular Emphasis on the Case of Yugoslavia." *Balkan Forum* 3, no. 2 (June), 149–76.

Taminiaux, Pierre. 1996. "Sacred Text, Sacred Nation." In *Text and Nation: Cross-Disciplinary Essays on Cultural and National Identities,* eds. Laura Garcí-Moreno and Peter C. Pfeiffer, 91–104. Columbia, S.C.: Camden House.

Tamir, Yael. 1994. *Liberal Nationalism.* Princeton: Princeton University Press.

Temperley, Harold W. V. 1919. *History of Serbia.* London: G. Bell and Sons.

Thompson, Mark. 1992. *A Paper House: The Ending of Yugoslavia.* London: Vintage.

Tito, Josip Broz. 1982. *Borba za novi svet* (The Struggle for a New World). Belgrade: Pres kliping.

Todorov, Tzvetan. 1984. *The Conquest of America: The Question of the Other.* New York: HarperCollins.

———. 1993. *On Human Diversity: Nationalism, Racism, and Exoticism in French Thought.* Cambridge, Mass.: Harvard University Press.

———. 1995. *The Morals of History.* Trans. Alyson Waters. Minneapolis: University of Minnesota Press.

Tomac, Petar. 1968. *Kosovska Bitka.* Belgrade: Vojnoizdavacki Zavod.

Tomasevich, Jozo. 1969. "Yugoslavia During the Second World War." In *Contemporary Yugoslavia: Twenty Years of Socialist Experiment,* ed. Wayne S. Vucinich, 59–118. Berkeley: University of California Press.

The Truth about the Plight of the Albanians in Jugoslavia. 1961. Tirana: Zeri i Popullit.

Udovički, Jasminka and James Ridgeway, eds. 1995. *Yugoslavia's Ethnic Nightmare: The Inside Story of Europe's Unfolding Ordeal.* New York: Lawrence Hill Books.

Urošević, Atanasije. 1990. *Kosovo.* Priština: Jedinstvo.

U.S. State Department. 1981–1997. *Country Reports for Human Rights Practices.* Published annually. Washington, D.C.: Government Printing Office.

Vasić, Miloš. 1996. "The Yugoslav Army and the Post-Yugoslav Armies." In *Yugoslavia and After: A Study in Fragmentation, Despair and Rebirth,* eds. David A. Dyker and Ivan Vejvoda, 116–37. New York: Longman.

Vasilijević, Vladan A. 1994. "Kosovo: Exercise and Protection of Human Rights." In *Conflict or Dialogue: Serbian-Albanian Relations and the Integration of the Balkans,* eds. Dušan Janjić and Shkelzen Maliqi, 69–107. Subotica: Open University.

Vejvoda, Ivan. 1996. "Yugoslavia 1945–91: From Decentralization Without Democracy to Dissolution." In *Yugoslavia and After: A Study in Fragmentation, Despair and Rebirth,* eds. David A. Dyker and Ivan Vejvoda, 9–27. New York: Longman.

Verdery, Katherine. 1991. *National Ideology Under Socialism: Identity and Cul-*

tural Politics in Ceausescu's Romania. Berkeley: University of California Press.

———. 1993. "Nationalism and National Sentiment in Post-Socialist Romania." *Slavic Review* 52, no. 2 (summer), 179–203.

Vickers, Miranda. 1994. "The Status of Kosovo in Socialist Yugoslavia," *Bradford Studies on South Eastern Europe*, no. 1, Research Unit on South Eastern Studies, University of Bradford.

———. 1995. *The Albanians: A Modern History*. London: I. B. Tauris.

———. 1998. *Between Serb and Albanian: A History of Kosovo*. New York: Columbia University Press, 1998.

Vickers, Miranda, and James Pettifer. 1997. *Albania: From Anarchy to Balkan Identity*. London: Hurst.

Vidović, Mirko. 1986. "Tito's Gulag and Human Rights." In *Human Rights in Yugoslavia*, eds. Oskar Gruenwald and Karen Rosenblum-Cale, 107–29. New York: Irvington Publishers.

Vojnić, Dragomir. 1995. "Disparity and Disintegration: The Economic Dimension of Yugoslavia's Demise." In *Yugoslavia: The Former and the Future: Reflections by Scholars from the Region*, eds. Payam Akhavan and Robert Howse, 75–111. Washington, D.C.: The Brookings Institute.

Volkan, Vamik. 1995. "The Transgenerational Transmission of Traumatized Self-Representations and Its Consequences: From Clinical Observations to Research on Large-Group Psychology." Paper presented at the Sixth International Psychoanalytical Association Conference on Psychoanalytic Research.

———. 1996. "Intergenerational Transmission and 'Chosen' Traumas: A Link between the Psychology of the Individual and That of the Ethnic Group." In *Psychoanalysis at the Political Border: Essays in Honor of Rafael Moses*, eds. Leo Rangell and Rena Moses-Hrushovski, 251–76. Madison, Conn.: International Universities Press.

Voutira, E., and S. Whishaw Brown. 1995. *Conflict Resolution: A Review of Some Non-Governmental Practices: A Cautionary Tale*. Uppsala, Sweden: The Nordic Africa Institute.

Vucinich, Wayne S., ed. 1969. *Contemporary Yugoslavia: Twenty Years of Socialist Experiment*. Berkeley: University of California Press, 1969.

Vucinich, Wayne S., and Thomas A. Emmert, eds. 1991. *Kosovo: Legacy of a Medieval Battle*. Minneapolis: University of Minnesota Press.

Vučković, Milan, and Nikolić, Goran. 1996. *Stanovništvo Kosova u razdoblju od 1918. do 1991. godine*. Munich: Slavica Verlag.

Vujačić, Veljko. "The Crisis in Yugoslavia." In *Dilemmas of Transition in the Soviet Union and Eastern Europe,* ed. George W. Breslauer, 95–117. Berkeley, Calif.: Berkeley-Stanford Program in Soviet Studies.

Vukadinović, Alex, ed. 1989. *Kosovo 1389–1989: Special Edition of the Serbian Literary Quarterly on the Occasion of 600 Years since the Battle of Kosovo*. Belgrade: Serbian Literary Quarterly.

Waltz, Kenneth. 1979. *Theory of International Politics*. Reading, Mass.: Addison Wesley.

West, Rebecca. 1941. *Black Lamb & Grey Falcon: A Journey Through Yugoslavia*. New York: Viking.

West, Richard. 1994. *Tito and the Rise and Fall of Yugoslavia*. London : Sinclair-Stevenson, 1994.

White, George W. 1996. "Place and Its Role in Serbian Identity." In *Reconstructing the Balkans: A Geography of the New Southeast Europe*, eds. Derek Hall and Darrick Danta, 39–52. New York: John Wiley & Sons.

Wilmsen, Edwin N., and Patrick McAllister, eds. 1996. *The Politics of Difference: Ethnic Premises in a World of Difference*. Chicago: University of Chicago Press.

Wilson, Duncan. 1970. *The Life and Times of Vuk Stefanović Karadžić: Literacy, Literature and National Independence in Serbia*. Oxford: Oxford University Press.

Woodhouse, Tom, ed. 1991. *Peacemaking in a Troubled World*. Oxford: Berg Publications.

Woodward, Susan L. 1995. *Balkan Tragedy: Chaos and Dissolution after the Cold War*. Washington, D.C.: Brookings Institute.

Ženski Centar. 1995. "Ženski dokumenti, 1990–93." In *Feminističke sveske*. Belgrade: Ženski Centar.

Žerjavić, Vladimir. 1989. *Gubici jugoslovenskog stanovništva u Drugom svetskom ratu*. Zagreb: Jugoslovensko viktimološko društvo.

Zimmerman, Warren. 1996. *Origins of a Catastrophe*. New York: Random House.

Index

Agence France Press, 22

Ahmeti, Sevdie, 46

Albania, xix, 19; break with Yugoslavia (1948), 288; cultural exchange with Kosovo, 17, 28–29, 291; emigration from, 123–24; "greater," 287; independence (1926), 286; isolationism, 38, 294; Kosovo Albanians hostile toward, 33; Kosovo Albanians on unification with, 33, 34, 38, 43, 53n113, 96, 293; Kosovo Albanians weakly identified with, 77; Kosovo border clashes (1948–1966), 289; Kosovo recognized as independent by, xvii; Kosovo relations after student demonstrations, 41; and Kosovo student demonstrations, 35–41, 76; "Marxist-Leninist," 33; poverty, 38; secret service Sigurimi, 39; WWII, 86n2, 287. *See also* Hoxha, Enver; Tirana

Albanian language, xix, 128–29; education in, 17, 28, 31, 41, 47n2, 285, 291, 302; and employment, 28, 128, 130; media in, 153–54, 201, 212n141

Albanian literature and culture: achievements (1970s), 292; Albania-Kosovo exchange, 17, 28–29, 291; creation of institutions of (1969), 291; festivals, 20; "forbidden books," 89, 90–91; vs. integration in Yugoslavia, 47n2; uni-versity courses, 17, 28–29. *See also* Albanian language; Albanians; education

"Albanian Mandela," Demaqi as, 200, 297

Albanian nationalism, 7, 19–21, 95–100; after constitutional changes, 183; Enverist / Titoist, 96; Kosovo Liberation Army (KLA), 6, 229, 278, 307, 308–9; League of Prizren and, 10, 15–16n40, 19–20; Martinović case and threat of, 12, 107–8; and Paraćin Massacre, 147, 149–51, 152–54, 162n74; and poisoning of Albanian school children (alleged), 189, 195, 217; and power struggle, 232–33; for republic status, 96–97; slogans, 96–97, 114–15n8; student demonstrations accused of working for, 31–32; in student demonstrations aftermath, 95–99, 293; taboo theme, 152; victimization and, 230, 232; young educated unemployed supporters, 29. *See also* "irredentists"; Kosovo Albanian underground; national identity

Albanians, xviii–xix, xxi; backlash against after student demonstrations, 41; Balli Kombeter resistance movement, 86n2; birthrates, 8, 11, 123–24; "boycotting" custom of, 154; crimes, 20–22, 97–98, 135–36, 164n113, 197; Čubrilović Memorandum on the Expulsion

ABOUT THE AUTHOR

Julie A. Mertus is Professor of Law at Ohio Northern University. She is the coeditor of *The Suitcase: Refugee Voices from Bosnia and Croatia* (California, 1997), coauthor of *Open Wounds: Human Rights Abuses in Kosovo,* and coauthor of *Local Action / Global Change.* She has written numerous academic and general interest articles on human rights, ethnonational conflict, and international law.

Author photo by Corley Gallow

Compositor: Binghamton Valley Composition
Type: 10/13 Galliard
Display: Galliard
Printer and binder: Maple-Vail Book Manufacturing Group